Palgrave Studies in Prisons and Penology

Series Editors

Ben Crewe
Institute of Criminology
University of Cambridge
Cambridge, UK

Yvonne Jewkes
Department of Criminology
University of Leicester
Leicester, UK

Thomas Ugelvik
University of Tromso - The Arctic Univer
Tromso, Norway

Aim of the Series

This is a unique and innovative series, the first of its kind dedicated entirely to prison scholarship. At a historical point in which the prison population has reached an all-time high, the series seeks to analyse the form, nature and consequences of incarceration and related forms of punishment. Palgrave Studies in Prisons and Penology provides an important forum for burgeoning prison research across the world.

More information about this series at
http://www.springer.com/series/14596

Laura S. Abrams • Emma Hughes • Michelle Inderbitzin • Rosie Meek
Editors

The Voluntary Sector in Prisons

Encouraging Personal and Institutional Change

palgrave
macmillan

Editors
Laura S. Abrams
Luskin School of Public Affairs
University of California Los Angeles
Culver City, California, USA

Emma Hughes
Department of Criminology
California State University, Fresno
Fresno, California, USA

Michelle Inderbitzin
Sociology, School of Public Policy
Oregon State University
Corvallis, Oregon, USA

Rosie Meek
School of Law
Royal Holloway University of London
Egham, Surrey, UK

Palgrave Studies in Prisons and Penology
ISBN 978-1-137-54214-4 ISBN 978-1-137-54215-1 (eBook)
DOI 10.1057/978-1-137-54215-1

Library of Congress Control Number: 2016936734

Printed on acid-free paper

This Palgrave Macmillan imprint is published by Springer Nature
The registered company is Nature America Inc. New York

This book is dedicated to prison volunteers around the globe, including those who have never been incarcerated, who are formerly incarcerated, and who are currently incarcerated. We want to acknowledge the important work that you do which often goes unnoticed, and which, as this book shows, can change the lives of individuals and institutions.

Acknowledgments

As coeditors we wish to acknowledge our editors at Palgrave Macmillan, Mireille Yanow and Mara Berkoff, for commissioning this volume and guiding us through this process. We could not have asked for a better publishing team. We also wish to extend our thanks to all of the contributors to this volume for their effort, and passion for this topic. We owe a huge debt of gratitude to Charles H. Lea III for his editorial acumen. He became master of formatting, reference checking, and our in-house manual of style. We could not have completed this work without him. Last, we wish to acknowledge the Economic and Social Research Council (ESRC) for awarding Rosie Meek the funding for the conference that led to this collection.

September 2015

Contents

Part I Background 1

1 **Introduction: The Significance of Voluntary Sector Provision in Correctional Settings** 3
Laura S. Abrams, Emma Hughes, Rosie Meek, and Michelle Inderbitzin

2 **Non-profit and Voluntary Sector Programs in Prisons and Jails: Perspectives from England and the USA** 21
Emma Hughes

Part II Prisoners as Volunteers 53

3 **Learning and Practicing Citizenship and Democracy Behind Bars** 55
Michelle Inderbitzin, Joshua Cain, and Trevor Walraven

4 **Leading by Example: Ways That Prisoners Give Back to Their Communities** 85
Michelle Inderbitzin, Trevor Walraven, and James Anderson

5 **Movements Towards Desistance via Peer-Support Roles in Prison** 115
Christian Perrin and Nicholas Blagden

6 **The Development of a Peer-Based Approach for Promoting Prisoner Health in an English Male Young Offender Institution** 143
Anita Mehay and Rosie Meek

Part III The Non-profit Sector and Prison Culture: Interactions, Boundaries, and Opportunities 171

7 **The Involvement of Non-profit Organizations in Prisoner Reentry in the UK: Prisoner Awareness and Engagement** 173
Rosie Meek, Dina Gojkovic, and Alice Mills

8 **Carceral Devolution and the Transformation of Urban America** 195
Reuben Jonathan Miller and Gwendolyn Purifoye

9 **From Ex-Offender to New Contributor: An Examination of How a Community-Based Reentry Program Addresses Racial Barriers to Employment** 215
Charles H. Lea III and Laura S. Abrams

10 **Penal Assemblages: Governing Youth in the Penal Voluntary Sector** 245
Abigail Tsionne Salole

Part IV Supporting the Supporters: The Voices of Volunteers 275

11 "Volunteers Welcome, That Is, Some Volunteers": Experiences Teaching College Courses at a Women's Prison 277
Kristenne M. Robison

12 Crossing the Color Line into America's Prisons: Volunteers of Color Reflect on Race and Identity in a College Service Learning Project 301
Jennifer R. Tilton

13 Developing Support and Self-Care Strategies for Volunteers in a Prison Writing Program 331
Tobi Jacobi and Lara Rose Roberts

Appendix 13.1 Assessing Compassion Satisfaction and Fatigue 354

Appendix 13.2 Creating A Self-Care Plan 355

Appendix 13.3 Writing-Based Self-Care Technique No. 1 356

Appendix 13.4 Writing-Based Self-Care Technique No. 2 357

Appendix 13.5 Sample Self-Care Writing Exercises 357

Afterword 363

Index 365

Contributors

Laura S. Abrams, Ph.D., is a professor of Social Welfare at the Luskin School of Public Affairs at the University of California, Los Angeles. Her research has focused on incarceration, reentry, and desistance from crime among youth and young adults. She is the author (with Ben Anderson-Nathe) of *Compassionate Confinement: A Year in the Life of Unit C* (2013) and is currently completing another book (with Diane Terry), *Life After Juvie: Young Men and Women on Desistance, Survival and Becoming an Adult* (forthcoming).

James Anderson is a prisoner at the Oregon State Penitentiary, serving a life sentence for a crime committed at the age of 17. He has been incarcerated for over 19 years straight. During his incarceration he has earned three college degrees, participated in numerous programs within the facility designed to better oneself, and achieved the goal of becoming a leader in both the Lifers' Unlimited Club and the RISE UP! Youth Empowerment Program.

Nicholas Blagden, Ph.D., is a senior lecturer in Forensic Psychology at Nottingham Trent University. Key achievements include delivering keynote presentations for the National Association for the Treatment of Sexual Offenders and the National Offender Management Service. One of his primary focus areas is denial among sexual offenders. Other projects have included explorations of rehabilitative climate sex offender prisons, deviant sexual interest, crime desistance, and the therapeutic climate of secure units.

Joshua Cain currently holds the elected position of Secretary in the Lifers' Unlimited Club at the Oregon State Penitentiary. He has been incarcerated since 1998 for a crime committed at the age of 18. During that time, he has earned an Associate's Degree and is working toward a Bachelor's. He also fulfills other leadership roles in education, peer-based cognitive skills classes, and employment. He is passionate about family, education, and equality.

Dina Gojkovic, Ph.D., is a research and evaluation lead at Associate Development Solutions in the UK. She is a psychologist by training and holds a doctorate in mental health. Dina has dedicated her career to research in challenging and complex settings, including hospitals, prisons, shelters for homeless people, and children's day care centers. She has published widely in international journals and authored a book on comparative offender rehabilitation.

Emma Hughes, Ph.D., is an associate professor in the Criminology Department at California State University, Fresno. She is the author of the book *Education in Prison: Studying through Distance Learning* published in 2012 and has contributed book chapters on offender rehabilitation to edited volumes. She is on the editorial board of the *Howard Journal of Criminal Justice.* She previously served as a lecturer at Birmingham City University, UK.

Michelle Inderbitzin, Ph.D., is an associate professor of Sociology in the School of Public Policy at Oregon State University. She primarily studies prison culture, juvenile justice, and transformative education. She is the lead author of the books *Deviance and Social Control: A Sociological Perspective* (2013) and *Perspectives on Deviance and Social Control* (2015). She regularly teaches classes and volunteers in Oregon's maximum-security prison for men and in state youth correctional facilities.

Tobi Jacobi, Ph.D., is an associate professor of English at Colorado State University. She specializes in the work of incarcerated women writers and teaches classes on writing and literacy. She also directs the CSU Community Literacy Center and trains student and community volunteers to facilitate writing workshops with incarcerated adults and at-risk youth in Northern Colorado. Her edited collection (with Ann Folwell) *Women, Writing, and Prison: Activists, Scholars, and Writers Speak Out* was published in 2014.

Charles H. Lea III,* M.S.W., Ph.D. *(candidate) is pursuing his doctorate in Social Welfare at the UCLA Luskin School of Public Affairs. His primary research areas include juvenile justice, reentry, education, and racial equity. He is specifically interested in contextual and individual influences on crime involvement and criminal desistance among boys and young men of color, particularly African Americans, and the protective processes and mechanisms that facilitate positive development.

Rosie Meek, Ph.D., is head of the School of Law at Royal Holloway University of London and is a chartered psychologist and prison researcher. She is a Fulbright Distinguished Scholar (University of California, San Diego) and her most recent book *Sport in Prison: Exploring the Role of Physical Activity in Correctional*

Settings was published in 2014. She has published widely on the role of voluntary and community organizations in criminal justice, with a particular focus on the transition from custody to community.

Anita Mehay, M.Sc., Ph.D. (candidate) is currently completing her Ph.D. at Royal Holloway University of London. She is primarily interested in Health Literacy and Health Promotion in prison populations. She is funded by the Economic and Social Research Council (ESRC) South-East Doctoral Training Centre under a CASE studentship, which is part funded by the National Health Service in England.

Reuben Jonathan Miller, Ph.D., is an assistant professor in the School of Social Work at the University of Michigan. He is broadly interested in punishment and social welfare policy, race and ethnic relations, and the urban poor. He has recently launched a study of prisoner reentry in Detroit, Michigan, and a study of the reintegration experience in the UK, Serbia, and Sweden.

Alice Mills, Ph.D., is a senior lecturer at the University of Auckland, New Zealand. She has extensive experience of researching voluntary and community sector involvement in criminal justice, including a 2-year project on the role of the third sector in criminal justice as part of the UK Third Sector Research Centre. More recently, she has completed research on the relationship between nongovernmental organizations and the state in criminal justice in New Zealand. She is currently examining the use of Tikanga Māori in indigenous youth courts and community sector housing support for ex-prisoners.

Christian Perrin, M.Sc., Ph.D. (candidate) is currently pursuing his doctorate at Nottingham Trent University in the UK. His research principally explores the application of peer-support schemes in prison, and how incarcerated sexual offenders make sense of meaningful roles while serving time. His varied role encompasses areas such as rehabilitative climates in prisons, resettlement strategies for sexual offenders, desistance, well-being in prisons, and sexual offender treatment.

Gwendolyn Purifoye, Ph.D., is an assistant professor of Sociology at Kent State University at Stark. She received her doctorate from the Loyola University Chicago Department of Sociology in 2014. Her research interests include social interactions, urban public spaces, and the criminalization of place.

Lara Rose Roberts is pursuing her Master's Degree in English Literature at Colorado State University. She is a strong advocate for the idea that mental health should be discussed more often and more openly, especially in academia. Her literary interests include understanding how women have been portrayed as psychologically dysfunctional in Early American Literature.

Kristenne M. Robison, Ph.D., is an associate professor of Sociology and Criminal Justice Studies at Westminster College in Pennsylvania. Her primary research interests include the intersection of gender with areas of the criminal justice system such as police work and prisons, as well as pedagogical issues in the criminal justice studies classroom. Robison is also active within the prison system teaching classes in both men's and women's prisons.

Abigail Tsionne Salole is a faculty member at Sheridan College, Canada. She is currently completing her Ph.D. in Criminology at Griffith University in Australia.

Jennifer R. Tilton, Ph.D., is an associate professor of Race and Ethnic Studies at the University of Redlands. She is the author of *Dangerous or Endangered? Race and the Politics of Youth in Urban America* and a contributor to *Childhood, Youth and Social Work in Transformation*. She is a founder of REACH, a community-service learning program that brings college students to volunteer with young people in a juvenile hall in Southern California.

Trevor Walraven is the youngest Lifers' Unlimited Club President in the history of the organization at the Oregon State Penitentiary extending back to 1968 when the club was founded. He was waived to adult court at the age of 14 and received a life sentence with the possibility of parole after 30 years. Trevor largely "grew up" inside, actively engaging in programs such as Inside-Out, club-related activities, family-orientated events, and youth-empowerment efforts. After a successful "second look," Trevor, aged 31, was released from prison shortly before this book went to press. He is now getting a chance to practice his leadership skills in the outside community.

List of Figures

Fig. 7.1	Percentage of respondents in each prison that had heard of/engaged with TSOs	181
Fig. 7.2	Reported reasons for not engaging with TSOs	183
Fig. 7.3	Awareness of and engagement with at least one TSO by pathway	185

List of Tables

Table 5.1	Prison information	124
Table 5.2	Participant information	125
Table 5.3	Superordinate and subordinate themes	127
Table 7.1	Summary of case study sites and survey response rates	178
Table 7.2	Prisoner self-reported awareness of and engagement with TSOs	181
Table 7.3	Number of TSOs operating in the eight prison research sites, by resettlement pathway	184
Table 9.1	Summary of program sessions observed	223
Table 10.1	Text–worker activation conversation: ABC worksheet	263

PART I

Background

CHAPTER 1

Introduction: The Significance of Voluntary Sector Provision in Correctional Settings

Laura S. Abrams, Emma Hughes, Rosie Meek, and Michelle Inderbitzin

The voluntary sector has had a long-standing relationship with prisons and prisoners in the USA and the UK and in many countries across the globe. Beginning with prison chaplains and later expanding to education, work training, and a range of rehabilitative services, the voluntary sector has played a significant role in providing programs for incarcerated people as well as in shaping the culture of penal institutions themselves. Yet never before has the study of the relationships between these sectors been more important or politically relevant.

L.S. Abrams (✉)
University of California, Los Angeles, CA, USA

E. Hughes
California State University, Fresno, CA, USA

R. Meek
Royal Holloway University of London, Egham, UK

M. Inderbitzin
Oregon State University, Corvallis, OR, USA

L.S. Abrams et al. (eds.), *The Voluntary Sector in Prisons*, Palgrave Studies in Prisons and Penology, DOI 10.1057/978-1-137-54215-1_1

More than 10.2 million people are incarcerated worldwide, one-fifth of whom hail from the USA. Put in perspective, the rate of incarceration in the USA is 712 per 100,000, while in England and Wales it is 148 per 100,000 persons, just slightly higher than the average of 144 per 100,000 persons worldwide (Walmsley, 2013). Although the USA is a clear outlier in criminal justice policies and incarceration rates, the overall global prison population has increased by over 25 % over the past 15 years. More and more individuals are affected by the institution of the prison; not only as inmates and their family members, but also as correctional and law enforcement officials, mental health professionals, educators, activists, and volunteers. The ripple effect of these unprecedented increases in the number of people either confined or under correctional supervision is virtually impossible to calculate in monetary or emotional value.

Based on its outlier status, the USA is currently facing the far-reaching consequences of "mass incarceration." This collection of harsh sentencing policies, stemming in part from the movement known as the "War on Drugs" of the 1970s and 1980s, has destroyed families and communities, exhausted public budgets, and created a new group of (primarily) men of color who are marginalized from voting rights, employment, and mainstream civic life based on their criminal records (Alexander, 2010; Manza & Uggen, 2006; Western, 2006). No longer able to sustain itself, the mass incarceration bubble is bursting (United States Department of Justice, 2013). While the countries that comprise the UK are not experiencing a crisis of this magnitude, still the rate of imprisonment has skyrocketed over the past 20 years. The British government is currently constructing new prisons, and prison reform organizations and activists are increasingly concerned that what has happened in the USA could happen in Europe as well.

Currently in 2015, there is increasing public and bipartisan governmental recognition in the USA that War on Drugs policies have largely failed to halt crime or create a climate of public safety (Raphael & Stoll, 2009). As such, we are witnessing a significant shift toward beliefs long held in other nations—particularly in Western European and Scandinavian countries—that incarcerated people need education, skills, and other forms of rehabilitation in order to succeed upon their release and that humane treatment of prisoners may contribute to a more peaceful society as whole. As such, public discourses have turned increasingly to softer terms, such as prisoner rehabilitation, education, job training, reentry, and resettlement. These discourses represent a significant shift for the USA in particular, where over the past several decades correctional facilities have become increasingly punitive and less rehabilitative at their core.

With the call for more supportive services in prisons and jails, one must recognize that a large portion of the rehabilitative umbrella in penal settings is currently provided by the voluntary sector, meaning individuals and groups who do not work directly for correctional agencies but who provide therapeutic, educational, skills training, spiritual, and an array of other supportive programs within prison and jail facilities. This sector encompasses unpaid volunteer work along with third sector nonprofit organizations that may or may not be contractually related to law enforcement or criminal justice agencies. While the voluntary (or "third") sector is largely responsible for a diverse range of service provision, there is limited scholarly conversation about the nature or limits of the voluntary sector as it operates in penal settings. Many questions remain unanswered about these exchanges, such as the extent to which the voluntary sector is truly able to change the institutions or the people whom they work with for the better. We also know little about volunteers themselves, who they are, and what their experiences are as they navigate their role in correctional settings. Moreover, there is limited critical conversation about volunteerism within prisons and jails or the role of volunteerism within the larger prison regime.

This edited collection seeks to address these knowledge gaps by providing a multifaceted exploration of the programming that the voluntary sector provides in encouraging institutional change in prisons as well as providing individual services and support to those who are housed behind bars. Rather than explore the voluntary sector's involvement with the criminal justice system more broadly (c.f. Hucklesby & Corocan, 2015), we have focused upon the sector's engagement with men and women behind bars through services provided within jails and prisons and upon reentry to society. This volume spans the USA, the UK, and Canada, juvenile and adult facilities, and prisons and jails. In doing so, it collectively demonstrates the exciting, groundbreaking, and yet often unrecognized work that the voluntary sector is implementing in correctional facilities. Even as we highlight promising practices, we also pose critical questions about the use of and in some cases, dependence on programs provided by the voluntary sector. For example, rather than relying on the energy of volunteers, nonprofit agencies, or prisoners themselves, should some of these important programs be funded by and built into the institutions themselves? On the flip side, what are the consequences of the voluntary sector becoming "too close" to the correctional sector? What does this clash and cooperation of sectors mean in an era of neoliberalism and more localized (i.e., state and county) control over services for offenders and ex-offenders?

We believe that the multiauthored nature of this collection, including two chapters coauthored with currently incarcerated men, is one of its unique strengths. There is a great diversity of programs created by the voluntary sector offered in correctional facilities in the USA, the UK, and beyond, and the chapters in this book offer insight into the current variety as well as the multiple possibilities that may exist for the future. In addition, the chapters contain rich diversity in regard to views, theories, and perspectives. The cross-national contributions include the perspectives of academics, some of whom are also volunteers (see Part IV of this volume). In Part II, we also uniquely highlight the essential but often unheard perspectives of incarcerated individuals as volunteers, some of whom are leading innovative programs within institutions themselves. Given that this volume considers the possibilities for personal change and institutional transformation through voluntary sector provision, there is particular significance when the programs are self-directed by those who are actually incarcerated. To our knowledge, this is one of few scholarly collections to consider the perspectives of prisoners themselves as volunteers, organizers, and leaders.

This volume also attempts to signal the positive efforts made to enhance the opportunities for incarcerated men and women to engage in constructive and rehabilitative activities while incarcerated and upon their reentry to society. All too often these stories of small gains are overlooked, contributing to correctional systems and volunteer programs operating in silos and reinventing the wheel when seeking to try new methods of programming or intervention. This book seeks to breakdown these boundaries, encouraging dialogue and discussion about the innovative work being carried out by volunteers in correctional facilities, programs that can help to offset the negative aspects of institutionalization that can hinder personal growth.

That said, the authors recognize the potential challenges and obstacles that can develop when nonstate actors provide programs within correctional facilities. The interface between the nonprofit and criminal justice sectors will be considered with this caution in mind and analyzed most specifically in Part III of this volume. As the hybridization of voluntary and penal sector services increases, the potential for correctional discourses of punishment and social control to influence voluntary service provision poses a potentially problematic set of consequences for workers, clients, and receiving communities. Still, the overall collection of essays will demonstrate the vulnerability of such programming if not properly acknowledged and supported by correctional staff, correctional officials, and policymakers. The potential consequences of a loss of such programming for the offenders themselves, and for society as a whole, are crucial. While rehabilitative endeavors are increasingly seen as necessary by governments, correctional systems, and the general public in the USA and the UK, vital questions must be asked about how such endeavors are best provided, supported, and sustained. This volume thus provides an important and timely contribution to a rigorous examination of these pressing social concerns.

Background to This Collection

The idea for this edited collection originated from a series of papers presented at an "Innovation in Prisons" workshop held in April 2014 at the University of California's (UCLA) Luskin School of Public Affairs in Los Angeles, California, in the USA. The UK's Economic and Social Research Council (ESRC) funded the workshop through a grant to Professor Rosie Meek, head of the School of Law at Royal Holloway University of London. The workshop activities were designed to appeal to policymakers, practitioners, academic leaders and activists in summarizing, discussing, and expanding on an existing but highly dispersed and fragmented body of academic and policy research on the changing role of the voluntary (or third) sector in criminal justice institutions. Thirteen academics from the USA, the UK, and Canada were invited to present at the workshop following a widespread call for papers via LISTSERVs and scholarly networks. Our exploration of third sector involvement in prisoner rehabilitation seeks to contribute to increased effectiveness of public services and policy, with a commitment to the *process* of generating impact (utilizing existing networks and collaborations, leading to high-impact opportunities to continue to provide formal advice and guidance to policymakers and practitioners), the *context* in which the academic messages are delivered (this subject area is especially relevant in the current economic and political climates of Europe and the USA), and the *content* of the scientific meetings, which encourage and build ongoing collaborations and relationships between researchers, policymakers, and practitioners.

The changing role of third sector involvement in criminal justice institutions in the UK and North America provides an especially significant and timely area of academic research. The workshop fueled rigorous discussions surrounding each paper, and the chapters proposed for this volume are, with a few exceptions, based on the papers presented at UCLA. The excitement generated by the original research shared at the workshop led to our decision to seek publication of this collective body of work. Thus nearly all of the evidence in this book is based on real-life examples, including empirical, ethnographic and qualitative case study research that "brings to life" the voices of volunteers and service providers as well as those who are recipients of these services.

There are also several areas not included in this fairly compact volume, but these deserve future attention. For example, with the exception of Emma Hughes's work (Chap. 2), we do not have many voices of religious volunteers, who comprise perhaps the largest sector of volunteers in prisons and jails around the globe. We also have limited information on arts and theater-based programs, animal-assisted therapies and programs, sport and numerous other examples of creative work in prisons. We hope that these and other types of voluntary sector programs will continue to be studied in a global context, as the scope of innovative programming in correctional facilities is rapidly evolving.

In addition, we want to make clear that we in no way wish to use this book as a platform to promote prisons as an optimal place to provide education, job training, health and mental health care, or other services to individuals in need. On the contrary and from a deeply held social justice perspective, we firmly believe that the voluntary sector should indeed reach people outside of prison and focus more on prevention than intervention. Indeed, the programs examined in this volume exist in the midst of complex and often damaging webs of social institutions. However, we believe that the voluntary sector has and will continue to have a role in making prisons and jails more humane and educational and less mundane and cruel. Deeply exploring these services is a worthy endeavor and one we are pleased to tackle in this volume.

The USA and the UK: Relevant Context for the Study of the Voluntary Sector in Prisons

In 2004, Tewksbury and Dabney, writing in the *Journal of Offender Rehabilitation*, identified a substantial need for further research on the role and effectiveness of volunteer programing in prisons and the experiences and perspectives of the volunteers themselves. Over 10 years later, with few notable exceptions, this call has gone largely unheeded, particularly within academic work generated in the USA (for two examples of US-based studies examining prison volunteerism see Camp, Klein-Saffran, Kwon, Daggett, & Joseph, 2006; Kort-Butler & Malone, 2014). Yet as Tewksbury and Dabney (2004) anticipated, "It is clear that there is an increased reliance on prison volunteers. It is also clear that this trend will continue to grow" (p. 181). While Tewksbury and Dabney wrote with specific regard to the USA, their call is applicable on a wider scale, and this growing level of interest is apparent in the UK where third sector involvement has recently received increased academic and policy attention. Indeed, as previously noted, the UK's ESRC funded the workshop on which this volume is based.

While little is known about the role and reach of volunteers in prisons, substantially more research has been accomplished in the UK in understanding the role of the voluntary sector in the criminal justice system. In Britain, third sector organizations (hereafter TSOs) currently provide a range of services to offenders and ex-offenders, including advice and advocacy, mentoring schemes, education and training, and watchdog and advocacy functions. TSOs are very much involved in the provision of core rehabilitative and resettlement services (such as drug and alcohol treatment, employment and training, housing aid and advice), and in some areas (such as debt and finance and assistance to offenders' families) services are almost entirely provided by TSOs.

Previous and current British governments have initiated a range of policies to facilitate and encourage third sector participation in services hitherto provided largely by the state (Home Office, 2005; NOMS, 2005), and the Ministry of Justice/National Offender Management Service has sought out numerous consultations with TSOs concerning their role in the criminal justice system. Recent legal changes (Offender Management Act, 2007), policy documents (NOMS, 2005), and initiatives such as "contestability" or tendering for the provision of a range of criminal justice services—including building and managing prisons, the provision of unpaid work, bail support, and resettlement services—signal a clear intention that core criminal justice services will be provided by a range of organizations outside the state sector, including TSOs (Neilson, 2009).

The benefits of the involvement of TSOs in criminal justice are gradually becoming more visible in the literature (Bryans, Martin, & Walker, 2002; HMPS/Clinks, 2002; Martin, 2002; Meek, Gojkovic, & Mills, 2010; Mills, Meek, & Gojkovic, 2012; Neuberger, 2009; NOMS/IVR, 2007; NPC, 2009; Silvestri, 2009). As several chapters in this volumes elucidate (e.g., see, Chaps. 2, 5, and 6), TSOs have a number of strengths in working with offenders, including diversity of provision and cost-effectiveness, independence, an increased ability to respond to the needs of service users, a more diverse workforce, and engagement with the views of service users at the planning stage of provision. However, these developments have not been without contention and controversy, as some professional criminal justice officials, such as correctional or probation officers, negatively view the contracting out of services that are historically in the law enforcement domain (Mills et al., 2012; Silvestri, 2009). Recognizing these potential complications, Part III of this volume grapples with an emerging concern about the infusion of the government's law enforcement agenda and mentality into a traditionally more independent, and potentially critical, voluntary sector.

Compared to the UK, it is harder to form an overall picture of official developments in regards to voluntary sector engagement in prisons and jails in the USA. This is partially due to the overwhelmingly large scope of the penal system and its fragmentation across 50 independent state prison systems, thousands of autonomous county-run jails, and an entirely separate federal prison system with facilities spread throughout numerous states. Published research has surveyed probationers and/or parolees in various cities to assess geographic access to services such as substance abuse, mental health, health care and/or job training programs, and the influence of such access on recidivism outcomes (Kubrin & Stewart, 2006; Taxman, Perdoni, & Harrison, 2007; Wallace & Papchristos, 2014). While making important strides in understanding key issues related to service access and provision, these are localized and point in time projections of how prisoners interface with the various types of social services and care providers upon release. Given the variation in political, cultural, and budgetary forces operating on each of these systems, it is not surprising that little is known about the size, character, and functioning of the voluntary sector in correctional settings in the USA as whole. To further complicate this scenario, a diverse range of local, state, national, and international voluntary and nonprofit organizations operate within these settings. While it is clear that efforts to undertake a national survey on voluntary sector provision in prisons and jails may be a valuable and fruitful area for future enquiry, the current volume cannot reasonably cover all of the variations in voluntary sector provision across federal, state, and county systems. However, we do include perspectives from five different states to provide just a glimpse of the possibilities for examining regional differences within the USA.

While regional differences surely exist, it would be naïve to suggest that no broader perspective can be achieved in regard to the US voluntary sector and its interface with corrections. For the first time in decades, in 2010 the prison population across the USA began to decrease. Moreover, with a burgeoning bipartisan interest in a "smart on crime" agenda that includes reforming harsh sentencing laws, reducing the nonviolent prison population, promoting alternatives to incarceration, and strengthening reentry programs (USA Department of Justice, 2013), there is a clear opportunity for greater voluntary sector involvement in the criminal justice sector as a whole. For example, the Federal Bureau of Prisons website proclaims, "You can make a difference," explaining that, "services and programs offered by Bureau staff can be supplemented by citizen volunteers, thereby supporting community re-entry efforts and promoting institution safety" (https://www.bop.gov/jobs/volunteer.jsp). Moreover, the state of California has recently issued grants to selected nonprofits with a view to encouraging expansion of voluntary sector involvement in facilities throughout its prison system (California Rehabilitation Oversight Board, 2015). Through the state-level office that fosters and supports volunteerism in California ("CaliforniaVolunteers"), efforts are underway to gather systematic data on the nature and extent of volunteerism in state prisons in order to fill recognized gaps in this knowledge base.

Unlike in the UK, where there is a whole body of knowledge on third sector involvement, there is wide variation across the USA in terms of existing data and comprehensive information. Kristenne Robison's work (Chap. 11) draws on a single state's data on prison volunteers, and Reuben Miller and Gwendolyn Purifoye (Chap. 8) reference national charity information on the rise of nonprofit reentry programs. However, comprehensive data on the work of the voluntary sector as a whole in prisons, jails, and juvenile facilities does not exist on a national scale. This volume thus renews Tewksbury and Dabney's (2004) call for more focused research on voluntary sector provision in correctional facilities, while also offering a sampling of innovative programs that are currently functioning across the USA and beyond. We hope that spreading examples of such practices will contribute to a broadening of perspectives across geographic and jurisdictional divides.

Organization of Volume

This volume consists of four parts that group together diverse submissions under key interrelated themes. This first section is intended to provide an overview and grounding in the issue of the voluntary sector in prisons.

Following this introduction, Emma Hughes's chapter (Chap. 2) provides a foregrounding for the book as a whole. The author accomplishes this by presenting the results of interviews and surveys with participants in a prison-based distance-learning program funded by a charity in the UK and interviews with current and former volunteers and participants in prison voluntary programs in California USA. From a cross-national perspective, her analysis locates ways that volunteers and the nonprofit sector enrich prison culture in a positive way, providing meaning to those receiving services and to the volunteers themselves. Additionally, the activities inspire some former prisoners to give back to the community with their own voluntary service. Hughes also ties these programs to encouraging hope, meaning, and criminal desistance among those who are incarcerated. At the same time as this information is presented, the author takes a critical eye toward disparities in volunteerism across various facilities and geographic locations and considers factors that may influence these differences.

Prisoners as Volunteers

This set of four chapters describes and comments on the role of prisoners serving as leaders, volunteers, mentors, and teachers within correctional facilities in the USA and the UK. Although prisoners have historically supported one another behind bars in many informal ways, little to no scholarship has examined the meaning and experiences of those who become volunteers and leaders in this capacity. As such, we invite the reader to absorb this collection of four chapters (two from the USA and two from the UK) as some of the first published work of its kind; of particular note, two of the chapters in this section are coauthored by prisoners themselves.

This collection of original empirical papers is united by several key elements. To begin, they showcase the idea that prisoners can and should serve as resources within penal institutions. While the correctional environment might appear to pose barriers to the reality of prisoners serving as volunteers and leaders, these chapters show how these opportunities can actually transform components of the prison culture itself. For example, Chap. 3 by Michelle Inderbitzin along with "lifers" Joshua Cain and Trevor Walraven describes, in Joshua and Trevor's own words, how prisoner-led clubs provide mechanisms for learning civic participation. As club members, incarcerated individuals are able to congregate, advocate, and promote leadership as a group. The next and complementary chapter by Michelle, Trevor, and fellow prison leader James (Chap. 4) Anderson illustrates how prisoners can work together in organized groups to make the prison a more humane environment and to shatter the barriers between insiders and outsiders. These two chapters are distinct yet united in that they take place in one maximum security facility in the USA that has provided these men, convicted of murder and other violent crimes, a clear opportunity to create meaningful lives while behind bars. In finding this meaning, they also benefit the prison and the outside community as a whole.

This section also uniquely speaks to the ways that prisoners serving as volunteers can dramatically change the lives of the volunteers themselves. Christian Perrin and Nicholas Bladgen's work (Chap. 5) on four UK peer-support schemes offers poignant examples of how these roles provide the volunteers with motivations as well as the skills to work toward desistance from crime. Taking on a peer-support role appears to offer those who participate new identities they can embrace after their release. The lifers referred to above (Trevor, Josh, and James) and some of the incarcerated men that Perrin and Blagden interviewed may not be able to exercise their leadership and citizenry outside the prison walls any time soon or perhaps not at all. Nevertheless, their roles as leaders of prisoner-led organization and peer-support schemes have provided positive outlets for their energy and enthusiasm to give back through direct support and engagement with fellow prisoners and the community at large. In essence, these roles and opportunities provide meaning, promote desistance, and positively influence the prison culture as a whole.

In addition to illustrating the power that prisoner-led initiatives can have in changing institutions and individuals, these chapters also showcase some of the barriers that arise in trying to launch and sustain these types of programs from the inside. The final chapter in this section (Chap. 6) provides information on considerations that may arise when launching a volunteer program involving prisoners. Anita Mehay and Rosie Meek present the results of an investigation into the development of a volunteer peer health promotion program in a young offender institution (YOI) for young men in the UK. The authors find that while many residents of the facility would welcome the opportunity to participate in such a program, institutional and personal barriers to discussing health matters in this setting are still present. While the young men largely felt that the program would be of benefit to them and the prison, they were still wary of how much the prison staff or institutional culture would support the idea of prisoners as leaders and champions of their own health. Thus while the prior three chapters offer examples of the positive benefits of existing programs, the final chapter in this group provides an alternative viewpoint as well as useful information for those seeking to develop or implement a peer-led support program in a prison or jail.

The Nonprofit Sector and Prisons: Interactions, Boundaries, and Opportunities

The third section of this volume contends with critical questions surrounding the paid voluntary sector and its interactions with probation, parole, and the rehabilitation of prisoners and ex-offenders as they transition out of correctional facilities. The chapters are united in examining the linking of the social welfare and criminal justice sectors through community-based reentry and resettlement organizations. Reentry work is often accomplished under the auspices of community-based nonprofit organizations and TSOs, either in concert or in cooperation with state governed parole and probation offices. The presence of workers who are outside of the constraints and training of law enforcement might appear to make the transition from prison to society a more supported experience for those receiving these services. This section of the volume problematizes this supposition by digging more deeply into some of the complex policies and practices that can arise from this type of hybridization.

We begin this section with a chapter that bridges "inside" and "outside" programs by defining the reach and utility of TSO involvement with reentering prisoners in the UK. Chapter Seven by Rosie Meek, Dina Gojkovic, and Alice Mills, reprinted from the *Journal of Offender Rehabilitation*, presents the results of a mixed methods English national survey that examined prisoners' involvement with third sector organizations for their reentry needs (services provided both in prison and in the community by the voluntary sector). This chapter both grounds the reader in the British TSO landscape and offers key suggestions for the future of these critical resettlement services. While there is no existing complementary national survey in North America from which to draw any comparisons, this chapter serves as a model of what can be done to provide a comprehensive portrait of third sector involvement in prison and reentry organizations.

While the chapter by Meek et al. calls for more readily accessible third sector involvement in reentry provisions to aid in criminal desistance and safety goals, Reuben Miller and Gwendolyn Purifoy's chapter offers a theoretical counterperspective from a US context. In Chap. 8, the authors lay out the history and potentially problematic process for "carceral devolution" in the USA, meaning the gradual transfer of rehabilitative services from the state to the nonprofit sector. They argue that through this shift, community-based reentry organizations have become agents of social control for the very large probation and parole populations that currently populate urban spaces. Miller and Purifoy's argument problematizes the new discourse of reentry and rehabilitation that seeks to make adults "employable" rather than to actually help them procure jobs. In essence, such programs focus more on personal, cognitive, and affective change among former prisoners, with a view to addressing perceived individual deficits, rather than changing structural conditions or barriers to employment. This trend, they argue, should be critically examined with regard to how the nonprofit sector now manages the lives of the urban poor.

The next two chapters add complexity and nuance to Miller and Purifoy's arguments by offering rich ethnographic examinations of reentry practices and programs in the USA and Canada. Through ethnographic analysis of an adult reentry program geared toward African American men and women in urban South Los Angeles, Charles Lea and Laura Abrams (Chap. 9) tease apart the discourses of the instructors (who are both paid and voluntary workers and all people of color) concerning barriers to employment based on the dual disadvantages of race and a criminal record. They find that despite the very bleak chances that this population has in the labor market, the program focuses on addressing personal change, the power of individual thinking, and prayer. Instructors rarely if at all address the structural barriers to obtaining a job. Nevertheless, the participants in this program find the messages encouraging and useful as they prepare themselves for lives in the community that will consist of employment and a more mainstream participation in society, rather than in crime.

Next, set in Canada and with a focus on youth on juvenile probation, Abigail Salole (Chap. 10) uses the perspective of frontline youth services workers in Canada to critically tease apart the place of the "penal voluntary sector" (PVS) in Canada's youth criminal justice system. Her chapter points to similar trends in Canada as in the UK in terms of third sector involvement in probation and resettlement services. Through her institutional ethnographic analysis, Salole argues that the voluntary sector workers both adopt and at times resist the language of the criminal justice sector that tends to dominate program materials, discourses, and practices. Thus both Chaps. 9 and 10 comment on clashes between reforming "people" or reforming "the system" in the hybridization of voluntary sector reentry and rehabilitation services. All of the chapters in this section thoughtfully consider the implications for the future of the voluntary sector as it continues to operate hand in hand within corrections and larger reentry organizations.

Supporting the Supporters: The Experiences of Volunteers

The final section of this book grapples with the experiences of volunteers themselves. It addresses important questions related to how to sustain volunteerism within prisons and jails and the range of issues that arise among volunteers themselves in doing this work. For example, what are the motivations for people seeking volunteer work in prisons and jails? How can we sustain their enthusiasm and energy to prevent burnout? What are some of the institutional barriers to bringing volunteers in? In various ways, all of the chapters in this section address these questions.

To begin this section, in Chapter 11, Kristenne Robison positions herself as the subject of her own qualitative analysis, examining her personal experience of working to establish sociology courses at a women's prison. She looks at the ways that power, culture, and key individuals shape the ways that volunteerism is structured at this prison. This work adds a useful perspective to this volume as so many of the positive practices described in earlier chapters rely on the opening of prisons to outsiders and particularly, to volunteers. It also provides the impetus to look at key questions surrounding access to prisons and jails and mechanisms for breaking down inside and outside barriers so that positive programming can occur.

The next two chapters are focused on the experiences of volunteers themselves, providing a glimpse into a largely untapped subject matter. In Jennifer Tilton's chapter (Chap. 12), as well as in Tobi Jacobi and Lara Roberts's work (Chap. 13), the authors interview volunteer instructors from their own programs in order to better understand how they relate to the work that they do inside various correctional systems. Jennifer Tilton focuses on college students of color, and how they come to understand their own race and class locations through their experiences volunteering in a juvenile hall. While Tilton recognizes that the literature on volunteers has more broadly examined the cross-cultural experiences of white people helping people of color, she turns this conversation in a different direction. For the college students of color, seeing people who might have been themselves, or their friends and siblings, locked in juvenile hall presents an opportunity to examine one's personal identities and social locations. Tilton astutely describes why it may be harder to sustain volunteerism among students of color based on the personal challenges that may arise from these complex identity negotiations.

Last, Tobi Jacobi and Lara Roberts's chapter (Chap. 13) describes the types of support that college students and community volunteers need to continue to offer their writing workshops within prisons. They address the very real issues of burnout and secondary traumatization that arise when volunteers repeatedly hear stories of rape, violence, and other distressing experiences. While the organized nonprofit sector might provide more institutional supports for workers to guard against burnout, grassroots volunteer programs do not always have these resources. As such, their chapter concludes with real-life "tools" that programs can use in order to better grapple with volunteers' own emotions and feelings. These last three chapters are thus critical to the volume in looking at ways that the prison sector can invite and sustain outside programs that are beneficial to the prisoners as well as to the volunteers themselves.

Conclusions

As coeditors, we invite the readers to think about some of the larger questions that undergird these various pieces. For example, what are correctional facilities trying to achieve, and what is the role of the third sector in the governing regime of the prison as a mechanism of control? If the state, particularly in the USA, is trying to reduce reoffending, why do they often (but not always) make it so difficult for volunteers to come in and stay involved, particularly those who are ex-offenders themselves? Why are these programs mostly operating in silos, with limited information about best practices or successes? What does it take to link larger goals concerning volunteerism to on-the-ground practice and for centralized policies to be implemented consistently even within the same systems? For prison administrators and policymakers, we hope that this volume provides valuable examples of proven, positive practices that are succeeding elsewhere, helping to reduce need for reinventing the wheel.

There are clearly a number of willing participants in volunteer organizations, both from the outside and on the inside, who wish to be involved in promoting personal and institutional change. There is also a real value as we can see in breaking down the barriers between the inside and outside of prison walls. But if the penal sector wishes to make optimal and continued use of innovations in promising and proven programs, we clearly need to rethink how to facilitate this in a way that allows for a meaningful experience. We also need to ensure that the values of the voluntary sector—and its commitment to community-based work and progressive social change—won't be usurped by the more punitive discourses and practices that often (but not always) characterize prisons and jails.

For volunteers or voluntary sector workers who are reading this book, we hope that the stories presented in these chapters provide ideas on meaningful ways to continue your involvement in prisons. There are excellent examples of good practice, but working in the trenches, we may not always be aware that there is indeed an international movement of volunteerism in the prison sector. Rest assured, your work is not being accomplished in a vacuum. Indeed, we anticipate that some of the examples herein will prepare volunteers and potential volunteers for some of the many ways they may encourage and sustain beneficial programs for both institutional and personal change.

Finally, we hope that the stories contained within the volume will shed light on what change is possible at both the institutional and personal level. We believe that voluntary work in prisons can help to ameliorate the destructive culture of the prison, break down stereotypes that marginalize the men and women behind bars, and ultimately offer them new skills and hope upon their release.

References

Alexander, M. (2010). *The new Jim Crow: Mass incarceration in the age of colorblindness.* New York: The New Press.

Bryans, S., Martin, C., & Walker, R. (2002). The road ahead: Issues and strategies for future joint working. In S. Bryans, C. Martin, & R. Walker (Eds.), *Prisons and the voluntary sector.* Waterside: Winchester, England.

California Rehabilitation Oversight Board (C-ROB) (2015). Annual report. September 15, 2015. Sacramento, CA: Office of the Inspector General. Retrieved from http://www.oig.ca.gov/media/crob/reports/C-ROB_Annual_Report_September_15_2015.pdf.

Camp, S. D., Klein-Saffran, J., Kwon, O., Daggett, D. M., & Joseph, V. (2006). An exploration into participation in a faith-based prison program. *Criminology & Public Policy, 5*, 529–550.

HM Prison Service/Clinks. (2002). Good practice guide: Prisons and the voluntary and community-based sector. London: Clinks. Retrieved from http://www.clinks.org/sites/default/files/Good%20Practice%20Guide%202002.pdf.

Home Office. (2005). Managing offenders, reducing crime: The role of the voluntary and community sector in the National Offender Management Service London: Author. Retrieved from http://www.pavs.org.uk/news/documents/VSUstrategy.pdf.

Hucklesby, A. & Corocan, M. (Eds.) (2015). *The voluntary sector and criminal justice*. London: Palgrave.

Kort-Butler, L. & Malone, S. E. (2014). Citizen volunteers in prisons: bringing the outside in, taking the inside out. *Journal of Crime and Justice*, *38*(4), 508–521.

Kubrin, C. E. & Stewart, E. A. (2006). Predicting who reoffends: The neglected role of neighborhood context in recidivism studies. *Criminology*, *44*(1), 165–197.

Manza, J. & Uggen, C. (2006). *Locked out: Felon disenfranchisement and American democracy*. New York: Oxford University Press.

Martin, C. (2002). Recent progress in community-based voluntary sector work with the prison service. In S. Bryans, C. Martin, & R. Walker (Eds.), *Prisons and the voluntary sector*. Winchester, England: Waterside.

Meek, R., Gojkovic, D., & Mills, A. (2010). *The role of the third sector in work with offenders: The perceptions of criminal justice and third sectors stakeholders* (Working paper 34). Third Sector Research Centre Briefing. Retrieved from http://www.birmingham.ac.uk/generic/tsrc/documents/tsrc/working-papers/working-paper-34.pdf.

Mills, A., Meek, R., & Gojkovic, D. (2012). Partners, guests or competitors: Relationships between criminal justice and third sector staff in prisons. *Probation Journal*, *59*(4), 391–405.

Neilson, A. (2009). A crisis of identity: NACRO's bid to run a prison and what it means for the voluntary sector. *Howard Journal of Criminal Justice*, *48*, 401–410.

Neuberger, B. (2009). Volunteering across the criminal justice system London: The Cabinet Office. Retrieved from http://www.oneeastmidlands.org.uk/sites/default/files/library/volunteers%20in%20cjs.pdf.

New Philanthropy Capital (NPC) (2009). *Breaking the cycle: Charities working with people in prison and on release*. London: New Philanthropy Capital.

NOMS (2005). *Action plan for the development of effective partnership with the voluntary and community sector 2005–2007*. London: NOMS.

NOMS/IVR (2007). *Volunteers can: Towards a volunteering strategy to reduce re-offending*. London: NOMS.

Offender Management Act. (2007). London, UK: HMSO.

Raphael, S., & Stoll, M. A. (2009). Why are so many 2 Americans in prison? *Do prisons make us safer?: The benefits and costs of the prison boom*, 27.

Silvestri, A. (2009). *Partners or prisoners? Voluntary sector independence in the world of commissioning and contestability*. London: Centre for Crime and Justice Studies.

Taxman, F. S., Perdoni, M. L., & Harrison, L. D. (2007). Drug treatment services for adult offenders: The state of the state. *Journal of Substance Abuse Treatment*, *32*(3), 239–254.

Tewksbury, R. & Dabney, D. (2004). Prison volunteers: Profiles, motivations, satisfaction. *Journal of Offender Rehabilitation*, *40*(1/2), 173–183.
United States Department of Justice. (2013, April). Smart on crime: Reforming the criminal justice system for the twenty-first century. Washington, DC: Author. Retrieved from http://www.justice.gov/sites/default/files/ag/legacy/2013/08/12/smart-on-crime.pdf.
Wallace, D. & Papchristos, A. V. (2014). Recidivism and the availability of health care organizations. *Justice Quarterly*, *31*(3), 588–608.
Walmsley, R. (2013). *World prison population* (10th ed.). London: International Centre for Prison Research.
Western, B. (2006). *Punishment and inequality in America*. New York: Russell Sage Foundation.

CHAPTER 2

Non-profit and Voluntary Sector Programs in Prisons and Jails: Perspectives from England and the USA

Emma Hughes

This chapter is about positive programs and interactions that can happen in prisons and jails. So often we hear of the negative aspects such as violence, gangs, fear, wasted time, and mental distress. In no way does this chapter seek to minimize these all too significant realities. Nor does it seek to support sentences of incarceration when community-based sentences could be more appropriately used. Instead, this chapter, and indeed this book as a whole, is largely about constructive outcomes that can be achieved within the parameters of imprisonment. It is about productive and worthwhile activities that might help to offset the still relevant "pains of imprisonment" that Sykes (1958) so vividly described, while also encouraging successful reentry for those who will be released.

In particular, this chapter will draw on qualitative research conducted in the USA and England to examine the role that non-profit organizations

Partial funding covering various aspects of this study was provided by Birmingham City University (UK), the Prisoners' Education Trust (UK), and a grant from the College of Social Sciences' Research & Creative Activities Awards, California State University, Fresno (USA). I would also like to acknowledge Hannah Riccardi for her assistance with this project.

E. Hughes (✉)
California State University, Fresno, CA, USA

L.S. Abrams et al. (eds.), *The Voluntary Sector in Prisons*, Palgrave Studies in Prisons and Penology, DOI 10.1057/978-1-137-54215-1_2

and volunteers from the community can play in providing positive opportunities that supplement official provision in prisons and jails, filling gaps that would otherwise exist. The consequences for the participants' future plans and for their experience of incarceration will be considered in depth. Exploring additional themes that emerged from this research, I will also examine how voluntary sector programming can help bridge the distance between the world of the prison and the world outside. I will assess possible implications of this connection for self-identity, reentry, and desistance from crime among incarcerated participants and will briefly consider how the experience of volunteering may affect the outside volunteers as well. I will go on to explore how voluntary sector involvement can engender a desire among incarcerated participants to give back to their communities, again assessing the significance for self-identity, reentry, and desistance. To better contextualize the findings, I will consider variations that exist between correctional institutions in terms of voluntary sector engagement. Last, I will examine the potential benefits of creating permeable cultures that leave prisons and jails more amenable to positive and constructive outside influences.

Background

This work originates from a qualitative research study of British prisoners involved in distance learning (correspondence courses) funded by the Prisoners' Education Trust (PET), a London-based charity (Hughes, 2009, 2012). The study incorporated 47 in-depth interviews with distance learners, 76 short-answer questionnaires completed by distance learners (including the interviewees), and an earlier analysis of unsolicited letters written by students to PET (Hughes, 2000). The interviews took place in nine adult prisons in England, representing a range of security classifications and geographical locations, and included one women's prison. The questionnaire and interview participants provided informed consent and were advised that their anonymous involvement with the research would in no way impact their future relations or funding opportunities with PET. Interviews were recorded and subsequently transcribed.

While the main focus of this study was on the students' motivations for taking correspondence courses as well as their actual educational experiences, a more recent line of enquiry has involved examining the role and impact of the charity itself. As with the original study, grounded theory (Strauss & Corbin, 1998) has continued to inform the analysis process, allowing themes to emerge from the participants' own words.

In addition to the British-based study, this chapter stems from research on the involvement of community volunteers and non-profit organizations in US prisons and jails, with a specific emphasis on voluntary sector provision in the state of California. Using a snowball sampling technique, I conducted 20 in-depth interviews with 13 female and 7 male volunteers in northern, central, and southern California. All but two of the interviewees are involved in faith-based programming or faith-based activities; the remaining two provide services related to substance abuse recovery. Of note, some of the volunteers have expanded into additional types of programming during their time of service. Significantly, seven of the interviewees were formerly incarcerated themselves, six of whom have volunteered in criminal justice settings post-release, and the seventh, like some of the other formerly incarcerated participants, helped to originate programming whilst inside. Between them, the formerly incarcerated participants took part in a range of volunteer-led programming whilst in prison and jail. All interviewees provided informed consent; interviews were recorded and transcribed. As with the British study, grounded theory has provided the basis for the analysis of the data.

The California study makes no claim to provide a representative sample of community volunteers in the state's prisons and jails. However, the interviewees' insights illuminate important themes that in turn demonstrate interesting parallels with the experiences of the British participants, despite geographical, national, correctional system, and substantive program differences. Additionally, I have been involved with other non-profits that provide education and mentoring to incarcerated and formerly incarcerated individuals within California and across the USA, and these experiences have also reflexively informed my research.

Taken together, the cross-national studies presented in this chapter seek to give volunteers and participants in these programs a voice in order to enhance our understanding of the potential positive influence that volunteers and the voluntary sector may have in correctional facilities. As the introduction to this volume points out, despite a flourishing role for volunteers and the voluntary sector in correctional facilities, there is a dearth of research investigating the involvement of non-state actors within jails and prisons. Tewksbury and Dabney (2004) identified the "paucity of literature" (p. 173) in this area over 10 years ago, but there have been limited developments since. Indeed it is an effort to address this need for further research that has informed this volume as a whole. However, before turning to consider ways in which voluntary-led provision can enhance the opportunities for incarcerated individuals to engage in productive and meaningful activities, I will begin with an examination of the overcrowding, limited budgets, and shortages in programs and services with which prison and jail facilities, and crucially their residents, must frequently contend.

Mind the Gap

The history of modern incarceration reflects ongoing shifts in sentencing policies that in turn have impacted correctional systems and the extent to which institutional regimes have prioritized rehabilitative activities. The latter decades of the twentieth century and the early years of the twenty-first are no exception in that significant swings of the sentencing pendulum have influenced the size, scope, and agenda of correctional systems, further compounded by broader political and economic forces (c.f. Blumstein, 2011). This section will provide a brief overview of the recent impact of these shifts in first, California, and then England and Wales, in order to provide a more specific backdrop to the study at hand.[1]

In 2005 the California Department of Corrections expanded its name, becoming the California Department of Corrections and Rehabilitation (CDCR). This marked a significant departure from previous decades in which rehabilitation had remained out of favor since the collapse of the rehabilitative ideal in the 1970s (c.f. Martinson, 1974), then followed by the ushering in of a retributive, "tough on crime" era and a rapidly increasing rate of incarceration (c.f. Blumstein, 2011; Cullen, 2007).

However, despite the more recent, burgeoning interest in the potential benefits of rehabilitative programs (see, for example, CDCR's [2007] *Master Work Plan for Rehabilitative Programming*), significant overcrowding and budgetary limitations in the California prison system restricted program availability (California Rehabilitation Oversight Board [C-ROB], 2008). Furthermore, the state's financial woes at the time of global economic recession led to substantial cuts of $250 million to CDCR's programming budget for adult prisoners in the 2009–2010 fiscal year (C-ROB, 2010).

The ongoing battle with overcrowding continued to have an impact on programming provision. In some facilities, space that was previously

[1] The prison system of England and Wales is combined under one governing body, but remains separate from that of Scotland, the third country constituting Great Britain.

used for recreational and rehabilitative activities had been transformed into makeshift dorms to accommodate the inflated population. Although CDCR (2007) had reported progress in repurposing some of these common areas for their originally intended use, it was not until the US Supreme Court ruled in *Brown v. Plata* (2011) that California must reduce its prison population to 137.5 % of design capacity that the state undertook radical measures to reduce its population level from the approximately 180 % of design capacity at which it then stood.[2]

CDCR has since reduced its population to the specified level of overcrowding largely through state legislation, specifically Assembly Bill 109 (AB 109). This 2011 law mandated that defendants convicted of low-level felonies be incarcerated in county-run jails rather than state-run prisons. Additionally, demonstrating a continued interest in rehabilitation and preparation for reentry, CDCR has developed "Reentry Hubs" within 18 of the state's 35 adult institutions. These hubs target eligible prisoners within 4 years of release, providing an array of programs designed to help individuals transition back to society (C-ROB, 2015). However, provision across California's prison estate as a whole remains variable, particularly for long-term prisoners, and efforts to rectify this are underway (c.f. C-ROB, 2014, 2015). Moreover, CDCR is seeking to expand the use of volunteer service provision (C-ROB, 2015). Significantly, Irwin's (2009) observation in his study of life-sentenced men in San Quentin, that some of the most innovative and purposeful programming within that San Francisco Bay Area prison derived from programs run by outside community groups, prisoner-volunteers, or a combination of the two, remains relevant today. As will be seen, participants within this study echoed this view.

Although this study is primarily concerned with prisons, it should be noted that county jails in California have experienced a sharp increase in population since the implementation of AB 109 (Petersilia, 2014). Furthermore, jails can now house men and women sentenced to more than the 1-year cap originally in place. Yet jails were not intended to provide long-term accommodation, and thus provision for rehabilitation services has not typically featured in the design of these facilities or their daily

[2] CDCR was compelled to make this reduction following the Supreme Court's finding that overcrowding was interfering with the state's ability to provide prisoners with acceptable levels of health care and thus was violating constitutional protections from "cruel and unusual" punishment.

regimes. However, regional variation exists, with some counties currently making greater use of community-based sentences and/or developing innovative rehabilitation services within their jails (Petersilia, 2014).

While not on the scale of overcrowding seen in Californian prisons, prisons in England and Wales have also experienced overcrowding, budget cuts, staff shortages, and resource pressures that have clearly limited rehabilitation offerings (c.f. Her Majesty's Chief Inspector of Prisons for England and Wales (HMCIP), 2015). A government-trumpeted policy of a "Rehabilitation Revolution" announced in 2010 is not yet underway according to the recent HMCIP (2015) report.

Funding for prisoner education programs in England and Wales did, however, increase in the early twenty-first century (Schuller, 2009), reversing budget cuts to prison education departments that had taken place in the 1990s. At that time the prison system experienced a contracting out of educational services, the influence of "tough on crime" attitudes like those in the USA and a system-wide focus on basic skills instruction, such as literacy and numeracy, at the expense of higher levels of education (Hughes, 2012). Despite an influx of additional funds in the early 2000s, prison education departments did not see a return to the depth and breadth of course offerings or to the higher range of academic levels that were more readily available prior to the 1990s. Of note, research shows an increased association between education and reduced recidivism the higher the level of education (c.f. MacKenzie, 2006). However, the emphasis has remained on basic skills tuition in literacy and numeracy and other key skills (Wilson, 2010). For those students wishing to advance their education beyond this level, their primary option is to apply to PET for a grant. Each year, PET funds distance learning courses for approximately 2000 prisoners throughout England and Wales. PET will consider funding any course offered by a recognized educational provider, suitable for independent completion within a prison environment, and not related to the student's offense. Since their founding in 1989 they have assisted more than 28,000 prisoners (Prisoners' Education Trust, 2015). To put the statistics in context, the prison population of England and Wales stood at approximately 85,000 in mid-2015 (Ministry of Justice, 2015).

A similar story in regards to education provision can be told of the USA, where the 1994 passage of the Violent Crime Control and Law Enforcement Act by Congress made prisoners ineligible for federal grants to assist students with college tuition. Although a brand new initiative is reintroducing Pell Grants for prisoners on a limited, trial basis

(US Department of Education, 2015), the loss of funds in 1994 resulted in the closure of most in-prison college programs (Batiuk, 1997; Gehring, 1997; Ubah & Robinson, 2003). In certain cases, programs staffed by volunteer college instructors, supported by an external university, or both, stepped up to fill in the gap (Irwin, 2009; Prison University Project, 2015).

In this chapter, I will describe how prisoners may turn to non-profits such as PET, or other volunteer-led provision, to expand their opportunities to engage in varied rehabilitative, constructive, and purposeful activities in prison. Whether in England and Wales, California, other geographic locations detailed throughout this volume, or beyond, the opportunity to engage in supplementary provision can offer incarcerated individuals a much sought after chance to address their current circumstances and consider their future directions.

Filling the Gap

Drawing on data from both the British and California-based studies described earlier, this section will explore how charity and volunteer-led programs and activities can enrich a prison or jail environment in ways that can appreciably impact the lives of those who take part. Notably, the enhanced provision can expand participants' opportunities to prepare for and gain insight into post-release lives, help reduce the negative impact of institutionalization, and aid the development of affirming and pro-social cultures within a facility.

Preparing for Post-release Lives

Participants described how the supplementary activities made possible by outside support have helped them to better prepare for employment after release, develop and clarify goals for the future, and find alternative ways of living their lives. In some cases these supplementary activities worked alongside state-run programs or complement personal transformations that the individuals are already experiencing. Significantly, participants reported gaining a greater sense of hope for their future as a result of their involvement with non-profit and voluntary sector provision.

A primary motivation for British prisoners to pursue distance learning is to improve their employment prospects post-release (Hughes, 2012). Students have consistently pointed to limited opportunities within prison education departments once basic skills classes have been completed, or if qualifications were held before entering prison, as motivation for seeking charitable funds to further their education through correspondence.

Trevor, who entered prison without educational qualifications, explained: "I've finished full-time education [in the department].... I've done a few extra courses that they had available ... I've completed them all."[3] He enrolled in a PET-funded introduction to the music industry course that he had heard about from a fellow prisoner. He said: "I wanted to get something that was going to benefit me in what I wanted to do when I get out...At the time, I still wanted to learn more things, so I opted to do that." Nick faced similar circumstances after completing all prison-based courses within 2 to 3 months of his arrival. With approximately 3 years left of his sentence, he found himself asking: "what's next?" and turned to distance learning.

The extensive range of available courses through PET can also overcome gendered stereotypes that may impact what prison-based courses are available (Bloom, Owen & Covington, 2003). The following quote is from Eileen, a student in an open prison who was able to leave the facility during the day for education and vocational training. She wrote in a letter to PET:

> I would like to thank you and the trustees for funding the forklift truck-driving course for me ... it was very interesting and took a lot of hard work.... Having passed, I hope this leads to further training on different trucks and possibly a job in the future. Thank you once again, if it wasn't for your funding, I would never have been able to attend the course.

Students who were focused on future job opportunities frequently pointed to the need to advance their education well beyond basic skills, given the challenges they anticipated encountering in obtaining employment on account of their criminal records. Students sought qualifications to show prospective employers that their time in prison was well spent, but also to boost their chances in comparison to other applicants. Joe, then aged 23 and serving a life sentence,[4] undertook distance learning with this in mind:

[3] Research participants' names have been changed in order to protect anonymity.

[4] In England and Wales, a "lifer" has a life sentence with a tariff that indicates the minimum time they are expected to serve before the Parole Board considers them for release. If they are released they remain on "life license," subject to recall to prison as long as they live. Most lifers, like Joe, and Bruce who will feature later, do not have a "whole-life tariff" that makes them ineligible for release.

"Because of the sentence I was doing … I thought I've got to give myself the best possible chance, not just of getting out but that when I do get out I'll have options open to me."

Indicative of the potential significance of the PET grants for helping to develop a new future based on enhanced education, Pam, a single mother of three, undertaking a business studies course, wrote on her research questionnaire:

> [The] Prisoners' Education Trust have really given me a big start, and I would like to take this opportunity to thank them. They have helped me in making a big change in my life. They have saved my life. Thank you!!!

For those still trying to imagine a different path in life, non-profit and voluntary sector provisions can help individuals to discover a new way forward. In their theory of cognitive transformation, Giordano, Cernkovich, and Rudolph (2002) argue that for persistent offenders to desist from crime, an important stage in the process revolves around selecting and using transformative opportunities, described as "hooks for change" (p. 992), that are available within their environment. Crucially, individuals must be able to perceive these hooks and recognize the potential meaningfulness for their lives. Living in a dynamic environment that offers vibrant and worthwhile activities increases the chances for such hooks to be found, whether that is specifically through education or through a wide array of other volunteer-led activities as demonstrated below.

Before prison, Dee said that her life as a musician was all about "sex, drugs, and rock and roll." While in a California prison she took a mandated state-contracted substance abuse treatment program and began developing her "relationship with God." She said, "It hit me like a ton of bricks … I'm going to have to change everything when I get out of here." Dee was "freaked out," worrying that "I don't know anything else" and wondering "what do I do?" However, she found an answer through one of the volunteer-led prison ministries that she regularly attended where she encountered a community volunteer, "with tattoos [and] spiked hair," playing a guitar. Dee recognized him from a punk rock band that he had performed with in the past. Watching him play music as part of this prison ministry she realized, "he's rocking for God!" For Dee this recognition meant: "'Whoa, I can still rock. But now I just rock for God,' you know."

For over 10 years Carl has been a volunteer associate chaplain at a California county jail, and for the past 5 years has also been running prison ministry programs in several California prisons. He developed his relationship with God whilst serving time in prison in the 1970s through the mid-1980s. He talks of experiencing a "born again" conversion halfway through his sentence that led to a profound transformation in his life. He removed himself from the prison gang warfare in which he had played an active role as a member of the Aryan Brotherhood and which had led to his conviction for a murder in prison. As part of his developing religious practice he began to attend prison ministries facilitated by outside community groups. He recalls knowing early on in his experience of participating in ministries that this would connect with his future life. Carl recounted how he spent the last 7 years of his sentence: "out of the gang and in the body of Christ, studying His word, [and] fellowshipping." He stated that: "the support that I received … to get me through the last 7 years was through Christian fellowships with other people." He has been working with ministries ever since his parole in 1985.

The community-led prison ministries that Dee attended six evenings a week whilst incarcerated also informed her desire to return to correctional facilities as a ministry volunteer, which shall be discussed in the "Giving Back" section below. However, it is noteworthy that the group Dee attended the remaining evening of each week, a Toastmasters meeting run by community volunteers, also helped her to prepare for her future plans. Like Toastmasters groups in the community, participants gather to practice public speaking by giving speeches and receiving feedback from fellow group members. Dee had already recognized that through ministry work in future she was "definitely going to be speaking and telling my story." She had thought: "I need to learn how to speak better" and had concluded that the Toastmasters meetings would help her achieve this goal.

Like other California research participants, both Dee and Carl talked about finding hope in prison, and they contrasted this with the despair they had previously experienced. Carl said of the early years of his prison sentence: "I saw the hopelessness, I had no hope." Dee said that she learned in prison that there is "hope after dope." For Dee and for Carl, the opportunity to partake in these optional activities complemented other personal or required pursuits and enhanced their optimism for the future. Their experience of finding hope resonates with accounts from the distance learners. Patrick echoed many of the students when he said that his PET-funded courses helped to provide "hope and direction" for the future. And Ed, who entered prison in England with no qualifications, said that: "When I first came here, it was 'my life is over …' the criminal record and all the stigma attached, but because of my education and my being able to move on, it has actually proved to be the most positive [thing] of my life so far."

Significantly, Burnett and Maruna (2004) have found that an increased sense of hope, which they equate with "the desire for a particular outcome and also the perceived ability and means of achieving the outcome" (pp. 395–396) is correlated with a lower return rate to prison. They argue that: "Participants with high hope scores [before leaving prison] seem better able to cope with the problems they encounter after they leave the prison walls" (p. 398).

Exposure to new ideas and activities through charity-funded education or volunteer-led provision may broaden horizons, influence goals, shape ideas about future directions, and help to inspire hope. These activities may work alongside other personal or state-run endeavors the individuals are involved with in prison (see also Hughes, 2012). The pursuits may foster imagination regarding what might be possible in future, enabling a vision of an alternative path. This can impact not only future lives, but also affect time spent in prison, as the next section will address.

Overcoming Institutionalization

Engaging in a range of positive activities whilst behind prison walls can help to offset negative experiences of incarceration such as boredom, depersonalization, and frustration. As this section will show, incarcerated individuals may use their time constructively, find ways to enhance their sense of self, cope with long sentences, and increase their self-confidence. Furthermore, these findings demonstrate that through taking part in rewarding activities that enrich their lives, the participants may potentially impact the lives of others around them as well.

Dee described the volunteer-based evening groups that she attended seven nights a week as "awesome" and "wonderful" because they provided "something else to do." She knew that she "wanted to do things different" and not be like "some people that just go out to the yard and do all of their crazy, stupid stuff ..." She found what Jim, studying math through distance learning in Britain, described as "options for the day." Similarly Will, who is studying Animal Behavior, expressed gratitude for having an alternative to watching TV in his cell on evenings and weekends. The decision to engage in constructive activities, where the option exists, can help to counter the monotony of prison life with potentially considerable positive consequences. According to Sean, engaging in distance learning courses kept him away from drugs. He stated: "the education has kept me busy and kept me occupied you know, where people will be bored and that and they'll start smoking heroin or whatever and they'll just get stoned." At the same time, the act of making choices about how time is spent may serve to reduce the loss of autonomy that Sykes (1958) identified as a main contributor to the "pains of imprisonment" whilst also better preparing prisoners for life beyond bars (see also Petersilia, 2003).

Because volunteer and charity-based provisions increase the chances that individuals will find opportunities and activities that align with their personal interests, participants may be better positioned to resist the "stripping of self" that Goffman (1961) notably associated with prison life (Wilson, 2003). For example, distance learning substantially broadens the range of academic and vocational courses to which prisoners have access, allowing students to explore individualized, specialized subjects that prison education departments could not possibly offer. Will has a particular interest in "herpetology—snakes and reptiles and things like that," hence his decision to take the course on animal behavior that gave him something to do besides watch TV. He would like to work in a zoo in future. Alan, studying the Enlightenment period, reported that: "it is probably something I have always wanted and never ever took up." Doug said he has "been in marketing and PR most of my life" and was taking related courses. Significantly, reconnecting with pro-social aspects of one's life before prison may help to restore or reinforce positive identities that are "spoiled" (Goffman, 1963) through incarceration (Crawley & Sparks, 2005; Jewkes, 2005).

For those who are serving very long or life sentences, there appear to be particular benefits to becoming involved in positive and constructive activities. Distance learners talk of setting personal goals that involve pursuing new or long-standing interests. For those who will be post-retirement when released, or who do not expect to be released, these interests are not intrinsically connected to future work plans. Alan, who is post-retirement age, said of his course on the Enlightenment, "I am not doing it to get a job.... It isn't that ... it is a personal thing, just for me." Bruce, a lifer, has plans to study a new language each year. Students recognized the benefit of using their courses for keeping their mental skills sharp (which some argue is not easy to do in prison) and noted that extended programs of study help to constructively delineate the passage of time (see also Cohen & Taylor, 1972). Dee reported that some of the participants in the numerous evening programs that she attended were lifers with little chance of release: "You know they're in for life," but reinforcing her earlier point, she praised the programs for "giv[ing] [them] ... something else to do, other than criminal behavior."

In a carceral world associated with failure, stigmatization, and condemnation, involvement in supplementary programs can also offer opportunity for praise, achievement, and positive recognition. As distance learner Martin suggested: "with people in prison a pat on the back goes a long way." Some of the prison ministry programs award certificates at the conclusion of educational courses and modules. One such program confers a certificate in Christian leadership upon completion of what Carl described as a "really rigorous" 4-year schedule of study involving 16 course modules. Carol, who volunteers and works with the ministry that oversees the program, remarked that:

> Certificates are so important to an inmate because they keep a portfolio of every single thing they have done to better themselves, you know, and to prepare themselves to get out. Men and women both do that.... They keep track of everything that they do.

For those who will be seeking employment, participants reported that certificates and other acknowledgements can be used as evidence of accomplishment to show prospective employers, but can also directly impact their sense of self. Trevor, studying in England, said: "Funnily enough, I've got a form with all the achievements I've done.... I was surprised that I accomplished so much." Kevin, studying psychology, explained that education has "give[n] me more self-worth" and added: "I feel better about myself." Research on desistance from crime has demonstrated that a greater belief in self and an improved sense of self-efficacy are associated with more positive outcomes post-release (Burnett & Maruna, 2004; Maruna, 2001). Additionally, recognition gained in prison can be used to show family and friends outside the facility that the time behind bars is being put to good use. This may serve to strengthen family ties, also associated with positive outcomes post-release (Light, 1993; Petersilia, 2003). Ed, for example, reported that his family is "amazed" by what he has achieved through his studies, and said that they are really "chuffed [very pleased] that I am using what I have got in a positive way."

The prisoners who participate in these varied activities may also inspire other prisoners. Jason decided to begin distance learning upon seeing a friend of his in the prison progress academically. Jason had thought to himself: "Well, okay, if other people can do it then I can do it." Dee, initially unfamiliar with Toastmasters, attended her first meeting because of her prison roommate, "[who] was like what they would call 'Polly Programmer.'" The roommate, knowing that Dee wanted to change her life, "was like, 'come to Toastmasters with me.'" In another example of prisoners reaching out to each other, members of a Catholic choir in a California prison spotted a man walking across the yard with a guitar in hand. They invited him to meet with the Chapel choir. "He t[ook] a leap ... and well, he became my lead singer and guitarist," explained Hilda, a community volunteer who assists the choir with their music every Sunday. She added: "I taught him everything I know about liturgical planning," something which the guitarist has practiced with community-based parishes since his release.

Relying on happenstance and word of mouth, as Hilda suggested, may make it hard for potential participants to "even find" what is available. Yet it is important to recognize the role that fellow prisoners may play in encouraging positive enterprise and supplementing official notifications of programming that may exist. The richer the environment and the more varied the opportunities through outside community involvement, the greater the likelihood of incarcerated individuals motivating each other in such ways. In turn, this contributes to a culture more representative of "mature coping" (Johnson, 2002), and more supportive of learning and purposeful activity, as detailed below.

Developing Cultures of Learning and Support

Within this study, current and former prisoners, as well as community-based volunteers who have not been incarcerated, recognized a humanizing quality that the outside provision can bring to facilities. This humanizing influence creates a space where incarcerated individuals may feel that they can lower personal barriers, share more of themselves than may typically be the case, engage in personal growth and learning, support one another, and feel treated as humans rather than prisoners.

Annette is a formerly incarcerated volunteer. She currently works with a Christian-based prison ministry that as part of its outreach runs 4-day retreats within prisons, bringing messages of love, forgiveness, and compassion through the teachings of Christ. Annette explained that through the retreats the participants "can go somewhere in a place that's [normally] so dark, so cold, so ugly, and just find peace for a few days." She described seeing participants' skin change from "ashen" to "glowing" over the course of the 4 days. The organizers hope that participants will continue their spiritual journey after the retreat through participation in prisoner-led, prison-based Christian study groups supported by future visits from ministry volunteers. Julie has found that in her experience of regularly volunteering with retreats in two women's prisons, 90 % of the women who take part choose to continue in study groups.

Elizabeth is another community volunteer assisting with the ministry's retreats. She observed how the women taking part "begin to start sharing things. Through the music, they start having some fun and letting some of their walls down," and the women sometimes tell her: "this doesn't feel like prison." Brian, who helps to facilitate the equivalent retreats in men's prisons, described seeing barriers between men of opposing gangs and different races and ethnicities break down whilst at a retreat. Speaking about race and ethnicity, he explained:

> I can't say it becomes a nonissue, but it becomes a very minor issue over the course of the weekend. And the first day, it's a big issue. By the end of the weekend, it's … very minor and I've heard inmates say, "you know, I am apologizing to my Black brothers or my Caucasian brothers or my Hispanic brothers."

Brian explained that apologies may be along the lines of "I've always either ignored you or I've not treated you well and I'm not going to continue that behavior."

Brian acknowledged that "when [the men] go back on the yard it's prison politics as usual. I don't think they're going up there hugging each other, but you know they might do a fist bump or at least a polite conversation." He recognized that outside of the retreat and the study groups "they have to be careful" because of how others on the yard might react, but noted "we understand that." Perry, who was formerly incarcerated, recounted similar experiences. He participated in numerous chapel-based programs in California prisons when he served time. For Perry, the chapel and the programs represented a "safe haven," offering a "break" from "all the crazy stuff on the yard," allowing him to feel that he had effectively "stepped out of prison." In the chapel, Perry, who is black, found that he could be friendly with prisoners of other races and ethnicities. While they did not feel able to "give [each other] a hug" when they met on the yard, there "would not be a stare of death either," because you "have a relationship with [each other] now." Echoing the comments of many of those involved with faith-based programs, Barbara, an outside volunteer, stated that these programs and retreats offer participants: "a sense of actually belonging" and for those who are "willing to work to have community," they can create "a safe place to share."

The British-based study also contains reference to the creation of supportive communities, specifically in regards to the informal study groups that some distance learners form to assist each other with their work. Doug, who regularly attended a study group in his prison, said: "if we can sit down together we can make more of it." Joan was studying the same course as another woman in her prison. She noted that: "if ever I get stuck on something I sit and discuss it with her. She'll give me her opinion on it and I'll give her my opinion on it and [we] try and work it out between us." Back in California, the musicians and singers who performed in the previously mentioned Catholic chapel choir were practicing approximately 14 hours per week. Hilda, the community volunteer who "assist[s] ... the inmates who are providing music for the mass or the communion service," said of the group of approximately 10 men who currently perform: "it's a group that is very committed. They set up their own practices during the week; they organize it. They work it out. They hold each other accountable."

Taken together, these examples illustrate how activities generated or assisted by outside parties may help to foster the development of pro-social communities, encourage the creation of spaces that are at least partially removed, either physically or figuratively, from the more negative environment of prisons (see also Wilson, 2003, 2007), and nurture the growth of a culture of support and assistance among those taking part. Indicative of the potential benefits, one distance learner wrote to PET saying:

> [Education in prison] really is the only place where you feel both human and confident.... It is therefore a godsend that Trusts such as yours exist. It is comforting to know that despite any obstacles we encounter, there are those who are prepared to a) help and b) support what is essentially a vital area of a prisoner's objective, to improve himself, and hence lessen his chances of returning to prison after release. Perhaps a far more important factor than the [P]rison [S]ervice is prepared to admit?

In subsequent sections I will explore how the development of pro-social cultures may ripple out toward others within the prison. However, in the section below I will examine more particularly what can happen when the outside comes in, when members of surrounding communities and non-profit organizations enter the largely closed world of a prison.

Building Bridges

Both the inside participants and the outside volunteers consistently discussed the benefits that accrue from the creation of bonds that transcend prison walls. It is important to note that these benefits are in addition to those already discussed above, and originate specifically in the relationships that community partnerships engender. The research demonstrates that building bridges with the outside world can have positive repercussions for incarcerated individuals' self-worth and self-identity, and there are possible consequences for desistance from crime and post-release transitions.

Christopher, who helped to run volunteer programs whilst incarcerated, explained: "No free person will ever understand how totally the prison system will shut you off from the world … psychologically, that can break you down." Involvement with volunteer-led programs and non-profit organizations can help prisoners to feel less isolated and lonely. For those who no longer have contact with family or friends outside of the prison gates, these connections may represent their only regular contact with people beyond the prison walls who are not prison employees. Julie said that whenever she and other volunteers are walking on the yard in one of the women's prisons she visits, shouts of "free world is on the yard" will echo around, and women will come over eager to talk. She added: "one of the things they are interested to see are the fashions that people are wearing." For Christopher, "the volunteers coming in … gave us a miniscule window on what was going on in the outside world."

As volunteers and inside participants are quick to point out, the significance of the connection extends beyond simply bridging a gap between two physically distinct worlds. The fact that the volunteers have chosen to visit a prison or jail, or that a charity on the strength of community-based donations has chosen to fund a prisoner, can help to ease the figurative separation that prisoners may feel based on anticipated or experienced stigmatization and condemnation from the outside world.

For example, Clive was taking courses funded by PET related to his goal of becoming a physiotherapist when I was doing my research. He described in his questionnaire being particularly affected upon "realis[ing] [that] people such as the Prisoners' Education Trust are willing to give me another chance." Clive's gratitude suggests that this support contrasts with the rejection that he may otherwise be expecting because of his prisoner and criminal status.

Formerly incarcerated interviewees in California consistently expressed gratitude for the involvement of volunteers, and surprise at their willingness to give up time that they could have spent with family and friends or in other activities. For Christopher, the volunteers' commitment had a "tremendous impact." He was "blown away," thinking, "you gave up all this for me?" Likewise, Perry said of a mentor who gave up time with family to visit him twice a month for 4 years across two different prisons: "this man made a conscious decision to reach out." Perry felt that the friendship and support "picked me up; he treated me like a human … and gave me a little touch of the outside that kept me sane." For Dee, the volunteers who ran the numerous programs she attended in prison are "just amazing people to give their time." Not only did she learn new skills, but the fact that the volunteers from the community wanted to be there, and that they "don't look at you like a lowlife," or like a "drug addict criminal" made an important difference.

The defining aspect of these interactions is that the volunteers treat the inside participants as people rather than prisoners. The potential consequences for participants' sense of self and identity were evident throughout this research. For Christopher, his interactions with the volunteers led to the realization that: "I'm not the worse thing that I ever did." He says: "I learned all that … because of the volunteers, because they were there to affirm me." Hilda says of herself and other volunteers who regularly attend mass at a prison's Catholic chapel:

> What our presence acknowledges is that [the incarcerated men] matter. That just because they are felons, and just because they're locked up, does not mean that they are forgotten…. I think what the visitors do is acknowledge their human dignity, their worth, our belief that they are important parts of our faith community.

Julie, a prison ministry volunteer, also articulated a common theme when she said: "Some of [the inside participants] will look at us and they'll say: 'Why do you come here? Why do you love us? How can you? Why?' And they're just amazed that somebody really will do that, and that grows and it changes people." Julie argued that regardless of the nature of the volunteer program, whether, for example, it is faith-based or education-based, "the bottom line [is] the fact that people from the outside care enough to come in; [that] makes all the difference."

For incarcerated individuals, community volunteers and non-profit organizations can act to affirm or reaffirm pro-social identities such as student, or person of faith, that can help to replace the stigmatized prisoner or criminal identity (Crawley & Sparks, 2005; Jewkes, 2005). This new sense of self helps to broaden horizons and open up new ways of being. According to Rumgay (2004), "successful desistance from crime may be rooted in recognition of an opportunity to claim an alternative, desired and socially approved personal identity" (p. 405). In turn, these identities can offer pro-social scripts for individuals to follow. The volunteers and outside organizations can serve to further validate and support these chosen scripts and roles (Rumgay, 2004; see also, Giordano et al., 2002; Harris, 2009; Hughes, 2009).

In this respect it is worth noting that the trustees and patrons of PET, individuals who thus oversee the charity's awarding of funds to prisoners for education, include senior judges and others who hold or have held prominent positions in the criminal justice system. As Clive intimated, it is significant that individuals involved with the system that convicted and sentenced the students to prison are also rewarding their efforts to use their time in positive ways. Indeed, Maruna (2011) has remarked upon the particular value of criminal justice professionals being involved in such a process of affirmation. Perry reinforced this point when a post-release volunteer mentor had a particular impact on his ability to see himself differently, precisely because the mentor was a lawyer: "It's a person who's a law person treating me like a human and just connecting with you" and he says that it feels "almost like getting a pardon or clemency … this person who somewhat worked to put you where you are … saying 'hey, you know you can change … and people will accept you when you make those changes.'"

The volunteers, whether formerly incarcerated or not, are well-positioned to identify a need for reentry support, especially for those individuals returning to communities after decades of incarceration and with few remaining family members or friends to offer assistance. In one prison, a 2-year collaborative effort involving weekly meetings between incarcerated men and outside volunteers resulted in a policy paper exploring how the Catholic Church could assist the reentry of former prisoners, a paper later distributed to all of California's Bishops. As Jane, a member of the project made clear, as important as the work is in prison, what happens in the community after release in terms of support, acceptance, and reducing stigma, is vital, too (see also Chap. 9, this volume).

The volunteers referred to regulations, informed by CDCR policy, prohibiting contact between volunteers currently assisting in a prison and those released from that facility on parole. However, examples emerged whereby direct support for reentry was offered through legitimate avenues. Barbara, a prison ministry volunteer who is engaged in letter correspondence with men and women in prisons around California, has created packets of information detailing community resources in each of California's 58 counties for distribution to correspondents soon to be released from the prison. She identified this need based on recurring questions in letters asking: "Where am I going to go when I get out? I have nowhere to go." She and her fellow volunteer writers in a central Californian prison ministry office "will probably write over a 1000 letters this year…many of those with packets."

Some of the formerly incarcerated interviewees in California have connected with community faith-based groups through their religious practice in prison, and they have reported continuing in substance abuse groups such as Alcoholics Anonymous and Narcotics Anonymous that they started on the inside. Some, like Perry, maintained contact with a mentor they were paired with during their sentence. Moreover, PET has established an alumni network for former prisoner-students they have funded, and encourages those who are released to remain in touch. For those distance learners in Britain still working on their courses at the time of release, the students are entitled to complete their course post-release, a benefit of being enrolled in an educational institution entirely distinct from their prison (Hughes, 2012). In these and other examples, individuals are able to continue their involvement in meaningful activities and practices begun behind bars, whilst reinforcing new identities. Crucially, such associations can also foster the development of new social bonds, correlated with the successful reintegration of former prisoners into the outside world and a reduction in reoffending (Laub & Sampson, 2003).

Building bridges between a prison and the outside community can bring significant benefits to those who are incarcerated. However, it would be wrong to suggest that these benefits only travel in one direction. The community volunteers consistently remarked that as much as they give, they get more in return. Hilda stated: "It gives us a great deal of joy and purpose, and that's why we do it…. I see redemption. I see compassion. I see forgiveness. I see friendship." Other volunteers reported their preconceived notions of criminals and prisoners shattering. As Julie put it,

"All of those stereotypical myths were blown to smithereens...it's incredibly impacting ... and your whole outlook, your whole belief system, everything just changes, and it's just so humbling." While the particular effects vary by person, the sense of mutual exchange remains significant. Perry found that whilst incarcerated he was able to provide assistance to the mentor who visited him regularly: "he went through some [difficulties] you know...and so it was just amazing how...being in the situation I was, I was able to be a good ear for him also." The following section will turn to explore in more detail how prison-based volunteer and charity-led activities can engender or reinforce a desire to give back.

Giving Back

The formerly incarcerated volunteers commonly identified that their desire to help others was informed by their own experiences of benefitting from voluntary sector support. As Carl, the volunteer chaplain who made it through the last 7 years of his sentence because of the help he received from prison ministries, explained: "I love to give back you know, [to] those who are in the same situation that I was in, that I found myself in." For Perry, now a certified substance abuse counselor in the community, the desire to "pay it forward" underpins, "why I do what I do," which includes voluntary talks with community groups and with incarcerated individuals about overcoming addiction.

In some cases the desire to give back is simultaneously driven by religious inspiration and spiritual guidance, and for some the process of volunteering is an integral part of addiction recovery. Sometimes it may be a combination of the two. Regardless of the particular origins of the impetus, an underlying theme that connects the participants' accounts is the sense that through their experiences, through their own surmounting of challenges, they may be able to assist others to achieve the same. Clive, the student taking the physiotherapy courses who was struck by the fact that PET was willing to help, said that that in itself: "makes me want to repay that trust, and one day I'll be able to help others who need help." Similarly, a student who received funds for art materials from PET wrote to the charity to say: "Maybe one day I can repay your valuable support—even send works for you to exhibit and inspire others to help change their lives."

Indeed there was a common perception among the formerly incarcerated volunteers that because of their histories, they are particularly well suited to helping others in need. For example, Al is a pastor in the community who returns to correctional facilities through a prison ministry, and like Carl, he serves as a chaplain in a jail. He has also established a ministry for at-risk youth. He said: "I couldn't reach the ones that I reach if I hadn't gone through it … I share with them what worked for me." He recalls meeting a formerly incarcerated ministry volunteer while in prison and seeing "a mirror image of mine … I was like 'wow, that worked for him,' you know … and I said 'wow, maybe I want that.'" Sally returns to correctional facilities to participate in 12-step recovery programs at least two nights a week. Like Al, she observed that: "it's always good with people that have, you know, 'been there, done that' … [to show] where you've gone to now."

Al further explained that: "when I stand in front of the guys, I don't pull no punches…. I share real stuff. And I go straight to the point and people say they never heard it shared that way." Drawing on his own experiences he warns people of "the rejections that they're going to get, the letdowns, the family members, the churches that tell them they're going to be there then don't … so they know how to deal with these things" so that they don't just go into "survival mode" and "go back to what [they] know." He says they "look at me you know, and think 'yeah, I can do that, that's attainable.'" "That," he adds, is "something special."

Maruna (2001) argued that finding a social purpose through making use of a troubled personal history is a successful strategy for maintaining desistance from crime, enabling former offenders to write "redemption scripts" of their lives. He noted a recurring interest in generativity (Erikson, 1968), or guiding the next generation, in the narratives of successful desisters. The relevance of his findings to the interviewees' narratives is readily apparent and helps to illuminate additional ways in which giving back may support the formerly incarcerated volunteers themselves. Of significance here, Maruna (2001) concluded that "the construction or reconstruction of one's life story into a moral tale might…itself, be an important element of maintaining significant behavioral reform" (p. 155), in part through the opportunity to reaffirm valued new identities. For former prisoners returning to jails and prisons as guest speakers or program volunteers, there is clear, official recognition of a new role and identity playing out. Annette was invited back into prison as a guest speaker only 13 months after release. Sally was invited to speak at a special event at a prison in which she once lived. She remarked: "I was told I would never be able to get back in there. Except as an inmate," but the security clearance came through. She observed of her visits to correctional facilities in general: "It's a good reminder, you know, I get to go in and walk out, so it's a good reminder."

These positive affirmations do not just emerge from official approval, but also most notably, from program participants. Following her release from prison, Dee moved into a residential drug treatment facility required by her parole conditions. There she connected with a local church group that provides Bible studies in the facility. Upon completing the program Dee maintained contact with this church. She now returns to the residential facility to co-lead the Bible studies. Dee reported that it is "awesome" when current residents of the facility exclaim in disbelief: "You were here?!" With a sense of amazement she remarks that among the residents: "I'm [known as] 'the church lady.'" Dee has applied for security clearance to return to prison with a ministry program. She hopes to show others that: "you can still find joy inside [prison]…. I became free on the inside." Dee, who said that she lives "an awesome life now," added that: "It means a lot to me just to be able to share my experience, strength, and hope" and to let others realize that: "This doesn't have to be it" for them. She hopes that the skills she learned through the Toastmasters group will further help her to share this message. In so doing, her identity as a contributor to society is reinforced.

The distance learners in Britain, still incarcerated at the time of their interviews, also expressed a desire to give back (Hughes, 2012). For some this desire has translated into volunteer work whilst serving their sentence, using skills they have learned or enhanced through their studies. Mike, who used to consider himself a "career criminal," has completed several distance learning courses on counseling skills alongside his participation in an intensive therapeutic community program within prison. He has put his knowledge to use through his volunteer work in the prison Listener scheme, a program run by the Samaritans charity whereby selected prisoners are trained to provide confidential support to prisoners experiencing mental or emotional crises. Mike said he is no longer the "horrible" person he was in the past, and he laughed that fellow members of the therapeutic community had given him the nickname of "counselor," further recognition of the changes that he has made in his life (for further discussion of the Listener scheme, see Chap. 5, this volume).

There are also distance learners who serve as peer tutors, providing assistance in particular to prisoners struggling with literacy and numeracy. Aaron, who earned a Certificate of Education during his incarceration, explained that he "got loads of satisfaction" from seeing his tutees "pleased with themselves … they've got this motivation … whereas at first they would mess you about, you see them flourish." Other distance learners reported teaching yoga and music, skills related to their educational studies. Others, like Mike, undertake counseling roles. Some direct their new skills toward work on their prison's magazine. Throughout, the distance learners' accounts offer evidence of a ripple effect, whereby the benefits the students gain from their studies extend out to others in the environment, further advancing a culture of learning and support within the prison. The programs and opportunities initiated and/or run by prison-based volunteers must not be underestimated for their enrichment potential, offering benefits as they do to the individuals providing the service, and to the recipients as well (for further information, see Part II, this volume).

For Carl, one of the formerly incarcerated volunteer chaplains in California, service is a central goal of the Christian leadership course that he teaches. The course focuses on: "getting th[e] student[s] to begin thinking of service … [and] getting out from themselves, because self has been their biggest enemy, that's why they're in prison. So come up out of that and reach out and minister to others." The benefits he observes for the men taking part in the programming are far-reaching:

> The positive changes that I'm seeing [are] the men getting self-worth. They begin to feel better about themselves and … I think that a poor sense of self-worth is one of the major reasons that guys are in prison.… Either there's no sense of self-worth [or] they drummed their worth out of them, with drugs or alcohol, or getting a sense of identity through … being a thief … gang affiliation, whatever … and maybe I'm just looking at it because of myself and my poor sense of self-worth that I had way back then … but I really believe that that is one of the keys to reaching men, is building them up through their self-worth.

In the meantime, Perry, out of prison for over 10 years, goes to the shopping mall every Christmas to make a donation to the Prison Fellowship Angel Tree fund that enables an incarcerated parent to provide a gift to each of his or her children. He said: "My daughter, every year she would get a present from me with my name on it, not something like grandma got, but something I actually got to [complete an application for and] pick out." Now, he says, he can "pay for it." "That" he adds, "is my whole basis of why I do what I do, the old 'pay it forward' syndrome."

Variation in Provision

Despite the potential benefits that can arise from voluntary provision, not all facilities are similarly situated in terms of the quantity or quality of volunteer-led programs. So why is it that some facilities have an abundance of programs, and some have relatively few? While this is a direction I intend to explore in future research, some preliminary thoughts are offered here.

Clearly, individual managers, wardens, correctional officers, and other staff at facilities make a difference (see also Chap. 11, this volume). For example, Dee credited the chaplain at her prison for the abundance of available programming, explaining: "She's really the heartbeat of [the prison]…. She's amazing." Annette complemented another chaplain who went out of her way to gain permission for Annette to speak with women in the prison chapel even though she had only been released from prison 13 months prior.

Prison wardens (or governors in Britain) are particularly singled out for the impact that they have. Brian, a long-term volunteer with both the CDCR and federal prison systems, offered: "you get down to the local level of the warden, and each prison … has its own differences." And in what was a common refrain, he noted that when the warden of the facility changes (a not infrequent occurrence), "life starts all over again."

When Annette was incarcerated in the CDCR system there were hardly any programs at her relatively newer facility. Now a community volunteer, she recognizes the impact that a warden can have on volunteer provision, especially in terms of the speed with which security clearances are processed for volunteers. Carol agreed and believes that delay in processing clearances "is probably one of the most frustrating things for a volunteer that there is," and can leave some volunteers seeking noncustodial settings to perform their community service. Reflecting on the warden's influence on staff she observed: "It starts at the top; it starts with the warden. If the warden is proactive and pro-programming … the acceptance of the programs will trickle on down … and yes, you can tell right away." Brian explained that under one former warden, who was particularly "hands on, committed, supportive" with the volunteer program, he was invited to present information about his organization at a staff meeting so that "the staff would understand" the work that they do. He said: "it was actually a rare thing. It will probably never happen there again." Julie reported that on one occasion she experienced a warden attending the opening evening of a ministry retreat and that that meant so much to those taking part. Although administration and staff may not share the same views, as Christopher, who helped to run volunteer programs whilst incarcerated explained, when a warden is supportive of programming: "that makes all the difference in the world."

The distance learners in Britain made similar observations. While funding is available through PET on a national basis, differences exist between prisons in regard to support for education from staff and managers, and in terms of security clearance practices for course-related materials, even across prisons of similar security classification (Hughes, 2012). Bruce, a lifer who has been housed in a number of prisons over the course of his sentence, is just one of the students who believes that the governor of the prison can have a considerable impact in setting the tone for the facility. He noted that the current governor of his prison was: "very forward thinking" in regards to his support for rehabilitation programs, but added: "you'll find some people in his position have very different views."

Not only may attitudes of senior staff and managers differ regarding the benefits of rehabilitative programming and/or volunteer-based provision in general, their values may also inform institutional judgments regarding which types of volunteer programs have merit. While not a commonly shared sentiment, one of the California interviewees felt that faith-based programs were less respected than secular-based ones (however, see Chap. 11, this volume, for a contrary view). Although this is evidently an area for future enquiry, it appears that the values of individual managers may inform the programs that volunteers bring into a facility.

Research participants also suggested that facility location plays a role in the nature and availability of volunteer provision. Perry, for example, reported volunteers having to drive a considerable distance from the nearest big city of Fresno to visit a rural prison where he was housed, and many of the volunteers reported making such drives from that city. However, nowhere does location feature more prominently in the interviewees' accounts than in regards to San Quentin, California's oldest and most well-known prison. Nestled on the San Francisco Bay, interviewees consistently described San Quentin as having an extraordinary range of volunteer-led provision, drawing on community members from neighboring locations including Berkeley and San Francisco (see also Irwin, 2009). As a long-standing volunteer at this prison explained: "San Quentin is unique. Because it's in the Bay Area, it has a wide variety of men and women who bring [all] kinds of programs." She pointed to the "[college] education, the worship, the athletics, the self-help programs" that are made possible by volunteers and argued that the rehabilitation that takes place in San Quentin takes place because of the volunteers: "... none of the programs that do anything to actually make some difference in the men's lives are run by the state." She continued: "I have great concerns about the wide number of prisons which are located in far away [areas], less located [near] populations." She also pointed out that the liberal inclination of the Bay Area population may further encourage volunteering in prisons. Ken, another long-standing volunteer at San Quentin, also observed that: "most of the prisons [in California] are in rural areas" making it challenging "finding a lot of volunteers in such places." He, too, noted the liberal persuasion of the Bay Area as another contributing factor.

Because San Quentin's population includes men serving very long sentences, the lower rate of turnover contributes to a more stable population, which Jane, another volunteer, argued further supports the growth of volunteer programming. Indeed, Jane was disappointed when she relocated to a different area of the state and was unable to make progress in her effort to provide voluntary programming in prisons, meeting attitudes and challenges that presented a stark contrast to what she encountered at San Quentin. Echoing sentiments shared by other Bay Area research participants, Hilda explained:

> Men know that ... if you're a lifer or you have a long terminate sentence [in California], the place to ... try to get into, because of the programs, is San Quentin. It's just phenomenal the amount of programs that men can participate in. They have to pick and choose. They can't do everything.

She continued:

> Many of [the men] are going to school...they're taking this class or that class. They're being trained, so that ... their educational life, their experience, their spiritual life is being fostered and challenged. And so ... they are not the people that probably did stupid, sometimes horrendous things, when they were young. They're not the same people.

Although requiring further investigation, preliminary analysis does suggest that the characteristics and perspectives of the community in which a facility is based may further affect the nature and availability of volunteer-led provision, leading to a confluence of inside and outside attitudes and cultures impacting that which is on offer inside.

Concluding Comments

While I am certainly not advocating that prisons and jails rely primarily on volunteers for the delivery of beneficial programs, the non-profit and voluntary sector can nevertheless provide a vital service, especially in the face of otherwise limited opportunities. There may be far-reaching benefits that extend substantially beyond the particular programs themselves. The programs may help to foster a culture of purpose within a prison or jail, a culture supportive of constructive and productive personal and community endeavor.

But in order to fully realize such purposeful cultures, correctional facilities need permeable cultures as well, cultures that are willing to embrace opportunities originating outside of the walls. Without ongoing institutional support, non-profit and voluntary sector provision risks marginalization and obstruction. Volunteers will lose hope, and prisoners will not find the benefits of these programs, unless delivery can take place in a consistent and cohesive fashion.

Christopher, formerly incarcerated, observed that when such permeability is achieved the impact on a prison is profound: "The volunteers coming in changes the society, the whole make-up of whatever prison. The people [who] participate in the programs that are being offered by the volunteers, they tend to have a broader outlook on what's going on, in their life; it opens [things] up." The volunteers and the participants alike referred to the increased levels of respect and humanity that the involvement of outsiders engenders. And whilst questions should rightfully be asked about why a shortage of these qualities may exist without voluntary sector engagement, when the outside comes in significant inroads are made.

Apart from the immediate benefits for those serving their sentences and the prison community as a whole, developing permeable cultures may have benefits for those who are released not only in terms of increased skills, qualifications, and enhanced self-esteem, but also through valuable connections to social networks and community institutions that can be further developed post-release. There are possible benefits for everyone, all of us, in return. While the outside community might benefit in terms of reduced recidivism, the measure that is typically of paramount importance to policy makers, corrections officials, and the public alike, the benefits of fluid and permeable cultures can transcend such measures. Reducing barriers may help to challenge stigma and stereotypes that can negatively impact formerly incarcerated individuals' efforts toward positive reintegration. Brian, who, has been volunteering in a prison ministry for over 10 years, offered this perspective. Asked why he has continued his volunteering over this length of time, he replied: "the reward is seeing change." That is, he explained: "what keeps most volunteers coming back." But as he also went on to say, he has "seen volunteers' hearts change [too]," his own included.

Reflecting on her own involvement with volunteering, Hilda observed that it has been "a wonderful experience in my life." She went on to express her hopes for the research in which she was taking part, and by extension, this broader volume. She remarked:

> I hope that somehow your project reveals the richness of volunteerism in the prison system, and how crucial [it is]. It needs to be amplified, and that's harder in communities more separated from urban environments. Because one thing, you know, a volunteer will feed another person who could become a volunteer. So if you don't have it, or you have it in very minimal ways, it's very hard to develop it.

But, Hilda believes, "it's always one person to one person to one" that can generally make the difference.

References

Batiuk, M. E. (1997). The state of post-secondary correctional education in Ohio. *Journal of Correctional Education*, *48*(2), 70–72.

Bloom, B., Owen, B., & Covington, S. (2003). *Gender-responsive strategies: Research, practice, and guiding-principles for women offenders*. Washington, DC: National Institute of Corrections.

Blumstein, A. (2011). Bringing down the U.S. prison population. *The Prison Journal*, *91*(3), 12S–26S.

Burnett, R. & Maruna, S. (2004). So 'prison works', does it? The criminal careers of 130 men released from prison under Home Secretary, Michael Howard. *Howard Journal of Criminal Justice*, *43*(4), 390–404.

California Department of Corrections and Rehabilitation (CDCR). (2007). *Master work plan for rehabilitative programming*. Sacramento, CA: Author.

California Rehabilitation Oversight Board (C-ROB). (2008). *Biannual report, July 15, 2008*. Sacramento, CA: Office of the Inspector General.

California Rehabilitation Oversight Board (C-ROB). (2010). *Biannual report, March 15, 2010*. Sacramento, CA: Office of the Inspector General.

California Rehabilitation Oversight Board (C-ROB). (2014). *Annual report, September 15, 2014*. Sacramento, CA: Office of the Inspector General.

California Rehabilitation Oversight Board (C-ROB). (2015). *Annual report, September 15, 2015*. Sacramento, CA: Office of the Inspector General.

Cohen, S. & Taylor, L. (1972). *Psychological survival: The experience of long-term imprisonment*. Middlesex, England: Penguin Books.

Crawley, E. & Sparks, R. (2005). Older men in prison: Survival, coping and identity. In A. Liebling & S. Maruna (Eds.), *The effects of imprisonment* (pp. 343–365). Cullompton, Devon, England: Willan Publishing.

Cullen, F. T. (2007). Making rehabilitation corrections' guiding paradigm. *Criminology & Public Policy*, *6*(4), 717–728.

Erikson, E. (1968). *Identity: Youth and crisis*. New York: Norton.

Gehring, T. (1997). Post-secondary education for inmates: An historical inquiry. *Journal of Correctional Education*, *48*(2), 46–55.

Giordano, P. C., Cernkovich, S. A., & Rudolph, J. L. (2002). Gender, crime, and desistance: Toward a theory of cognitive transformation. *American Journal of Sociology*, *107*(4), 990–1064.

Goffman, E. (1961). *Asylums: Essays on the social situation of mental patients and other inmates*. Middlesex, England: Penguin Books.

Goffman, E. (1963). *Stigma: Notes on the management of spoiled identity*. New York: Simon & Schuster.

Harris, M. K. (2009). Identity change through the transformation model of the public safety initiative of LIFERS, Inc. In B. M. Veysey, J. Christian, & D. J. Martinez (Eds.), *How offenders transform their lives* (pp. 143–164). Cullompton, Devon, England: Willan Publishing.

Her Majesty's Chief Inspector of Prisons for England and Wales. (2015). *Annual report, 2014–2015*. Retrieved from https://www.justiceinspectorates.gov.uk/hmiprisons/wpcontent/uploads/sites/4/2015/07/HMIP-AR_2014-15_TSO_Final1.pdf.

Hughes, E. (2000). An inside view: Prisoners' letters. In D. Wilson & A. Reuss (Eds.), *Prison(er) education: Stories of change and transformation* (pp. 138–157). Winchester, England: Waterside Press.

Hughes, E. (2009). Thinking inside the box: Prisoner education, learning identities, and the possibilities for change. In B. M. Veysey, J. Christian, & D. J. Martinez (Eds.), *How offenders transform their lives* (pp. 87–103). Cullompton, Devon, England: Willan Publishing.

Hughes, E. (2012). *Education in prison: Studying through distance learning*. Farnham, Surrey, England: Ashgate Publishing.

Irwin, J. (2009). *Lifers: Seeking redemption in prison*. New York: Routledge.

Jewkes, Y. (2005). Loss, liminality and the life sentence: Managing identity through a disrupted lifecourse. In A. Liebling & S. Maruna (Eds.), *The effects of imprisonment* (pp. 366–388). Cullompton, Devon, England: Willan Publishing.

Johnson, R. (2002). *Hard time: Understanding and reforming the prison* (3rd ed.). Belmont, CA: Wadsworth/Thompson Learning.

Laub, J. H. & Sampson, R. J. (2003). *Shared beginnings, divergent lives: Delinquent boys to age 70*. Cambridge, MA: Harvard University Press.

Light, R. (1993). Why support prisoners' family-tie groups? *Howard Journal of Criminal Justice*, *32*(4), 322–329.

MacKenzie, D. L. (2006). *What works in corrections: Reducing the criminal activities of offenders and delinquents*. Cambridge: Cambridge University Press.

Martinson, R. (1974). Nothing works: Questions and answers about prison reform. *The Public Interest*, *35*, 22–54.

Maruna, S. (2001). *Making good: How ex-convicts reform and rebuild their lives.* Washington, DC: American Psychological Association.

Maruna, S. (2011). Reentry as a rite of passage. *Punishment & Society, 13*(1), 3–28.

Ministry of Justice. (2015). *Prison population figures: 2015.* Retrieved from https://www.gov.uk/government/statistics/prison-population-figures-2015.

Petersilia, J. (2003). *When prisoners come home: Parole and prisoner reentry.* Oxford: Oxford University Press.

Petersilia, J. (2014). *Voices from the field: How California stakeholders view public safety realignment.* Stanford, CA: Stanford Criminal Justice Center.

Prison University Project. (2015). *About us.* Retrieved from http://www.prisonuniversityproject.org/about-us.

Prisoners' Education Trust. 2015. *What we do.* Retrieved from http://www.prisonerseducation.org.uk/index.php?id=home.

Rumgay, J. (2004). Scripts for safer survival: Pathways out of female crime. *Howard Journal of Criminal Justice, 43*(4), 405–419.

Schuller, T. (2009). *Crime and lifelong learning: IFLL thematic paper 5.* Leicester, England: NIACE.

Strauss, A. & Corbin, J. (1998). *Basics of qualitative research: Techniques and procedures for developing grounded theory* (2nd ed.). London: Sage.

Sykes, G. (1958). *The society of captives: A study of a maximum security prison.* Princeton, NJ: Princeton University Press.

Tewksbury, R. & Dabney, D. (2004). Prison volunteers: Profiles, motivations, satisfaction. *Journal of Offender Rehabilitation, 40*(1/2), 173–183.

Ubah, C. B. A. & Robinson Jr., R. L. (2003). A grounded look at the debate over prison-based education: Optimistic theory versus pessimistic worldview. *The Prison Journal, 83*(2), 115–129.

U.S. Department of Education. (2015). *U.S. Department of Education launches second chance pell program for incarcerated individuals.* Retrieved from http://www.ed.gov/news/press-releases/us-department-education-launches-second-chance-pell-pilot-program-incarcerated-individuals.

Wilson, A. (2003). Researching in the third space—Locating, claiming and valuing the research domain. In T. Lillis & J. Maybin (Eds.), *Language, literacy and education: A reader* (pp. 293–307). Clevedon, England: Open University Press.

Wilson, A. (2007). 'I go to get away from the cockroaches:' Educentricity and the politics of education in prisons. *Journal of Correctional Education, 58*(2), 185–203.

Wilson, A. (2010). *Goodwill and good fortune: Obstacles and opportunities for level 2 learners in local jails—Extended report.* London: Prisoners' Education Trust.

PART II

Prisoners as Volunteers

CHAPTER 3

Learning and Practicing Citizenship and Democracy Behind Bars

Michelle Inderbitzin, Joshua Cain, and Trevor Walraven

Introduction

Even as the USA locks away and punishes its people in unprecedented numbers, the impact of mass incarceration extends beyond those sitting in prisons and jails to their families and communities who feel their loss and are deeply affected by it. As Gottschalk (2014) explains:

> Today the United States is the world's warden, incarcerating a higher proportion of its people than any other country. The United States has built a carceral state that is unprecedented among industrialized countries and in U.S. history. The emergence and consolidation of the U.S. carceral state is a major milestone in American political development.... Its reach is truly breathtaking. It extends well beyond the nearly 2.3 million people sitting in jail or prison today in the United States. It encompasses more than 7 million people—or 1 in 31 adults—who are under some form of state control, including jail, prison, probation, parole, or community sanctions. (p. 289)

M. Inderbitzin (✉)
Oregon State University, Corvallis, OR, USA

J. Cain • T. Walraven
Oregon State Penitentiary, Salem, OR, USA

L.S. Abrams et al. (eds.), *The Voluntary Sector in Prisons*, Palgrave Studies in Prisons and Penology, DOI 10.1057/978-1-137-54215-1_3

Our democracy is necessarily weakened by the loss and possible estrangement of millions of citizens through their involvement in the criminal justice system. Harcourt (2014) writes about the "invisibility of the prison in democratic theory" (p. 6), noting that "one can only wonder about the much broader impact of such a massive prison system on the democratic citizenship of large segments of our communities" (p. 9).

Many prisoners were convicted of crimes and incarcerated at a very young age; as such, they may not have had the opportunity to develop a clear understanding of what it means to live and participate in a democratic society before they were forcibly removed from it. As adults, much of what these young men and women know about democracy and citizenship has been learned within the prison environment (Inderbitzin, Walraven, & Cain, 2013). This chapter is coauthored by two juvenile lifers and focuses on their experience as elected leaders in the Lifers' Unlimited Club at the all-male, maximum-security Oregon State Penitentiary (OSP). The prisoners who volunteer their time and energy as elected leaders are charged with representing the voices and the interests of the club members with prison administrators and other prisoner-led clubs; these leaders work closely with staff advisors to organize events and panels, partner with outside community agencies and stakeholders as they have the opportunity to do so, raise and distribute funds, and put forth proposals for new programs.

Participation in such prisoner-led clubs reinforces principles of democracy by showing incarcerated individuals that their votes and voices can be made to count and that they can make a difference in their own daily lives and the lives of others. Leaders in these prisoner-run clubs are often the "good citizens" of the prison, recognized as such by both their fellow prisoners and the prison staff, and they consistently make efforts to give back to the larger community by participating in fundraisers and contributing to organizations that work with children and at-risk youth on the outside. These young men deal with the deprivation of liberty through positive means, "rejecting the rejectors" (Sykes, 1958) by becoming stronger and better citizens in prison, partnering with and embracing the outside community with their charitable deeds.

Justice and Meares (2014) suggest that public schooling and the criminal justice system are two central pathways by which the state interacts with its citizens, providing formal and informal education to the individuals passing through their ranks. They further argue: "for an increasing number of Americans, the criminal justice system plays a powerful and pervasive role in providing a civic education, in anticitizenry, that is the reverse of the education that public schools are supposed to offer" (p. 159).

Similarly, Weaver, Hacker, and Wildeman (2014) argue that imprisonment can be a debilitating experience for individuals, noting the many areas of their lives that can be affected after release. They write:

> Criminal justice interventions make people less prepared and capable of being engaged citizens, regardless of their desire to do so, by making them more troubled in a host of social domains: their ability to maintain jobs, housing, and stable families; their access to the social safety net; and their risk of poverty, joblessness, homelessness, and other disadvantages that make civic engagement more difficult. (p. 12)

While we appreciate the additional challenges a felony record or prison sentence can have on an individual's efforts at civic engagement, we also understand that many men and women in prison work hard to develop relationships with their families or other community stakeholders through visits, educational opportunities, classes, and clubs within correctional facilities.

Incarcerated men and women are capable of developing their marketable skills by working in various jobs within the prison environment and accessing educational literature and texts. As an example, men in OSP, where two of the authors of this article currently reside, can develop contacts with community and find parole-friendly housing opportunities through transitional services classes and through agencies and volunteers who work within the prison. They are able to work on their ability to maintain a stable family through classes like Parenting Inside-Out, Responsible Fatherhood, and Keys to Loving Relationships.[1] Within this particular prison, special interest groups like Family First—a program created and maintained by both prison staff and incarcerated men—help the men inside develop skills in parenting and caregiver support, while also providing opportunities to share and exercise those skills during special visiting opportunities.

[1] The programs available in the Oregon State Penitentiary are a combination of regional programs run by nonprofit organizations contracted by the Department of Corrections to develop and deliver the curriculum (Parenting Inside-Out is one example), national programs with curriculum available for purchase with classes led by staff or volunteers from the prison and larger community, and programs developed and implemented within the prison by prisoners, volunteers, and staff members.

An informal social safety net also commonly develops among releasing prisoners who share positive attitudes and goals. Released prisoners often go out of their way to help each other: to attain employment, to find housing, to navigate family assistance, to secure aid in emergencies, to understand the use of social media to respond to roadside emergencies, and to generally find mentorship, sponsorship, and other daily necessities. As Weaver et al. (2014) suggest, released prisoners face a greater likelihood of poverty, stigma, and homelessness, but a sense of community is often developed between those who share the prison experience with all the accompanying stress and challenges of living under the state's control.

In his classic book, *Society of Captives*, Gresham Sykes (1958) described several pains of imprisonment, one of which is the deprivation of liberty:

> For the great majority of criminals in prison, however, the evidence suggests that neither alienation from the ranks of the law-abiding nor involvement in a system of criminal value is sufficient to eliminate the threat to the prisoner's ego posed by society's rejection.... The prisoner is never allowed to forget that, by committing a crime, he has foregone his claim to the status of a full-fledged, *trusted* member of society. The status lost by the prisoner is, in fact, similar to what Marshall has called the status of citizenship—the basic acceptance of the individual as a functioning member of the society in which he lives. It is true that in the past the imprisoned criminal literally suffered civil death and that although the doctrines of attainder and corruption of blood were largely abandoned in the 18th and 19th Centuries, the inmate is still stripped of many of his civil rights such as the right to vote, to hold office, to sue in court, and so on. But as important as the loss of these civil rights may be, the loss of that more diffuse status which defines the individual as someone to be trusted or as morally acceptable is the loss that hurts most.
>
> In short, the wall which seals off the criminal, the contaminated man, is a constant threat to the prisoner's self-conception and the threat is continually repeated in the many daily reminders that he must be kept apart from "decent" men. Somehow this rejection or degradation by the free community must be warded off, turned aside, rendered harmless. Somehow the imprisoned criminal must find a device for rejecting his rejectors, if he is to endure psychologically. (pp. 66–67)

In this chapter, we argue that one way current prisoners can and do "reject their rejectors" and prove their value to the community is by embracing the ideals of democracy and citizenship, becoming leaders of the prison population and exemplars for those in the outside society.

Sibley (1995) claims that, "We cannot understand the role of space in the reproduction of social relations without recognizing that the relatively powerless still have enough power to 'carve out spaces of control' in respect to their day-to-day lives" (p. 76). We now move to explore the many ways that prisoners serving time in correctional facilities can act as volunteers, working separately when it is necessary and alongside outside volunteers when it is possible to affect positive change. We offer an inside look at current prisoners' efforts to carve out their own spaces of control and to make meaning of their lives during the long and difficult years of their incarceration. Their positive attitudes and good works in extremely constricting circumstances can create an empowering ripple effect on their families, the prison staff members, and the larger community.

An Unlikely Path to Citizenship: Prison as a (Trans) formative Experience

> contact with the criminal justice system is not value-neutral. Deliberately or inadvertently, it teaches citizens about their state and how their state sees them. In these senses, the criminal justice system is the primary forum for "civic education"—how one learns about rights, responsibilities, and expectations as a citizen—for many poor young men. (Weaver et al., 2014, pp. 8–9)

Many of the men currently serving long prison sentences in the USA came to prison when they were very young, some in Oregon beginning their incarceration as young as 13 for sentences that will stretch for decades. Those who were teenagers at the time of their crimes had generally never had the chance, or even the inclination, to vote. In practice, many had not yet attained full adult status, and having not even been old enough to purchase or consume alcohol legally, were not yet considered full citizens. Many of the men and women in prison came from working-class or lower-class families that did not vote. They may have participated and invested in communities in other ways such as through church groups, little league teams, or public schools, but faith in the democratic system and importance of voting/representation may have been lacking. It can be difficult to appreciate the value of the symbolic actions of democracy in the midst of a hardscrabble life.

Prison shapes conceptions of citizenship and democracy for those incarcerated at a young age; prisoners learn about politics, power, and compromise while serving time. As Justice and Meares (2014) state: "for an increasing number of Americans, the criminal justice system plays a powerful and pervasive role in providing a formal education in what it means to be a citizen" (p. 160).

Aging in prison is inevitable; growth is optional. The prison system is largely designed to control its residents. As such, it inhibits growth, decreases personal agency, and reduces the likelihood of prisoners really gaining the skill set required to successfully take productive control of their own lives. There are, however, opportunities for growth within prisons for those who seek them. Every person who enters prison must choose how he or she is going to serve their time; individuals can choose whether to get involved with positive programs and become the gleaners that Irwin (1970) described, or they can choose to dabble in contraband and trouble, or to simply get by. Leaders emerge through their own efforts, attitudes, and achievements.

Those who choose to enter the fray of prison politics fully understand they must work within the constraints of the prison. As Scharf (1975) rightly noted: "almost any effort at prison democracy is, in fact, limited democracy. Inmates cannot vote themselves out of jail, nor can they vote to jail their captors. 'Prison democracy' exists within the limits defined by the inmate's captivity" (p. 21). Scharf identified two dimensions helpful in understanding political participation in prison: the range of influence of prisoners' participation and the mode of power. In his description power can be advisory, representative, or direct, and the influence can be in a single living unit or workplace, or prison-wide. These are helpful distinctions four decades later as prisons continue to hold their populations captive and to limit prisoners' abilities to advocate for themselves and others and to create change.

The impact of prisons, both negative and positive, reaches beyond the walls in many different ways. For example, along with shaping the experience and conceptions of the men and women inside, the prison experience often affects political attitudes and behavior of incarcerated individuals, their friends and families, and the larger community. We concur with Lee, Porter, and Comfort (2014), that "the criminal justice system serves as an important institution for political socialization for the families of those imprisoned, affecting their attitudes and orientations toward the government and their will and capacity to become involved in political life" (p. 44).

Our goal for the remainder of this chapter is to explore the political participation and leadership of prisoners in the state of Oregon's maximum-security prison. We will show the different pathways available to those who want to get involved in order to make a difference in their own lives and in the larger prison population. And, importantly, we'll show how prisoners grow, change, and learn about citizenship and democracy even while serving long sentences behind bars. We believe this process is important to understand for the leaders, themselves, the more than 2000 men they serve in the prison, the staff members they work with, and the larger community that often benefits from prisoner-led efforts.

Method

This work grew out of a collaborative relationship between Michelle, a college professor who has taught classes and worked with prisoner-led clubs in OSP for more than 8 years, and Trevor and Josh, biological brothers who are currently serving time in the penitentiary. The penitentiary is the oldest of Oregon's prisons and is the only maximum-security facility in the state. It holds more than 2000 men, primarily in double-bunked cells, and operates several major industries within the cement walls, including an enormous laundry facility that serves both public and private businesses. Men serving time in the penitentiary generally work in the industries or in the upkeep of the facility, take educational and life skills classes, participate in prisoner-led clubs and recreational sports, and enjoy visits from family and friends. While approximately 225 men are housed in a special mental health unit, and roughly another 200 are on 23-hour lockdown (including 34 men on death row and approximately 160 in the disciplinary segregation unit at any given time), the remaining 80 % of the prison's population move between their jobs, activities, and recreation, and interact regularly with their peers and staff members. Privilege level determines the amount of time prisoners are allowed outside of their cells: for example, those on the most basic behavioral level (Level 1) are only outside of their cells for approximately 3 hours per day; those on Level 2 may be outside of their cells for 6 hours per day in the winter and 8 hours per day in the summer (in summer there is additional time allowed in the outside yard at night); while those on Level 3—the highest level that can be earned in the prison—may be outside of their cells for 8 hours in the winter and 10 hours in the summer.

Incarcerated for the same crime, Josh was 18 and Trevor was 14 when they began serving their long sentences. Now with more than 17 years served in correctional facilities, Trevor is the President of the Lifers' Unlimited Club and Josh serves as the Secretary of this club. While much of the history of the Lifers' Club has been lost due to poor record-keeping and/or the idiosyncrasies of a maximum-security prison, to the best of our knowledge, the Lifers' Club was one of three prisoner-led clubs created in response to a riot that took place in OSP in 1968 to give prisoners an avenue to represent themselves and improve their environment. The Lifers' Unlimited Club has run continuously since 1968 and its members have helped to start and sustain several of the other 10 clubs that currently exist in the penitentiary. There are approximately 150 members in the Lifers Club, each of them serving long-term sentences for murder, and they hold democratic elections every 2 years to choose the five members of their executive body.

The current officers of the Lifers' Unlimited Club are striking for their relative youth and their focus on positive change. Three of the elected leaders were young teenagers at the time of the crimes that brought them to prison, and they have literally grown up in state correctional facilities. Trevor, first elected while in his mid-twenties and having been reelected twice, is the youngest President in the club's more than 40-year history. Along with serving as elected leaders of the Lifers' Club, Josh and Trevor both hold high-level jobs in the prison's enormous laundry industry, serve as teaching assistants in college classes in the prison, participate in a wide range of programming, and have a broad view of the workings of prison culture at the OSP.

The three of us have previously published a piece on "Juvenile Lifers, Learning to Lead" in an earlier book (Inderbitzin et al., 2013), examining how teenage prisoners develop into citizens and leaders while serving long sentences, and we knew we had much more to contribute concerning the more positive and hopeful happenings and developments inside of state prisons. This project developed out of many, many hours of conversation and interaction between the three authors. Each author wrote portions of the manuscript, Josh and Trevor based on their lived experience and personal observations, and Michelle pulled it all together into an academic format. Each author had the chance to look over the manuscript numerous times, making changes and suggestions until we all agreed it is an accurate representation of our views and perspectives on learning leadership, citizenship, and democracy while behind bars.

Learning Leadership and Citizenship in Prison

Prisoners learn much of what they know about leadership and citizenship from their peers. To begin, their very first experiences with what leadership looks like in prison come from observations of how their fellow prisoners and staff conduct themselves. Leadership in prison can take many different forms, including:

- *Leaders of clubs.* By the time they rise to leadership roles in prisoner-led clubs, these men tend to have acquired many managerial skills that include an ability to delegate responsibilities to others and to train those delegates to take on the assigned task; "each one teach one" is a common theme among prisoners, and such delegation and mentoring serves the function of an informal apprenticeship. Leaders of clubs must also develop an understanding of how to best prioritize their time, goals, and energy, and they must become fluent in the function and form of business-like documents such as e-mails,[2] proposals, and memos. Additionally, they need strong public speaking skills and the ability to communicate effectively with staff members, including prison administrators who are commonly considered out-of-reach by prisoners.
- *Leaders and teachers of educational classes and cognitive-behavioral programs.* The staff and educators who hold classes in prison teach leadership skills and also demonstrate what being a leader looks like. They share knowledge while also teaching patience, time-management, empathy, and understanding. Effective teachers work with students to help them to develop themselves and bring the best out of them without degrading them or frustrating them. This is a delicate balance

[2] While prisoners generally do not have access to the Internet in Oregon, club leaders find it very useful to be able to communicate with outside community partners and organizations electronically. All e-mail and phone communication with outside community members are run through prison staff members. As an example, when Trevor needs to send an e-mail, he writes the message with the following statement prominently displayed at the beginning of each e-mail: *This is (Staff Advisors' Name), Recreation Specialist at the Oregon State Penitentiary. I am sending this on behalf of (Trevor's Name), a prisoner here at OSP and the President of the Lifers' Unlimited Club.* The message is generally written on an older computer on the prison's "Activities" floor, saved to a club-owned thumb drive, transferred to a staff member's computer, and then sent through the staff advisor's Department of Corrections' e-mail account. Responses to the e-mail are printed and the hard copies are given to the club's officers.

that is not easy to achieve and is extremely valuable to learn, both in prison and the larger community.

- *Leaders of peer-taught classes.* These men commonly share many of the same skills as club leaders and professional educators, with an emphasis on training/teaching, public speaking, and time-management. They offer good examples to other prisoners of how to speak effectively and respectfully with each other. They demonstrate how to manage groups and inspire a deeper level of thinking and reflection.
- *Leaders of prison gangs.* Interestingly, it is common to see many of the same types of management skills in gang leaders as we see in other forms of prison leadership. Gang leaders tend to display strong people management skills and have a well-developed sense of hierarchy and bureaucracy. They understand and share an understanding of democracy and politicking. They also tend to have a family-oriented style of interaction taking a great deal of pride in caring for each other like a brother would. There is commonly a familial element to the leadership style they adopt, demonstrate, and teach.
- *Lead men in prison jobs.* These men teach others who work under their leadership how to do the task at hand. Again in an apprenticeship type of way, they share their knowledge and skill in on-the-job training sessions. To reach these trusted work positions, lead men need to develop and demonstrate good communication and time-management skills. They also need to effectively liaise between the prisoner laborers that work under their tutelage and the staff/production coordinators that oversee and manage the lead men.

In addition to these more formal roles, there are also informal leaders within the prison who are just people with strong personalities and charisma that others naturally gravitate to and follow. These are the popular individuals who don't necessarily have strong management skills but definitely have influence among their peers. This can be good or bad in that what they demonstrate can be antisocial behaviors or prosocial behaviors, but either way, they are likely to be admired and emulated by their peers.

Each of these types of leaders also teaches citizenship through their leadership. They demonstrate a way to coexist that others can learn from and emulate. Beyond those leaders described above, the men in prison learn about what citizenship looks like from their "cellies" or cellmates, their neighbors, dining-table partners, and others they come into contact with on a daily basis. The etiquette of citizenship is constantly being reinforced with instructions from other prisoners about not looking into someone's cell that is not yours, about how to respect the spaces that have been claimed by other groups, and about respectfully excusing oneself after bumping into or passing closely by another person. These are some of the things that define citizenship in prison, that make up the ways in which interactions are conducted within the confines of confinement.

Some of these ideas about prison citizenship are taught in Admissions and Orientation (A&O) classes held for prisoners just coming into the facility. A long-term, more experienced prisoner teaches the majority of the material in 32 hours of class sessions. Topics include how to access areas of the prison in order to meet one's needs—including an overview of the particular prison's Medical, Dining Room, Clothing Room, and so on. The peer leader offers encouragement to new arrivals to seek out educational and religious opportunities. In these ways, a leader of the prison population provides a number of models of citizenship, while also demonstrating their own leadership style.

Many of the ways individuals learn to be citizens while in prison are comparable to conduct that is generally taught outside of prison: do not look into someone else's home, respect the spaces that have been claimed by other groups (police stations, college campuses, gated communities), treat interactions with others respectfully, and be kind. We note, however, that in some cases the men in prison conduct themselves with better citizenship and sense of community than do those in freedom. For example, men who have paroled often share their view that there is a great deal more disrespect among those in freedom; rudeness and disrespectful language are common and generally go unaddressed in the community, and abuses of power and position are vividly splashed across the media.

Much of the above also applies to the staff members who work in prison. The ways in which they lead and manage are examples to both prisoners and other staff members, and that can be either positive or negative. When staff treats prisoners poorly, some may be inclined to lash out and treat other prisoners and other staff badly, as well. Generally, however, most staff members demonstrate a more positive attitude that serves to model patience and rational understanding. The Oregon Department of Corrections and the administrative team at the penitentiary make an effort to teach principles of democracy and representation in the daily running of the state's correctional facilities; prison is very structured and there is a clear hierarchy of power that is supposed to be worked through starting at the lowest level for each issue.

Regardless of their particular role, leaders in the prison population must learn and practice patience and persistence, and they must learn to deal with the cumulative effects of ongoing frustration. In his role as President of the Lifers' Unlimited Club, Trevor explains:

> I've gotten permission for this or that to occur and days later been told that it can no longer happen … by the same folks who had just signed off! Same person who signed off now saying "no" and if you take that stuff personal or develop the idea that it is of no use, you will burn out and lose the drive that is so paramount to affect the change we desire. To "be the change you want to see in the world" you really have to dedicate yourself and continue to work towards the efforts you believe in while knowing when to pull back and approach the issue from a different direction. The skills acquired through navigating this environment can greatly help you succeed in the free world I've no doubt.

Prisons as Political Places

Many prisoners have had educational experiences that left them unaware of their rights, roles, and responsibilities as citizens. Josh explains his limited understanding of government, democracy, and citizenship as he was growing up:

> I was raised in a family that didn't believe in voting and neither of my parents voted until after my arrest. I was also arrested at 18, before I'd even had a chance to vote, not that I would have anyways. I didn't have much faith in democracy, nor did I think about it much. Both of my parents spoke openly about their feeling that citizens didn't really vote presidents in or pass laws, the powers that be decided those things before the first ballot was cast and I subsequently followed that same mindset.… Interestingly, it was my incarceration that spawned a belief in personal effect on the system in my parents. I think they felt a need to try everything in their power to help my brother and I get out of jail, even if it meant participating in something they hadn't previously believed in, such as voting. Once they started putting some faith in the system, so did I. I obviously couldn't vote myself but I began to do

> all I could to convince my friends and family to vote, and which way they should vote, that is on laws and for governor, and so on, that would positively affect my situation.

Within the prison setting, democracy is learned largely by opportunities to vote and see the results of one's vote in action. Some of the examples that Josh and Trevor have experienced within the prison include: electing executive body members for prisoner-led clubs, voting for the items they would like to see provided by the prison's commissary, voting for the most- and least-liked menu items from the prison chow hall, and offering input on other issues that affect the quality of daily life within the institution. Prisoners also learn about governmental democracy by understanding how bills and laws that affect criminal sentences and conditions of incarceration work their way through state and federal legislation—they may have a personal stake in the outcome of these laws or they likely know someone who does. They see the influence of elected officials on the passage or failure of such bills and laws, and they come to understand that who the current state Governor is affects chances for clemency, the viability of a potential pardon, and the probability of an execution being carried out in states that still allow the death penalty.

Practicing Democracy in Prisoner-Led Clubs

Prisoner-led clubs are a large part of how prisoners voice concerns in OSP. Because prisoners do not have direct access to forms of public communication, it is difficult to assess the presence and influence of prisoner-led clubs in other states and facilities in the USA. The Louisiana State Penitentiary at Angola has perhaps the best record of prisoner-led clubs for academic purposes when one pieces together information found in three books: one written by a long-term prisoner and editor of the prison newsmagazine (Rideau, 2010); one written by a journalist who started out exploring Angola's prison rodeo but delved much deeper into the culture of the prison and the experiences of the men inside (Bergner, 1998); and another by a writer focused on Warden Burl Cain's efforts to transform "America's Bloodiest Prison" into a redemptive environment (Shere, 2005). While not all prisons have prisoner-led clubs within them, the clubs are a very important aspect of life inside OSP. There are 11 formally recognized prisoner-led clubs at the penitentiary, some of which have been around for nearly 50 years. Prisoners can choose to be a member in up to three clubs at any given time, and outside community volunteers often serve as sponsors of a particular club, attending meetings and offering support as they are able. The clubs represent different cultural groups, needs, and interests within the prison.

Candidates for club leadership are nominated by their peers and elected by popular vote; the elected leaders are then responsible to represent the voice of their members, to negotiate with administration and other clubs, and to advocate for prisoners who may not be capable of advocating for themselves. Club leaders champion improvements in prisoners' pay, educational opportunities, privileges at each prison incentive level, and living conditions within the facility. The elected leaders have to be able to communicate with prison administrators about issues such as what kind of food is served in the prison, how much time prisoners can spend in the fresh air, how often they are allowed to see family and friends, and other issues that directly correlate to the quality of life.

Voting for ideas and plans of action in prisoner-led clubs can be one of the most powerful ways to reinforce a belief in democracy: to see a group have their "yeas" and "nays" counted and a decision immediately reached based upon majority vote makes the impact of democratic processes tangible. While advocating for their membership and the larger prison population, club leaders are also tasked with fundraising, distribution of funds, organizing events and panels for the clubs' regularly scheduled meetings and special events, and working closely with staff advisors.

Formally Recognized Prisoner-Led Clubs at the OSP

In this section, we provide a brief overview of each of the officially recognized clubs that currently exist in OSP:

Narcotics Anonymous (*NA*). Narcotics Anonymous is a drug treatment group geared toward providing tools and support for drug addicts. This local chapter of NA within the prison uses the 12-step program and offers sponsorship for struggling individuals; this helps both the sponsor (to give back to the program) and the struggling individual (to maintain their sobriety). They hold bimonthly meetings, book studies, and other associated programs.

Alcoholics Anonymous (*AA*). Alcoholic Anonymous is a treatment group geared toward providing tools and support for alcoholics. Similar to Narcotics Anonymous, this local chapter of AA within the prison uses the 12-step program and offers sponsorship for struggling individuals; this helps both the sponsor (to give back to the program) and the struggling individual (to maintain their sobriety). They hold bimonthly meetings, book studies, and other associated programs.

Asian Pacific Family. The Asian culture club is one of the newest officially recognized clubs in OSP, and it is geared toward investing in the Asian community within the walls of the prison. They sponsor/facilitate a Japanese language study class, practice traditional dance, and have monthly meetings to conduct club business.

Lifers' Unlimited Club. The mission statement of the Lifers' Unlimited Club reads as follows: "The purpose of the Lifers' Unlimited Club is to unite the incarcerated men of OSP with a goal of improving the quality of life for those inside and outside of these walls. The club will work with charity programs, informational services, youth speaking panels and other positive programs. We cannot change the past, however, we believe through rehabilitation and pro-social behavior we can create a more productive future." To be eligible for membership of the Lifers' Unlimited Club, one must be convicted of some form of murder (barring any form of manslaughter or attempted murder.) The Lifers' Club holds monthly meetings to conduct club business, and its members run a monthly youth-speaking panel emphasizing the importance of good choices and positive decision-making skills.

Uhuru Sasa. The African-American culture club is geared toward investing in the African-American community within the walls of OSP. They hold monthly meetings to conduct club business, and they also host special meetings to celebrate holidays such as Martin Luther King, Jr. day, Kwanza, and Juneteenth.

Seventh Step. The Seventh Step club is a community of men that aims to assist fellow prisoners in preparing for their return to the outside world. The club's mission is to reduce recidivism through the promotion of educational opportunities, and self-reflection practices. The Seventh Step club hosts community impact meetings and victim impact meetings, they sponsor and facilitate a codependency class, and they generally work to support one another in positive activities. They are also the largest and most consistent donor to a local homeless youth resource center, regularly contributing both hygiene products and monetary donations. They hold monthly meetings to conduct club business.

Athletic Club. The Athletic Club organizes and operates all intramural sports within OSP. The club conducts nine tournaments yearly: three softball tournaments, three soccer tournaments, and three basketball tournaments; all of these tournaments bring outside teams into the institution to compete against inside teams made up of participants from the prison population. They also hold quarterly Sport Lunches where champions are recognized by the attendees during a special meal that simultaneously raises funds for additional sporting equipment. The Athletic Club oversees a chess league, a pool league, and card game tournaments and other sporting events within the facility. They hold monthly meetings to conduct club business.

Toastmasters International. Toastmasters International focuses on leadership development, speech crafting, debate, teamwork, and generally improving communication skills. It is an internationally recognized organization with chapters around the world, and outside community volunteers and supporters are heavily involved with OSP's club functions. The club hosts debate tournaments and local college teams pay an entry fee to participate. They conduct six peer-led classes yearly, all geared toward developing communication skills. Members of Toastmasters speak in A&O (Admissions & Orientation) meetings for new prisoners in order to further develop their communication skills, and the club holds monthly meetings to conduct club business.

Veterans Association. Another of the newest clubs to be officially approved and recognized by OSP, the Veterans Association is focused on supporting the needs of military veterans who are incarcerated in the facility. The club sponsors a Post-Traumatic Stress Disorder (PTSD) class and works to ensure that releasing veterans have their benefits in order before returning to the outside community. They work with a number of outside volunteers and supporters, and they hold monthly meetings to conduct club business.

Latino Club. The Latino culture club is geared toward investing in the Latino/Hispanic community within the walls of OSP. They hold monthly meetings to conduct club business and run a monthly youth-speaking panel emphasizing the importance of culture and good choices.

Lakota Club. The Lakota Club is a Native American culture club geared toward investing in the Native American community within the walls of OSP. Along with regular meetings to conduct club business, they hold weekly sweat lodge ceremonies, organize yearly powwow celebrations and a Spirit Run, and run a monthly youth-speaking panel emphasizing the importance of culture for teenagers in the community.

Presidents' Meetings With OSP Administration

On a monthly basis, the presidents of each of the officially recognized prisoner-led clubs meet with the penitentiary's superintendent, administrative team, and other invited guests. These meetings provide an opportunity for the prison population's elected representatives to discuss matters concerning the institution, upcoming events, policies and procedures, desired improvements, and other relevant topics. Trevor offers his insight as a club president who has been elected to multiple consecutive terms; he explains his perceived responsibilities and the potential difficulties in carrying them out:

> As an elected official in this environment you have a certain level of responsibility to your membership and even to the population. The Lifers' Club mission is to "improve the quality of life for those inside and outside of these prison walls," and, as President, I look at that as even extending to the staff that work here. Why? Well, they are both inside and outside of these prison walls, and just as in any environment, the safer and more positive the day-to-day operation the more likely it is to be productive in that environment. My public relation practice extends to all encountered because it is only through relationships and networking that ultimate efficiency can be achieved. No one person can do it all. In any small community, the person(s) who have the greatest number of connections and the best reputations are going to be the most successful at affecting positive change. As one's ability to do so grows, so too does the understanding that there are responsibilities that cross all cultural lines and all lines of rank. What I mean is that just because I am the Lifers' President, that doesn't mean I only work to help fellow lifers. This is the community that I reside in and therefore it is this community that I likely have the greatest ability to positively affect. It is further not lost on me that however I am able to improve this community, ultimately I am giving back to the community that I harmed in the commission of my crime, for if men leave prison as better human beings than they came here as, then I've helped to prevent further crime, thereby giving back. If I can somehow accomplish this task, I've a responsibility to do so.
>
> It requires tremendous patience and foresight to truly work in this environment in a productive fashion. If you expect swift results, while these can come at times, that is certainly not the norm. Largely the negative things are thought to occur quickly but I would suggest that even most of those take years to fully unfold. Similar to laws that come into effect in the community, most if not all rule changes occur with opportunity to comment, or have

> a voice in the process. The fact of the matter is that it requires our willingness to invest, to educate ourselves on what changes are being proposed or coming into effect so that we can be adequately informed and educated on pertinent issues. In recent years the Lifers' Unlimited Club has taken upon itself the responsibility to investigate each rule proposal put forth so that we may weigh in on it as an executive body and consider whether or not it is worth better informing membership/population on what is being discussed and figure out what our suggested stance is. It's amazing how something as simple as an e-mail can bring about the realization that prisoners can have a voice, can have access, and are intelligent enough to reach out and seek positive change.

As Trevor suggests, leadership within prison requires patience, focus, perseverance, and the ability and willingness to evaluate situations and know when to push an agenda. Trevor has found that one valuable strategy is to assign project leaders for specific ideas and issues, allowing club members to feel ownership over different projects and play to their individual strengths. In this way, current leaders are able to mentor their peers and also help to strengthen networks throughout the prison and the larger community.

Further, as Trevor's quote illustrates, prison politics and decision-making share many challenges with those processes in the larger community. It requires serious and sustained effort to be educated and informed on policy issues and to choose to engage and be a useful voice in the process. The stakes of leadership may be particularly high in prison where one's reputation is critically important to one's well-being and where escape from difficult situations and volatile environments are literally impossible.

Connections with and Investment in the Outside Community

Regular interactions with family members and community members are vital for keeping prisoners connected to the outside world. The leaders and the men in OSP actively work to give back to the community in whatever ways that they can (see also Chap. 4 in this volume).

A large percentage of income generated in the prison is donated to worthy causes; this is particularly significant given low prison wages, which top out at approximately $150 per month for the best jobs in Oregon's prison industries. There are numerous examples of successful projects that the men in prison have conducted for and with community members. For example, the men in OSP participated in a Girl Scout Cookie Drive that over the course of 3 years resulted in a total of 1859 boxes sold to the men inside, generating $7436. This project was beneficial for all involved, providing prisoners the option to buy Girl Scout cookies at the same cost they would pay for them in the community, and providing all proceeds to the Girl Scouts Beyond Bars Troop that serves Oregon and Southwest Washington. This troop utilizes these funds in their efforts to coordinate with prisons housing female offenders to organize events that connect families.

The men in the penitentiary also coordinate a backpack project that provides free backpacks filled with school supplies to all school-age children that come to the prison to visit their loved ones in the month of August. This helps to reduce the cost associated with children's return to school and thereby eases some of the burden of having one less contributor in the household.

In addition, multiple groups conduct hygiene drives within the prison throughout the year to provide necessary items like toothpaste, socks, combs, and deodorant to those in the outside community who are most in need. The local homeless youth shelter and a Native American outreach group are the primary recipients of these efforts; the men from the penitentiary have been among the most consistent and generous contributors to these agencies over the last several years.

It is clear that the prison population values participation in fundraisers and charities that help children. A desire to give back to communities and veer away from selfishness and toward compassion and selflessness is especially common among the good citizens of prison. Many men in OSP and perhaps in the Lifers' Club, particularly, carry the burden of their past decisions and actions and feel a responsibility to make a difference in a positive way when they are able to do so.

Along with contributing goods and money to agencies serving vulnerable populations, leaders of the prison population often work to invite outside community members and stakeholders into the facility to interact with their members. This can be a complicated process, as it requires careful planning, permission from several layers of prison staff and administration, and criminal background checks on all visitors. Yet despite these barriers, leaders persist in these efforts because they believe it is important for prisoners to have opportunities to discuss what led them to the commission of their crimes and how they have grown throughout their lives. They arrange speaking panels to interact with victim advocacy groups and invite community members to engage in frank discussions about the real impact of crimes, prisons, and the criminal justice system, and the harms suffered by individuals and communities. As another form of community interaction, college students are occasionally allowed one-time visits into the institution to talk with prisoners in order to gain valuable perspectives that may be useful for them in their future careers as judges, corrections officers, counselors, parole and probation officers, police officers, attorneys, social workers, teachers, voters, and as parents.

Other events that provide opportunities to interact with outside community members can be as simple as a race for track enthusiasts held inside the walls with runners from the outside running alongside men from the prison (Heald, 2015), basketball or softball tournaments with teams from the community participating, or a debate with outside teams, college students, and community members coming into the facility to compete with the men inside. Any event that brings people from the community into the prison can provide an opportunity for transparency and growth. Individuals who are incarcerated can share their life experiences with those who may be from very different environments, perhaps leading to better and more complex understandings on both sides of the prison wall.

As one example, the Lifers' Unlimited Club recently hosted a Legal Seminar in hopes of providing members with information that could be used to help them channel their energy in positive directions during the remainder of their incarceration and hopefully into their eventual release. Trevor explains how these goals and activities represent a distinct shift in the direction of the club's leadership:

> The current executive body came into the club when the atmosphere was somewhat volatile and subdued (an interesting combination!). Basically the majority of membership was older, especially compared to the incoming executive body, (all 20's and 30's with most being convicted of their crimes, murder, in their teens) the past number of presidents had been removed or gotten into trouble for one reason or another, and most of the meetings had been for a number of years relatively uneventful and filled with complaining about what administration was taking from us, how we should be standing up more for ourselves than we were, and why was this happening. Stepping into that lead role our collective goal was primarily to create "fun" environments that engaged our membership to the point of actually wanting to attend meetings and as attendees, enjoy the time spent there, and look forward to what was going to come next.

> Having largely succeeded at creating this environment, the voice of membership has been geared now toward advocacy, and while not so much the voice of old complaining about why are we not doing this or that, but instead how about doing this or that? As such, we've begun reaching out to organizations, individuals, legal folks, and so on. In May we hosted two former Parole Board Members, a trial attorney out of Portland, two representatives from the Board of Directors of Oregon CURE (Citizens United for the Rehabilitation of Errants), a number of counselors from here at OSP, and a local professor specializing in the judiciary, constitutional rights, and the American Government. This was a more informative type of event where speakers presented and then broke into small groups where discussions ensued that were focused on the particular speakers' expertise. Gaining insights from former Parole Board members on how to properly prepare to go in front of the Board, thinking differently about how media portrays incarceration and crime, and talking with a trial attorney who is not familiar with your individual case, can and did shed light on different issues that can have impacts on how someone moves forward legally. In the future we are hoping to bring in organizations such as Oregonians for Alternatives to the Death Penalty, Oregon Innocence Project, Psychologists, and so on These efforts are being made primarily to provide information to the members so that if they choose to advocate on their own behalf, they can do so with a proper understanding of what needs to be done.

The meeting succeeded in its goal to be informational in nature and for the good of all members, with community participants explaining processes of the law rather than working with individuals seeking help on their particular cases.

Benefits of Leadership and Citizenship Within Prison

As leaders of and in the prison population, Trevor and Josh are familiar with both the benefits and challenges of choosing to put themselves in the forefront in order to serve others. Part of what they believe can be learned through these efforts is the idea that power exists through service. Many men in prison have not been exposed to opportunities for service prior to incarceration and, as such, they aren't aware of how empowering it can be. Trevor notes that service to others can really change one's perspective. At the heart of that learning curve is the power and self-fulfillment that occurs when one is able to affect positive change and to give back in some way. It is empowering to realize that you as an individual can have a positive impact on your community. Recognition and being acknowledged for your work is nice, but it is rarely a sustaining force in serving others.

Trevor explains his perspective on leadership, citizenship, and service within prison as follows:

> You don't do it for the praise you get, or even necessarily the immediate results that you are able to see. You do it because you are drawn to that kind of service work. Because you ultimately believe that the work you do is what matters. There really is an amazing sense of accomplishment associated with service work, you simply have to be doing it ultimately because it's the right thing to do, not for any rewards that may or may not accompany the position.

Josh adds his appreciation for even small gains made in prison: "In an environment as controlled as prison, it is easy to feel powerless when you send *kytes*[3] (or written communication) to the authorities that are never returned, make complaints that go without a response, and can be locked down or taken to the hole at the whim of your oppressors. On the other hand, this makes each small victory or obvious improvement all the more sweet and encouraging."

Risks of Leadership Within the Prison Setting

There are real dangers to being perceived as having too much power or influence in the prison population. Individuals with influence over their fellow prisoners can be viewed as threatening by staff and administration (Scharf, 1975), and also irritating to the men inside the prison who may have long histories of dealing with conflict through violence. It is a calculated risk to make oneself both visible and vulnerable by taking on leadership responsibilities for a volatile population.

Prisoners walk a thin line when trying to improve their environment. Ultimately, to productively and nonviolently work toward creating a better and improved community inside prison, leaders have to be able to communicate effectively with staff and administration, as well as their peers. They need to serve as the voice of those who are incarcerated, not just highlighting their own individual voices or perspectives, but representing the populace as a whole, to the extent that is possible. In doing this work,

[3] "Kytes" are an accepted form of prison communication; in the Oregon State Penitentiary kytes are often notes sent through formal channels to administrators requesting information or a meeting.

leaders have to build appropriate and respectful relationships with those on both sides of the fence—staff and other prisoners alike.

The pitfalls that can arise from leadership roles can be damaging to prisoners. As Josh explains:

> The most glaring of these is a development of what might be called "over-empowerment." In this situation, a prisoner may grow so far in his leadership roles that he sees himself as above or in charge of many of the other prisoners. He is so accustomed to operating within a leadership role that he may begin seeing himself as outside of the need to respect institution rules. Pride generally cometh before the fall, however, and it is not usually long before the over-empowered prisoner finds himself in a heap of trouble and scratching his head in befuddlement as to why. Staff can feel as though an over-empowered prisoner threatens their authority. The already-present friction between line-staff and prison administration can further aggravate this. At times, the rapport that a leader has developed with administration can afford the opportunity to be "saved" from a punishment imposed by line-staff. This can create frustration on the part of the line-staff who end up feeling undermined. Jealousy can also develop and play into this as line-staff feel as though a prisoner may have a better relationship with their boss than they do.
>
> There are issues with other prisoners as well. It is an interesting dynamic to balance when a leader has some prisoners pushing him to do more and be involved in more, while at the same time other prisoners develop distaste for the amount of influence and involvement the leader has. Some prisoners try to encourage the use of access to administration to find solutions, while other prisoners view this as a version of informing and suspect that the relationship between the staff and the leader is inappropriate or a "violation" by "convict code" standards. The politics of being involved in anything, in freedom or in prison, always requires delicate and thoughtful navigation. However, some unique risks are present in the prison community where violence is frequently considered a viable solution to perceived violations.

Because prisoners may feel the need to join groups and gang up for protective purposes, there are often disagreements that arise between these informal groups or between the formally recognized clubs. The leaders of each group must then work through these issues until some sort of resolution is reached. Prisoners who may be forced to deal with such situations more frequently than they would like learn the essentials of politics in this fashion. There is, too, the temptation for corruption in situations where power or privilege is at stake. Leaders of groups sometimes go back on their agreements and do whatever they choose. These betrayals can further shake one's faith in the legitimacy of the larger system, and make it even more challenging for leaders in the prison to continue working to resolve problems and improve the daily environment.

Encouraging Prisoners' Citizenship and Leadership Opportunities

Concerns about the challenges facing prisoners in learning citizenship, democracy, and leadership during their incarceration go back at least 75 years. As Hayner and Ash (1940) wrote: "If the function of a prison is to protect society, the convict must learn, during his period of incarceration, how to live in society.... If he is to be accepted as a law-abiding person on his return, he must learn in prison to play the role of a citizen" (p. 577).

The prison experience can greatly impact the perspective of all those that are affected by it, including victims and families (Harcourt, 2014; Lee et al., 2014; Weaver et al., 2014). Many have fallen by the very laws that they voted into existence, mostly due to a misunderstanding of what they were voting on or the "it won't happen to me" mentality. Most of those who are incarcerated did not expect to come to prisons; it wasn't "part of the plan." Those releasing from prison frequently get caught up in simply trying to reestablish themselves—attempting to regain former positions in the community and a seat at the family table, to rebuild careers, and to somehow make up for lost time. They may simply want to put the prison experience behind them.

It can be difficult and frustrating to translate prisoners' hard-won skills of leadership and citizenship to the larger society. Felony convictions can limit participation in social institutions and professions. Public distrust of ex-prisoners and fear of manipulation may close doors and limit valuable opportunities for civic engagement. In addition, felon disenfranchisement in some states bans those on parole and/or ex-felons from voting (Uggen & Inderbitzin, 2010); because disenfranchisement laws are poorly understood by both prisoners and citizens, even in states where felons are allowed to vote after prison, they may miss the opportunity to do so.

To validate the humanity of prisoners, society needs to recognize and honor their circumstances; to encourage citizenship of prisoners and former prisoners, we must provide relevant experiences and encourage opportunities for growth. Scharf (1975) makes this case simply but elegantly: "If we expect inmates to become politically involved citizens we must provide at least some experiences in democratic life" (p. 32).

We view education as an important step in the personal development and growth of individuals in prison. While not all prisoners will choose or be able to participate, by offering more quality educational opportunities to those who are incarcerated, we increase the possibilities for men and women convicted of serious crimes to raise their sense of awareness, explore their own views, and better understand the larger society. From our experience, college courses can offer hope to those who need it most; an education can empower individuals in dark circumstances and emphasize the rights and privileges of citizenship to those in prison (Inderbitzin, 2012, 2015).

In encouraging prisoners to adopt a larger perspective and to feel empowered to work toward positive change within the institution, prison staff members must also be accountable for following up on issues that are raised through the proper channels. We believe that knowing and showing that those in power will not arbitrarily disregard one's voice is key in establishing a belief in the legitimacy of the system.

As Scharf and Hickey (1976) explain, learning citizenship and democracy within prison goes far beyond concerns with recidivism and extends to the rights of human beings to have some level of control over their own actions and future:

> The reason why experiments in prison democracy should continue is not simply a matter of efficacy. Rather the issue should be posed in terms of society guaranteeing to the inmate the social right to participate in the decisions critical to his life … an effort to create a prison democracy rests on a philosophic foundation broader than simply its recidivism ratio as compared with other programs. (p. 121)

Implications for the Voluntary Sector Working Within or in Partnership with Prisons

> It should not be forgotten that criminal justice institutions, whatever else they are, are pain-delivery mechanisms. Moral beings permit others to suffer as little as possible; civic beings treat one another as fellow citizens who all have a rightful place alongside them in the public world. Dysfunctional institutions that punish too much, or carelessly, or with bias, are shameful reminders of our humanitarian and democratic failings. (Dzur, 2014, p. 4)

The first thing that those in the voluntary sector can do in working with prisoners is to simply recognize the humanity of prisoners and recognize that prisoners are and should be an important resource and voice in the community. Those from the community should think of *partnering* with prisoners rather than simply working or doing *for* them. There are many motivated and talented men and women in prisons who would benefit from encouragement, mentoring, and enhanced opportunities to participate in positive groups and programs. The voluntary sector might also work to create or facilitate partnerships between prisoners, their families and loved ones, and community agencies in order to improve living conditions both inside correctional institutions and in the larger society.

While we are writing from experiences based in one state and confined largely to one maximum-security prison, we note that other academics and activists are making similar points and arguments (Edgar, Jacobson, & Biggar, 2011). One reason for the virtual invisibility of the good work going on in prisons and prison partnerships stems from the fact that prisoners may be viewed as a separate category of beings, unworthy of attention or the efforts of more conforming citizens:

> prisoners have few or no advocates, not even among those who traditionally represent the underrepresented.... We tend to think of the convict as someone of inferior moral worth, and this rubs off on our judgments of citizenship. We tend to think of those caught in the carceral mesh as less worthy citizens, whose exclusion from the political arena is therefore less troubling. (Harcourt, 2014, p. 10)

We hope those in the voluntary sector are and will be very troubled indeed by the exclusion of prisoners from the social fabric. By partnering with prisoners and their family members, we can bring a lost voice to the table, help to empower a discouraged segment of the population, and reap the benefits of a more representative society.

The academic literature shows different views of prisoners' families and how they may react to the incarceration of their loved ones. Lee et al. (2014) argue: "People affected by a family member's incarceration may already feel disenchanted with the democratic process and perceive attempts to improve their (or their loved one's) life circumstances as futile" (p. 49). While we fully understand how some become disenchanted with the system and overcome with inertia, we have seen the opposite, as well, where family members of prisoners become more motivated and politically active when their loved ones are in prison. They take seriously the responsibility to speak for the men and women inside who may not be able to advocate for themselves in the community. Loury (2014) helps to represent this perspective in noting that: "the incarcerated and their families are not passive in their alienation. Rather, they construct meaningful worlds for themselves amid the storm" (p. 181). Volunteers and community agencies can work with prisoners and their families to help ensure that those caught up in the system are exposed to opportunities for leadership, democracy, and citizenship so that they can construct those meaningful worlds on a foundation of hope.

Owens (2014) shares our view that there is important work already being done by the "good citizens" within prisons, and that more can be accomplished if they and their families are able to partner with active community organizations:

> Yet many people under and after correctional control seek to restore themselves as full citizens.... They engage in political work, challenging notions of low civic interest and weak democratic commitments by felons and ex-felons. They do it to broaden and better circumstances for themselves and others. In doing so, they are "good citizens".... The best organizations focused on persons with felony convictions not only develop the capacities of ex-offenders to reconnect in positive ways with their families, obtain stable and licit employment, and remain free, they organize and mobilize felons and ex-felons and their families to rehabilitate (or habilitate) citizenship in their communities. (p. 258)

Perhaps our most important piece of advice for volunteers and agencies working within prisons is that you must learn and practice patience. Anyone hoping to do work within prisons must abide by the rules and idiosyncrasies of the prison staff and administration, which can fluctuate wildly from visit to visit. Volunteers and guests may be denied access or have ideas rejected with no explanation; you must keep persisting and playing within the rules—lessons well-learned with the prisoners who will be working at your side to improve conditions in the community both inside and outside of prison.

As an outside supporter you must have an understanding of the greater good we all hold out hope for and trust that your investment working in the prison is worthwhile. Without a willingness to move forward productively in the face of frustration and aggravation, the roadblocks will seem insurmountable. Compromise is and will always be paramount in seeking to affect positive change in any prison system. Yet, the better you understand a problem, the more likely you will be able to improve the situation. It takes meaningful and consistent investment to make a positive impact in a prison environment. We believe it is worth the effort, and we hope that you are encouraged to continue in this work. It makes a difference.

References

Bergner, D. (1998). *God of the Rodeo: The quest for redemption in Louisiana's Angola prison*. New York: Ballantine Books.

Dzur, A. W. (2014). An introduction: Penal democracy. *The Good Society*, *23*(1), 1–5.

Edgar, K., Jacobson, J., & Biggar, K. (2011). *Time well spent: A practical guide to active citizenship and volunteering in prison*. London: Prison Reform Trust.

Gottschalk, M. (2014). Democracy and the carceral state in America. *The ANNALS of the American Academy of Political and Social Science*, *651*, 288–295.

Harcourt, B. E. (2014). The invisibility of the prison in democratic theory: A problem of "virtual democracy". *The Good Society*, *23*(1), 6–16.

Hayner, N. S. & Ash, E. (1940). The prison as a community. *American Sociological Review*, *5*(4), 577–583.

Heald, M. (2015, June 25). For inmates "the wall" has a totally different meaning. *Runner's World*. Retrieved from http://www.runnersworld.com/runners-stories/for-inmates-the-wall-has-a totally-different-meaning.

Inderbitzin, M. (2012). Prisons as places of hope and transformative learning. *Appreciative Inquiry Practitioner*, *14*(1), 20–25.

Inderbitzin, M. (2015). Active learning and educated hope: College and prison partnerships in a liberal education. *Liberal Education*, *101*(3), 46–51.

Inderbitzin, M., Walraven, T., & Cain, J. (2013). Juvenile lifers, learning to lead. In D. Hartman & C. Uggen (Eds.), *Crime and the punished* (pp. 171–185). New York: W.W. Norton.

Irwin, J. (1970). *The felon*. Berkeley, CA: University of California.

Justice, B. & Meares, T. L. (2014). How the criminal justice system educates citizens. *The ANNALS of the American Academy of Political and Social Science*, *651*, 159–177.

Lee, H., Porter, L. C., & Comfort, M. (2014). Consequences of family member incarceration: Impacts on civic participation and perceptions of the legitimacy and fairness of government. *The ANNALS of the American Academy of Political and Social Science*, *651*, 44–73.

Loury, G. C. (2014). Detention, democracy, and inequality in a divided society. *The ANNALS of the American Academy of Political and Social Science*, *651*, 178–182.

Owens, M. L. (2014). Ex-felons' organization-based political work for carceral reforms. *The ANNALS of the American Academy of Political and Social Science*, *651*, 256–265.

Rideau, W. (2010). *In the place of justice.* New York: Vintage Books.

Scharf, P. (1975). Democracy and prison reform: A theory of democratic participation in prison. *The Prison Journal*, *55*, 21–33.

Scharf, P. & Hickey, J. (1976). The prison and the inmate's conception of legal justice: An experiment in democratic education. *Criminal Justice & Behavior*, *3*(2), 107–122.

Shere, D. (2005). *Cain's redemption.* Chicago: Northfield Publishing.

Sibley, D. (1995). *Geographies of exclusion: Society and difference in the West.* London: Routledge.

Sykes, G. M. (1958). *Society of captives.* Princeton, NJ: Princeton University.

Uggen, C. & Inderbitzin, M. (2010). The price and the promise of citizenship: Extending the vote to non-incarcerated felons. In N. A. Frost, J. D. Freilich, & T. R. Clear (Eds.), *Contemporary issues in criminal justice policy: Policy proposals from the American Society of Criminology conference* (pp. 61–68). Belmont, CA: Cengage/Wadsworth.

Weaver, V. M., Hacker, J. S., & Wildeman, C. (2014). Detaining democracy? Criminal justice and American civil life. *The ANNALS of the American Academy of Political and Social Science*, *651*, 6–21.

CHAPTER 4

Leading by Example: Ways That Prisoners Give Back to Their Communities

Michelle Inderbitzin, Trevor Walraven, and James Anderson

I came to prison at the age of 17 as a first time offender, and the truth is, I wasn't trying to be a criminal. Not at all. I was just a teenager trying to fit in and part of that resulted in me making some extremely poor choices. Choices that led to a prison sentence of 25 years to life.

I never wanted to be the prisoner who just sat in his cell twiddling his thumbs waiting for time to slowly pass by. That's torture. Instead, I knew that I wanted to somehow make a difference in this community, to be part of something positive, and to contribute on a level that shows I'm more than who I was on my worst day.

So, knowing that this was my home for the next several decades, I set out to better myself. I worked my way into one of the top job positions in the entire prison, became the Vice President of the Lifers' Club, earned three college degrees, and then aimed for and achieved the goal of becoming a member of a group that talks to struggling youth about the importance of wise-decision making and effective goal-setting.—James

M. Inderbitzin (✉)
Oregon State University, Corvallis, OR, USA

T. Walraven • J. Anderson
Oregon State Penitentiary, Salem, OR, USA

L.S. Abrams et al. (eds.), *The Voluntary Sector in Prisons*, Palgrave Studies in Prisons and Penology, DOI 10.1057/978-1-137-54215-1_4

The Drive to Give Back

Too often when the public thinks of prisons and the souls held within them—if they think of them at all—the image that comes to mind is wholly negative. Fed by the popular press that relies on bloody incidents and salacious details to sell stories, we rarely hear about the good work being done in prisons or the men and women who have grown up, matured, and changed their lives while incarcerated. This chapter offers a look inside one maximum-security prison with the explicit intent to shine a light on the positive programs created, sustained, and supported by the men inside these walls. In spite of the harsh environment, charitable efforts and individual transformations can and do flourish in prisons, providing an example to the larger community of generosity and empathy under difficult conditions.

While others have recognized that many prisoners create and participate in positive programs and rehabilitative activities during their incarceration (Carter, 2008; Franklin, 2000), academics have been slow to recognize or focus on the ways that prisoners "give back" while living inside prison walls. A few types of programs—including hospice, where prisoners offer palliative care for those dying in prison (Hoffman & Dickinson, 2011), and animal training programs, where prisoners train animals for new homes and duties (Strimple, 2003)—have garnered attention for their positive contributions. Yet still, on the whole prisons are generally portrayed as negative, criminogenic, and violent environments.

We focus our work on the Oregon State Penitentiary (OSP) in the USA where coauthors Trevor and James have each lived for over a decade, and we offer an account of the many ways that prisoners are learning to lead from within (Inderbitzin, Walraven, & Cain, 2013), striving to make positive contributions to both the inside and the outside community while serving their sentences. In this chapter we detail a number of programs and events that prisoners have built and nourished, often with little or no direct benefit to themselves. The men who feed their life's blood into these positive programs in prison aspire to make the most of their time and to give back to the community in whatever ways they can. They are the "gleaners" of the prison population (Irwin, 1970), the individuals who want to ensure that the prison sentences they are serving are ultimately "time well spent" (Edgar, Jacobson, & Biggar, 2011).

As long-standing members and elected leaders of the Lifers' Unlimited Club, Trevor and James have thought deeply about their own inclinations to give back and make positive contributions to the community, and they share their thoughts and experiences in this chapter. Each member of the Lifers' Unlimited Club has been convicted of some form of murder, and they take seriously the club's mission statement: "The purpose of the Lifers' Unlimited Club is to unite the incarcerated men of OSP with a goal of improving the quality of life for those inside and outside of these walls. The club will work with charity programs, informational services, youth speaking panels, and other positive programs. We cannot change the past, however, we believe through rehabilitation and pro-social behavior we can create a more productive future." Members of the Lifers' Unlimited Club generally spend decades in prison; while some are serving life without the possibility of parole, the vast majority will have the opportunity to return to the community after spending a significant portion of their lives in prison.

Trevor believes that Lifers in particular owe a significant debt to society. While not the case for every Lifer, many give generously of their time, resources, and talents to try to make a positive contribution to their community, both inside and outside of prison. Trevor explains his view:

> The compulsion to "give back," particularly with "Lifers" exists in my mind because we have taken away what cannot be overcome. What I mean by that is in every other crime, the individual who is the victim, has some level of ability to *choose* how they will react to what has been done to them. With those of us who have taken a life, especially on purpose, there is an unwavering weight that bears down on our shoulders. As we collect years inside, as we lose loved ones, as our families have struggles that we are unable to assist with in any way, shape or form, as we grow and mature, as we look at ourselves in the mirror each day and have to face that fact that we are incarcerated for removing *choice* from another human being, as we feel dehumanized by the very environment that we put ourselves in by dehumanizing someone else through placing less value on their life than we placed on our own, realizations set in. Empathy develops, sorrow and regret become more pronounced while oddly enough, simultaneously they fade. It is that constant realization, however, that causes so many to reinvest, to give back, to make a difference in a positive way when they are able to. These are often guys who don't make a big deal of what they are doing as well. They will donate for years on end to some organization and they are also the ones who, when a group or club is soliciting for funds, for whatever cause, are the first to contribute.

The generosity of prisoners often goes unnoticed. We believe this is in part because they do not have direct communication with the outside community.

Prisoners do not typically have access to social media or other platforms to share their fundraising goals or to raise awareness of the causes they champion. In addition, many prisoners have experienced bitingly negative media exposure, and they are reluctant to open themselves to renewed attention or to advertise tenuous ties to the community. Instead, they choose to donate to worthy causes quietly, wanting to help but fearing their intentions may be misconstrued if such acts become public.

James offers a personal example of how and why he donates more than 10 % of his income from his job to charitable organizations:

> For approximately six years I was donating twenty dollars out of my monthly earnings to a local homeless shelter. Then, in 2009, another prisoner told me about an organization, Angels in the Outfield, which helps children who've been the victims of crime and abuse. I knew that my small monthly donations could be better utilized with them so I've been doing that for over five years now. Being able to contribute to an organization like Angels in the Outfield and knowing that they have the capability of making such huge differences in the lives of youth means a lot to me. I feel like I'm making a difference and it's a feeling I've needed for a long time because of the guilt I feel for the mistakes that I've made in life. Contributing doesn't lessen my guilt and it doesn't minimize the shame I feel, but it does provide me with a sense of worth and the understanding that I can make seemingly small amends by paying it forward.

Trevor and James and many others in their situation are driven to make positive contributions to society. They know that they can never clear the ledgers of their crimes, but they aspire to help others and give back to the community in whatever ways they are able to do so. At a young age, Trevor came to a clear understanding of his ability to choose to "make good" (Maruna, 2001) even while in prison and to leave a positive footprint on the community. He shares the reason for his personal drive and his efforts to bring the prison community and the voluntary sector together in efforts to improve the larger society:

> I also want to ensure that I make a difference with my life. I've done some horrible things that I can't ever fix or give back. That said, I can and do work towards redemption, even if I don't feel as though full redemption is possible, I can, I need to do what I can to give back, to lead by example now, to improve whatever my environment looks like at any given time, to give rather than to take away, to contribute, to invest, because it's my responsibility to do so and because there's actually real joy in it. I'm a big believer in

> our own personal agency surrounding the quality of life we live, regardless of our circumstances…we have the ability to learn, grow, explore, and give back! We are only going to become a better community if we work together. We are far stronger together than we are apart. We have a responsibility for those ahead of us, to create rather than destroy, to give rather than take, to provide rather than deprive, to move forward collectively rather than individually.

We will spend the rest of this chapter outlining various programs that the men in OSP have created, built, and sustained. Some of these programs primarily benefit the men inside the prison, while others are focused on contributing to vulnerable populations in the outside community. The men inside appreciate partnering with outside organizations or individuals from the community whenever they are able to do so; the programs can and do benefit from the support of the voluntary sector. We conclude this chapter with advice and suggestions for community-based volunteers who may be willing to partner with current prisoners in such efforts.

Method

This chapter is a collaborative effort between Michelle, a professor of sociology who has taught classes and volunteered with various clubs and activities at OSP for more than 8 years, and Trevor and James, who are currently serving long sentences in the penitentiary. Incarcerated for life sentences for crimes committed as juveniles, Trevor was 14 years old and James was 17 years old when they began serving the decades-long sentences handed down to them by their judges. Now with more than 17 years and 19 years served in correctional facilities, Trevor is the elected President and James is the elected Vice President of the Lifers' Unlimited Club. Along with leading one of the prison's oldest and most influential clubs, they are both involved in many other positive programs and activities in the prison. Through their own experiences and observations, they have developed a broad view of the workings of prison culture at OSP (for more information on the Lifers' Unlimited Club and OSP, see Chap. 3, this volume). Each of these men has literally grown up behind bars, and they have both made significant efforts to find positive ways to serve their time and their communities.

As a long-time volunteer, Michelle has taught nearly 20 college courses in OSP and has worked with and helped to develop a number of programs with her collaborators in the prison. She offers a sociological perspective on the culture of the prison and the important contributions that volunteers—from both the prison population and the free world—can and do make in improving individual lives and the larger environment.

This chapter developed out of many, many hours of conversation and interaction between the three authors. Each author wrote portions of the manuscript, Trevor and James wrote and commented on material based on their lived experience and personal observations, and Michelle brought in her outside questions and observations as well as the limited academic research she could find about positive programs created or run by prisoners. In pulling these perspectives together into a unique chapter, we chose to highlight Trevor's and James's individual voices through lengthy quotes. We believe prisoners' voices are too often lost in academic work about prisons, so here we seek to share their views directly from their current place in OSP. Each author went over the manuscript multiple times, making changes and suggestions until we all agreed that we presented an accurate representation of our views on the many different ways prisoners lead by example and give back to their communities.

Programs Initiated or Run by the Men in Prison for Their Peers

We have separated the positive programs that we will be discussing into those that primarily benefit other men in the prison, those that primarily benefit segments of the outside community, and those that bring the outside community into the prison for meaningful interactions. These are useful but largely artificial distinctions as many programs benefit both those on the inside and those on the outside. Moreover, given that the vast majority of prisoners will be released back into the community, any new skills or increased competencies developed by the men in prison will transfer outside of the penitentiary's walls. In addition, any program that helps the men inside likely helps their families, and actions and programs that benefit families and communities may be helpful to the men in prison sooner or later. In all cases, programs that are created in prison are developed only through the sustained efforts of prisoners with the cooperation of staff members and administration.

Trevor notes that some events and programs take extraordinary effort on the part of the men, especially those leading programs, inside the prison. It can take months and years of patience and compromise to ultimately navigate the bureaucracy of the prison and attain approvals from staff members, the security team, and layers of administration. When asked whether such programs are worth the effort and the grappling with the prison's strict security measures, Trevor replied: "so long as you are doing it for the right reasons and there isn't something of greater value that could be getting done in place of whatever event is in question, absolutely it's worth the effort."

Hospice

The first prison hospice program opened in 1987, and a recent study counted 69 known prison hospice programs in the USA (Hoffman & Dickinson, 2011). While they operate with procedures and standards very similar to those in the community, Hoffman and Dickinson (2011) found that prison hospices utilize a more stringent screening process for volunteers and require more training prior to interacting with a hospice patient.

Oregon began hospice programs in its state prisons in the late 1990s. An interdisciplinary team including representatives from health services, security, programs, religious services, administration, and inmate volunteers helped to design and implement Oregon's statewide model for prison hospice programs (Cahal, 2002). The health service manager of the penitentiary at the time explained the decision to train and use prisoners as hospice volunteers: "We decided to use inmate volunteers in the model in the hope that the participation of volunteers would have a positive effect on the program, on the inmate population as a whole, and on the volunteers themselves" (Cahal, 2002, p. 127).

Now, more than a decade later, men in OSP who are incarcerated and expected to die in the near future are placed on hospice and a team of prisoner volunteers spend time caring for them and attending to their needs. This includes constant bedside care, feeding, cleaning, and a general effort to provide improved quality of life care as well as advocacy for their patients. The prisoners who volunteer in this program must go through extensive training developed and conducted by staff and current hospice workers as well as going through an interview with institutional administration. This program provides meaningful engagement for participants and allows for introspection and a way to give back to their own community.

In research conducted at Louisiana State Penitentiary at Angola, where the prison hospice program has been in continuous operation since 1998, Cloyes, Rosenkranz, Wold, Berry, and Supiano (2014) investigated the transformative potential of prisoners' service as hospice volunteers. They found that for prisoners working in hospice, "the sense that volunteering service to others—especially vulnerable others facing death—is a defining characteristic of 'true humanity' that brings value to life" (p. 746).

When the prisoners who volunteered in hospice at Angola were asked what they felt others should know about the program and the role of prisoner volunteers, their responses fell into the following categories:

> (1) Hospice volunteering is a way to express authentic compassion that is truly within us; (2) hospice confirms our shared humanity with each other and the free world; and (3) volunteering and giving of yourself, especially when to do so is difficult or demanding, leads to personal change and redemption; (4) hospice provides a safe place to make and keep close connections with others and to become family; and (5) providing reliable, high-quality, patient-centered EOL [end-of-life] care should be a shared social responsibility. (Cloyes et al., 2014, p. 742)

In OSP, the men inside say it is easy to see how volunteering in hospice has affected their fellow prisoners. While James has not been directly involved in the hospice program, he is able to explain the value for both the patients and the volunteers:

> Hospice volunteers learn firsthand how precious and very delicate life can be, and the empathy for the dying men they care for helps to put their own struggles into perspective. To learn how to put yourself second and another first in prison is about as abnormal as it gets, especially when considering that this environment fosters selfishness for the sake of personal comfort and survival. But these men give selflessly to provide comfort for others whose situations are dire at best. I remember hearing about the joy a prisoner on hospice displayed when a handful of LemonHead candies made their way into his shaking hands. Simple gestures of kindness like that, gestures that most would never think twice about, are often what those on hospice talk of before passing. I've seen hardened convicts take part in the hospice program and freely shed tears in the middle of the yard each time one of their "patients" has passed.

From our perspective, prison hospice programs staffed with prisoners who assist their fellow men through the end of life appear to be beneficial to all concerned. Frail prisoners do not have to feel like they are dying alone, their peers who serve as hospice volunteers are able to connect deeply with their own humanity, and correctional facilities are able to provide better and more extensive end of life care to their population than would otherwise be possible.

Prisoners as Peer Teachers

While many prisoners have hard-earned knowledge and practical skills that they might like to share with their peers, prison administrators are wary of giving any individual prisoner sanctioned power or influence over others. Manipulation can and does happen when prisoners with bad intent take advantage of their peers, so staff and administrators keep a close eye on any opportunities for the men inside to have control over one another.

Nevertheless, many prisoners have extremely useful skills and knowledge that can be shared to benefit their peers. Trevor, who has become a strong leader in the Lifers' Unlimited Club and many other programs in the prison, offers his perspective:

> The sharing of knowledge in a productive and pro-social manner can be extremely effective on a number of levels. Without those who have come before us, teaching us how to navigate the system, we are limited in our abilities to grow. In addition to sharing information in a peer-based fashion, this provides an opportunity for those learning to get inspired about what can be accomplished through time and effort. Improving communication, learning a new language, learning a new skill, motivating others, showing others an easier way so that they don't make the same mistakes you did! This is both empowering on a personal level and for the individual receiving this knowledge. Feelings of humanity surface when you reach out in this way, and also when you are reached out to.

Prisoner-led Classes

OSP has 11 officially recognized and approved prisoner-led clubs, and each of the clubs elects prisoners to its executive body to lead and represent the members' voices and concerns. The clubs serve many functions in the prison (for further information on leadership and prisoner-led clubs see Chap. 3 in this volume), and they offer an important avenue for prisoners to share their skills with each other.

Administration and staff have come to recognize and appreciate the value of these clubs, and they were receptive to ideas on how to encourage effective and responsible leadership. A Club Leadership class was developed and is taught by a veteran prisoner who offers ideas and advice and encourages motivated individuals and elected leaders to invest in club activities. This class is offered to Club Executive Body members so that knowledge and brainstorming opportunities can be presented to those who are in leadership positions. We believe this course is unique to OSP and shows the potential of prisoners as leaders, role models, and teachers; the Club Leadership class was organically created and fine-tuned by the men inside in order to support and mentor their peers.

Toastmasters International focuses on communication and leadership development and has thousands of chapters all over the world. The chapter in OSP holds multiple prisoner-led classes yearly, focusing on leadership, team building, and mental flexibility. Toastmaster International members facilitate the classes, wherein the participants and the facilitators are able to learn and improve their communication and leaderships skills.

Uhuru Sa Sa is one of the one of the longest running clubs at OSP; created primarily to serve African-American prisoners, Uhuru Sa Sa sponsors a program called Understanding Self Equals Life's Foundation (U-SELF). A former member of Uhuru Sa Sa (who has been released and is doing well in the community) wrote the curriculum with the guiding philosophy of "each one teach one," or that men who had the opportunity to learn, grow and succeed should share the lessons they have learned with their peers. This program encourages participants to really look at who they are and why they are the way they are. Then it empowers participants by offering them tools for positive self-reflection and change.

Another prisoner-led class is Admissions and Orientation (A&O), which is offered to all new prisoners of OSP. Prisoners and staff cofacilitate the A&O class to offer information about the institution, provide an opportunity for questions and answers, and offer suggestions and the perspective of peers on how to make the most of one's time in prison.

Supporting Classes in the Inside-Out Prison Exchange Program

Michelle taught the first Inside-Out Prison Exchange Program college class in OSP in 2007. The Inside-Out program brings college students from the outside community into the facility to share class with students from the prison for a full term (Pompa, 2013). The "inside" and "outside" students do all of the same readings and course work. However, it can be difficult for inside students to reach the professor to ask questions or to receive clarification on assignments. To deal with these communication issues and to retain involvement of highly motivated students,

Michelle started using inside students as teaching assistants for her college classes. Having prisoners serve as teaching assistants allows tremendous opportunities for those individuals to build leadership skills, become comfortable facilitating group activities, and tutor their peers. Students in the classes—both from the college and the prison—also find it helpful when they can hear the perspective of both their inside teaching assistant and their professor when discussing or writing about class materials.

Fundraising for Prisoners with Special Needs

The prisoner-led clubs in OSP routinely raise money for prison events and club functions; for example, the Lifers' Unlimited Club holds bimonthly "senior days" for members of the prison population who are over the age of 50. In addition, a recent collaborative effort of the prisoner-led clubs was a fundraiser specifically benefitting those who are housed in the Special Housing Units (often called SHUs). These units house prisoners suffering from mental and behavioral health issues who require a greater level of supervision.

The clubs, after meeting with staff members and administrators, conducted a fundraiser selling donuts to the men in the general population (fundraisers are planned, approved, and advertised far in advance; generally the men inside can choose to pay to attend the event, and with staff members' cooperation and help, food is ordered and brought in from outside restaurants in order to raise funds). The proceeds in the first year were used to purchase donuts for everyone housed in the mental health SHU, a treat they otherwise would not have received.

In the second year, the clubs again sold donuts to the general population and used the profits to purchase security-approved basic hygiene products for care packages for men in the mental health SHU. The care packages contained either better quality items than those provided by the state—such as toothpaste rather than the straight baking soda the prison provides—or items not provided at all like shampoo or deodorant.

Creative Writing and Book Projects

A creative writing group called "Penned Thoughts" meets weekly in OSP to work together, share inspiration, and cultivate their writing skills. A professor from a local community college volunteers her time and energy to facilitate and supervise the group. Once a year they host an event where families and outside guests are able to come together for a reading by the authors and a celebration of their collective, self-published work.

James was one of the founding members of the "Penned Thoughts" group and participated until his work schedule no longer allowed it. He explains how important the group was in providing an outlet to express himself:

> I was fortunate to be a part of the creative writing group Penned Thoughts for many years. I found my voice as a writer while with Penned Thoughts and I can never adequately show the appreciation deserved for the many hours spent helping me fine-tune this craft. Coming to prison as young as I did meant I missed out on a lot of the experiences that would have helped shape me, and yet it was with Penned Thoughts that I discovered my experiences while incarcerated still amounted to a story that needed to be told. Being naturally shy, it's through my writing that I've found the comfort needed to really open up and describe the feelings I have.
>
> One of my fondest memories while with the Penned Thoughts group was when we got to see the book of creative writing we made for the first time. I did the artwork on the cover and when our writing teacher handed me a copy of it I just held it in my hands and stared at it; it was amazing to see something we had all put so much effort into. I helped create it! That was huge for me; it helped me understand that creativity can be an amazingly therapeutic tool. It helped spark conversations with my family, which is always a welcomed bonus when considering how mind-numbingly boring prison life can be.
>
> Another aspect of the writers group that I always enjoyed was when we'd meet with our families in the prison visiting room for our annual summer poetry readings. During those nights we managed to make that room our home, a stage in which each of us was able to step up and say with words the things our actions rarely did. Expressions of sorrow for the pains inflicted on our loved ones by way of our selfish actions, declarations of love, and heartfelt descriptions of places we'd gone or hoped to one day go.

James and the Lifers' Unlimited Club are currently working on a book called "Wisdom within the Pen." The idea was simply that Lifers, who often spend decades in prison, have a wide variety of experiences and a lot of wisdom to share for other incarcerated people as well as the public. James agreed to lead the book project, which included securing permission from the administration for the project, soliciting poems, essays, and artwork from potential contributors, and editing all of the submissions. James had a clear vision for the book and for how it might be used to benefit others:

> I wanted to create an opportunity for the men and women of the DOC (Department of Corrections) to have their voices be heard. Their true voices. With this book you read proof of the incredible talents that exist behind these walls. Our book will be printed soon and what we're most proud of is that all the proceeds from this project, after cost, will go towards helping a local charity called Angels in the Outfield that we're closely aligned with (As mentioned earlier, Angels in the Outfield is a local non-profit agency serving children who have been affected by crime and abuse, either as victims themselves or as the children of victims or offenders).

Informal Mentoring of Incoming Prisoners

Much of the peer teaching and service that occurs within OSP takes the form of informal mentoring. Men who are older and/or wiser offer guidance and advice to younger men or those who may not be younger, but are seeking to change their lives in a positive direction and would like support. Trevor and James have both benefited from being mentored by their peers, and they have both moved into mentoring and leadership roles. Trevor, who has been incarcerated since he was 14, has a fairly unique perspective on what it is to grow up and mature in prison. As one of the youngest people in Oregon to be convicted of murder in adult court, Trevor was sentenced to 30-years-to-life. Because he was only 14 at the time of the crime, however, he was too young under state law to be given a mandatory-minimum sentence. Trevor hopes to benefit from a rare "second look" which would allow him to return to the community under supervision if he is judged to have matured and grown into a responsible citizen during the first half of his sentence. Now at age 31, Trevor has taken on key leadership roles within the maximum-security prison for several years. With the possibility of release in his near future, he has put real thought into mentoring others and hoping they will step up to continue the positive momentum he has helped to create. Trevor writes:

> In here, if we don't mentor others, if we don't share the knowledge of how to accomplish this or that, what we have worked towards is lost. I was fortunate to have that philosophy taught to me early on in my years at OSP. It was a combination of creating for yourself a place where it's as enjoyable an environment to do time as possible and teaching others so that they maintain those improvements in your absence … While students are not as eager or readily available as I'd like them to be, I'm happy to teach so long as the student is interested and willing to learn.

James, who was given a mandatory-minimum sentence of 25-years-to-life for the crime he committed at 16, has been both a partner in helping to lead the Lifers' Unlimited Club over the last several years and also a willing student as he transitions into leadership of the RISE UP! (Reaching Inside to See Everyone's Unlimited Potential) youth empowerment program. James explains what these leadership roles and the encouragement of other leaders has meant to him:

> I'm one of the lucky ones in terms of being a prisoner because with these leadership positions I'm being afforded the opportunity to learn valuable skills that will be beneficial both here and in the outside community. I'm learning computer, communication, and time management skills. I'm learning how to write effective proposals, gather groups for activities that will involve heavy doses of teamwork and cooperation, and ways to work out conflicts without it devolving into confrontation. These leadership requirements are things that don't necessarily come easily to me, I have to work really hard at it because by nature I feel more at ease in the background. But again, I want to grow and I understand that to do so means I have to step outside my comfort zone, and it becomes a little easier each time I'm encouraged by my peers.

While formal leadership opportunities are available to prisoners in good standing if they choose to pursue them, it is more common and certainly easier for prisoners to share their experiences and advice with their peers informally. James shares one such interaction:

> About a year ago a fellow lifer brought a prisoner to me who had just arrived with a 25-to-life sentence. He had just completed the orientation portion of being a new arrival and was brought to me because, like him, I arrived here very young with a very long sentence. I recognized myself in this new prisoner from all those years ago; the fear he was obviously feeling, the anxiety that courses through the body for what feels like a hopeless situation, and more than anything else the fear of not knowing what to do in a new environment that's usually anything but inviting.

I introduced myself to this new lifer, talked briefly about the 19 years I've done since arriving at the age of 17, and gave a lengthy description of the do's and don'ts that determine a prisoner's likelihood for institutional success. And then I waited. I watched him from a distance for a few months because I learned long ago that you can talk until you're blue in the face about positive ways to do time, but ultimately it's up to them to determine what type of prison time they want to do. I was encouraged one day when this same new prisoner came up to me on the yard and said I was one of the only men who talked to him about taking accountability for his actions and growing from them. He said he was still confused as to how that could be done after committing the crime he's here for, but that he wanted to try. He could have gone several different routes upon entering the prison system: join a gang, start getting horrible tattoos that he'd surely regret, or run with the drug crowd and create a revolving door for himself in the disciplinary segregation unit. But he didn't. Instead he enrolled in classes to earn his GED, joined a few positive, goal-oriented clubs, and got a really good first job. That's success from the start compared to the alternatives.

Situations like that mean a lot to me because it shows that I'm in a position to make positive impacts on the lives of those around me. Whereas I was once the youngster who sought out advice from the old school convicts, I'm now the "old man" who imparts wisdom on some of the newbies. Yeah, and I'm only 36 years old. It's kind of cool. Especially since I've been here for 19 years and I'm still about five years younger than the average age of the men imprisoned here.

Such informal and positive mentoring surely happens in prisons much more than the public will ever hear about. While the "pains of imprisonment" (Sykes, 1958) are undoubtedly real and the environment can be extremely harsh, at least some good can and does occur within the prison community through such mentoring processes. We hope the above examples helped to shed light on the fact that as challenging as the prison environment can be, during the time inside some men learn leadership, empathy, and how to truly care for their peers.

Programs Created or Run by the Men in Prison to Benefit the Outside Community

Many men in OSP have a strong desire to give back to the larger community that they may have harmed. They often feel particular affinity for disadvantaged, at-risk, or troubled youth and they have created a number of programs to offer advice and/or material goods to vulnerable youth in the community.

Youth Empowerment Programs and Speaking Panels

Three of the prisoner-led clubs sponsor speaking panels that bring youth into the prison to share conversations and receive advice from the men inside. Club leaders reach out to community organizations including schools, churches, after-school programs, and parents who are looking for advice and help, and they invite them to bring youth to their monthly speaking panels. Two of the panels focus on culturally specific issues and youth; one group focuses on Native American youth, and another reaches out to Latino youth. The Lifers' Unlimited Club sponsors The RISE UP! youth empowerment program, and both Trevor and James are members and leaders of that group. James explains the potential of such groups and the youth speaking panels they host:

> The youth empowerment programs in this prison, though few in number, reach a significant number of youth in the surrounding communities. A message of hope is always the main theme when talking to youth during our small group sessions. No matter the struggles they're currently going through, no matter the troubles they've already started to accumulate, we relay to them that there's always the chance to stop and start over with wise decision making. It's possible, and we talk with them about attainable goal setting so that they can see the clear fruit of their efforts. It's always amazing to start with a group of shy, quiet, and reserved youth and then be able to see them open up and talk openly about the pains they're holding inside in a matter of an hour or two. I think they realize that the prisoners involved in these programs truly care about their futures and that they find comfort in knowing they can be honest without fear of being judged. That's huge.
>
> The small number of men who take part in the RISE UP! program do so knowing the only payback they'll get is the satisfaction that comes from knowing they may have helped change a youth's life for the better. The wisdom that we share with these youth is different than what parents, teachers, counselors, or others in the community can offer, in large part because they seem to respect us for the sheer fact that we've been there and done it. They listen to us attentively, they ask questions in our small group sessions, and when we turn the questioning around and get them to understand that poor choices can land anyone in prison, they can't argue against that because they're sitting with men who've done decades in prison. Men who received life sentences as juveniles and were younger than a lot of them are now. When their eyes get big after hearing how long some of us have been incarcerated, when we describe with honesty the shame and remorse we feel, or when their eyes well up with tears as their own realities become

> clear, progress can begin to be made with these youth. The most important thing to remember, and a line that I really enjoy hearing Trevor, our Lifers' club president, say is that we should never give up on someone because no matter how far gone or how disruptive they may seem, at the end of the day who are we to say when that person will become something of value?

Trevor offers his perspective on the youth empowerment programs, the motivation for men in prison to participate, and the potential impact of this volunteer service:

> If you look at almost all of the Youth Speaking Panels, the majority of those involved are serving long prison sentences. Most participants are Lifers, just looking for another way to give back, to have an impact, to contribute. We share a deep-seated desire to prevent others from making some of the same poor decisions that we made, ultimately leading us to prison. However, it isn't necessarily the prison experience that so drives us to make these efforts, I think there is a strong desire to do these things because we know how devastating the effects are to everyone involved. We come to realize that our victims encompass not just those the criminal system labels as such, but every single person we engage with as a result of our crime. Judges, lawyers, police, detectives, fathers, mothers, sons and daughters, neighbors, family members, communities, correctional officers, pen pals, cellies (cell-mates), the list goes on and on! As we realize these things we are forced to recognize our duty to make amends to whatever degree possible, unsuccessful as they may be at complete restoration, maybe it's even at times less than partial restoration, regardless we have to make that attempt. The old adage, "once you know, you owe" drives me at least daily!

Finally, James gives a first-hand account of what he is thinking and hoping for each night he participates in a youth speaking panel:

> During the nights we speak to youth I always go out there hoping to make a difference in the life of a youth who is maybe going through some of the same struggles, feeling some of the same insecurities, and who's maybe making some of the same poor choices I was making at that age. I want to encourage them. If I can be the person to sit with them and talk about life, the choices we make on an everyday basis, and about the importance of school and the benefits that come with seeking higher education, I feel I'm providing that voice of reason that I could have used myself when I was a youngster. It's my way of giving back after so many people rallied around me during my 19 years of incarceration.

I'm not the greatest speaker in the world, and I'm definitely not one of the best in our group, but I think I speak in a way that youth can relate to because I'm willing to be completely transparent and show vulnerability. I believe it's important to show that side of myself because more often than not it seems like youth, males in particular, seem to be heavily influenced by the culture of "machoism." Seeing another male spill tears over mistakes can let them see that it's okay to let it out, it's okay to hurt inside, and it's okay to seek the support of others whenever hardships arise. They need to know that it's okay. I just try to be real with them and explain why I was doing some of the things I was doing at that age, what need I was trying to meet by way of those behaviors, and how hindsight can be a very heavy thing to carry when you look back later in life and contemplate the poor choices made and the people affected by them.

I'm encouraged, and I'm just really thankful for the opportunity to be in a position that can potentially help change the lives of youth for the better. Doing time this way is much more fulfilling than just sitting on my bunk twiddling my thumbs. That's for sure.

Partnering with Community Agencies

Men in OSP are eager to work with community partners whenever they are reasonably able to do so. It can be a lengthy process for the men inside to establish interest and communication with community agencies, and any individual volunteers from the community who wish to enter the prison regularly must train as volunteers for the Oregon DOC, pass the criminal background checks, and be fully approved by the administration. In order to reach out and offer support to worthy causes, the men inside regularly donate money to community-based organizations—as an example, along with numerous donations to agencies and families in need, in 2014 the Lifers' Unlimited Club donated $1200 to the nonprofit agency Angels in the Outfield and $650 to a local high school to sponsor a drug-free graduation event. They also invested money and effort to fill backpacks with school supplies and to hand them out to the children who visited their loved ones in the prison. If community agencies or volunteers come to them with an idea or a good cause, the leaders of the prison population will generally seek support from their peers, staff members, and prison administrators to figure out what they can do to help. Over the past several years through their persistence in pursuing avenues to make a positive contribution to the larger society and their strong desire to give back, prisoners in the penitentiary have developed ongoing relationships with a number of community partners.

HOME Youth Resource Center: Donations and Encouragement for At-Risk/Homeless Youth

For a number of years, the men in OSP, led by the Seventh Step club, have been the largest and most consistent donor to the HOME Youth Resource Center, a drop-in center catering to at-risk and homeless youth in the city where the prison is located. The Seventh Step club (for more information on prisoner-led clubs in OSP, see Chap. 3 in this volume) regularly holds hygiene drives, where prisoners can purchase new, practical items such as toothpaste, combs, and deodorant from the prison canteen/shop and donate them to HOME. They also coordinate cash donations from the prison population to support the important work that HOME is doing to help youth who are either on the streets or at-risk of ending up on the streets. Staff representatives from HOME are regularly invited into meetings of Seventh Step and other prisoner-led clubs in order to receive the checks and donations for the youth they serve. In addition, the RISE UP! youth empowerment program has also started working with HOME to bring youth from the street into the prison to attend one of the youth empowerment program's speaking panels; in these visits, the men from RISE UP! share parts of their own histories in order to discuss life choices and offer new perspectives with the youth who attend.

Working to Build a Partnership with the Oregon Youth Authority

Michelle has had significant experience in volunteering with and teaching within the Oregon Youth Authority (OYA) (Inderbitzin, 2014), and Trevor served significant time in an OYA facility before being transferred to adult prison. Based in part on these experiences, we have been working for the past several years to develop an official relationship between OYA and the RISE UP! youth empowerment program. We believe that men who have served many years in prison and matured and grown in the process have real wisdom to offer young men facing similar paths. In hopes of making the transition from OYA to the DOC as productive as possible, we have proposed a program where adults in custody (and formally incarcerated individuals) will share their personal experiences, perspectives, and advice with currently incarcerated youth. Incarcerated youth tend to have many questions, fears, and misperceptions about life inside a state prison; talking with men who have survived the transition and are currently leading productive lives in prison may help the youth in their own transition to a DOC facility.

This partnership is a work in progress. Michelle initiated contact with the Director of the OYA, and he and key members of his administrative team have come to the prison to meet with Trevor, James, and other men who could potentially serve as role models/mentors to youth and young adults in OYA custody. There are still many details to be worked out concerning staff supervision of any interactions and ensuring compliance with all federal regulations, but everyone who is involved believes this is a promising partnership and continues to invest time developing the idea and potential program.

Working with Citizens United for the Rehabilitation of Errants

Citizens United for the Rehabilitation of Errants (CURE) is an international grassroots organization that works to improve the criminal justice system, and its members advocate on behalf of both prisoners and victims. The Oregon chapter of CURE is an all-volunteer organization that has committed to working with the Lifers' Unlimited Club at OSP. Because the men inside raised questions and concerns about the policies and practices of the Oregon Board of Parole and Post-Prison Supervision, members of CURE regularly attend Parole Board hearings and provide valued feedback. They correspond with the Lifers' Unlimited Club through e-mails sent and moderated by a prison staff advisor and by attending club meetings and speaking with the members.

James sees promise in the partnership with CURE and feels hope in knowing that the members of CURE care what happens inside the state's courtrooms, parole hearings, and prisons:

> I've been fortunate in that I've had the opportunity to meet with the representatives of CURE on a regular basis. To hear their thoughts, to take part in discussions about the immediate concerns they have regarding incarceration in general, and to be present when the hopes they have for effective change within the current prison system are voiced gives me hope. Why hope? Because right now the system punishes each person as if each is exactly the same, yet each of us is distinctly different in a myriad of ways. To incarcerate for the sole purpose of throwing away a problem doesn't solve the problem in the long run; it only warehouses it. There are better ways to deal with people who've made horrible choices, and being able to work side by side with those

from CURE who are actively stumping for change is rewarding because the two sides are learning so much from the other. Ideas are being shared and with the right approach I think amazing things are on the horizon.

Family First

Family First is a program that started in at least two Oregon prisons due to the efforts of the prison chaplains, men inside, and community volunteers. While families and children may be able to attend regular visiting hours, Family First allows its members to spend quality time interacting and making memories. The Family First program seeks to bring fathers, father figures, and/or other male role models together with the children in their lives for meaningful visitation opportunities. Men in the penitentiary must first complete a parenting education program before they can apply to be part of Family First; once in the program, they can practice their skills while spending time with their children in special family events. Because regular visiting at OSP is limited to morning and afternoon sessions, Family First events take place on Friday nights and offer unique opportunities for children to spend time in the prison with their loved ones. Important bonding time is created as families are able to sit down and share stories and a meal together.

Trevor is a participant in Family First and shares what it has meant to him personally:

> For me, Family First has allowed me to connect with my high school sweetheart's oldest daughter who has lived with my mom for the past several years. Having gone through the Parenting Inside-Out class, which is a prerequisite for Family First, I learned a lot of the skills I now employ while providing a parental role to her. Sometimes she needs a big brother, sometimes a dad, sometimes just a friend, and having the opportunities that are provided through these programs I've been able to be there as she needs and when she needs.

While James has not been personally involved in Family First, he sees the value of the program in the lives of his friends, and he finds hope in such interactions:

> A close friend of mine is involved in the Family First program. He lights up whenever I ask him how the most recent family function went, it's pretty cool to see. Though incarcerated, most of his daily conversations seem to

revolve strongly around the positive strides he's made in regards to strengthening his family ties. This man, roughly 40 years old and with a bum hip, turns into a kid himself whenever the chance arises for horseplay with his children. I take photos at some of the Family First events and I'm always encouraged to see the amazing bonds being formed when dads, equipped with parenting skills learned while on the inside, interact with their children. It would make anyone smile and say there's hope for all.

Interactions Between Community Members and the Men Inside

Leaders within the prison population strongly believe in the benefits of bringing members of the outside community into the prison to interact with the men inside. Such personal interactions can help to break down barriers and stereotypes between individuals on both sides of the prison walls. Club leaders in particular work with their staff advisors to meticulously plan events involving a wide variety of volunteers, speakers, performers, and guests from the community. Once they have developed a plan, the leaders write and submit formal proposals in hopes they will get approval from security staff and prison administrators.

Inviting the Outside Community Inside

Hosting Victim Impact and Community Impact Meetings

A number of the prisoner-led clubs invite professors from local universities to bring groups of college students into their meetings. The Lifers' Unlimited Club, Seventh Step, Toastmasters, and the Asian Club all bring in groups at least once each year. The purpose of such meetings vary: some groups come in for debates, some for community impact meetings, some for victim impact meetings, and some simply for students and prisoners to interact in an honest forum where questions can be asked and answered with impunity.

The meetings with college students help to break down stereotypes for all involved, but especially those associated with prisons, prisoners, and people with criminal histories. These interactions can be extremely valuable for all participants because they help show the college students that prisoners are human beings with many positive characteristics even if they made bad decisions at some point in their lives. From the prisoners' side of things, social interactions with the outside are highly restricted and can be nonexistent for years on end, especially for lifers. Meetings with college students can provide a valuable opportunity for the men inside to think about and talk about what brought them to prison, perhaps offering new perspectives or new ways to articulate their experience. Further, these meetings may also help current prisoners to realize that college students are not that different from the men inside, and college may be an attainable goal for them as well.

James has been involved in many community and victim impact meetings and meetings with college students. He shares his perspective on why they are worthwhile:

> I really enjoy taking part in the discussions with college students because it's an opportunity to show them that prisoners are human. It seems like every new group comes in with a set of preconceived notions as to who they think prisoners are, and it's just nice when towards the end of the evening students speak up about the different attitudes they'll be leaving with. Most people see the nightly news, or their local newspapers, and they're quick to buy in when they describe us as monsters that deserve nothing more than a dark cell and a lifetime confined to our own thoughts. When these students come in and sit with us, when they ask questions about our lives and learn our stories, they're able to see the humanity inside each of us. We're human beings who make mistakes just like everyone else, and that's easy to forget when most people only see the news highlighting who we were during the worst moments of our lives. We're fathers, husbands, sons, grandparents, and uncles. We're poets, business owners, artists, and counselors. We're responsible for the poor choices we've made, we'll never argue against that, but we're also capable of some very positive things and I oftentimes think it's too easy to just throw people away for large chunks of time without putting real thought into it.
>
> Victim Impact meetings are done every year and I've had a chance to attend a few of them myself. It's pretty intense. I've had to face the fact that my own actions have had a similar impact on an innocent person and their family. So badly I wish I could apologize and take back what I've done. When someone's right there in your face describing in detail how they were harmed and how it made them feel, how it's affected the rest of their lives as a result, it really humbles you and makes you realize the scope of your poor choices.
>
> A question I always struggle with is: Do I deserve forgiveness? I've worked hard over the last two decades to grow into a better man than I was on that day at age 17, but self-forgiveness is something I struggle with

> mightily because I never wanted to be a criminal in the first place and I'm horrified that I'm the cause of someone's death. I didn't wake up that morning thinking that before the day would end an innocent person would be dead. I was just a naïve kid trying a drug for the first time, and I couldn't handle it. The next thing I knew I was on the nightly news as the latest teenage disappointment. It hurts. It's something I can't make better. It's something I can't go back and fix even though every ounce of my being aches to do just that.

Inviting Community Groups, Sports Teams, Debate Teams, and Entertainers into One-Time Meetings

While religious groups of all denominations come into the institution regularly to hold services, other community groups are invited in for special purposes. Runners come in for races held on the prison yard (Heald, 2015), college debate teams come in to compete with teams from Toastmasters, and intramural sports teams from the community can arrange to play teams from within the prison. In addition, community groups, speakers, writers, and entertainers may come in for club meetings and special events; for example Sister Helen Prejean, the author of *Dead Man Walking* (Prejean, 1994), came in for a writing workshop, and Jennifer Thompson-Cannino, author of *Picking Cotton* (Thompson-Cannino, Cotton, & Torneo, 2009), came in to speak with the Lifers' Unlimited Club.

As Vice President of the Lifers' Unlimited Club, James has spent a good deal of time arranging for entertainment and special events. He shares why these interactions with the outside community are so important to the men inside:

> I've been blessed with the opportunity to arrange concerts and comedy nights, and to have live animal exhibits brought into the prison on many occasions. The live animal exhibits are always a hit: snakes, alligators, snapping turtles, lizards, eagles, parrots, owls, you name it. It's amazing to see grown men go from hardened convicts to lovable animal cuddlers in a span of a few minutes, but it happens, and I'm glad that it does because those are therapeutic moments that we need in order to still feel human. What's also really gratifying is seeing how quickly guys step up and help out whenever events like these take place. Our guests routinely make comments as they're leaving about how well they were treated, how helpful we were, and just

how comfortable they felt while with us. Hearing these comments is an achievement in and of itself considering we're in large part the same men who society has given up on by way of long prison terms.

Annual Car and Bike Show

The largest community event that OSP regularly hosts is an annual "Car & Bike Show," an all-day event occurring on the main recreation yard with owners bringing as many as 200-vehicles to showcase their cars, trucks, and bikes. Up to 300 outside guests may come in during an event of this nature. There is a raffle of donated items provided by sponsors or created on the prison grounds, and trophies are created on site and awarded to the top vehicles as selected by a prisoner-run judging panel.

The Car & Bike show is a huge undertaking in terms of logistics, and the prisoners in charge of the event often spend a full year planning it. Trevor has been at the center of the planning process for the Car & Bike show, and he can speak to both how much work it is and why it is generally worth it:

> Things like the Car & Bike Show bring in vehicles that some men may otherwise never see. We're surrounded by 30-foot tall concrete walls; men can go years and even decades without seeing anything from outside of the walls without events like the Car Show occurring. It does take a lot of effort for sure, but if you see the value in it, not just for those short-term benefits but for the longer-term and bigger picture benefits of exposure, humanization, community, and so on, if you can see these things for what they are, then you realize the effort is absolutely worth every ounce of work that has to be invested. You learn and develop leadership qualities, communication skills, stress management, delegation techniques, teamwork, and a host of other unexpected benefits. You can also gain the respect of community members, both inside and outside, staff and prisoner alike, as well as make connections with those coming inside to experience the show that may later result in sponsorship of some kind, support or other benefits/involvement.

James serves as a volunteer during the Car & Bike show, and explains his role:

> The car show is an awesome day for prisoners at OSP. Men love cars, enough said. For the last eight years I've been a "greeter" during the Car & Bike Show, which means it's my job to welcome the guests to OSP and engage in conversations that help them feel at home for the day. Usually the guests

> want to know about prison life: "Is the food really as bad as it looks on TV?" "How do prisoners get tattoos?" "What types of jobs are there on the inside?" and many other inquisitive questions that we're all happy to answer.
>
> I've always been really into cars so I enjoy being able to ask questions. Since I've been here for so long every car that comes in made after the early nineties seems like a brand new car to me. It's always amusing to see the outside guests do a double take when I tell them how long I've been here and the age that I came at.

The events that bring community members into the prison are important for a number of reasons: they give the men inside something to look forward to by offering a vital infusion of fresh energy and opportunities with each guest that walks through the cement walls; they offer guests from the community a chance to meet the men inside and see them as fully dimensional human beings rather than stereotypes or media headlines; and finally, they can provide a synergy of new possibilities and partnerships by enabling men who want to change their lives and contribute to the community to meet individuals who may be able to partner with them in those efforts.

Implications for the Voluntary Sector Working Within or in Partnership with Prisons

> *Prisons can often feel like insular worlds with their own culture and dynamics. Terms such as "total institution," proposed by Erving Goffman, suggest that some institutions, such as prisons are almost hermetically sealed and exercise a powerful, dominating influence over those inside. However, such a polar view could never be entirely sustained. There is always space, even if constrained and circumscribed, for the outside to seep in and for people to express and enact their own individual and collective will.* (Editorial Comment, 2014)

We want to conclude this chapter by stating as clearly as possible that many men inside are eager to work with community partners. They do what they can from inside to make space for personal growth and the ability to give back, but their power to create programs and positive change is greatly enhanced when they are able to partner and combine resources with agencies and volunteers from the larger community. We speak from experience when we tell you that the resulting synergy can empower and energize participants on both sides of the prison walls.

It can be difficult for men inside prisons to reach out to community agencies—they have very few avenues for direct communication. For security reasons, leaders of programs and prisoner-led clubs at OSP always have to work through prison staff members to make phone calls, send e-mails, or do any kind of outreach; because of this, communication can be slow and frustrating and sometimes shut down entirely for no clear reason. The men inside, however, are always happy to respond when community members make the effort to reach in and allow them to extend their goodwill and their reach outside of the prison.

While it can be challenging, communication between leaders inside the prison, staff members, and community volunteers is key. Trevor finds that he has to be both flexible and persistent in working with different community partners as each group presents different rewards and challenges:

> It can be both challenging and empowering to work with community groups. Work with the HOME Youth Resource Center, for example, is mostly empowering because of the willingness they have to communicate how our efforts are received. They have come in and given video presentations, they e-mail updates to our staff advisor, they've brought some of their youth to our RISE UP! youth empowerment program, and overall there's a *feeling* of support from them reciprocated through the work that they do and the work that we do. CURE has been great from the engagement level as regular dialogue occurs back and forth. For me personally it is rewarding to bring in a resource such as CURE and simply be a conduit for the interactions that occur. Empowering club members to sit down at the table and put in their two cents, productively, and, more often than not, for the improvement of others who will come after them—that for me is the joy. College and university students are our prospective movers and shakers of the next generation. Their ideas matter; they are still learning and developing. These are our judges, lawyers, counselors, teachers, police, medics, and the list goes on and on. Beyond that these are everyday people whose opinion matters, they are more likely to vote, and they will shape our world by their actions and deeds.

Communicating and partnering with community agencies and volunteers creates a set of challenges, including difficulty with timely communication, the need to help community agencies understand prison protocol and regulations, and a lack of follow-through on ideas and promises. Still, working closely with prison staff members entails a whole different set of challenges and requires the use of different skills. James has found working with staff members to be one of the largest challenges of taking on leadership roles within the prison. He explains:

> One of the hardest things I've had to learn, and which I'm still learning, is how to deal with the personalities of various prison staff when the stars aren't aligning. There have been many times when I've honestly felt like throwing my hands in the air and just walking away from the many programs that I'm involved in. Not because quitting is something I embrace, or because I'm getting burnt out on volunteering for things that rarely come with appreciation, but rather because sometimes the stress just doesn't seem worth it while trying to maintain mental health. I've managed to accumulate over 14 years of clear conduct to date (no disciplinary infractions within the prison), which I'm super proud of, but it hasn't been an easy road by any means and it's always in jeopardy of being lost.... I enjoy using my time to better this community, it means a lot to me and allows me to use my creativity for positive purposes. But at times it can be extremely difficult as rules change from day to day, new policies are constantly being enacted, each staff interprets these rules and policies differently, and the mood of staff is always unfortunately in question from minute to minute. Maintaining security is the ultimate standard, period. I get that. But trying your hardest to do positive things in an environment where staff routinely take their problems out on you is taxing. It really is.

Community members and agencies, too, have to learn to deal with authority, administration, and staff members when entering or attempting to enter any prison or correctional facility. You are there by the administration's grace and permission, and you must respect the rules and the environment in order to do the good work that brings you to the prison in the first place. It can be very frustrating to be turned away without clear explanation or to be treated poorly by a member of the staff, but you must be both patient and persistent. A lot of ideas won't fly the first time around. That's okay. Try to learn from the experience without giving up—a modification just might make your program or idea successful the next time you propose it.

As an outside volunteer, Michelle offers the following advice: try not to step on anyone's toes, including other volunteers who may have invested years in starting or building programs. Take some time to learn the lay of the land in that particular prison before pushing forward with your well-intentioned agenda. Listen to those who have put in significant time in the institution—the prisoners, staff, administration, and other volunteers—their thoughts, advice, and goodwill could prove priceless. Be respectful to all and be extremely conscious of personal boundaries; try to ensure that your motivation and actions are beyond reproach. Your intentions may be questioned, but choose your battles. You will almost certainly get at least a small taste of the frustration that the prisoners feel as you suggest new ideas but have to wait on the approval of several layers of bureaucracy before finding out whether you will be allowed to try to implement them. Try to see the big picture and understand the concerns of everyone involved. Emphasize the positive points and it will help you to keep coming back. Trust that your efforts ultimately do matter.

We also note that there is the possibility for manipulation and corruption within prison settings. You will learn as you go, but any major mistakes—especially those regarding personal boundaries—may be irrecoverable. Trevor offers the following advice and perspective to close this chapter:

> Not everyone is as they appear, and there are people inside who have yet to reach the point of transformation or may never reach it. There those who are still committed to criminal activity inside prison walls, and there are folks who have deep-seated negative behaviors instilled in them—that's part of prison, too. Boundaries are important for everyone involved, so be careful to maintain personal boundaries and follow all institutional rules.
>
> Be patient! It is worth the effort for sure and there is a great deal of good that can and does come from partnerships. Each institution is different, administration changes, staff can come and go, so just because you were able to do this or that the last time you were here, that doesn't mean you'll be able to do it the next time. Sometimes even when it's the same staff, you don't know what has transpired since your last visit, new rules could have been enacted, old rules may have been reinstated, you just never know! Again, it's worth the effort, there's really good people inside and they can use all of the help and support that they can get!

It can be a great experience for all involved to contribute to positive programs, growth, and development with those who have been locked away in state prisons and correctional facilities. If prisons are willing to allow such programs within their walls, volunteers can make a huge difference by working with the men and women inside to provide the spark, the help, and the connections to allow them to thrive.

References

Cahal, W. (2002). The birth of a prison hospice program. *Journal of Correctional Health Care*, *9*(2), 125–129.

Carter, S. (2008). HOPE, 'repair,' and the complexities of reciprocity: Inmates tutoring inmates in a total institution. *Community Literacy*, *2*(2), 87–107.

Cloyes, K. G., Rosenkranz, S. J., Wold, D., Berry, P. H., & Supiano, K. P. (2014). To be truly alive: Motivation among prison inmate hospice volunteers and the transformative process of end-of-life peer care service. *American Journal of Hospice & Palliative Medicine*, *31*(7), 735–748.

Edgar, K., Jacobson, J., & Biggar, K. (2011). *Time well spent: A practical guide to active citizenship and volunteering in prison*. London: Prison Reform Trust.

Editorial Comment.. (2014, November 3), *Prison Service Journal*, 216, 2.

Franklin, P. (2000). "Read to succeed": An inmate to inmate literacy program in Washington state. *Journal of Correctional Education*, *51*(3), 286–292.

Heald, M. (2015, June 25). For inmates "the wall" has a totally different meaning. *Runner's World*. Retrieved from http://www.runnersworld.com/runners-stories/for-inmates-the-wall-has-a totally-different-meaning.

Hoffman, H. C. & Dickinson, G. E. (2011). Characteristics of prison hospice programs in the United States. *American Journal of Hospice & Palliative Medicine*, *24*(4), 245–252.

Inderbitzin, M. (2014). "A lot of life ahead": Connecting college students with youth in juvenile justice settings through service-learning. *Currents in Teaching and Learning*, *7*(1), 100–107.

Inderbitzin, M., Walraven, T., & Cain, J. (2013). Juvenile lifers, learning to lead. In D. Hartman & C. Uggen (Eds.), *Crime and the punished* (pp. 171–185). New York: W.W. Norton.

Irwin, J. (1970). *The felon*. Berkeley: University of California.

Maruna, S. (2001). *Making good: How ex-convicts reform and rebuild their lives*. Washington, DC: American Psychological Association.

Pompa, L. (2013). One brick at a time: The power and possibility of dialogue across the prison wall. *The Prison Journal*, *93*(2), 127–134.

Prejean, H. (1994). *Dead man walking: An eyewitness account of the death penalty in the United States*. New York: Vintage Books.

Strimple, E. O. (2003). A history of prison inmate-animal interaction programs. *American Behavioral Scientist*, *47*(1), 70–78.

Sykes, G. (1958). *Society of captives*. Princeton, NJ: Princeton University.

Thompson-Cannino, J., Cotton, R., & Torneo, E. (2009). *Picking cotton: Our memoir of injustice and redemption*. New York: St. Martin's Press.

CHAPTER 5

Movements Towards Desistance via Peer-Support Roles in Prison

Christian Perrin and Nicholas Blagden

Introduction

Many peer-support programmes are currently operating in prisons across the UK. Through these programmes, prisoners are able to access support for issues ranging from emotional distress and addiction to practical and educational needs. Although such programmes have existed in UK prisons for decades, limited research has focused on those who occupy peer-support roles. This chapter aims to generate a deeper understanding of how adopting a peer-support role in prison can shape offenders' experiences of imprisonment. This chapter will highlight how individuals carrying out such roles in prison can reshape their lives and will thus illuminate some of the broader implications of peer-support volunteer programmes in prison contexts. This book recognises the financial constraints suffered by criminal justice systems worldwide and the resultant growth of volunteer-based programmes. Simultaneously, it is recognised that little research exploring such programmes exists, and it is therefore difficult to speculate upon the potential impact and trajectories of such programmes. This chapter aims to assist in the bridging of this knowledge gap and in

C. Perrin (✉) • N. Blagden
Nottingham Trent University, Nottingham, UK

L.S. Abrams et al. (eds.), *The Voluntary Sector in Prisons*, Palgrave Studies in Prisons and Penology, DOI 10.1057/978-1-137-54215-1_5

doing so offers an insight into peer-support volunteer roles as opportunities for offenders to gather meaning and purpose in prison and begin to make some movements towards desistance.

The Rise of Peer-Support in Prisons in the UK

Peer-support programmes in the UK have traditionally operated in high-risk environments, such as areas with high rates of crime, unemployment, poverty, and a high density of ethnic minority members (Devilly, Sorbello, Eccleston, & Ward, 2005). Research has consistently revealed positive effects of peer-support programmes in distressed communities. These benefits include enhanced community cohesion, reduced feelings of isolation and loneliness, and increased perception of social and emotional support (Bean, Shafer, & Glennon, 2013; Field & Schuldberg, 2011; Walker, & Bryant, 2013). For example, some research has positively assessed the use of effectively structured neighbourhood watch programmes on the grounds that they provide members of local communities with a sense of control over the crime and deviance occurring near their homes (Bennett, Holloway, & Farrington, 2009).

Perhaps the best recognised peer-support programme, and one that typifies the notion of mutual reciprocity and shared problem-solving, is Alcoholics Anonymous (AA). The AA programme encourages recovering alcoholics to share their stories of alcohol addiction and their transitional experiences that led to sobriety. Individuals who are in recovery invite newcomers to share their stories and adopt a mentoring role that involves guiding new members through the Twelve Steps programme. The mentors themselves benefit from this exchange, in that they remain in a position of heightened self-awareness regarding their own history with alcohol and are surrounded by people who can support them, should they relapse or lose hope. Experts have suggested that the system of giving and receiving help lies at the heart of peer-support (c.f., Devilly et al., 2005). Peer-support programmes can therefore be defined as involving reciprocal emotional exchanges and the sharing of experiences of overcoming great personal challenges (Mead, Hilton, & Curtis, 2001). Whilst there is a clear direction of support (there is a provider and receiver of support) the provider may also benefit from exchange because of the sense-making process involved in giving support and the natural requirement for self-reflection and experiential learning (Solomon, 2004). By providing support to others, individuals may reflect upon their own experiences and coping strategies. Mead et al. (2001) has argued that this can result in a sense-making process whereby effective self-regulation strategies are practiced and solidified. For these reasons, one can see how peer-support programmes have emerged in prisons and how they could have a positive effect on both the recipients and providers of such support. Indeed, there is a need to develop interventions that address the well-documented problems associated with prisons, such as high rates of suicide and self-harm; increased levels of violence, drug taking, sexual assault, and bullying; and higher incidences of severe mental illness compared with the general population (Dye, 2010).

There are many types of prison peer-support programmes in the UK. Such programmes focus primarily on the areas of HIV/AIDS and health education, drug and alcohol abuse, sexual assault/offending, prison orientation, anti-bullying and anti-racism, and suicide/violence prevention (Devilly et al., 2005). In general, peer-support in prison encompasses a range of different structures and approaches including training, facilitation, counselling, modelling, and helping (Parkin & McKeganey, 2000). This chapter focuses on the most widely implemented peer-support programmes in operation: the Listener scheme (Foster & Magee, 2011), the Insiders programme (Boothby (2011), Toe-by-Toe (also known as the Shannon Trust programme) (Shannon Trust, 2005), and the RAPt (Rehabilitation of Addicted Persons Trust) mentoring programme (Kopak, Dean, Proctor, Miller, & Hoffmann, 2014).

The Listener Scheme

The Prison Service Headquarters established the Listener scheme in 1991 in collaboration with the Samaritans. The Samaritans operates a 24-hour, volunteer hotline across the UK and the Republic of Ireland (ROI) that aims to provide people with an outlet for their emotional distress. Given that prisoners would otherwise be unable to access such a service whilst confined, the Listener scheme was introduced to help tackle especially high rates of suicide in prisons. Via the Listener scheme, prisoners suffering distress, despair, and suicidal ideation are able to talk face to face about their feelings without judgement and with utmost confidentiality. Prisoners who volunteer to become Listeners go through several weeks of training. This training covers the same modules as the community-based course and is delivered similarly, with adjustments made according to the context of prison and prison rules. Listeners receive a certificate upon completion of their training, and they sign a contract that binds them to the same policies to which Samaritans working in the community also adhere.

The Listener team establishes a rota within each prison with the aim of providing a 24-hour service to any prisoner in need (referred to as a "caller"). Callers have two options to contact a Samaritans Listener: (1) they can use a Listener phone in the prison to call a Listener working in a community branch, or (2) they can request to speak to a prison Listener. The majority of prisons in the UK now have cordless phones that prisoners can access at any time of the day or night to call Samaritans. This phone is capable only of calling Samaritans branches, and the officers control the use of the phone. The callers in these circumstances are connected to community-based branches of Samaritans and are able to speak to a Listener working in one of these branches. If a prisoner prefers to speak face-to-face to a prison Listener (they are still referred to as a caller), they can do this by speaking to an officer and requesting to meet with a Listener. In these circumstances, officers will use discretion to arrange the meeting in the most convenient and safest way possible. When feasible, face-to-face meetings are held in a private environment to allow complete confidentiality (either in a Listener suite if one is available, or in the caller's cell if staff consider this safe). Prisoners either wishing to make a telephone call to a branch or speak to a prison Listener in person must approach prison staff first. Staff will then facilitate the process by providing a private space and the time to either contact a Listener by phone or speak to a prison Listener in person. Prison Listeners needing to debrief after a face-to-face meeting (referred to as a call), or needing confidential support, can ask to contact their supporting Samaritans branch by telephone privately (NOMS & MoJ, 2012). Community volunteers from supporting Samaritans branches attend Listener meetings every 2 weeks at their allocated prison(s) in order to provide emotional support for Listeners and to regulate the programmes and address any emerging issues. The Listener scheme is currently the foremost peer-support programme in prisons (Samaritans, 2012).

In addition to listening, members of the programme also meet weekly to discuss issues relating to "caller care" and the general running of the scheme. Furthermore, every prison Listener has a chance to coordinate the programme, to be involved in the recruitment and training of new members, and to serve as a representative at safer custody meetings which address prisoners' rights and safety issues (Foster & Magee, 2011). Prisoners are not paid for becoming Listeners or for occupying other similar volunteer roles. However, employment in prison is categorised in bands, and each band is associated with different levels of privilege (i.e. extra and improved visits, access to in-cell television, the opportunity to wear one's own clothes). Listeners and Insiders, discussed below, operate within the "red band" and have the highest level of privileges (NOMS & MoJ, 2011).

The Insiders Programme

Research has revealed that initial experiences for new prisoners are traumatic, with around 50 % of all prison suicides occurring within the first week of custody (Shaw, Baker, Hunt, Moloney, & Appleby, 2004). The Insiders programme operates in prisons throughout the UK and aims to address this problem through reducing anxiety experienced during prisoners' early days in custody. Much of this work involves preventing and addressing bullying issues, and Insiders often promote themselves as anti-bullying mentors. Volunteers also provide basic information and reassurance to new prisoners shortly after their arrival. Insiders are not an alternative to Listeners; they offer a different but complementary peer-support service. As such, it is crucial that Insiders and Listeners understand each other's roles and are able to refer distressed individuals to each other. As with the Listener scheme, the Insiders programme also involves the vetting and selection of prisoners (carried out by Safer Custody Departments in UK prisons) who then go through extensive training. Insiders are not bound by the same confidentiality procedures as Listeners, and the Insiders programme is directed more towards providing practical advice and support. In terms of the setup, the Insiders programme works very similarly to the Listener scheme. Each volunteer not only fulfils a weekly shift commitment, but also has the opportunity to run different elements of the programme, attend standardisation and continual improvement meetings, and represent the programme at safer custody meetings. For such reasons, staff view Insiders, like Listeners, as holding positions of responsibility within the facility.

Toe-by-Toe

A 2008 Prison Reform Trust study found that 48 % of prisoners had a reading level at or below Level 1 (equivalent to a reading age of 14–15), and 65 % had a numeracy level at or below Level 1. Additionally, 67 % of all prisoners reported being unemployed at the time of imprisonment (Clark & Dugdale, 2008). There is no shortage of research that highlights the need for educational interventions in prison. Indeed, a broad body of research suggests that educated prisoners are less likely to return to prison (King, 2010; Kim & Clark, 2013).

Toe-by-Toe is the leading programme addressing literacy tutoring in prisons and began in 2000 at Her Majesty's Prison (HMP) in Wandsworth. Whilst this programme only operates in England and not all parts of the UK, it is regulated by the Shannon Trust, a UK-wide charity. The charity's vision is to help prisoners to better engage in their rehabilitation journeys by helping them to read. Once the Shannon Trust has helped to establish a Toe-by-Toe programme within a prison, prisoners run the programme, supervised and facilitated (in terms of resources, allocation of rooms, and so on) by prison staff via monthly meetings. The foundation of the programme lies in a "buddy system" through which older, fluent readers adopt mentor roles and coach lesser able students through a reading programme.

In prisons, the Shannon Trust trains volunteer prisoners on a needs basis and equips them with the materials (principally a Toe-by-Toe manual) required to carry out the role. Trained mentors are allocated a small number of mentees, whom they meet with for hourly sessions each week. During these sessions, mentees receive support to develop basic literacy skills, in a journey that aims to enhance the self-esteem of both the mentee and mentor (Trust, 2005). To the best of the researchers' knowledge, there is currently no research on the Toe-by-Toe programme. Furthermore, there is limited information concerning the scale of these programmes across English prisons. Nevertheless, the Shannon Trust website reports that in 2005, Toe-by-Toe covered 95 % of English prisons, with 80 % of the programmes in place considered active. The website also reports that at this time, 954 active mentors were working with mentees across English prisons.

RAPt Mentors

RAPt (Rehabilitation of Addicted Persons Trust) provides a range of services in prisons across England and Wales (it does not currently run throughout other parts of the UK) but is particularly well known for its drug and alcohol treatment programmes. The RAPt Substance Dependence Treatment Program (SDTP) is a rolling, abstinence-based treatment programme lasting between 16 and 22 weeks. This programme is based on the Twelve Steps principles of AA and Narcotics Anonymous (NA) and has been adjusted specifically for prisoners and offending populations. RAPt trains recovered prisoners (those who have completed the Twelve Steps programme) to serve as mentors. These mentors provide support to recovering prisoners through advice, guidance, and effective modelling of pro-social recovery attitudes and behaviours.

Peer-Support and Criminal Desistance

Research in the area of prison peer-support has generally focussed on the recipients of the support, posing questions about the extent to which such support can alleviate the negative emotional impact of imprisonment. Many studies have found that peer-support programmes are indeed effective in reducing stress and anxiety for those who utilise these services (e.g. see Boothby, 2011; Jaffe, 2012; Sirdifield, 2006).

Although research has principally focussed on the recipients of peer-support programmes, some studies have found that such programmes are also beneficial for the peer-supporters themselves. For example, such programmes may increase peer-supporters' insight into their own lives and empower them to change their offending behaviour and lifestyles (Keller, 1993; Maruna, 2001; Parkin & McKeganey, 2000; Sirdifield, 2006; Snow, 2002). Due to this process of self-reflection and the contribution that being a peer-support volunteer can have on the self-change process, some have argued that peer-support may assist with an offender's desistance journey (e.g. see Jaffe, 2012; Perrin & Blagden, 2014). Although criminal desistance can be defined as the cessation of all criminal activity, a more sophisticated conceptualisation of crime desistance is that it is a non-linear process of change involving a blend of multiple internal and external factors. Thus, desistance is directly tied to the psychological mechanisms that drive changes in criminal behaviour patterns. In short, desistance appears to rest on the interactions between internal psychological mechanisms (e.g. a constructive and positive self-identity) and external frameworks (social support and capital) (Serin & Lloyd, 2009).

Desistance researchers have also emphasised the need for individuals to address protective factors (goals that people can achieve) as well as risk factors (the offender's criminogenic needs) (de Vries Robbé, Mann, Maruna, & Thornton, 2015). Being a peer-support volunteer may help to promote and maintain certain protective factors, such as traits or social factors that assist or enable desistance from offending (de Vries Robbé et al., 2015). Protective factors include positive self-identity and personal autonomy, sobriety, being believed in, hope, stable relationships, closeness to others, constructive social support networks, and receiving emotional support (de Vries Robbé et al., 2015; McNeill & Maruna, 2007).

There are several ways in which being a peer-support volunteer may help with the desistance process. Boothby (2011), for example, explored Insiders' views of their roles. In this qualitative study, participants described elements of personal growth and increased self-confidence resulting from their work. Scholars have suggested that these outcomes represent a constructive resource that may assist offenders' desistance processes by contributing to redemption scripts (a desire to give something back) (Blagden, Winder, Thorne, & Gregson, 2011; Vaughan, 2007). Perrin and Blagden (2014) found that having a meaningful peer-support role in prison enabled prisoners to "counter negative prison emotions," gain perspective, and forge supportive relationships (p. 913). The ability to form and foster supportive relationships is crucially important to the desistance process. Involvement in a peer-support programme could help prisoners foster such social relationships, help provide meaning and purpose for prisoners, and assist them in building a range of skills and attributes (e.g. social skills) (Stevens, 2012). Being a peer-support volunteer is a trusted position and often involves social interaction with prison officers. Such interactions allow for an offender's self-identity and personal change process to be validated. Vaughan (2007) has argued that change narratives require continuous validation. This validation provides desisting offenders with hope and belief when things become especially difficult. The reciprocal nature of interactions within peer-support roles (both between peer-supporter and mentee and peer-support and prison staff) can constitute a source of validation for prisoners. Whilst more research is needed in this area, the literature discussed here points to the relational properties in the "self-change" process (Mead et al., 2001) and how peer-support roles might influence such dynamics.

In light of this available research, it appears that peer-support programmes may represent an innovative approach in terms of offender rehabilitation. Traditionally, the offender rehabilitation framework views the offenders themselves as passive recipients of treatment (Devilly et al., 2005), with the offender being externally advised and coached through a professional's proposed course of action. Some studies have found this approach to elicit frustration and resentment among the targets of the interventions (Perrin & Blagden, 2014), who feel they deserve to contribute towards their own process of change. This aligns with McHugh's (2002, in Snow, 2002) assertion that offenders themselves represent an expert yet underused resource, capable of positively influencing their own desistance journey. This chapter will build on this idea by examining how peer-support roles can influence an offender's experience of rehabilitation.

Although the overarching aims of peer-support programmes are conceptually linked with protective factors, they are not directly linked with reducing re-offending. However, there is evidence to suggest that holding a peer-support role may help offenders build self-esteem and a sense of belonging. Thus, the protective elements of peer-support and their link with desistance are aligned with the good lives model (GLM) of rehabilitation. The GLM is a model of offender rehabilitation that builds on the traditional risk, need, and responsivity approach (see Andrews & Bonta, 2006) and focuses more on offenders' strengths rather than deficits. In the GLM, "goods" are positive states or experiences that are obtained via legitimate means (Ward, Mann, & Gannon, 2007). Destructive behaviours result when offenders are socially isolated, become frustrated with finding their place in society, and consequently rely on criminal behaviours as a social outlet. As such, the GLM centres on enabling the formerly incarcerated person to achieve "goods" through pro-social activities and behaviours. When an offender is able to do this, he or she is more likely to see rewards such as a sense of autonomy, purpose, friendship, and excellence in work and play (Ward et al., 2007). In terms of rehabilitation, the GLM would assert that offenders should be afforded opportunities to attain meaningful primary goods through pro-social means (Ward et al., 2007). Peer-support roles, such as those under investigation here, may represent such opportunities. Nevertheless, few scholars have examined peer-support programmes in the context of desistance or their potential contribution to offender rehabilitation. Therefore, this chapter will highlight key findings from research that the authors conducted as part of a broad investigation into prison-based peer-support and desistance.

Method

Setting and Participants

This research took place in five adult male prisons in England, all varying in terms of risk category and size. Prisons in England and Wales are categorised based on the type of prisoners they hold, the type of crime they committed, the length of their sentence, the likelihood of their escape, and the potential danger to the public if escape were to happen. The four categories are (A) escape from this category of prison would be considered highly dangerous to the public or national security; (B) prisoners in this category do not require maximum security, but escape for such prisoners still needs to be very difficult; (C) prisoners here cannot be trusted to reside in open conditions, but are considered unlikely to try to escape; (D) open prison conditions in which prisoners are reasonably trusted not to try to escape. Table 5.1 contains key information relating to all of the prisons included in this study.

Table 5.1 Prison information

Category/risk	*Type*	*Operational capacity*	*Cell occupancy*
C	Sex offender treatment facility	841	Mainly single, some double and multiple
C	Local	770	Single and double
C/D	Resettlement	798	Mainly double
D	Open	581	Single and double
Uncategorised	Young offenders institute (YOI)	550	Shared residential units

The Governor at each research site and the National Research Committee regulated by the National Offender Management Service (NOMS) approved this study. The psychology departments within the prisons and occasionally the peer-support programme coordinators facilitated recruitment and data collection. Resettlement staff nominated participants and subsequently, the researchers sent recruitment letters to nominees outlining the research and inviting them to participate. The researchers then sent letters to all active members of each programme (92 potential volunteers in total), and a final sample of 17 responded stating that they were interested in participating. All refusal reasons related to clashes of appointments, treatment sessions, or education commitments. Eligibility requirements included 6 months or greater volunteer experience, current participation as a volunteer, and at least 2 years served in prison. These eligibility criteria assured that quality information concerning peer-support roles in prison could be generated. The researchers did not offer participants any benefits in exchange for their involvement, and participation was purely voluntary. To minimise the risk of potential participants of coercion, we made each aware at all stages of the research (on the information sheet, at the first meeting regarding the subject area, when gaining consent, and before interviews began) that their participation was entirely voluntary. The written consent form reiterated the voluntary nature of the study.

Among the sample of 17, participants' crimes were varied and time spent in prison ranged from 2 years and 4 months to over 27 years. Table 5.2 presents further demographic information, including age and sentence length.

Table 5.2 Participant information

	Pseudonym	*Role*	*Age*	*Offence details*	*Sentence*	*Time served*
1	Andy	Listener	29	Drug related	6 years	3 years 4 months
2	Kyle	Listener	39	Drug related	5 years	2 years 4 months
3	Steve	Listener	52	Drug related	IPP sentence	6.5 years
4	Ben	Listener	48	Murder	Life (99 years)	27 years 4 months
5	Cliff	Listener	64	Murder	Life (99 years)	27 years 1 month
6	Jason	Listener	28	Violent	IPP sentence (recommended 5 years)	4 years 3 months
7	Jason	Toe-by-Toe	W*	Sexual	W*	W*
8	Charles	Toe-by-Toe	W*	Sexual	W*	W*
9	Jamie	Toe-by-Toe	W*	Sexual	W*	W*
10	Ash	Insider	W*	Sexual	W*	W*
11	Charlie	Insider	W*	Sexual	W*	W*
12	Stewart	Insider	W*	Sexual	W*	W*
13	Simon	Insider	W*	Sexual	W*	W*
14	Drew	Insider	W*	Sexual	W*	W*
15	Harry	12 Steps	35	Attempted robbery	W*	W*
16	Joel	12 Steps	52	Murder	W*	W*
17	Victor	12 Steps	38	Robbery	W*	W*

Note: *W = withdrawn. The lead researcher and the prison liaison officers at specific sites agreed that certain demographic information be omitted to ensure the protection of participants' identities

Data Collection

The lead researcher (and first author of this chapter) carried out all of the semi-structured interviews in private interview rooms at the prisons. These interviews were recorded using a password-protected digital Dictaphone, and they lasted 62 minutes on average (range: 34–88). The interview schedule was divided into four sections and covered the following areas:

- Introductory questions—arrival into prison, initial perceptions of prison life, first encounters with peer-support programmes.
- Views and attitudes regarding peer-support work—initial perceptions of peer-support programmes, first involvement, motivations for volunteering.

- Impact of programme involvement on the person—thoughts and feelings regarding peer-support role, exploration of how the role impacted on the individual and their experiences of imprisonment.
- Future—views of future in the context of the peer-support role, exploration of how this role has shaped thoughts about future self.

The lead author transcribed all of the data and engaged in discussions with the second author that helped to identify potential themes. The researcher also took some brief notes relating to emerging thoughts and ideas during the data collection period.

Analytic Technique

This study adopted Braun and Clarke's (2006) phenomenologically oriented approach to thematic analysis. We selected this method of analysis as the sample size ($n = 17$) exceeded that recommended for studies taking a traditional phenomenological stance.

The goals of phenomenological enquiry are to generate a detailed perspective of personal lived experience, develop an understanding of the meaning of experience to participants, and explore how participants make sense of that experience. As such, phenomenologically oriented analysis is particularly useful when examining experience which is of "existential import to the participant" (Smith, 2011, p. 9). This strand of analysis necessitates the detailed analytic attention of each transcript and the search for emerging patterns across all transcripts. It requires a rigorous qualitative analysis of rich personal accounts.

Initially, notes relating to interesting thoughts and ideas were made in the left-hand margin of the transcripts. The next level of analysis involved focussing on more psychologically based concepts and turning initial thoughts and ideas into more specific phrases or labels. The aim here was to generate a summary of the data, in the form of a broad range of labels and phrases relating to key concepts. Finally, we carried out a data reduction strategy whereby emerging concepts were redefined and categorised under superordinate and subordinate themes. Superordinate themes represented particular phenomena evident within the data set through analogies, metaphors, or free discourse (Larkin, Watts, & Clifton, 2006). Subthemes were clustered and assigned to superordinate themes based on how participants' expressions interweaved with other subthemes, and how they shaped their parent (superordinate) themes. This entire process was repeated for all transcripts, with equal attention dedicated to each. Of course, as qualitative researchers, we remained vigilant of the possibility of blurring the boundaries between the participant's account and our own interpretations (Smith, 2011). In order to ensure quality in this regard, we both read through a sample of transcripts independently and made separate notes regarding emerging themes. These notes were contrasted against each other and disputes resolved through conversation and re-examination of the findings.

Findings

Following transcript coding and analysis, we identified two superordinate themes, each comprised of three subordinate themes. These themes are presented in Table 5.3.

Change and Transition

The analysis illuminated various ways in which the participants had changed during imprisonment. These changes appeared to be directly related to the peer-support roles in that carrying out such a role acted as a form of validation that change had occurred. As such, "change and transition" seemed most appropriate as a label encompassing the subordinate themes in this section.

New Me

The first of these subordinate themes is "new me." In outlining some of the internal changes that participants experienced, they often made

Table 5.3 Superordinate and subordinate themes

Superordinate themes	*Subordinate themes*
Change and transition	New me Earning trust Giving back and making meaning
Keeping sane	Acquiring a stake in conformity Addressing personal trauma through helping Channelling

comparisons between their past and new lives. Participants' recognition of past lives and a subsequent process of change allowed them to reflect on their "old me" and differentiate the "new me." Research has emphasised the importance of these types of narratives (Abrams & Aguilar, 2005) and has argued that offenders who experience qualitative shifts in their attitudes towards themselves are more likely to commit to pro-social "possible selves" (Stein, Roeser, & Markus, 1998, p. 102). Participants consistently described their old offending selves as "bad," "destructive," or "hindering" and their new selves in terms such as "good," "calm," and "positive." In this sense, peer-support roles appeared to have a transformative effect on enhancing positive views of the self. The following interview with a Listener illustrates this theme:

Interviewer: What does it mean to you to be a Samaritan Listener?

Steve: If you're out through life causing destruction and distress to people and yourself, you can quite quickly fill your bank up with negative ways of thinking and negative thoughts.... It's like having a big tub of dirty water, that's negative. And then someone gives you a positive drip, and eventually, with more drips, the water gets less murky, overflows, and then it's just nice and clean. That's what happens basically. It's learning to accept that positive.

Interviewer: So Samaritans was a big drip?

Steve: I believe so yeah.

In this extract, Steve conceptualises his old self as a tub of dirty water, full of negativity. Over time, he has learned to accept help and support and has undertaken a range of courses within the prison, which he tags as "drips" of positivity. Everything he has learned as he has completed his sentence has diluted the negativity in his life. He talks about his experience as a Listener as being very influential, and it appeared throughout his interview that listening may have assisted the beginning of his movement towards his "new me." Crucially, the positive drips in Steve's life have also allowed him to reflect on the negative behaviours associated with his old ways. In this sense, "being" a listener has allowed for a momentum of change (Göbbels, Ward, & Willis, 2012) in that he is learning to accept a positive view of himself through purposeful activity. For Steve, listening appears to catalyse self-evaluation and promote profound personal realisations.

Steve's role may also represent a turning point, or at the very least an influential factor in his experience of transformation. In this respect, although offenders may be motivated to change before becoming peer-support volunteers, such roles seem to provide the perfect environment for change to actually happen. Steve's analogy of the tub of dirty water gathering drips illuminates this point well; he is allowing many positive influences into his world, and this is enabling him to re-story that world. Other participants echoed a similar viewpoint. Kyle, a listener, stated thus:

> I was more ignorant before. I mean, judgemental. "Don't wanna talk to him, don't need to know him" ... that kinda attitude. That's all I knew for so many years so there was nothing I could really do about it. When I did eventually learn something else being a Listener, it had a big impact. Just on general day-to-day life, like, how I deal with people from how I would before. Even some of my mates, "pftt, that's not the same guy." I'm a good boy now.... I don't do the things I used to do. Listening calms you down as a person, 'cos you realise, that person here's going through this and he's going through that.... When you listen to people it's different. You really help without actually doing anything. Just listening, it's empowering.

Kyle here distinguishes between his old and new attitudes. Ignorance and resistance were all he knew, and sensing limited opportunity to change, he was unable to break loose. Being a Listener prompted Kyle to reflect on his "self," and he has found reward in the new way in which he's able to deal with people. Interestingly, Kyle comments on how he's "a good boy now." This self-construal of being "a good boy" represents a narrative shift from "bad boy, who does bad things," to a "good boy capable of doing good things and making amends." Such narratives are important as they allow offenders to portray "good selves" and assert that the person who offended is not really who they are, such shifts in narratives have been associated with redemptive episodes and personal change (Maruna, 2001; Presser, Veysey, Christian, & Martinez, 2009).

Participants also appeared to be very connected to their peer-support roles. Crucially, the requirements associated with these roles encourage the individual to form a new, law-abiding life in prison. Whilst behaviours and realisations that emerge in prison are not forced to travel through the gate with offenders, the analysis revealed a strong suggestion that the participants were able to practice pro-social behaviours via their peer-support roles in prison. Hence, Kyle doesn't "do the things he used to do." These movements towards a changed self-identity offer some hope for reintegrating offenders, who may be galvanised by their peer-support roles to implement the necessary controls to lead law-abiding lives on the outside.

Earning Trust

Participants emphasised the importance of earning the trust of staff in the prison. Indeed, researchers have discussed how earning trust in the context of prison can prompt positive change in offenders and feed into their narratives of desistance (Blagden, Winder, & Hames, 2014; Vaughan, 2007). The quotations listed within this subordinate theme illustrate how important it was for participants to build trust and in doing so, to nourish their transitioning selves. Stewart, an Insider, explained:

> You kind of get a bit of rapport with the staff, because when the staff see that you can do a job and you can do a job well … you then … kinda get a bit of trust with them – they trust you to deal with things … so the way some wings work … you're not allowed to go to other landings and stuff like that … so if you've got a rapport with them and you're doing your job correctly and efficiently … they'll allow you to go onto the other wings, or to the other landings … and talk to people who've come on if they've got any issues and help … so it's about kind of building up that trust with them so they can see you can do a job, you're not messing them around and not swapping things or dealing stuff or whatever … it's about taking it seriously.

Here, Stewart discusses how his role as an Insider has enabled him to build rapport with staff members in the prison and gain trust and freedom. What he is describing is akin to a cycle of positive behaviour, reinforcement, and continued positive behaviour. It is in Stewart's best interests to behave well within his role and to follow prison rules, as he is rewarded for doing so by earning trust and some freedom. As such, peer-support roles in this context appears to create an environment whereby prisoners can actually "do" trust (not just feel trusted) and enact "good" and "moral" selves. Receiving trust, appraisals, and validation from others in a prison context can inspire positive change towards desistance (Göbbels et al., 2012). Jamie, a Toe-by-Toe volunteer, illustrates this idea in the quote below:

> You get a bit more trust. And I think … looking at it where you get that trust level that shows that you are improving yourself. You are still treated as if you're a prisoner but you get that slight better respect and you get that much better rapport with the officers and the staff … it makes you feel a bit like a human still. Again it's all about that rehabilitation, I am a strong believer in that if you're treated poorly by officers or staff then you can't really be rehabilitated.

Jamie's extract suggests that earning trust and some recognition for "doing good" equates to a form of validation that he is "improving himself." Jamie inadvertently describes a process of self-assurance, via which he does good things, earns trust and recognition, and consequently lives up to his objective to change. All of this makes Jamie feel more human, and whilst he is not looking to log favours, this process of doing good and receiving appraisals appears to be giving him hope that he is changing for the better. There is a body of literature within the realm of desistance that encourages this kind of process. For example, the enhanced expectation and trust in Jamie appears akin to the Pygmalion effect (high expectation equals high outcome) that Maruna, LeBel, Naples, and Mitchell (2009) describe. Peer-support-role holders seem to become recognised as good people, and this seems to have a self-fulfilling effect.

Giving Back and Making Meaning

Along with the establishment of "new selves" and positive self-images, participants also evidenced a desire to give back in some way. In exploring criminal desistance, Maruna (2001) posits that offenders who are going straight construct a redemption script. This script is typified by a desire to "give something back" and an acceptance that although they cannot change the past, they can contribute positively in the future. These redemption scripts are also linked to successful community reintegration (Marsh, 2011). Across all of the interviews, participants provided descriptions of how they thought they had given something back through their peer-support roles. These thoughts provided them with deep satisfaction, as evidenced in the two excerpts below:

> You could see someone was upset or whatever, and after you speak to them they've perked up a bit ... they start relaxing a bit and they say "yeah, I'm ready to go back out to the prison" ... and when you see it happen it makes you feel good because you've done something good and given something back. I'm not saying it makes up for the crime you've committed, but you are giving something back and you're turning something into a positive. Even if it's just for that hour or that day, you know you've tried.
>
> —Andy (Listener)

> I would be extremely gutted if I lost it (the Insider role). I'm very proud to be an Insider and to help other people.... I feel it's a role which I should be doing, with the experiences I've got of prison life ... and I see it as putting

> something back into the prison. It's about being human in a sense ... and about being a normal person, not the criminal aspect of "oh it's always take, take" ... but actually to be a real human on the outside. And it's something which this program does ... it allows me to give something back into the prison system. Even if that's just mentoring somebody who's come on to the wing and going and having a chat with them ... that in some instances can mean all the difference to that person ... so this role allows me to be able to do that on a sort of legitimate basis ... Obviously if you try and do it out of that ... then all questions can be asked as to what you doing in there and things like that ... so it's just more, a legitimate way of being able to help somebody.
>
> —Stewart (Insider)

A key theme in this analysis was that peer-support roles provided meaning and purpose in prison, and this seemed to come as a by-product of "giving back" and "earning trust." In 2010, the Prison Reform Trust asserted that "prisons should not allow offenders to simply mark their time in a purposeless fashion. Rather, prisons should be seen as places where prisoners are engaged in challenging and meaningful work" (Edgar, Jacobson, & Biggar, 2011, p. 5). Peer-support roles certainly appeared to help prisoners establish meaning and build purposeful lives in prison. This appears complimentary with the principles of the GLM, which is influenced by self-determination theory, and which asserts that humans naturally seek autonomy and connectedness, and have an intrinsic desire to effect the environment around them, not just exist within it. When these needs are not met, individuals construct illegitimate substitute strategies. However, when these needs are met, individuals become motivated to reflect and realise change (Ryan & Deci, 2000). Through peer-support roles, participants were able to generate meaning and purpose. More than that, though, participants were pointing to the benefits of "owning their own rehabilitation." The following extracts highlight how participants moulded themselves important roles and gained a feeling of being needed:

> I've got more experience and understanding of some of the stuff than some of the guys, so I'll give my feedback and that's what I'm here for, just try and give a bit of constructive feedback as well, try and build them up a little bit. So I'm just there to give a bit of feedback, and offer them a bit of hope as well. That's part of my job.
>
> —Victor (Twelve Steps)

> These people have spilled their heart out to you. And you've got that, in a little box, just there, never to be revealed. So he's put his life (pause).... He's took everything and he's put it in this basket here (hand gestures a box and passes the box to the researcher). "Please look after it" (whispers). That's what it's like. Like, don't let no one see it. You've gotta protect that.
>
> —Kyle (Listener)

Keeping Sane

This superordinate theme relates to avoiding the negativity traditionally associated with imprisonment (Dye, 2010). The subordinate themes here can be viewed as strategies that participants use to distance themselves from the stresses and strains of imprisonment. As noted previously, involvement in constructive and positive activities provided the impetus and tangible opportunities for participants to construct desirable new selves (Perrin & Blagden, 2014). Furthermore, the mechanisms underlying these subthemes also appeared to help the participants address personal issues that may have been previously unaddressed. Via peer-support roles, volunteers seemed able to create space in which to experience personal growth and a sense of inner peace and calm through times of adversity.

Acquiring a Stake in Conformity

This subtheme categorises extracts relating to how participants perceived their peer-support roles as valuable and as something they did not want "to lose." Laub and Sampson (2001) have neatly tagged these types of processes as striving to "acquire a stake in conformity"—a legitimate social bond via which individuals can satisfy basic human needs. In these narratives, participants were clearly investing in legitimate and normative behaviours via their roles and indirectly making sure they didn't "slip up." Having this focal point appeared important for participants, who were able to carve out some satisfaction from their roles and thus maintain a level of well-being in prison. Stewart, an Insider, explained:

> I wouldn't have met the people I have ... so ... the other Insiders ... I wouldn't have known them like I do ... the safer custody department. I wouldn't have known them ... as well as kind of higher ranking, if you like, governors and that when I go to the meetings ... I know all the governors and they kind of know me ... and, whenever I see them in the corridor they'll ask me how I am ... so to have that kind of rapport in the place is in

> some ways beneficial ... not something to be abused ... but to kind of be proud that I'm in that kind of position.

In this extract, Stewart discusses how his volunteer role has enabled him to forge positive relationships with staff. He takes pride in the fact that he knows everyone, and they know him, even the higher-ranking staff (governors). Stewart enjoys his status as an Insider, which appears to give him a feeling of being appreciated. He values his role so much that he would never do anything to compromise his position, which he respects as "not to be abused." Stewart's narrative, in which he describes how he has something good to potentially lose, perfectly exemplifies this theme. Many participants viewed their roles in the same way—they respected their privileged position as peer-support role holders, and this appeared to be influential in keeping them moving forward.

Addressing Personal Trauma Through Helping

Another subtheme in this category was the notion that helping others (listening, teaching, supporting emotionally) could elicit realisations about personal challenges and past difficulties. Through supporting others, many participants seemed to be double sense-making, that is—they were assisting people with their specific issues whilst also reflecting on the difficulties and personal traumas they had experienced in the past. This experience was a prominent feature in the data and appeared to contribute to many powerful realisations: The following quotes from Gary and Drew illustrate this theme:

> I was on constant watch every four minutes, I was that low ... I'd hit rock bottom, I didn't know where to turn to or who to talk to.... I was on A1 or A2 [wings] ... and then they moved me on here and I just didn't know what was happening I felt like I'd been punished, guilt ... everything ... and I just didn't know where to turn to, who to speak to at the time and.... I think you know, with the Listeners ... and the staff ... I don't think I'd be here today if I didn't get the help and support and so ... that's why I decided I wanted to become a Listener, once I knew I was ready.
>
> —Gary (Listener)

> I thought, "well I've been through that experience," and I know it wasn't very nice and I managed to come through it and I managed to keep stable

> … so I'm using my experiences and the way I've dealt with it to try and pass it on and to help somebody else. So yeah … I think it makes you a stronger person too. Erm, you know 'cos obviously I had to deal with my own personal problems and if I've helped somebody who's had a similar problem and it's worked for them then I can take what I've used on them for myself and learn from that as well. You sort of realise what sort of person you actually was and where you are today and where you wanna be tomorrow.
>
> —Drew (Insider)

Channelling

This theme refers to the notion that peer-support roles kept prisoners focused on constructive and legitimate activities. The nature of imprisonment, often characterised by loss of liberty, deprivation, and a range of antagonistic conditions (Dye, 2010), cannot only cause despair but can also result in destructive behaviours. Indeed, a vast body of research cites the volatility of the prison environment and the heightened presence of social issues such as gang violence, drug use, violent and sexual abuse, bullying, and discrimination (Carpentier, Royuela, Noor, & Hedrich, 2012; Fleisher & Decker, 2001). Prisoners overwhelmed by such conditions often re-offend due to this negative socialisation (Cullen, Jonson, & Nagin, 2011). In this study, participants spoke of a protective element associated with their peer-support roles; their work prevented went some way to inoculating them against to the destructive forces and pains of imprisonment:

> I suppose there's the possibility that I would've been in a lot of trouble … because the Shannon Trust has given me the opportunity to seize the amount of patience I have … and for me to recognise that that actually affects everything I do … without that … I'd be an impatient bugger … you know … if I asked a member of staff for something and I didn't get it straight away then … I would tend to lose my rag … you know.
>
> —Charles (Toe-by-Toe)

Here Charles recognises that he may well have found himself getting "into a lot of trouble" had he not been able to "seize" positive traits via his mentoring role. He goes on to identify that an inclination towards impatience could have led him astray and that his Shannon Trust role occupied the space where destructive traits might have otherwise prevailed. Through this role, Charles is actively addressing a behaviour that he has recognised as harmful. Charles is able to let trivial annoyances pass by and avoid getting into trouble. For many participants, this investment in peer-support roles kept them focussed and enabled them to harness constructive traits and skills as the quote below shows. This apparent feature of peer-support roles is once again reminiscent of the GLM and again further emphasises how being involved as a peer-support volunteer may act protectively, in that positive behaviours that may exist, but lay dormant, are unearthed via engagement in pro-social activities (Ward et al., 2007).

> To be able to sort them out, get them through that it's just enjoyment really, for me, at least I've done something good for that day … which is what we need to do … it makes you feel good, it just raises you up, your sense of responsibility and your sense of awareness around you which is what we need to do. So I find it gets you through the day, otherwise you're just gonna be bored out your head all day … and obviously that can lead onto something else so being able to do something, be involved (erm) you know no matter how small it is … (stutters) … it is a good feeling.
>
> —Drew (Insider)

In this extract, Drew echoed Charles' experience of peer-support roles as protective, but also introduced the idea of peer-support roles raising awareness and increasing a sense of responsibility. Again, it appears that having such a meaningful role places individuals in the present moment and enables them to stake stock of their situation and surroundings. This type of focus not only gets prisoners "through the day," it also prevents boredom and "something else" from happening.

Summary, Implications, and Trajectory

Using the GLM as a guiding model, this research aimed to generate a phenomenological understanding of how prison peer-support volunteers experience their roles in the context of imprisonment. Participants from four different peer-support programmes described their experiences in very positive terms and appeared to be having deep realisations and life-changing revelations through their work. In addition to cultivating constructive relationships with prison staff and other prisoners, enjoying personal growth from "doing good," honing positive skills, and keeping busy, participants were also able to have a more generally positive experience of prison life because of their volunteer roles. This experience was a product of meaning making, positivity gathering, and the avoidance of negative labels and destructive stigma. All of these benefits appeared to protect participants against the negativity associated with imprisonment and enable them to serve their sentences more constructively than if these opportunities were not present. As such, this study supports prior research suggesting that peer-support in prisons goes beyond basic peer-to-peer helping and actively assists the process of offender rehabilitation (e.g. see Davies, 1994; Boothby, 2011; Perrin & Blagden, 2014).

There was an interlocking nature to the subordinate themes discussed in the analysis. "Earning trust," for example, appeared to result from participants channelling their energies into something positive and in turn generating more and more positivity and a sense of belonging. This acquisition of positivity and enhanced self-esteem placed participants into a position where they were able to focus on doing good deeds and occupying positive roles in prison, and this in turn appeared to drive their experiences of transition and change.

Furthermore, participants were able to carve out meaningful and purposeful roles for themselves, through which they could feel autonomous, independent, and more human. There are clear links to the GLM here, and it appears that being involved in peer-support roles could encourage desistance in this context. This places this area of research in front of broader questions about prisons as institutions of well-being. Helliwell (2011), for example, argued that prisons are generally constructed as "schools for criminals rather than creators of wellbeing" (p. 255). This author draws on Singaporean prison reforms, which have led to the re-conceptualisation of prisons as "schools for life," which emphasise the importance of prisoner well-being, social context, benevolence, trust, building positive outcomes, and top-to-bottom engagement in a shared purpose. These factors underpin and best fit the interview data in this study. Whilst Helliwell's research is not seamlessly transferable to peer-support, it offers an insight into the possible future of peer-support in prisons.

Indeed, the participants unanimously spoke about ways in which they managed to cope with the strains of imprisonment, and this seemed connected with improving general well-being. The meaningful and purposeful roles that participants developed through their peer-support roles significantly helped to counter negative prison emotions and experiences. Participants were coping and developing via their roles as well as accumulating positivity and "meaningful goods" (Ward et al., 2007). Participants' narratives were akin to those discussed more broadly in the desistance literature in that they focused on meaningful personal change, and qualitative shifts in identity towards more pro-social and positive self-images. Indeed, being involved and invested in peer-support roles allowed for momentums of change and the development of new selves. This is vitally important as LeBel, Burnett, Maruna, and Bushway (2008) found that self-identification and positive self-image were significant predictors of post-prison outcomes. In contrast, feelings of stigmatisation predicted recidivism. It may be that peer-support roles are a positive "drip" in the self-change process (Perrin & Blagden, 2014, p. 916).

A fundamental aspect of the desistance literature, and in line with the GLM, is that desistance is about discovering agency. Interventions thus need to encourage and respect self-determination (McCulloch, 2005). Peer-support roles, at least in this study, allowed for personal agency, as this is something participants wanted to do and be a part of, not something they had to confirm to in order to meet institutional demands. It appears that peer-support deserves a space for discussion in the ever-growing research field of desistance. Furthermore, current penal policy objectives align with what peer-support roles appear to offer to volunteers. For example, a 2011 Ministry of Justice policy document identified that providing purposeful activity was a key aim in order to improve rehabilitation, and meaningful prison work is now ingrained in political narrative concerning prisons. In line with these propositions, this study asks for peer-support schemes across UK prisons to be acknowledged on a wider academic and political scale.

This current research adds, albeit incrementally, to existing understandings of how personal and institutional change can occur vis-à-vis peer-support roles. Such programmes appear to have a positive impact in terms of prisoners' views of themselves, their experiences of prison, and their perceptions of life beyond prison. Many respondents made an explicit connection between their peer-support role and reduced offending, and all participants expressed a strong desire to become better people and reintegrate successfully after serving time. Whilst this study cannot claim that peer-support roles might reduce re-offending, it has been argued that such roles can assist desistance by enabling individuals to develop better images of themselves, to help prisoners obtain basic human needs, and to prevent prisoners from becoming "institutionalised" or consumed by harmful labels. Ultimately, peer-support roles offer prisoners a chance to "re-story" their lives. Nevertheless, there still exists a gap in knowledge regarding the relationship between positive roles in prison and the impact on re-offending, and further research should begin to unpack this interaction.

References

Abrams, L. S. & Aguilar, J. P. (2005). Negative trends, possible selves, and behavior` change: A qualitative study of juvenile offenders in residential treatment. *Qualitative Social Work*, *4*(2), 175–196.

Andrews, D. A. & Bonta, J. (2006). *The psychology of criminal conduct* (4th ed.). Newark, NJ: LexisNexis.

Bean, K. F., Shafer, M. S., & Glennon, M. (2013). The impact of housing first and peer-support on people who are medically vulnerable and homeless. *Psychiatric Rehabilitation Journal*, *36*(1), 48–50.

Bennett, T., Holloway, K., & Farrington, D. P. (2009). A review of the effectiveness of neighbourhood watch. *Security Journal*, *22*(2), 143–155.

Blagden, N. J., Winder, B., Thorne, K., & Gregson, M. (2011). 'No-one in the world would ever wanna speak to me again': An interpretative phenomenological analysis into convicted sexual offenders' accounts and experiences of maintaining and leaving denial. *Psychology, Crime & Law*, *17*(7), 563–585.

Blagden, N., Winder, B., & Hames, C. (2014). "They treat us like human beings"—Experiencing a therapeutic sex offenders' prison: The impact on prisoners and staff and implications for treatment. *International Journal of Offender Therapy and Comparative Criminology*, *58*(10), 1–29.

Boothby, M. (2011). Insiders' views of their role: Toward their training. *Canadian Journal of Criminology And Criminal Justice*, *53*(4), 424–448.

Braun, V. & Clarke, V. (2006). Using thematic analysis in psychology. *Qualitative Research in Psychology*, *3*(2), 77–101.

Carpentier, C., Royuela, L., Noor, A., & Hedrich, D. (2012). Ten years of monitoring illicit drug use in prison populations in Europe: Issues and challenges. *Howard Journal of Criminal Justice*, *51*(1), 37–66.

Clark, C. & Dugdale, G. (2008). *Literacy changes lives: The role of literacy in offending behaviour: A discussion piece. Part 1.* London: National Literacy Trust.

Cullen, F. T., Jonson, C. L., & Nagin, D. S. (2011). Prisons do not reduce recidivism the high cost of ignoring science. *The Prison Journal*, *91*(3), 48S–65S.

Davies, B. (1994). The Swansea listener scheme: Views from the prison landings. *The Howard Journal*, *33*(2), 125–136.

de Vries Robbé, M., Mann, R. E., Maruna, S., & Thornton, D. (2015). An exploration of protective factors supporting desistance from sexual offending. *Sexual Abuse: A Journal of Research and Treatment*, *27*(1), 16–33.

Devilly, G. J., Sorbello, L., Eccleston, L., & Ward, T. (2005). Prison-based peer-education programmes. *Aggression and Violent Behavior*, *10*(2), 219–240.

Dye, M. (2010). Deprivation, importation, and prison suicide: Combined effects of institutional conditions and inmate composition. *Journal of Criminal Justice*, *38*(4), 796–806.

Edgar, K., Jacobson, J., & Biggar, K. (2011). Time well spent: A practical guide to active citizenship and volunteering in prison. London: Prison Reform Trust. Retrieved from http://www.prisonreformtrust.org.uk/Portals/0/Documents/Time%20Well%20Spent%20report%20lo.pdf.

Field, R. J. & Schuldberg, D. (2011). Social-support moderated stress: A nonlinear dynamical model and the stress-buffering hypothesis. *Nonlinear Dynamics, Psychology, and Life Sciences*, *15*(1), 53–85.

Fleisher, M. S. & Decker, S. H. (2001). An overview of the challenge of prison gangs. *Corrections Management Quarterly*, *5*(1), 1–9.

Foster, J., & Magee, H. (2011). *Peer-support in prison healthcare: An investigation into the listening programme in one adult male prison.* Retrieved from http://www.samaritans.org/pdf/The%20role%20of%20Listeners%20in%20an%20adult%20male%20prison.pdf

Göbbels, S., Ward, T., & Willis, G. M. (2012). An integrative theory of desistance from sex offending. *Aggression and Violent Behavior*, *17*(5), 453–462.

Helliwell, J. F. (2011). Institutions as enablers of wellbeing: The Singapore prison case study. *International Journal of Wellbeing*, *1*(2), 255–265.

Jaffe, M. (2012). Peer support and seeking help in prison: A study of the listener scheme in four prisons in England (Doctoral Dissertation). Keele University.

Keller, R. L. (1993). Some unanticipated positive effects of a juvenile awareness program on adult inmate counsellors. *International Journal of Offender Therapy and Comparative Criminology*, *37*(1), 75–83.

Kim, R. & Clark, D. (2013). The effect of prison-based college education programs on recidivism: Propensity score matching approach. *Journal of Criminal Justice*, *41*(3), 196–204.

King, M. (2010). In-prison education and recidivism: A narrative inquiry on the impact of in-prison education on former inmates in the state of Texas. *Dissertation Abstracts International Section A*, *70*, 4043.

Kopak, A. M., Dean, L. V., Proctor, S. L., Miller, L., & Hoffmann, N. G. (2014). Effectiveness of the rehabilitation for addicted prisoners trust (RAPt) programme. *Journal of Substance Use*, *20*(4), 1–8.

Larkin, M., Watts, S., & Clifton, E. (2006). Giving voice and making sense in interpretative phenomenological analysis. *Qualitative Research in Psychology*, *3*(2), 102–120.

Laub, J. H. & Sampson, R. J. (2001). Understanding desistance from crime. *Crime and Justice*, *28*, 1–69.

LeBel, T. P., Burnett, R., Maruna, S., & Bushway, S. (2008). The 'chicken and egg' of subjective and social factors in desistance from crime. *European Journal of Criminology*, *5*(2), 131–159.

Marsh, B. (2011). Narrating desistance: Identity change and the 12-step script. *Irish Probation Journal*, *8*, 49–68.

Maruna, S. (2001). *Making good: How ex-convicts reform and rebuild their lives.* Washington, DC: American Psychological Association.

Maruna, S., LeBel, T., Naples, M., & Mitchell, N. (2009). Looking-glass identity transformation: Pygmalion and Golem in the rehabilitation process. In B. Veysey, J. Christian, & D. J. Martinez (Eds.), *How offenders transform their lives* (pp. 30–55). Cullompton, England: Willan.

McCulloch, T. (2005). Probation, social context and desistance: Retracing the relationship. *Probation Journal*, *52*(1), 8–22.

McNeill, F. & Maruna, S. (2007). Giving up and giving back: Desistance, generativity and social work with offenders. In G. McIvor & P. Raynor (Eds.), *Developments in social work with offenders* (pp. 224–339). London: Jessica Kingsley.

Mead, S., Hilton, D., & Curtis, L. (2001). Peer-support: A theoretical perspective. *Psychiatric Rehabilitation Journal*, *25*(2), 134.

National Offender Management Service (NOMS), & Ministry of Justice (MoJ). (2011). *Incentives and earned privilege.* Retrieved from http://www.justice.gov.U.K./downloads/offenders/psipso/psi-2011/psi_2011_11_incentives_and_earned_privileges.doc.

National Offender Management Service (NOMS), & Ministry of Justice. (2012). *Management of prisoners at risk of harm to self, to others and from others (safer custody).* Retrieved from http://www.justice.gov.U.K./search?collection=moj-matrix-devweb&form=simple&profile=_default&query=Management+of+prisoners+at+risk+of+harm+to+self%2C+to+others+and+from+others.

Parkin, S. & McKeganey, N. (2000). The rise and rise of peer education approaches. *Drugs: Education, Prevention Policy*, *7*(3), 293–310.

Perrin, C. & Blagden, N. (2014). Accumulating meaning, purpose and opportunities to change 'drip by drip': The impact of being a listener in prison. *Psychology, Crime & Law*, *20*(9), 902–920.

Presser, L., & Kurth, S. (2009) 'I got a quick tongue': Negotiating ex-convict identity in mixed company. In B. M. Veysey, J. Christian, & D. J. Martinez (Eds.), How offenders transform their lives (pp. 72–86). Devon, England: Willian.

Ryan, R. & Deci, E. (2000). Self-determination theory and the facilitation of intrinsic motivation, social development, and wellbeing. *American Psychologist*, *55*(1), 68–78.

Samaritans. (2012). *Information resource pack.* Retrieved from http://www.samaritans.org/pdf/2012%20Information%20Resource%20Pack.pdf.

Serin, R. C. & Lloyd, C. D. (2009). Examining the process of offender change: The transition to crime desistance. *Psychology, Crime & Law, 15*(4), 347–364.

Shannon Trust. (2005). *Toe-by-Toe: Prison project.* Retrieved from http://www.Toe-by-Toe.co.U.K./prison_project.html.

Shaw, J., Baker, D., Hunt, I. M., Moloney, A., & Appleby, L. (2004). Suicide by prisoners: National clinical survey. *The British Journal of Psychiatry, 184*(3), 263–267.

Sirdifield, C. (2006). Piloting a new role in mental health—Prison based health trainers. *The Journal of Mental Health Workforce Development, 1*(4), 15–22.

Smith, J. A. (2011). Evaluating the contribution of interpretative phenomenological analysis. *Health Psychology Review, 5*(1), 9–27.

Snow, L. (2002). The role of formalised peer-group support in prisons. In G. Towl, L. Snow, & M. McHugh (Eds.), *Suicide in prisons* (pp. 102–120). Malden, MA: Blackwell Publishing.

Solomon, P. (2004). Peer-support/peer provided services underlying processes, benefits, and critical ingredients. *Psychiatric Rehabilitation Journal, 27*(4), 392.

Stein, K. F., Roeser, R., & Markus, H. R. (1998). Self-schemas and possible selves as predictors and outcomes of risky behaviors in adolescents. *Nursing Research, 47*(2), 96–106.

Stevens, A. (2012). 'I am the person now I was always meant to be': Identity reconstruction and narrative reframing in therapeutic community prisons. *Criminology & Criminal Justice, 12*(5), 1–21.

Vaughan, B. (2007). The internal narrative of desistance. *British Journal of Criminology, 47*(3), 390–404.

Ward, T., Mann, R. E., & Gannon, T. A. (2007). The good lives model of offender rehabilitation: Clinical implications. *Aggression and Violent Behaviour, 12*(1), 87–107.

Walker, G., & Bryant, W. (2013). Peer support in adult mental health services: A multisynthesis of qualitative findings. *Psychiatric Rehabilitation Journal, 36*(1), 28.

CHAPTER 6

The Development of a Peer-Based Approach for Promoting Prisoner Health in an English Male Young Offender Institution

Anita Mehay and Rosie Meek

Introduction

This chapter examines the views of young adult men held within a prison setting concerning a prospective peer-based approach for health promotion. The authors developed this study in collaboration with the prison healthcare team as part of a wider initiative to promote health through greater participation of the young adults held in the prison, and this study was intended to inform the development of this initiative.

The poor health status of incarcerated populations has received public attention both in England and Wales (HM Prison Service, 2003; Joint Prison Service and National Health Service Executive, 1999) and internationally (WHO, 2014). The health status of prisoners is particularly important given that there are a record number of people residing within prison establishments worldwide (Ministry of Justice, 2014; Walmsley, 2011), presenting with a high prevalence of complex health needs (Senior & Shaw, 2007). These include high rates of mental health issues (Fazel & Danesh, 2002), chronic health conditions (Herbert, Plugge, Foster,

A. Mehay (✉) • R. Meek
Royal Holloway University of London, London, UK

L.S. Abrams et al. (eds.), *The Voluntary Sector in Prisons*, Palgrave Studies in Prisons and Penology, DOI 10.1057/978-1-137-54215-1_6

& Doll, 2012; Lewis & Meek, 2013), substance abuse (Brunton-Smith & Hopkins, 2013; Light, Grant, & Hopkins, 2013), and communicable diseases, such as Tuberculosis, Hepatitis C, and HIV (Health Protection Agency and Department of Health, 2011).

Although the primary aim of incarceration is not health improvement, prisons provide an opportunity for health services to access a hard-to-reach and underserved population (Bridgwood & Malbon, 1995; Marshall, Simpson, & Stevens, 2001), and for many offenders, prison may be the first time that they consider their health needs and make contact with health services (Social Exclusion Unit, 2002). Confinement thus represents an opportunity to address larger health disparities (Department for Health, 2002) by returning prisoners back to their communities with better health than when they entered (Watson, Stimpson, & Hostick, 2004). Consequently, understanding and promoting health among young adult offenders is particularly important as it may contribute to a generation-level reduction of poor health outcomes (British Medical Association, 2014).

Prisons in England and Wales currently provide (through commissioned services) health assessment and treatment as well as health promotion activities. Yet prisoners also represent an untapped resource, capable of a powerful and positive influence on their fellow prisoners (McHugh, 1996; South & Phillips, 2014). The use of peers to promote health in prison is a recent development in prisons in England and Wales and requires insights to inform its future development within the prison context, particularly within young offender institutions (Bagnall et al., 2015; South et al., 2014). This chapter will draw on the theory and current application of peer-based approaches in prisons. Using interview data collected from incarcerated young adults, we aim to provide an insight into the challenges and the potential impact of peer-based approaches to inform the future development of these services within young adult prisons.

Young Adults in Prison

As is the case with prisons internationally, men comprise the vast majority of the prison population in England and Wales, with approximately 6 % of them being young adult men, defined as ages 18 to 20 (Ministry of Justice, 2015). For young adult offenders, courts can impose a custodial sentence to be served in a Young Offender Institution (YOI)[1] which are establishments run by the Prison Service in much the same way as adult prisons except with increased staff–prisoner ratios (Home Office, 2000). Although the number of young adult men in custody in England and Wales has decreased since 2010, those serving custodial sentences represent the most vulnerable young adults, with complex health and psychosocial needs (Harris, 2015). Although young adults share many of the same high levels of health needs as those seen within the general prison population, including mental health issues, chronic health conditions (particularly asthma and musco-skeletal problems) (Meek & Lewis, 2014; Meek, Lewis, & Mehay, 2015), and substance abuse disorders (Lewis & Meek, 2013; Meek & Lewis, 2014; Meek et al., 2015; Williams, 2015), many have increased vulnerabilities relating to histories of violence, abuse and neglect, and time spent in local authority care (Bradley, 2009; Harris, 2015).

The complexity and multiplicity of the health needs of young adults in YOIs might suggest these young adults have histories of extensive contact with health and social care agencies prior to incarceration. Yet for many, this is not the case. The contact they have had is often negative (e.g. contact with the criminal justice system) and fails to provide the support for their needs (Bradley, 2009). Once incarcerated, meeting the health needs of an already vulnerable and disadvantaged patient population can be challenging in a secure environment that is not always conducive to well-being. Tensions can arise between obligations to secure and detain whilst protecting and providing rehabilitation for the young adults held in custody. This conflict may be particularly acute for health professionals within prison settings, wherein the primary obligation to promote the welfare of patients can come into conflict with the more punitive and rank and files mission of the institutions. Furthermore, some have criticised prison health policies and practices for being too preoccupied with the practical dangers such as self-harm and the prevention of suicide rather than prevention and health promotion (Caraher et al., 2002).

Young adults tend to report poor satisfaction with prison healthcare, regarding it as ineffective with little impact on their overall health (HM Chief Inspector of Prisons, 2013; HM Inspectorate of Prisons, 1997;

[1] Young adults categorised as requiring high security and those on remand can find themselves placed in both local prisons and YOIs. Analysis from Ministry of Justice, 2013 data found that 48 % were held in single-use YOIs, and 52 % in dual designated establishments, which are certified to hold both young adults and older prisoners (Ministry of Justice, 2013).

Meek & Lewis, 2014; Meek et al., 2015). Few studies have focused on peer health promotion among younger offenders, as young adults are generally healthy, and as such, they do not use the healthcare system as extensively as adults (Newacheck, Wong, Galbraith, & Hung, 2003). However, developing the knowledge, skills and confidence to enable young adults to adopt healthier behaviours could be an important step in supporting informed health-seeking lifestyles that stay with young people into adulthood (Macdonald, 2006), thus contributing to a generation-level reduction of negative health outcomes (Flecha, García, & Rudd, 2011).

Peer-Based Approaches for Prison Health

'Peer-based' is an umbrella term covering a range of different approaches including peer education, peer support, representative and bridging roles (South et al., 2010). Typically, these approaches all involve some degree of support by a social network member (the 'peer') who possesses experiential knowledge of a specific behaviour or stressor while sharing similar characteristics (e.g. age, sex, disease status) as the target population (Dennis, 2003). The support provided through peers can be emotional, affirmational, informational, and/or practical where enhanced self-esteem and connection to services can operate to improve health (Harris et al., 2015). Within a health context, peers have worked in communities to help with navigating health services, taken on buddy-type roles to connect groups, provided support for health management, and developed self-help groups for rehabilitation (South et al., 2010).

Peer-based approaches aim to improve health outcomes in a number of ways. First, peers often have more credibility within a community because of homophily, which suggests that contacts are more frequent (Chiu & West, 2007), communication is of better quality (Milburn, 1995), and relationships have more meaning between people who share attributes or specific experiences (South & Phillips, 2014). Second, peers provide an opportunity for the mentee to observe and practice modelled behaviour until they feel confident in performing it effectively (Milburn, 1995; Turner & Shepherd, 1999). The extent to which individuals are influenced by modelled behaviour depends on the characteristics of the models, the attributes of observers, and the perceived consequences of adopting similar behaviour (Bandura, 1985; Turner & Shepherd, 1999). The closer that individuals can identify with the peer, the more likely that they are to change their behaviour (Bandura, 1985). Third, peer-based approaches are closely linked to the notions of empowerment where through collective action, peers and communities can develop a greater awareness of the factors influencing their health in the broader environment, and the potential to change them. This may include improved information flow between the community and service providers, more accurate identification of community needs, improved engagement with services, improved networks of support and social capital, and changes to the social, cultural, and environmental factors which affect lives, (Batterham et al., 2014; National Institute for Health and Care Excellence (NICE), 2008; South & Phillips, 2014).

Peer-based approaches have only recently expanded into the prison health context in the UK (Edgar, Jacobson, & Biggar, 2011) as well as internationally (Wright et al., 2013). In the UK, a few notable peer-based approaches for prison health include the Department of Health Prison Health Trainer scheme, the Irish Red Cross Volunteer Inmates programme, and the Samaritans' Listener scheme, each of which is discussed in more detail below.

Prison Health Trainer Scheme

The Prison Health Trainer scheme is one of the most widely implemented peer-based approaches for prison health in England and Wales. The British government's Department for Health introduced this scheme to engage people from some of the country's poorest communities and support them to make lifestyle changes, with the strapline *support from next door rather than advice from on high* (Department for Health, 2004). In 2006, the Department of Health expanded the scheme to include prison populations, which was subsequently piloted in five adult prisons.

The prison Health Trainer role does not differ significantly from trainers who are based in the community. The role consists of a combination of 'signposting,' where peers work with clients to establish the nature of their health problems and use their knowledge of resources to refer them onto the appropriate prison service (e.g. dentist, gym staff, optician, drug and alcohol misuse teams, smoking cessation worker, counsellor, or any other specific health programmes and groups); and a health promotion/ behaviour change role, where peers are trained to assess a client's readiness to and ability to change and provide support in achieving a healthier lifestyle. The scheme is designed to be flexible enough to meet local needs whilst providing a structure to guide prisons. Once in post, Health

Trainers are required to complete an accredited course which covers four core competencies including (1) making relationships with communities, (2) communicating with individuals about promoting their health and well-being, (3) enabling individuals to change their behaviour to improve their health and well-being, and (4) managing their own time and activities. As part of the training, Health Trainers are required to present evidence (e.g. case studies, tutor observations, reflective accounts, role-plays, tests) to show that they have the knowledge and understanding required to undertake the various aspects of the role and have applied that in their practice. Upon any contact with clients, Health Trainers complete a clinical activity form which monitors details of the health services that the client is already engaging with, their identified health problem, the intervention offered/referral made, and whether the prisoner/client made a further appointment with the Health Trainer.

The Department of Health commissioned a process-and-impact assessment of the Health Trainer prison pilot scheme (Brooker & Sirdifield, 2007). A total of 11 Health Trainers had been recruited across the five sites, although more had applied and had failed the security check process. Prison staff reported that they generally selected those who had already held similar positions in the prisons or who had demonstrated relevant skills in communication and motivation when attending other courses in the prison. Recruiting in this manner helped to ensure the selection of individuals considered trustworthy, knowledgeable, and skilled for the role. The evaluation reported positive benefits for the Health Trainers in their level of knowledge across a variety of health topics. Health Trainers also stated that the role had given them an incentive to lead a healthy lifestyle themselves and most wanted to continue employment as a Health Trainer upon release.

The evaluation collected a sample of clinical activity forms from all five prisons sites to explore the effect on clients. A total 127 forms were collected which reported positive effects for Health Trainer clients. For nearly half the clients, the Health Trainer was the first health service they had chosen to engage with whilst in prison. The clients discussed a wide range of health issues with the Health Trainer with the main topics being exercise, healthy eating, and weight. The peers referred clients to a variety of services, most frequently gym staff and healthcare. Furthermore, 75 % of clients said they would like another appointment with a Health Trainer. Prison-based staff reported an increase in service use in some areas such as smoking cessation clinics and the gym. Health Trainers also reported that they were meeting a need in service provision by offering advice to improve self-esteem and to manage and cope with a prison sentence.

Senior prison administrators reported that the scheme was positive for the prison as the roles enabled prisoners to engage in purposeful activities and improve employability prospects upon release. The scheme did not seem to have an adverse effect on staff time or workload in terms of escorting prisoners to training or to see clients, but staff involved in the implementation of the scheme felt that managing future Health Trainer roles would need to be the responsibility of a whole department rather than an individual. Furthermore, the administrators reflected that the Health Trainer roles had raised the staff's awareness of health issues and the services available. Since this pilot phase, prison Health Trainer schemes have now spread to a number of prisons across England and Wales.

Irish Red Cross Volunteer Inmates Programme

The Irish Red Cross established a Health and First Aid prison volunteer scheme in one prison in Ireland in 2009 (Betts-Symonds, 2012), which was subsequently rolled out across all 14 prisons in Ireland by 2014. The scheme utilises groups of prisoners as peer-to-peer educators to promote health, hygiene, and first aid. Volunteer prisoners also work as an auxiliary to the professional healthcare team, focusing on health awareness and information sharing in the prison community. The Red Cross runs the volunteer training, which includes seven modules: the history and the structure of the International Red Cross, communication and building relationships, assessment of the community needs, first aid, preventing and responding to epidemics, disease prevention and health promotion, and module for supplementary topics depending on local needs. The programme uses an Action Learning approach where volunteer prisoners identify topics of interest based on an assessment of health risks in the prison.

In 2011, the Red Cross conducted a formative evaluation of the programme (Betts-Symonds, 2012). At the point of this evaluation, 6 of the 14 prisons in Ireland were currently involved in the scheme with 140 volunteer prisoners in post. Prison volunteers had reached an estimated 2000 prisoners through relevant health awareness and safety messaging with further effects likely to have been achieved through the indirect spread of messages to staff, relatives, and family members. Prison volunteers were involved in a number of projects, some emerging directly from volunteer prisoners and others as a result of management or health department initiatives. Projects included sharing relevant health messages to the prison community (e.g. TB awareness, swine flu prevention, and stomach bug awareness), transforming health promotion materials into easy to understand formats and different languages, and advocating for a rapid voluntary HIV testing campaign. Furthermore, during a particular outbreak of TB in some prisons in Ireland, volunteer prisoners were active in managing responses and preventing the spread of the disease. Prison volunteers also reported positive changes in their knowledge and personal development (Betts-Symonds, 2012).

The Samaritans' Listener Scheme

The Samaritans is a leading national helpline for emotional support in the UK. In 1991, they established a peer-support scheme for prisoners, recognising that prisoners are high risk for suicide and self-harm. Listeners are now an established peer-support scheme providing the most common peer role for prisoners in England and Wales. The goal of the Listeners scheme is to provide prisoners in distress with access to emotional support at any time of day or night. Chapter 5 in this volume has a detailed account and analysis of the Listener scheme.

These three established peer-based approaches provide useful insights into how to develop such schemes and their potential for positive effects in volunteers and clients. However, it is still important to consider the implementation of approaches across various populations and institutions. YOIs, where violence, racism, and bullying are widespread (Harris, 2015; Ireland, 2000), present particularly challenging settings to implement a peer-based approach to health. The existing literature on peer schemes has largely focused on adults, as many prison health professionals worry that young offenders may not be emotionally ready to support others and may lack the experience and maturity required to take on these roles (Woodall, South, Dixey, de Viggiani, & Penson, 2015). While a recent systematic review of peer-based approaches for prison health demonstrated the positive influence of peer education and support (Bagnall et al., 2015), much of the research focused on the positive effects of taking on a peer-deliverer role among adults. Few studies have examined the potential reach of these approaches within the prison community and the acceptability of peer-based approaches to those receiving support (Bagnall et al., 2015). This study examines the acceptability, utilisation, and potential challenges in developing and implementing peer-based approaches with young offenders.

Method

There are currently 130 prison establishments in England and Wales, of which 16 are YOIs. This study focuses on young adult men within a single YOI that incarcerates an average of 400 young adult men, with around 15 new young men entering the establishment each month. This represents a lower turnover than what has been previously reported, largely as a result of recent policy changes meaning that unsentenced and therefore more transient young men were no longer held in this YOI. With the greater stability of their population, the healthcare team based in this YOI expressed an interest in developing peer-based approaches as part of a wider health promotion initiative. The healthcare team envisioned the future peer role as 'Health Champions' and members were keen to gain early insights from the young men to inform its conception, development, and subsequent implementation. Embedded within a larger study concerning attitudes towards health at the YOI, the present study sought to elicit from the young adults their perceptions of peer-based approaches for promoting health.

Design

Royal Holloway University of London and the Ministry of Justice both granted ethical approval for the study. The researcher (first author) conducted individual, semi-structured qualitative interviews specifically relating to peer-based approaches for promoting health. We selected a qualitative approach as the best method to draw out some of the complexities and nuances of developing such programmes. The semi-structured guide for the qualitative interviews was designed to elicit the views of young adults in their own words and through the lens of their lived experiences. We conducted interviews with 37 young adult prisoners over a 3-month time period (February–April 2015) with each interview lasting up to 1 hour in duration. Due to security constraints within the prison, electronic items were prohibited. As such, the researcher conducted the interviews whilst taking written notes as close to verbatim as possible. The researcher reviewed the notes directly after each interview to ensure completeness and when necessary, obtained subsequent clarification from the participant. This followed similar prison-based research designs where the use of electronic equipment is often restricted and pragmatic designs are required (Schlosser, 2008; Wilson, 2006).

Sample

We selected participants through convenience sampling where the researcher entered the prison units where the young men reside and introduced the wider study (exploring attitudes towards health) to potential participants. The prison officers on duty were consulted during the recruitment process where they gave approval to approach specific young men to introduce the study. This was partly to support the safety of the researcher as well as minimise disruptions to the prison regime. The researcher, however, used a sampling framework to ensure that a range of young men (e.g. by ethnicity, age, and prisoner status)[2] was offered the opportunity to take part in the study. All young men who were approached to take part in the study agreed to an interview that was subsequently held in a private room on the unit. The age of participants in this sample ranged from 18 to 21, reflecting the full range at the YOI (where those aged 21 were either close to release or were due to be transferred to adult prisons), with a mean age of 19 years. In this sample, 71 % (n = 26) self-identified as being from a Black or Ethnic Minority or mixed ethnicity group with the remaining 29 % (n = 11) self-identifying as being of White ethnicity, also broadly reflecting the YOI population. Participants across the range of prisoner levels were also represented (46 % Standard, 40.5 % Enhanced, and 13.5 % as Basic level). Young men had spent an average of 10 months (ranging from 1 to 36 months) at the YOI.

Analysis

Written notes taken during the interview were typed into electronic format. We conducted a thematic analysis through coding and indexing. In this process, sets of categories were developed to reflect the overarching themes of the data (Ritchie, Spencer, & O'Connor, 2003). Themes were then discussed with a second researcher, a pragmatic version of double-coding

[2] Prisons in England and Wales set a status of Basic, Standard, or Enhanced for each prisoner under the 'Incentive and Earned Privileges' Scheme (IEPS). Prisoners are automatically allocated to 'Standard' level status after 14 days of entering a prison establishment. With good and compliant behaviour, prisoners can apply for 'Enhanced' status, where if awarded, they are eligible for additional privileges such as more and longer visits and increases in the amount of money they can spend in the prison. Prisoners can also be allocated 'Basic' level as a punishment level for those who do not comply with prison regulations and protocols.

(Barbour, 2003). The researcher also selected examples from the transcripts to illustrate the themes.

Findings

Data analysis resulted in four major themes relating to the acceptability and use of peer-based approaches. These themes included: taking on a peer role, utilising peers, challenges to utilising peers, and the prison commitment to bottom-up approaches.

Taking on a Peer Role

Most participants were enthusiastic about peer-deliverer roles that might be developed within the YOI. They were motivated to take on the role for personal development, personal health gains, to perform a civic duty, and to gain status and credibility.

Personal Development

The young men in this study were keen to take part in prison activities that allowed for personal development. They described frustrations with the lack of activities and the heightened security restrictions imposed on them characterised by long periods of lock-up; one participant reflected that, 'mentally it's shit. It's depressing. Soul crushing. Stagnating my mind. It's the whole prison in general.' Participants described the prison experience as merely passing time (what the literature often describes as 'doing time' or 'surviving prison,' e.g. Crewe, 2011; de Viggiani, 2006; Van Ginneken, 2015) rather than engaging in rehabilitative activities.

Concerns that they were spending a crucial part of their developmental stages in prison were common; one participant stated: 'I feel like I came in here at the pinnacle of my youth—it's like a transitional age for me. You are building a life, which is what I was doing before coming in here. I see coming in prison as a speed bump' Some participants were also aware that they were expected to develop into adulthood and learn valuable skills that they would require upon release:

> 'I just don't want to come out the same person as I came in. When any of us get out, we will be full adults—yes, young adults, but still adults. We will have to adjust to doing adult stuff like paying bills, and getting a job. So we need to be able to do that.'

According to the narratives, current opportunities within the prison did not adequately support them in their developmental needs and did not provide them with any transferable skills for use on release. One young man stated: 'they do all the courses in here and then you're just on servery. Which is a good position to have in here but it's nothing on the outside and gives you no skills for the outside.' As such, they viewed peer-approaches for health as an opportunity for personal development, particularly when the training was externally provided and led to a certificate of qualification, which could help their future job prospects.

Personal Health Gains

Peer-based approaches also had the potential for personal health gains. Training to undertake the role would provide health information that the young men could use for themselves. They also viewed being a positive role model as important, particularly with regards to health behaviours such as exercise, diet, and smoking. This in itself was a motivation to be healthy where, 'It would make me be healthy 'cos I have to play the position. There's no point if I'm not healthy myself.' Furthermore, participants highlighted that taking on a responsible role could have a positive impact on their own confidence and self-esteem: 'It's a great title and position to have, I would tell my mum I am a Champion!'

Perform a Civic Duty

In addition to the personal gains associated with taking on peer role, many respondents reported that they wanted to perform a civic duty; as one explained: 'I would like to give back to the community—like the prison community.' A peer role represented an opportunity for personal redemption, as, 'it gives me a chance to help other people not just myself. It's time for a change as I used to think about myself a lot and I want to now help others.' Participants who had previous negative experiences with healthcare were highly motivated to take on the role because: 'I know what it is like be let down by healthcare so I can help others.' These participants expressed a high level of empathy and a strong will to provide support to ensure that their peers didn't experience similar problems. One young man shared his desire to use his experience to help others: 'I know it would be hard for others to quit smoking so I could help as been through it. Especially in prison when your health is all you think about.'

Gaining Status and Credibility

All participants reflected that prison roles were highly sought after and subject to fierce competition. They described the prison as a hierarchical system where they were constantly seeking to elevate their status and viewed the process of taking on a formal role in the YOI as a way to bolster their status. For example, they saw Listeners and 'Red Bands'[3] as high-ranking positions due to the prison privileges the roles afforded, including greater freedom of movement around the YOI, more time out of their cell, extra gym sessions, and increased earnings through a prison wage. A health peer-deliverer role was particularly attractive to the young men if it provided them with a similar status within the prison. Participants thought the peer role should provide a wage and extra incentives although as one young man stated, 'the status of being a health champion is more important than getting paid.' Other valuable incentives in the prison included 'time out of my cell, more freedom, more gym time.' Furthermore, participants reflected that anything that distinguished the role from others in the prison, such as bright T-shirts and name badges, also bolstered the status of the role. Some participants specifically viewed the title of the peer-deliverer as an important aspect of creating greater status. Two participants found the proposed 'Health Champion' title appealing; it resonated with the participants, symbolising a high status and being the best. However, for two other participants, the 'Champion' title seemed patronising, and they felt 'Health advisor … would be better as sounds more professional … Champion is like childish.'

The status associated with the role was deemed crucial for the acceptability and use of peer-approaches. First, without an incentive, most participants felt that few prisoners would undertake the role because, 'No one does anything here without getting something out of it—it's like outside but magnified in prison. There has to be an incentive like 1-day work then 1 day gym. No one does it just for the money—it's the perks.' The young men reflected that this was the reality of prison life where prisoners were forced to negotiate the hierarchical system to gain control, power, and positioning where, 'you work towards the job you want in prison.' Second, participants viewed these incentives as a way of providing credibility to the role within the prison to ensure that both the peer-deliverer and the wider prison population 'took the role seriously.'

Utilising Peers

All participants acknowledged that their prison sentence provided them with an opportunity to take stock of their health and address some of

[3] Red bands are allocated to prisoners who have demonstrated exceptionally good behaviour and are given special privileges such as freedom to move around the prison.

their health concerns. Prison had a detoxifying effect for many of the participants, 'Prison has helped me, it's cleansing my body.' Moreover, for many participants prison was seen as a respite from their chaotic lives in the community where they were comparatively safe. One young man stated: 'I feel kinda happy here as I'm away from my area. I know there's no way I'll get stabbed or shot in here. I think being here has affected my health in a positive way.' All participants were therefore highly motivated to seek information and support to maintain and improve their health in the prison context since 'everything in your life is related to your health.' They tended to view peers as a suitable avenue to access certain information and support as well as provide an auxiliary healthcare service.

Access to Information and Support

Participants unanimously reported that the YOI currently did not provide enough health information and support and that access to prison healthcare was challenging. Peer-based approaches were welcomed as a response to redressing these gaps. For example, one respondent viewed prison health as 'all about paracetamol (acetaminophen) and creams—that's all,' which was reactive and ineffective. They tended to view peer-based approaches as a potential way to increase access to broader health information when needed. Participants stated that they wanted more general health promotion information and support on a wide range of health topics including diet and nutrition, exercise, smoking cessation, personal hygiene, disease prevention and vaccinations, sexual health, mental health and coping, and primary care problems (such as sleep problems, pain management) whilst at the YOI. Many participants felt that peers could provide some of this information around key themes such as weight control, building muscle-mass, maintaining personal hygiene, preventing illnesses, and self-management tactics as well as more general information regarding accessing prison healthcare services and support for new prisoners when first entering the prison. A few participants also felt that peers could provide more information around disease prevention such as vaccinations. For example, one young man stated: 'when I first came in, they just jabbed me but I had no idea what it was really.' For others, the lack of information meant they refused vaccinations. One participant said: 'I don't know what's in them and I don't trust it.' Thus for those who were distrustful of the system, peer-based approaches represented not only a convenient avenue for providing this type of health information and support, but also one which would be more credible, relevant, and meaningful for them.

In the current scheme, many viewed the information and support from the healthcare team as lacking relevance and empathy. For example, one young man stated:

> I get that they are trying to help—like I know smoking isn't good but they don't really understand what we are going through in here. It's boredom and stress really and it's hard in here to deal with it all. They really don't understand so when they say, 'Oh stop smoking' or do this and that, it's not that easy.

Current health promotion posters and leaflets were considered mostly irrelevant, as one respondent stated, 'no one reads a leaflet in here—you just think, "what do they know giving you this leaflet!" It's pointless.' Some participants felt that the lived experience of peers would mean that they were in a position to understand their concerns, in that 'you can relate to other people in your position and they would be more approachable.' Participants also thought they would likely receive the information and support from peers more positively as it comes from a more empathetic and relevant source.

Auxiliary Healthcare Service

Most participants reflected that there were also a number of difficulties in accessing prison healthcare services that peer-based approaches could supplement. In this way, peers were not just a source of health information and support, but they could also take on a bridging role to prison healthcare and provide some of the health services directly on the wings. They described access to healthcare as a long and inefficient process where 'there is none of this information [health promotion], you have to put in an app [application] and wait and then try and get the information yourself. It's not easy.' The prison application system required young adults to complete a form and post into a healthcare box on the units, which were then collected by healthcare each evening. A nurse or healthcare assistant contacted each young person within 24 hours of picking up the form to assess the health issue and treat or triage where appropriate. Participants felt that they had to wait long periods of time before being seen by healthcare staff because, 'It's just so slow here and by the time they come, you are OK—but then you had to suffer in that time waiting. If it was quicker it would be OK.' This waiting provoked anxiety, as one young man explained: 'in your cell, you just think and think and think and you got nothing to do to get it off your mind.' Peers could relieve some anxiety by providing support and acting as a contact point for finding out information, such as when an appointment might be scheduled or when they might receive test results. In this capacity, as one participant stated, 'a health champion is good as they can give reassurance—just giving a face of healthcare and making you feel someone is there who is involved with healthcare and knows you are there.' Having someone readily available and based on the wing who was also able to contact healthcare was deemed a positive asset for peer-based approaches. Although this could be anyone, a peer may show more urgency and understanding.

Peer-based approaches could provide a cooperative service with the healthcare team by providing self-help information and support and diverting these concerns away from the health service. One participant stated that a peer 'can give general advice for little things that you wouldn't normally need healthcare. This would free up doctors to see people about proper things.' Furthermore, some of the participants were keen for healthcare to be more flexible with a stronger presence on the wings. They viewed peer-based approaches as potentially facilitating this need through providing health screenings on the wing (such as height-and-weight checks and screening for infectious disease) and being a more constant source of information without a lengthy application processes.

Challenges to Utilising Peers

Although most participants were keen to utilise peers for access to health information and support as well as auxiliary healthcare services, many young men noted that there were a number of challenges associated with seeking help from peers. These challenges included the perceived motivations of the peers, role-modelling and behaviour change in the prison context, and the social environment at the YOI.

Peer Motivations

Most participants stated that they would speak to a health champion about certain health issues, but they would really like to take on the role themselves. As stated earlier, participants reflected that high status roles were highly sought after but they were also sometimes divisive in creating strong competition between the young adults for the limited positions. Young adults were motivated to take on the peer role for a combination of reasons including for both personal gains (e.g. personal development, to gain status in the prison) and for the benefit of the prison community (e.g. to provide support and perform a civic duty). However, they were largely sceptical to the motivations of other individuals who held prison roles. One participant stated:

> I wouldn't talk to a health champion as all these things just look good for parole—like being a Listener. You get privileges and you get perks and people don't do them for the right reasons.

Participants also reflected that prison roles were often allocated to those who 'got in with the govs [prison staff]' rather than through a fair selection processes. This reduced the credibility of the role because participants questioned why they should seek help and support from someone whose motivations may be purely self-serving.

Behaviour Change in the YOI Context

Participants discussed the challenges for changing behaviour within the prison context and the effects of peers as healthy role models. Some felt that peers had to be healthy themselves as, 'what's the point of having bad health and trying to preach to others about good health?' However, all the young men noted that keeping healthy in the YOI was challenging because boredom and stress encouraged unhealthy behaviours such as smoking. Furthermore, a few participants noted that it was difficult to make changes to be healthy in the YOI because they could not readily undertake exercise and they were largely reliant on unhealthy prison foods. They suggested that gaining information and knowledge through a peer or through other avenues was not always effective in changing behaviours. For example, one young man stated:

> In here, even if you bring someone in who had a bad experience and nearly died or something [from taking drugs] we will just think, whatever—I don't care. It's like if you put one million pounds in front of you in a box and you tell them, don't take it, it's bad—you will always take it! It's like Satan is on your shoulder tempting you—you can't resist!

Therefore, the extent to which peers could influence behaviour change through role-modelling was considered challenging within the restrictions and health contexts of the YOI.

The Social Environment

Most participants expressed caution in seeking support from peers for health topics that were deemed as 'sensitive' including sexual health and mental health. They viewed these as important issues to address, but felt that others in the prison may not be trustworthy. One participant stated:

> mentally, it is a bit of a mind game…trying to form a bond with prisoners and the staff, feeling part of something and having people around you. I see health as part of that. Being able to share things and talk—but not personal things. Personal things you should talk to those you trust. I don't know people in here from Adam.

The common view was that 'confidentiality is an issue … inmates can't be trusted.' Participants suggested that seeking support from others in the prison was unusual where the norm was, as one person stated, 'people don't talk about their problems so I don't talk about mine.' The young men were concerned that by revealing too much personal information, they left themselves open to unwanted attention within the prison environment which could lead to exploitation: 'Then they tell this person, and then that person and suddenly you're on the big screen!'

As a barrier to a peer health scheme, some participants reflected that the prison culture did not allow them to show their true selves. One respondent stated: 'in here, people see me as a laughing and joking guy but I just don't feel like that inside, I'm not that person' and 'the people here…they know too much about me, I don't want them knowing anymore.' Many of the issues concerning trust and confidentiality were also driven by the YOI culture of bullying and violence where 'in prisons, it's not a place where people are soft for each other.' One participant stated, 'I have major trust issues, I know. I can't trust anyone.' Some participants also sensed a lack of maturity with some of the other young adults in the YOI, making the prison a precarious environment, subject to flare-ups of violence:

> The lads here are stupid…they are immature and do my nut in [British slang, to annoy]…they think they are special. It's like a fight for survival in here. Everyone is trying to be better than everyone else. You have a few days when it's all fine and then someone will just say something and then it all kicks off. It's bad if someone gets in trouble as then everyone gets involved.

As such, one participant expressed that the lack of maturity within the YOI meant that peer-approaches 'might work in adults but youths don't care as they all think they're gangsters.' Those who were interviewed overall felt that their own level of maturity was much greater than that of the YOI population, in general, but acknowledged that the YOI prison regime had also created a culture of mistrust and violence. As one young man stated: 'this is a kids' place—a Kindergarten! I was in [name of adult prison] before. It was adults there and here its typical kids' behaviour. If you put them in [name of adult prison], they would behave differently.'

This limited the reach of peers in creating supportive networks where participants felt that, for example, 'the support bit [of peer-approaches] for others wouldn't happen. Other peer support doesn't happen. It's a very hostile environment—no one will talk to them.' There was clearly a desire for an environment which was more supportive and trusting, where participants wanted, for example 'someone I know and can trust' and felt that 'if I could talk to more people and be open it could help—it would help—but I won't do that. I'm not here to make friends.' However, many participants did not believe that peer-based efforts to tackle sensitive health needs could counteract these dominant features within the social culture of the YOI.

Prison Commitment to a Bottom-Up Approach

Most participants were keen to express the potential use of peers as a core component of wider bottom-up approaches which seek to engage with, learn from, and collaborate with young people in prison to develop health promotion initiatives in the prison since, as one participant explained, 'no one really asks about what we think ... It's 100 per cent a good idea!' With more open communication, participants reflected that prison-based staff could learn more about them, their daily challenges and the value of the unique insights they possessed. The young men proposed ideas which they thought could change the prison culture, with one saying, 'all of us are born philosophers in here...I could make big changes that wouldn't benefit just me but everyone.' Through listening to their ideas, participants believed that the prison administrators could implement changes for the benefit of the organisation. For example, one participant described how healthcare often worked to meet the health workers' priorities, which he felt sometimes neglected his own needs:

> I've got scars on my face from when I got attacked in prison. It still worries me as I got attacked from behind by a few people so now when I am out;

> I sit and stand against a wall so no one is behind me. So I went to healthcare as I wanted some cream and oils for my scars. They just came and were worried about my asthma. But the scar thing really bothered me. I hate myself when I look in the mirror. I just wanted some oil or something—even if I had to buy it myself.

For the most part, the young men perceived staff within the prison healthcare service as lacking engagement and collaboration, as one participant stated, 'it's like he's done the working out but doesn't show you how he did it—just the end result.' Most participants therefore described changes they would like to see in both prison staff and within the healthcare team as a whole where peer-based approaches could be used to guide and develop the service. They wanted greater involvement in their care and hoped peers might help to change the views of them from prisoners to patients who should be involved in decisions about their care. In other words, peer-based approaches represented an opportunity to shape healthcare services through consultation with the people involved and tailoring the service accordingly.

Importantly, some participants stated that this engagement had to provide a genuine opportunity and priority for the prison staff to 'listen to prisoners and what they need. Like not just random things but properly listen to us and listen to what we need and the reasons why.' Participants were aware that the notions of involvement and engagement were at odds with the overall function of prison as a punitive institution. However, some respondents felt that opening up discussions to create shared understandings was important, because, as one person stated 'some things they will agree on, on what we need. But others they won't but then it opens the discussions. They can tell us why they can't do stuff and at least we will understand. Like if they really can't give us more time out of our cells, then just think about stuff you can do in your cell instead. Every kid hated homework, but in here it would be good!' Such discussions would require commitment from the prison where 'people need to voice their opinion especially to a manager who has authority to do something. Not just anyone.'

Although most participants expressed the view that greater involvement in developing services could be a valuable aspect of peer-based approaches, many young men were also dubious of the motivations of the prison staff and prison healthcare team in developing the role in this way. Some had already experienced disappointments from similar initiatives that aimed to create changes within the prison culture (e.g. equality representatives, prison listeners).

Where participants perceived these initiatives as ineffective, they doubted the realistic implementation of the peer health scheme as well. One young man stated: 'it won't work—they have these things already like equality officers but you don't see any of them doing anything.' Furthermore, some of the participants evidently did not think that the prison staff were motivated to make these changes. As one respondent stated, 'nothing's gonna make it better. They have been here too long and are just here to do their job and go back home. They just want to make sure I stay alive and don't hurt anyone else.' More widely, participants questioned their own role as prisoners and the motivations for prisons to make significant changes to their lives and their health since, as one participant expressed, 'we are not the cream of the crop as citizens so no one cares a lot about us.'

Discussion

This study provides insight into potential facilitators and barriers to implementing a peer-based health scheme for young adult offenders in English prisons. These findings support previous research that indicates the potential for positive effects for individuals who take on peer roles along with the recipients of these services (Bagnall et al., 2015; Devilly, Sorbello, Eccleston, & Ward, 2005; South et al., 2014; Woodall et al., 2015; Wright et al., 2013). Overwhelmingly, the young adults interviewed in this study were keen to take on the role of a peer 'Health Champion,' which they appeared to view as an opportunity for personal health gains and personal development during their sentence rather than just 'doing time.' The young men were also open to seeking support from a peer on diet, smoking cession and exercise, and signposting/bridging to healthcare services. However, sensitive health topics (such as mental health and sexual health) were viewed as more problematic.

Most of the young adults wanted to be Health Champions and cited personal and civic motivations even as they questioned the motivations of others in similar high status roles. They felt that a commitment from the prison and the healthcare teams as part of a wider bottom-up approach had the potential to create wider social and environmental changes for improving prison health. However, the young adults were largely dubious about the prison changing its culture towards health promotion. There appears to be great potential for developing peer-based approaches for individual personal development (i.e. for the peer or the client), yet the likelihood of creating wider changes within the social and organisational culture that supports these schemes within prison is less clear.

This study was developed in conjunction with the prison and the prison healthcare team at the YOI as an initial step to develop and potentially implement a peer-based approach. Therefore, we offer a number of initial recommendations to guide the future development of peer-based approaches. First, prisons and healthcare teams ought to be committed to developing and maintaining peer-based approaches and willing to provide adequate resources and staff time. Teams should be mindful that people in prison have had prior experiences of similar schemes and roles producing little opportunity and impact and therefore should strive to counteract the negative perceptions within prison populations. Furthermore, once committed to developing peer-based approaches, prison and healthcare staff should seek to engage with people in prison early on to inform its conception and ensure the scheme is tailored in line with their needs and priorities and with consideration for the prison context. Young adults in this study raised concerns in selecting the 'right' individuals to be peers in light of the varying maturity levels within the YOI population. Indeed, evaluations of other peer-based approaches—such as Health Trainers, Listeners, and the Red Cross Volunteers initiative—report recruiting those who already held prison positions and were trusted to minimise the risk issues associated with introducing a role into the prison (Betts-Symonds, 2012; Brooker & Sirdifield, 2007; Jaffe, 2012). Security is clearly an important consideration within the prison context; however, selecting from a limited pool of individuals can create contempt and feelings of injustice within the wider prison population. Roles should be open to a diverse range of individuals who may not be already engaged in other prison roles.

Whilst the young adults in this study anticipated many potential positive benefits of being associated with being a peer, schemes should be realistic as to the potential for wider effects on the prison community. The basic assumption of peer-based approaches is that of responsibilisation, that people in prison must take charge of their own reform and be active help-seekers. However, by placing the onus on the individual, we tend to ignore the negative effects of imprisonment and the constraints of the prison environment in achieving behaviour changes. The young adults were keen for prison to be a place of rehabilitation where they could lead healthy and purposeful lives that would equip them on release into adulthood. Echoing similar findings from independent inspectorate reports (HM Inspectorate of Prisons, 1997, 2012), the young men in this study present a bleak picture of prison life in the YOI with long periods of being locked up with little purposeful activity. Clearly peer-based approaches are not the only way people in prison can be engaged in purposeful activity, and prisons should ensure adequate rehabilitation provisions for all people in prison. Young adults also described the functions that peer-based approaches could provide within the YOI, including providing information, support, and health services as well as being a reassuring contact point for the young adults. In this study, there were high levels of dissatisfaction with the healthcare service, and peer-approaches were viewed as an avenue to provide what participants felt was lacking. Peer-based approaches should not be viewed as a way to fill in the gaps and should not excuse improvements that could be made in prison healthcare.

Peer-based approaches have great potential for positive change at both an individual (i.e. for the peer) and an organisation level if prisons commit to a bottom-up approach in engaging and involving people in prison. Prisons and prison healthcare need to be willing to invest resources, time, and support through this process and ensure that they listen and involve people in prison into the discussions and reasons. In sum, these schemes could be a valuable part of a wider prison approach to creating supportive and healthy settings.

Conclusion

Peer-based approaches are increasingly common in prisons in England and Wales, with evidence pointing to their potential effectiveness as an approach to tackling health disparities in the prison population (Bagnall et al., 2015). This study provides insights into the perceived benefits and challenges of utilising peer-based approaches with young adult male prisoners, a population often overlooked in the literature on peer-based initiatives in prison. In light of the health needs and inequalities observed within the young adult prisoner population, the findings support the development of peer-based approaches with caution about the types of setting or environment that would be conducive to this type of scheme. The potential use of peers in responding to sensitive health topics, such as mental health and sexual health, may be less acceptable as a source of support. Prison clearly has a part to play in meeting the health needs of a marginalised group of people and more is required to address the current gaps in services and opportunities for health. More widely, a commitment to creative approaches that seek to act on the wider social and environmental factors associated with health may be required to create supportive and healthy cultures within prisons.

References

Bagnall, A. M., South, J., Hulme, C., Woodall, J., Vinall-Collier, K., Raine, G., et al. (2015). A systematic review of the effectiveness and cost-effectiveness of peer education and peer support in prisons. *BMC Public Health*, *15*(1), 290.

Bandura, A. (1985). *Social foundations of thought and action: A social cognitive theory* (1st ed.). Englewood Cliffs, NJ: Prentice Hall.

Barbour, R. S. (2003). The newfound credibility of qualitative research? Tales of technical essentialism and co-option. *Qualitative Health Research*, *13*(7), 1019–1027.

Batterham, R. W., Buchbinder, R., Beauchamp, A., Dodson, S., Elsworth, G. R., & Osborne, R. H. (2014). The OPtimising HEalth LIterAcy (Ophelia) process: Study protocol for using health literacy profiling and community engagement to create and implement health reform. *BMC Public Health*, *14*(1), 694.

Betts-Symonds, G. (2012). *Community based health and first aid in action in Irish prisons: 3 year evaluation*. Ireland: Irish Prison Service, Irish Red Cross and Vocational Education Committee. Retrieved from https://www.redcross.ie/resources/?cat_id=8.

Bradley, K. (2009). *The Bradley report. Lord Bradley's review of people with mental health problems or learning disabilities in the criminal justice system*. London: Department of Health. Retrieved from https://www.rcpsych.ac.uk/pdf/Bradley%20Report11.pdf.

Bridgwood, A. & Malbon, G. (1995). *Survey of the physical health of prisoners 1994: A survey of sentenced male prisoners in England and Wales*. London: Stationery Office Books.

British Medical Association.. (2014). *Young lives behind bars: The health and human rights of children and young people detained in the criminal justice system*. London: British Medical Association. Retrieved from http://bma.org.uk/-/media/files/pdfs/working%20for%20change/improving%20health/vulnerable%20people/po-younglivesbehindbars-31-10-2014.pdf.

Brooker, C., & Sirdifield, C. (2007). *New futures health trainers: An impact assessment*. London: Department of Health. Retrieved from http://eprints.lincoln.ac.uk/2535/1/OHTR_final2.pdf.

Brunton-Smith, I., & Hopkins, K. (2013). *The factors associated with proven re-offending following release from prison: Findings from Waves 1 to 3 of SPCR*. London: Ministry of Justice. Retrieved from https://www.gov.uk/government/uploads/system/uploads/attachment_data/file/261620/re-offending-release-waves-1-3-spcr-findings.pdf.

Caraher, M., Dixon, P., Carr-Hill, R., Hayton, P., McGough, H., & Bird, L. (2002). Are health-promoting prisons an impossibility? Lessons from England and Wales. *Health Education*, *102*(5), 219–229.

Chiu, L. F. & West, R. M. (2007). Health intervention in social context: Understanding social networks and neighbourhood. *Social Science & Medicine (1982)*, *65*(9), 1915–1927.

Crewe, B. (2011). Depth, weight, tightness: Revisiting the pains of imprisonment. *Punishment & Society*, *13*(5), 509–529.

Dennis, C. L. (2003). Peer support within a health care context: A concept analysis. *International Journal of Nursing Studies*, *40*(3), 321–332.

Department for Health.. (2002). *Health promoting prisons: A shared approach*. London: Department for Health. Retrieved from http://webarchive.nationalarchives.gov.uk/+/www.dh.gov.uk/en/Publicationsandstatistics/Publications/PublicationsPolicyAndGuidance/DH_4006230.

Department for Health. (2004). *Choosing health: Making healthier choices easier* (No. Cm 6732). London: The Stationary Office. Retrieved from http://webarchive.nationalarchives.gov.uk/+/dh.gov.uk/en/publicationsandstatistics/publications/publicationspolicyandguidance/dh_4094550.

de Viggiani, N. (2006). Surviving prison: Exploring prison social life as a determinant of health. *International Journal of Prisoner Health*, *2*(2), 71–89.

Devilly, G. J., Sorbello, L., Eccleston, L., & Ward, T. (2005). Prison-based peer-education schemes. *Aggression and Violent Behavior*, *10*(2), 219–240.

Edgar, K., Jacobson, J., & Biggar, K. (2011). *Time well spent: A practical guide to active citizenship and volunteering in prison*. London: Prison Reform Trust. Retrieved from http://www.icpr.org.uk/media/4426/time%20well%20spent.pdf.

Fazel, S. & Danesh, J. (2002). Serious mental disorder in 23 000 prisoners: A systematic review of 62 surveys. *The Lancet*, *359*(9306), 545–550.

Flecha, A., García, R., & Rudd, R. (2011). Using health literacy in school to overcome inequalities. *European Journal of Education*, *46*(2), 209–218.

Harris.. (2015). *Changing prisons, saving lives report of the independent review into self-inflicted deaths in custody of 18–24 year olds* (The Harris Review). Retrieved from http://dera.ioe.ac.uk/23552/1/moj-harris-review-web-accessible.pdf.

Harris, J., Springett, J., Croot, L., Booth, A., Campbell, F., Thompson, J., et al. (2015). *Can community-based peer support promote health literacy and reduce inequalities? A realist review*. London: NIHR Service Delivery and Organisation Programme. Retrieved from http://www.journalslibrary.nihr.ac.uk/__data/assets/pdf_file/0019/135604/FullReport-phr03030.pdf.

Health Protection Agency and Department of Health.. (2011). *Prevention of infection and communicable disease control in prisons and places of detention: A manual for healthcare workers*. London: Health Protection Agency. Retrieved from https://www.gov.uk/government/uploads/system/uploads/attachment_data/file/329792/Prevention_of_infection_communicable_disease_control_in_prisons_and_places_of_detention.pdf.

Herbert, K., Plugge, E., Foster, C., & Doll, H. (2012). Prevalence of risk factors for non-communicable diseases in prison populations worldwide: A systematic review. *Lancet, 379*(9830), 1975–1982.

HM Chief Inspector of Prisons.. (2013). *Report on an unannounced inspection of HMP/YOI Feltham (Feltham B - young adults)*. London: HM Chief Inspector of Prisons. Retrieved from https://www.justiceinspectorates.gov.uk/hmiprisons/wp-content/uploads/sites/4/2015/01/Feltham-B-YA-web-2014.pdf.

HM Inspectorate of Prisons.. (1997). *Young prisoners: A thematic review by HM chief inspector of prisons for England and Wales.* London: HM Chief Inspector of Prisons. Retrieved from https://www.justiceinspectorates.gov.uk/hmiprisons/wp-content/uploads/sites/4/2014/08/young-prisoners-rps.pdf.

HM Inspectorate of Prisons.. (2012). *HM chief inspector of prisons for England and Wales annual report 2011 to 2012.* London: HM Chief Inspector of Prisons. Retrieved from https://www.justice.gov.uk/downloads/publications/corporate-reports/hmi-prisons/hm-inspectorate-prisons-annual-report-2011-12.pdf.

HM Prison Service.. (2003). *Prison service order (PSO) 3200 on health promotion.* London: HM Prison Service. Retrieved from https://www.justice.gov.uk/offenders/psos.

Home Office.. (2000). *Powers of criminal courts (sentencing) act 2000* (Pub. L. No. 31/2000). Retrieved from http://www.legislation.gov.uk/ukpga/2000/6/contents.

Ireland, J. L. (2000). 'Bullying' among prisoners: A review of research. *Aggression and Violent Behavior, 5*(2), 201–215.

Jaffe, M. (2012). *Peer support and seeking help in prison: A study of the listeners scheme in four prisons in England.* Unpublished doctoral dissertation, Keele University, UK.

Joint Prison Service and National Health Service Executive.. (1999). *The future organisation of prison health care.* London: HM Prison Service and National Heath Service. Retrieved from http://webarchive.nationalarchives.gov.uk/20130107105354/http:/www.dh.gov.uk/prod_consum_dh/groups/dh_digitalassets/@dh/@en/documents/digitalasset/dh_4106031.pdf.

Lewis, G. & Meek, R. (2013). *A comprehensive health needs assessment of prisons and IRCs on behalf of NHS England (London).* London: Royal Holloway University of London.

Light, M., Grant, E., & Hopkins, K. (2013). *Gender differences in substance misuse and mental health amongst prisoners.* London: Ministry of Justice. Retrieved from https://www.gov.uk/government/uploads/system/uploads/attachment_data/file/220060/gender-substance-misuse-mental-health-prisoners.pdf.

Macdonald, W. (2006). *The health needs of young offenders.* The National Primary Care Rese arch and Development Centre. The University of Manchester. Retrieved from http://www.ohrn.nhs.uk/resource/Research/PCSysRevYO.pdf.

Marshall, T., Simpson, S., & Stevens, A. (2001). Use of health services by prison inmates: Comparisons with the community. *Journal of Epidemiology and Community Health, 55*(5), 364–365.

McHugh, M. (1996). Managing the stress of strategic change. *Strategic Change, 5*(3), 141–150.

Meek, R. & Lewis, G. (2014). *HMP/YOI Portland health needs assessment.* London: Royal Holloway University of London.

Meek, R., Lewis, G., & Mehay, A. (2015). *Health heeds assessment: HMYOI Feltham (b side young adults aged 18–21).* London: Royal Holloway University of London.

Milburn, K. (1995). A critical review of peer education with young people with special reference to sexual health. *Health Education Research, 10*(4), 407–420.

Miller, R. J., Williams Miller, J., Djoric, J. Z., & Patton, D. (2015a). Baldwin's Mill: Race, prisoner reentry and the pedagogy of repression, 1965–2015. *Humanity and Society, 39*(4), 456–475.

Ministry of Justice.. (2013). Transforming management of young adults in custody. London: Ministry of Justice. Retrieved from https://consult.justice.gov.uk/digital-communications/young-adults/user_uploads/transforming-management-of-young-adults-in-custody.pdf.

Ministry of Justice.. (2014). *Prison population projections 2014-2020 England and Wales.* London: Ministry of Justice. Retrieved from https://www.gov.uk/government/uploads/system/uploads/attachment_data/file/380586/prison-population-projections-2014-2020.pdf.

Ministry of Justice.. (2015). *Offender management statistics quarterly: January to March 2015.* London: Ministry of Justice. Retrieved from https://www.gov.uk/government/uploads/system/uploads/attachment_data/file/449528/offender-management-statistics-bulletin-jan-mar-2015.pdf.

National Institute for Health and Care Excellence (NICE).. (2008). *PH9 community engagement guidance.* National Institute for Clinical Excellence. Retrieved from www.nice.org.uk/guidance/PH9.

Newacheck, P. W., Wong, S. T., Galbraith, A. A., & Hung, Y. Y. (2003). Adolescent health care expenditures: A descriptive profile. *The Journal of Adolescent Health, 32*(6), 3–11.

Ritchie, J., Spencer, L., & O'Connor, W. (2003). Carrying out qualitative analysis. In J. Ritchie & J. Lewis (Eds.), *Qualitative research practice: A guide for social science students and researchers* (pp. 219–262). London: Sage.

Schlosser, J. A. (2008). Issues in interviewing inmates navigating the methodological landmines of prison research. *Qualitative Inquiry, 14*(8), 1500–1525.

Senior, J. & Shaw, J. (2007). Prison healthcare. In Y. Jewkes (Ed.), *Handbook on prisons* (pp. 377–398). London: Routledge.

Social Exclusion Unit. (2002). *Reducing re-offending by ex-prisoners*. London: Office of the Deputy Prime Minister. Retrieved from http://www.prisonstudies.org/sites/default/files/resources/downloads/reducing_report20pdf.pdf.

South, J., Bagnall, A.-M., Hulme, C., Woodall, J., Longo, R., Dixey, R., et al. (2014). A systematic review of the effectiveness and cost-effectiveness of peer-based interventions to maintain and improve offender health in prison settings. *Health Services and Delivery Research*, *2*(35), 1–218.

South, J., Meah, A., Bagnall, A.-M., Kinsella, K., Branney, P. E., White, J., et al. (2010). *People in public health—A study of approaches to develop and support people in public health roles*. London: NIHR Service Delivery and Organisation Programme. Retrieved from http://www.leedsbeckett.ac.uk/health/piph/documents/PIPH%20Final%20Report.pdf.

South, J. & Phillips, G. (2014). Evaluating community engagement as part of the public health system. *Journal of Epidemiology and Community Health*, *68*(7), 692–696.

Turner, G. & Shepherd, J. (1999). A method in search of a theory: Peer education and health promotion. *Health Education Research*, *14*(2), 235–247.

Van Ginneken, E. F. (2015). Doing well or just doing time? A qualitative study of patterns of psychological adjustment in prison. *The Howard Journal of Criminal Justice*, *54*(4), 352–370.

Walmsley, R. (2011). *World prison population list* (9th ed.). London: International Centre for Prison Studies.

Watson, R., Stimpson, A., & Hostick, T. (2004). Prison health care: A review of the literature. *International Journal of Nursing Studies*, *41*(2), 119–128.

WHO. (2014). *Prisons and health*. Geneva, Switzerland: World Health Organisation.

Williams, K. (2015). *Needs and characteristics of young adults in custody: Results from the Surveying Prisoner Crime Reduction (SPCR) survey*. London: Ministry of Justice. Retrieved from https://www.gov.uk/government/uploads/system/uploads/attachment_data/file/449586/Young-adults-in-custody.pdf.

Wilson, D. (2006). Some reflections on researching with young black people and the youth justice system. *Youth Justice*, *6*(3), 181–193.

Woodall, J., South, J., Dixey, R., de Viggiani, N., & Penson, W. (2015). Expert views of peer-based interventions for prisoner health. *International Journal of Prisoner Health*, *11*(2), 87–97.

Wright, N., Bleakley, A., Butt, C., Chadwick, O., Mahmood, K., Patel, K., et al. (2013). Peer health promotion in prisons: A systematic review. *International Journal of Prisoner Health*, *7*(4), 37–51.

PART III

The Non-profit Sector and Prison Culture: Interactions, Boundaries, and Opportunities

CHAPTER 7

The Involvement of Non-profit Organizations in Prisoner Reentry in the UK: Prisoner Awareness and Engagement

Rosie Meek, Dina Gojkovic, and Alice Mills

Introduction

Discussions regarding the definition of nonprofit organizations in the UK have developed considerably over the past two decades. A wide range of terms have been used, including *voluntary sector*, *nongovernmental sector*, *charitable sector*, and *community sector*; all of which draw our attention to different attributes of the sector and draw intersector boundaries along slightly different lines (Buckingham, 2009; Halfpenny & Reid, 2002).

Originally published in *Journal of Offender Rehabilitation*, Vol. 52, No. 5, pp. 338–357.

R. Meek (✉)
Royal Holloway University of London, London, UK

D. Gojkovic
University of Southampton, Southampton, UK

A. Mills
University of Auckland, Auckland, New Zealand

L.S. Abrams et al. (eds.), *The Voluntary Sector in Prisons*, Palgrave Studies in Prisons and Penology, DOI 10.1057/978-1-137-54215-1_7

The term *third sector* was largely promoted by the British New Labour government as an inclusive term (Alcock & Kendall, 2010) but one that carries few assumptions about the characteristics of organizations or the origin of their funding sources. It is, therefore, considered appropriate to use this term to represent the variety of organizations that are involved in the criminal justice system (CJS), ranging from charities and social enterprises to nonprofit organizations, cooperatives, faith groups, and clubs.

Approximately 84,000 people are currently in prison in England and Wales: over 95 % of these are men, 25 % are from Black, Asian, and minority ethnic communities; 8 % are young adult offenders (between the ages of 18 and 21); and 1.5 % are juveniles[1] (Ministry of Justice [MOJ], 2013a). In 2012, over 86,000 offenders were discharged following a prison sentence[2] (MOJ, 2013a), but latest estimates indicate that approximately half of all offenders released from custody will reoffend within a year[3] (2013b). In 2002, the Social Exclusion Unit's (SEU) report, *Reducing Re-Offending by Ex-Prisoners* (SEU, 2002), concluded that prisons were failing to turn offenders away from crime, with reoffending costing the state at least £11 billion per annum (for recorded crime). The report identified nine factors that influence reoffending, which were then transformed into the seven reducing reoffending pathways formulated by the Reducing Re-Offending National Action Plan (Home Office, 2004), which would guide reentry—or "resettlement"—service provision. These pathways are organized as accommodation; education, employment, and training; health; drugs and alcohol; finance, debt and benefit, children and families; and attitudes, thinking, and behavior. Offender managers were established by the National Offender Management Service to coordinate these pathways and provide "end-to-end" management of offenders for the duration of their sentence, with the aim of managing risk and addressing criminogenic needs to reduce reoffending. Offender managers in England and Wales work with 260,000 offenders every year who are either in one of the

[1] As well as the 989 15- to 17-year-olds held in young offender institutions, there are currently 366 children as young as 10 years of age held in secure children's homes and secure training centers.

[2] This figure excludes discharges following recall after release on license, noncriminals, persons committed to custody for nonpayment of a fine, persons reclassified as adult prisoners, and deported prisoners.

[3] A proven reoffense is defined as any offence committed in a 1-year follow-up period and receiving a court conviction, caution, reprimand, or warning in the 1-year follow-up or a further 6-month waiting period. The data source is the extract of the Police National Computer held by the MOJ.

137 prisons in England and Wales or are serving a community sentence in one of the 35 probation trusts.

However, British resettlement policy and the assumptions behind it have been criticized for a number of reasons. Firstly, resettlement (and a similar concept, reintegration) remains a contested term as it tends to assume that offenders were well settled or integrated in the community before prison, when they were often excluded from society (SEU, 2002), and fails to recognize that the communities in which they were settled or integrated may value criminal activity (Raynor, 2007). Secondly, the pathways approach risks compartmentalizing resettlement practice and commissioning, potentially creating barriers for more holistic services (Hucklesby & Hagley-Dickinson, 2007). Thirdly, resettlement policy has tended to focus on the provision of practical services to offenders to meet their social needs but the links between these and the actual reduction of reoffending is not clear. It is argued that more focus should be given to offenders' mental processes and self-motivation to desist from crime, as any future offending is likely to be influenced by offenders' thinking as well as their circumstances (Maguire & Raynor, 2006).

In order to tackle high rates of recidivism, the Reducing Re-Offending National Action Plan promoted partnership working with third-sector organizations (TSOs) as a means of achieving the best results. This has been supported by a myriad of further strategic documents (MOJ, 2008; MOJ/NOMS, 2008a, 2008b), reflecting the wider government agenda of increasing the involvement of the third sector in service planning and delivery. The role of TSOs in providing a range of services to offenders and their families, both in prisons and the community is historically well established, but their involvement has been placed on a more formal footing in the context of developments that mean they can be commissioned to provide services at a local and regional level. The numerous benefits of TSOs' engagement with this population are well rehearsed in national and international literature (see Dodson, Cabage, & Klenowski, 2011; Meek, Gojkovic, & Mills, 2010), but research examining their efficacy, particularly in comparison to other providers, has been more limited. The evaluation of the resettlement pathfinders, which ran from 1999 to 2005, found that probation-led projects which included a cognitive-motivational program were more likely to produce higher levels of continuity of contact with offenders postrelease from prison and higher levels of positive change in attitudes and beliefs than the voluntary sector-led projects which did not include a cognitive-behavioral element but focused more on welfare needs and facilitating offenders' access to services, and provided volunteer mentors (Lewis, Maguire, Raynor, Vanstone, & Vennard, 2007; Raynor, 2007). In two of the probation-led projects, both of which contained a cognitive-behavioral program, participants had significantly lower reconviction rates. However, prisoners attending voluntary-sector-led schemes who maintained postrelease contact with volunteer mentors had lower reconviction rates than any other group of prisoners analyzed and statistically significant lower rates than prisoners in a comparison group (Clancy et al., 2006). This suggests that ex-prisoners may benefit from contact with volunteers who have the time to be able to provide more personal and emotional support (Lewis et al., 2007).

Little formal data exists in terms of the extent of third-sector involvement in work with offenders in the UK. Previous attempts by the MOJ to measure the number of TSOs working with offenders have produced incomplete and varied data, partly due to the inconsistent ways that criminal justice agencies record TSO involvement. The work of TSOs may be commissioned or authorized by a variety of different actors in a prison or probation service area, and senior management may not be aware of who is working within their establishment/service, particularly in the case of smaller, volunteer-led TSOs. Seeking to measure the number of TSOs working with offenders, therefore, largely depends on three key factors: (a) which part(s) of the sector are measured (registered charities or other TSOs); (b) whether or not organizations consider offenders to be one of their main client groups; and (c) whether or not only the organizations whose primary area of work is the criminal justice system are included. The most comprehensive estimates to date have been generated by Gojkovic, Mills, and Meek (2011) who used two UK datasets, the ission (a nonministerial governmental body charged with the regulation of charities) dataset, and the 2008 National Survey of Third Sector Organizations (NSTSO), commissioned by the then Office of the Third Sector and carried out by Ipsos MORI (2009).

A preliminary search of some 200 TSOs known to work with offenders identified several keywords used to describe their activities: prison, "offen-" (root of words such as offense and offender), inmate, and legal restriction. Grant-awarding bodies and organizations specifically for prisoners of war were excluded from the analysis. Applying these in a keyword search to the aims and objectives, and published material on an organization's work, client/service user/beneficiary groups, and total income led to the identification of 769 organizations from the Charity Commission dataset. A broader analysis of the NSTSO dataset revealed more varied estimates: 18,380 organizations identified offenders, ex-offenders, and their families as one of their client groups, a more modest 4916 identified criminal justice as one of their areas of work, and 1744 indicated that offenders, ex-offenders, and their families represented one of their main client groups.

It is apparent that establishing the number of TSOs working with offenders in England and Wales is a complex and challenging task, leading to different figures depending on what constitutes "working with offenders." Indeed, aside from analyses of existing datasets, very little is known about the levels of offender engagement with the TSOs that purport to work with them. As Maguire and Raynor noted, the resettlement pathways seem to assume that "offenders who are assessed as 'needing' services … are also likely to *want* them, and hence that they largely share the goals of those assisting them: they want to attain a crime-free life" (2006, p. 27, emphasis in original). To this end, the current research aimed to investigate, predominantly through prisoner self-reports, the extent to which a national sample of prisoners were aware of, and reported engaging with, TSOs operating in the prison in which they were being held, alongside the reasons why they had chosen to engage with such organizations.

Method

Procedure

The survey was distributed in eight prisons across England, as a supplement to a wider study involving qualitative semistructured interviews with prison staff, third-sector representatives, and offenders. The eight prisons were chosen to represent the diversity of the prison estate, in terms of the population held, the function of the prison, geographical location, and the prison providers. It is not possible to name the prisons for confidentiality reasons, but Table 7.1 gives details of their function and the category of prisoners they hold, along with the survey response rates for each establishment.

As well as a request for demographic information and brief details of their custodial sentence, participants were presented with a list of TSOs concerned with reentry services that operated in their prison. This list was obtained from the offender management unit, psychology team, or from the resettlement office, and ranged between 15 and 31 organizations across the different establishments. For each organization listed, the respondents were asked to indicate whether or not they had heard of or

Table 7.1 Summary of case study sites and survey response rates

Prison	*Description of prison (Two of these prisons were privately run)*		*Survey response rate*
ID	*Population*	*Type of prison*	*N (% of prisoners in establishment)*
1	Female	Closed	85 (18)
2	Male	Open, training	50 (10)
3	Male	Closed, local	90 (9)
4	Male	Juvenile	19 (4)
5	Female	Open, training	16 (11)
6	Male	Closed	66 (12)
7	Male young adults	Closed	46 (10)
8	Male	Closed, local	308 (25)
			$N = 680$

engaged with it. If they had heard of an organization but not engaged with it, they were offered a choice of six possible explanations for why this was so. The respondents were also asked open-ended questions such as whether there were any services which were not available in the prison but which they considered helpful to them in their resettlement needs. Prisoners in the open prisons and the juvenile establishment—which were likely to have voluntary or work placements for inmates—were asked additional questions relating to those placements, specifically whether or not the offenders engaged in any voluntary or paid work during their sentence and, if so, for which organization.

All participants were informed that the completion of the questionnaire was voluntary and anonymous. The survey was distributed to prisoners through the resettlement, offender management, or education offices, by placing them under the cell doors or including them with weekly menus for prisoners. The completed surveys were then collated either by staff or by dedicated prisoner representatives.

Survey Participants

Approximately 12 % of the questionnaires were returned completed (680 in total), and the response rate ranged from 4 % to 25 % of the total prisoner population in each prison surveyed. Compared to customary return rates for self-completed prisoner surveys (Fazel & Danesh, 2002), this response rate is fairly typical.

The mean age of respondents was 32 years (SD = 10.75), ranging from 15 to 78 years. Reflecting national prison population figures, 85 % of the participants were male, 3 % were juvenile offenders, and an additional 7 % were young people 18 to 21 years old. In terms of the establishment type, 10 % of respondents were held in open prisons and the rest were in closed institutions. Fifty-nine percent were repeat prisoners, 70 % of whom had served a previous sentence in the prison where they were surveyed. A statistically significant difference was found between gender, type of prisoner (first-time or repeat), and type of prison establishment, whereby repeat prisoners were more likely to be men and to be serving in a prison of a higher category of security ($\chi^2 = 17.2$, $p < .01$; $\chi^2 = 95$, $p < .01$).

In terms of ethnicity, 60 % of the respondents identified themselves as White British or Irish, 12 % as Black British, 7 % as Asian British, 6 % as mixed race, and 15 % as White Other or Other. At the time of participating in the research, respondents had been in their respective prisons for an average of 3 months (interquartile range: 6.5). The majority of respondents were sentenced (73 %) with a considerable portion of prisoners on remand (19 %). These figures are fairly similar to the national prison population figures, whereby 15 % of prisoners are on remand and 83 % are sentenced (MOJ, 2012).

Sentenced prisoners were serving an average sentence of 14 months (interquartile range: 21). Female prisoners were found to have sentences that were, on average, almost twice as long (Median = 25 months, interquartile range: 26) as male prisoners' sentences (Median = 13 months, interquartile range: 23), although this is likely to be a result of including only two women's prisons in the sample, one of which was an open prison and the other a closed establishment with a high-security unit. Furthermore, there was a statistically significant difference between sentence length and ethnicity, with people of mixed and Black ethnicity (but not Asian) serving sentences that were on average 25 % longer than people who identified themselves as White ($t = 8.9$, $p < .01$).

Qualitative Interviews

Across the eight prisons, qualitative semistructured interviews (n = 254) were held with offenders (n = 102), criminal justice staff (n = 74), and third-sector-agency representatives (n = 78) to examine the value and effectiveness of third-sector involvement in the reintegration of offenders. The age of interviewed offenders ranged from 16 to 65 years, with a mean age of 36 years (SD = 11.6). There were no age variations between men and women. Over 70 % of offender interviewees declared themselves as White British and additional 8 % as Black British. The rest of the respondents were predominantly foreign nationals from a variety of ethnic backgrounds.

A purposive sampling method was adopted to include offenders who were in contact with TSOs, either as service users or volunteers, and a wide range of criminal justice staff who work with TSOs, for example, resettlement officers, safety custody officers, diversity officers, case managers, and wing correctional officers. TSOs were selected for interview to ensure that a broad mix of organizations was covered, including smaller, local volunteer-led organizations, and larger, national/regional organizations which employed paid staff. Interviews lasted between 20 minutes and an hour and were carried out in person or, in the case of some TSO interviews, over the telephone. Semistructured interviews were used to ensure that key themes such as contact with TSO services, strengths and limitations of TSO work with offenders, and the barriers and challenges to TSO service provision were covered in all interviews, enabling a degree of comparability between responses, but respondents also had the latitude to bring up matters of concern and importance to them (May, 2001). Most interviews were audio-recorded and then transcribed verbatim. Where this was not possible, notes of the interview were written up immediately. Transcripts and interview notes were then analyzed using framework analysis (Ritchie & Spencer, 1994), a form of content analysis where data are coded in a way that reflects the dominant themes emerging from the data.

For the purpose of this chapter, the data categories examining the aims and remit of TSOs, barriers to offender engagement with TSOs and how services users came to be aware of TSO services were interrogated and analyzed for common themes, patterns, and conflicts.

Results

Engagement Between TSOs and Offenders

The number of TSOs that each prison claimed was active in their establishment at the time of data collection ranged from 15 to 31. However, the respondents reported having heard of, on average, just four organizations, and had engaged with an average of only one. The results for each establishment are presented in Table 7.2 and Fig. 7.1. They indicate low overall engagement levels with TSOs, with minor variations between prisons.

Table 7.2 Prisoner self-reported awareness of and engagement with TSOs

Prison ID	*No. of TSOs per prison*	*Median no. and range of TSOs that respondents had engaged with*		*Median no. and range of TSOs that respondents know of*	
		No.	*Range*	*No.*	*Range*
1	22	1	0–21	6	0–22
2	15	1	0–6	8	4–15
3	24	0	0–16	6	0–24
4	15	1	0–4	2	0–9
5	18	1	0–4	4	0–17
6	31	1	0–17	10	0–28
7	31	0.5	0–6	6	0–13
8	20	0	0–13	3	0–18

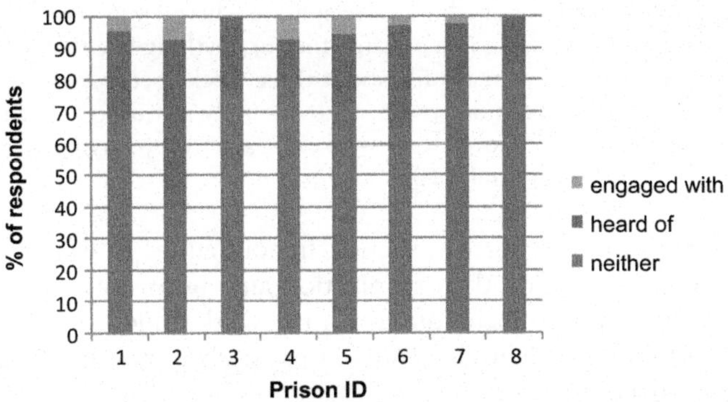

Fig. 7.1 Percentage of respondents in each prison that had heard of/engaged with TSOs

In the qualitative interviews with TSOs, we examined some of the key barriers that TSOs reported in trying to engage with offenders. Many TSOs reported a reduction in funding and staffing, and several confessed that they are no longer able to provide "what it says on the tin" (i.e., what their aims and objectives dictate):

> It's just me now providing the housing advice unfortunately. So people say "Oh [the name of the organization] is here. There is someone providing housing options. That's all right then we can tick that box." And then prisoners wait and wait for weeks to see me and when they do they ask, "Well why did I have to wait so long to see you?" They don't realize it's really just me now. (Participant T405)

Also, a number of organizations reported that working in a prison setting often meant access to very limited resources, which often prevented them from making their services known in the prison as well as from accessing prisoners. As a consequence, several organizations talked about experiencing significant difficulties in trying to establish a continued presence, which would put them on the radar of the prison staff and offenders alike:

> On a site like this, it is actually quite difficult, as we don't have an office with a phone, which is a bit of a nightmare. Which is why I tend to work from home. This means that getting hold of people [that is, offenders] can be quite difficult.... We've had staff, not obstructive, just ... we're not on their radar if you know what I mean. And it's really difficult to get them to see us as a helpful service. (Participant T401)
>
> There are also a few practical difficulties, because I'm based in the visitors center. I still don't have any kind of telephone where I can actually talk to people privately so I'm not in a private office or anything like that. I haven't been able to access my emails for about three weeks because there's been staff training in the computer room, so I've simply not been able to get in there. So I just sit here not able to work, not able to do anything. So why am I here then? (Participant T106)

Several organizations reported experiencing difficulties in trying to engage prison staff in promoting the organization among prisoners. They noted that staff often showed little interest in the work done by TSOs and did not make appropriate referrals or strive to raise awareness of organizations among prisoners:

> We also have barriers of prejudice amongst certain members of the staff. Prejudice is probably too strong, it's just disinterest. A lot of prison staff know about [the name of the program], they're not anti-[the name of the program], but they're not really interested in facilitating it. They just don't really care at all, so it's like, "I am not against you, it's just, I've got too many things to do." (Participant T208)

If the offender respondents had heard of an organization but not worked with it, we asked them why this was so. They were offered a choice of six answers and were asked to select the most appropriate one for each organization.

As shown in Fig. 7.2, the primary reasons that survey respondents reported for not engaging with organizations that they were familiar with

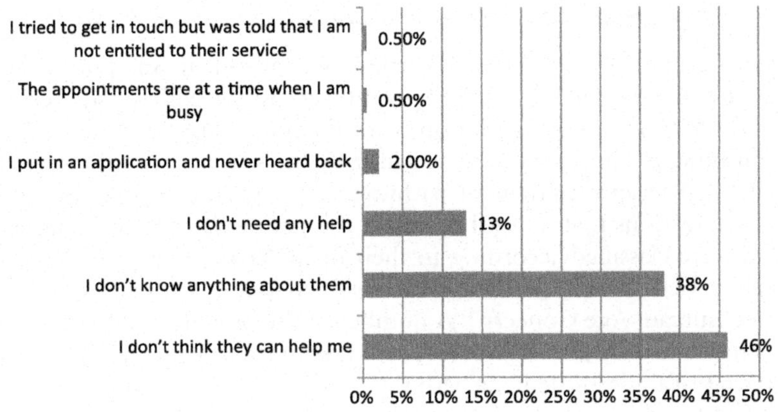

Fig. 7.2 Reported reasons for not engaging with TSOs

were that they did not know anything about the particular organization, or that the organization was not deemed relevant to their needs ("I don't think they can help me"). There were no significant variations in answers between the seven resettlement pathways.

Data from the qualitative interviews with offenders revealed the reasons why they chose to engage with TSOs and the services they provide. The most common reason was that prisoners felt they needed the help that TSOs potentially offer:

> I just needed to ... I got addicted to crack and this is why it's left me in prison. So I just thought I've got to clean up.... It's done me the world of good. (Participant O808)
>
> They are trying to help me with two problems: the housing benefit and the finance, which I cannot pay when I am in prison. (Participant O210)

In a small number of cases, respondents reported engaging with TSOs due to boredom and the hope that it might give them something to do. But engagement with TSOs was also seen to help offenders to form links with organizations outside of prison with the hope of continuing such connections on release, "I thought it would be quite useful to join an organization that I could then link up to on the way out" (Participant O117).

Engagement with TSOs According to Resettlement Pathway

From the information generated from each prison, it was found that a total of 116 different TSOs were operating across the eight prison research sites at the time of data collection, with many working in more than one establishment. The TSOs were classified by the authors according to their remits into seven resettlement pathways. An eighth category was added for organizations that did not fit any of the pathways or for organizations which were classified according to their main activity, but provided additional services which could not be classified (e.g., Samaritans, Citizens Advice Bureau, Age Concern). A number of the organizations included in the study had wide remits which enabled them to provide services in more than one of the resettlement pathways, and these were counted for each pathway to which they were classified (i.e., more than once). Table 7.3 and Fig. 7.3 present the number of organizations in each pathway and the proportion of respondents who were aware of their existence and reported having engaged with each category of TSO.

Table 7.3 Number of TSOs operating in the eight prison research sites, by resettlement pathway

Resettlement Pathway	*No. of TSOs (categories not mutually exclusive)*	*% of prisoners who have heard of one / more organisation in this pathway*	*% of prisoners who engage with one / more organisation in this pathway*
1. Accommodation	37	21	4
2. Education, employment, and training	28	27	8
3. Health	7	19	1
4. Drugs and alcohol	18	28	10
5. Finance, debt, and benefit	8	30	7
6. Children and families	17	30	4
7. Attitudes, thinking, and behavior	21	30	6
8. Other	27	25	5

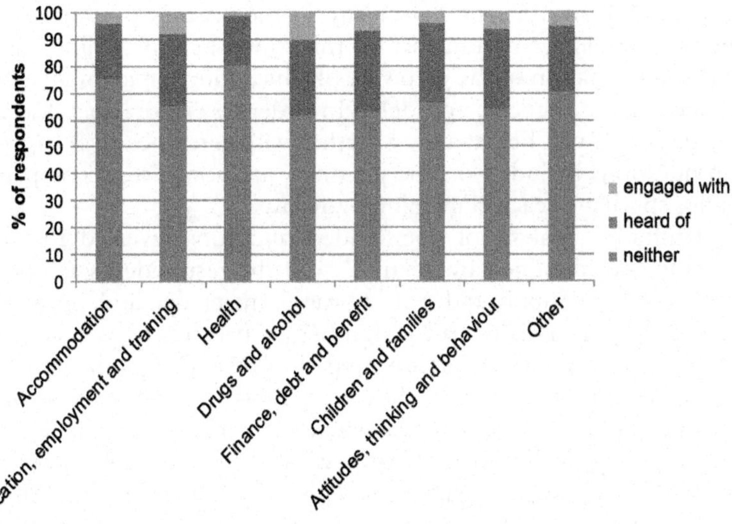

Fig. 7.3 Awareness of and engagement with at least one TSO by pathway

We also investigated the proportion of respondents who claimed to have engaged with organizations across the resettlement pathways, and the extent to which these figures varied between prisons and between pathways. Although the health pathway appears to have virtually no representation in TSOs, this is somewhat balanced out by the Drugs and Alcohol pathway, which has the most consistent representation across the prisons and use by prisoners. This may represent the involvement of a high number of TSOs in providing CARATS (counseling, assessment, referral, advice, and through care services), which exist as part of prison-based drug treatment programs and receive statutory funding. The interviews revealed that in several prisons, it was mandatory for substance misusers to have at least one appointment with CARATS.

It was also discovered that five of the prisons had two or more TSOs that none of the respondents reported having worked with or had heard of. These TSOs were most likely to be operating within the accommodation pathway. Thus, despite the high number of TSOs who claim to work with offenders, a large proportion of the surveyed prisoners had not heard of—or engaged with—the majority of the TSOs that each prison claimed to be operating in their establishment. As previously noted, reductions in staffing and insufficient advertising in the prison as reported in TSO interviews, could account in part for this contradiction. A similar problem was noted in relation to the pathways of education; employment and training; and finance, benefit, and debt. In order to explore this discrepancy, these pathways will be examined further with reference to data from the open questions included on the prisoner questionnaire, accompanied by findings specific to each remaining pathway.

Quantitative analysis of open-ended questions revealed that accommodation was identified by nearly 7 % of the respondents as one of the key areas where supply did not appear to meet demand. It was found that each prison already had a number of organizations that provided housing, yet awareness of accommodation-related organizations among the respondents was low. As shown in Table 7.3, an average of 20 to 25 % of respondents claimed to have heard of accommodation organizations operating in the prison they were held in, one of the lowest levels of awareness among the pathways. This is perhaps somewhat surprising given the target that NOMS has to ensure that 81.3 % of offenders are in settled or suitable accommodation at the end of their sentence (NOMS, 2011). Of the respondents who identified accommodation as one of the key areas for improvement, nearly half of these ($n = 21$) emphasized the need for better links with housing organizations, especially those which cover areas outside large cities. It was noted both in the survey and interviews that housing organizations often had strict eligibility criteria which could hinder access to the services by certain groups of offenders, such as people on short sentences, women offenders with children, people with substance misuse issues, and young people, and often only covered the local area surrounding the prison and were therefore of no use to anyone from outside of that locality:

> I asked them if they could help me with accommodation so when I get out I'll have a roof over my head … they came back two weeks later, "You don't fit the criteria, we're going to make you an appointment on the day of release to go to some housing in [area] and they are going to sort something out from there." (Participant O813)

Female respondents ($\chi^2 = 33$, $p < .01$) and those from non-British Black, Asian, and mixed ethnic backgrounds ($\chi^2 = 41$, $p < .01$) reported significantly less engagement with accommodation TSOs, despite being equally aware of these TSOs as the rest of the prisoners. In addition, young adult and juvenile respondents reported less awareness of, and less involvement, with accommodation TSOs than adult respondents ($\chi^2 = 45, p < .01$). This is in line with previous research (Gojkovic et al., 2011; Maguire & Nolan, 2007), which illustrates an underrepresentation of housing organizations offering housing to some of the most vulnerable subpopulations of prisoners, such as female offenders, young people, and offenders from Black and minority ethnic backgrounds. Indeed, interviews with prison staff provided accounts of the challenges of trying to provide a service to some of these groups:

> The biggest challenge is particularly where people have really very low support needs and they have no fixed abode. They're reasonably young, fit and they have no mental health problems or substance misuse problems and it's really trying to find them accommodation. (Participant S205)

Analysis of open-ended survey questions revealed that 22 % of the survey respondents reported a need for more organizations that specialize in providing employment, training, and voluntary- and paid-work placements for prisoners in the community. To further support this, the analysis of the additional questions for prisoners in the open prisons revealed that only 30 % did any voluntary or paid work during their sentence. Voluntary work placements varied from work in charity shops to the care of the elderly. As for the very few offenders who were employed, they worked in large supermarkets, stocking the shelves or transporting goods. The offenders who were interviewed about their experiences clearly saw these opportunities as an important step toward resettlement into the community:

> Taking part in either voluntary or paid work outside of prison is a way to prepare you for release. When you have been in prison for a long time you can forget what the outside world is like. Especially what it's like to work. (Participant O205)

Sentenced prisoners and prisoners on recall were significantly more likely to be aware of TSOs operating in this pathway than prisoners on remand ($\chi^2 = 26, p < .01$). Similarly, respondents from open prisons, more particularly the female prison, were more likely to engage with these TSOs ($\chi^2 = 53.6, p < .01$) as were respondents on longer sentences (over 12 months), ($\chi^2 = 7, p < .05$) and women respondents ($\chi^2 = 53.6, p < .05$). Although many of the prisons in this study operate in partnership with a number of outside organizations to offer employment and training, survey findings confirm that offenders' engagement with and awareness of these organizations remain low. Indeed, as demonstrated in Table 7.3, an average of only 27 % of respondents had ever heard of an employment and training TSO operating in their establishment.

Further analysis of the survey and qualitative interviews confirmed that offenders emphasized the need for more organizations that specialized in debt and benefits advice, particularly those in closed establishments who were significantly less likely to engage with these organizations than respondents from open establishments ($\chi^2 = 9.3, p < .01$). In some prisons this issue had been tackled by employing a dedicated finance and benefits manager/officer, and in others by contracting the services of cooperative banks, credit unions, and/or financial groups to meet the needs of prisoners. Since financial matters are often linked to housing, it was not uncommon to have the same representative for both finances and housing, regardless of whether they were a member of prison staff, or an employee of a private or third-sector organization. It was found that the financial concerns of short-sentence prisoners ($\chi^2 = 7.3, p < .05$) and nonsentenced prisoners ($\chi^2 = 2\ 6.9, p < .01$) were more often reported as being unmet compared to other groups of prisoners, but it could be argued that this is to an expected result of them spending shorter periods of time in custody.

In terms of drugs and alcohol, nonsentenced respondents had greater awareness of and contact with TSOs operating in this pathway than sentenced prisoners ($\chi^2 = 23.4, p < .05$). Furthermore, respondents from closed prisons ($\chi^2 = 24, p < .01$), and male prisoners ($\chi^2 = 6.8, p < .05$) were more likely to be users of these organizations than other respondents. With regards to children and families, it was found that sentenced prisoners ($\chi^2 = 22.5, p < .01$) and those serving sentences in closed establishments ($\chi^2 = 13, p < .01$) were more likely to work with TSOs in this pathway, as were women ($\chi^2 = 9, p < .01$) and foreign nationals ($\chi^2 = 47, p < .01$).

There were no statistically significant differences in awareness of, and access to, health services. This is likely to be due to a very low number of health-related TSOs operating in the eight prisons and low levels of engagement generally. Lastly, it was found that women had more awareness of and engagement with TSOs operating in the attitudes, behaviors, and interventions pathway ($\chi^2 = 6.9, p < .05$).

Due to the low reported awareness of TSOs among offenders and the low proportion of prisoners who report engaging with TSOs, it is worth considering the routes by which offenders come to hear about

TSOs and their services. In the qualitative interviews, offenders reported hearing about TSOs from a range of different sources, including publicity, families and friends outside prison, and other TSOs. In some cases, prisoners had experienced contact with the TSOs before prison and foreign national offenders at one of the women's prisons were given automatic appointments with a support TSOs. The two most common sources of information, however, were prison staff and other prisoners:

> The first morning I was here somebody comes to you and asks you if you have any debt problems or if you are on benefits [welfare]. So I just got told about it through staff. (Participant 0311)
>
> A friend was excitedly discussing what he'd done that morning and I overheard him so I jumped in and found out about this. (Participant O809)

Some respondents recounted having been informed about various services during an induction to the prison, usually held the day after they had arrived. However, due to the shock experienced by some in the early stages of their incarceration, this was perhaps not always the most constructive timing:

> When I first came in I was told about different organizations and things like that but to be perfectly honest, it just went straight over the top of my head. I've never been in prison before. I was totally terrified. I think 99 percent of what I got told, I possibly forgot anyway (Participant O308).

In two of the prisons "resettlement fairs" were held periodically, where all the TSOs who offered reintegration services were invited to come into the prison and set up a stand where offenders could come and talk to them. This was seen as a more productive approach and was highly valued. However, it was also recognized that they needed to be held more often to ensure that short-sentence prisoners could make productive use of such opportunities.

Discussion

This chapter contributes a new perspective on the role and profile of TSOs involved in the seven resettlement pathways for offenders, and the general overrepresentation of TSOs working with offenders in the seven areas compared to the national figures serves to mirror the level of need in this population and the focus of reentry/resettlement policy to provide services to meet offenders' criminogenic needs. However, the findings presented in this chapter indicate that despite the recent emphasis on working in partnership with TSOs in providing prisoner resettlement services, and a large number of TSOs claiming to work with offenders, levels of awareness of resettlement-focused TSOs in prisons remains low. The average number of TSOs per prison was approximately 20, yet our findings showed that on average, respondents were aware of only four TSOs operating in their prison and engaged with no more than one. When juxtaposed against the findings from existing datasets, that revealed that nearly 20,000 TSOs claim to work with offenders, these findings provide a clearer picture of the actual levels of involvement of TSOs in work with offenders during their time in custody. Indeed, a number of TSOs had no or very few users among our respondents, despite the prisons reporting a working relationship with them.

The findings from the survey and the interviews suggest that there is an established need for access to services provided within the seven resettlement pathways, but that they are often underpublicized or difficult to access. On average, no more than 25 % of the prisoners surveyed reported awareness of at least one TSOs per resettlement pathway. Prisoner awareness may be moderated by poor literacy, which is likely to limit the effectiveness of TSO publicity materials, but also a lack of staff knowledge, particularly among those working on prison wings, which are likely to have the most contact with prisoners. Other research in this area has also shown mixed levels of support for TSOs among prison staff and management which may make it difficult for them to publicize their work and may also affect staff willingness to refer prisoners to third-sector services (Lewis et al., 2007; Mills, Meek, & Gojkovic, 2011, 2012). It might, therefore, be useful to improve prison staff awareness to promote these services more widely in the prison and to improve communication between offenders and TSOs. This should fall within the remit of a third-sector coordinator (or "VCS coordinator," as they are referred to in policy), as stipulated by Prison Service Order 4190 (HM Prison Service, 2002). However, this order has not yet been implemented in a standardized manner across the prison estate: many prisons still lack a third-sector coordinator (Clinks, 2010) and others have coordinators who also fulfill other duties in prison, which may lead to role conflict, marginalization of third-sector work when they are needed elsewhere, ambiguity in the extent of their authority, and unclear links with senior staff and managers. The implementation and operation of this role should be reviewed on a national level, especially in terms of its potentially valuable strategic position in building cross-sector alliances. This could be a significant milestone in ensuring greater awareness of and access to TSOs for prisoners.

The findings revealed low levels of engagement with services provided by TSOs, with on average only 5 % of prisoners engaging with at least one TSO. This may be explained not only by the lack of awareness of third-sector services highlighted in this chapter, but also by the high levels of need within the prison population and the consequent high demand for some services, particularly in the fields of accommodation; education, employment and training; and finance, debt, and benefit (see SEU, 2002). In the evaluation of the resettlement pathfinders, Lewis et al. (2007) found that long waiting lists and the limited time spent in custody could affect access to prison-based services. TSOs are likely to have only limited resources to meet such demand, and thus the proportion of prisoners that they are able to help will remain low, a situation that is likely to be exacerbated by expected budget cuts (Clinks, 2011). Indeed, a recent report by Clinks (2012) indicated that 95 % of organizations have experienced, or expect to experience, a reduction in income and 77 % are using their reserves. Furthermore, an important issue that needs to be recognized when interpreting the results is that there are differences in how TSOs approach engagement with prisoners. Some TSOs will only offer services to those who fit their selection criteria, for example, if they reside in a particular area. These criteria are often stipulated as conditions of the grant/contract funding. For these TSOs, lack of awareness among general prisoner population may be less of an issue than for an organization that aims to provide services to a broader offender population. The findings also identified significant differences in access to organizations, with particular groups being less likely to access certain pathways than others (such as accommodation), particularly BAME and foreign nationals, short-sentenced prisoners, nonsentenced prisoners, women, and young people.

However, the limitations of the prisoner survey and the low response rate should be considered when interpreting these findings. Reasons for low response rates for self-completed prisoner surveys include low literacy levels in prisons (50 % of prisoners have reading skills, and 80 % have writing skills, at or below the level expected of an 11-year-old; SEU, 2002), a degree of apprehension among the prisoners about persons who request information from them, and a lack of motivation to complete surveys if there is no perceived immediate benefit to participating. In terms of the implications of the potential nonresponse bias, it is possible that those who did not answer the survey may have had acute needs which prevented them from completing it, for instance in literacy, and it may be that these people are particularly targeted by TSOs. Thus, there may be a nonresponse bias toward underestimating the extent of awareness/engagement with TSOs. Alternatively, nonresponse bias may be overestimated if those who did respond to the survey are generally more "engaging" than other prisoners and are therefore more likely to engage with or be aware of TSOs.

Despite these limitations, the prisoner survey proved to be a valuable tool in gaining a wider picture of the involvement of TSOs with offenders and in supplementing the qualitative interviews. The measures were designed so as to include predominantly multiple-choice questions where the chosen response was ticked or where a number was entered, thus reducing the need and time for writing to a minimum. It remains possible (but unlikely) that nonrespondents contained a higher proportion of service users than the survey sample. Indeed, reasons for nonengagement with third-sector services remains an important area for future research that should be prioritized in order to complement the quantitative and qualitative data presented here.

References

Alcock, P., & Kendall, J. (2010). *Constituting the third sector: Processes of decontestation and contention under the UK Labour governments in England* (WP 42, TSRC). Retrieved from http://www.tsrc.ac.uk/LinkClick.aspx?fileticket=H8ue2VjymLw%3d&tabid=500.

Buckingham, H. (2009). Competition and contracts in the voluntary sector: Exploring the implications for homelessness service providers in Southampton. *Policy and Politics, 37*, 235–254.

Clancy, A., Hudson, K., Maguire, M., Peake, R., Raynor, P., Vanstone, M., et al. (2006). *Getting out and staying out: Results of the prisoner resettlement pathfinders.* Bristol, England: Policy Press.

Clinks. (2010). *Clinks' response to the Government's proposals for a 'rehabilitation revolution'.* London: Author.

Clinks. (2011). *Changing times—Challenging times.* London: Author.

Clinks. (2012). *When the dust settles: An update.* London: Author.

Dodson, K., Cabage, L., & Klenowski, P. (2011). An evidence-based assessment of faith-based programs: Do faith-based programs "work" to reduce recidivism? *Journal of Offender Rehabilitation, 50*, 367–383.

Fazel, S. & Danesh, J. (2002). Serious mental disorder in 23,000 prisoners: A systematic review of 62 surveys. *The Lancet, 359*, 545–550.

Gojkovic, D., Mills, A., & Meek, R. (2011). *Scoping the involvement of third sector organisations in the seven resettlement pathways for offenders* (WP57, TSRC). Retrieved from http://www.tsrc.ac.uk/LinkClick.aspx?fileticket=JnJy2cVtyx0 percent3d &tabid=500.

Halfpenny, P. & Reid, M. (2002). Research on the voluntary sector: An overview. *Policy and Politics*, *30*, 533–550.

HM Prison Service. (2002). *Strategy for working with the voluntary and community sector* (Prison Service Order 4190). London: Home Office.

Home Office. (2004). *The reducing re-offending national action plan*. London: Author.

Hucklesby, A. & Hagley-Dickinson, L. (2007). Conclusion: Opportunities, barriers and threats. In A. Hucklesby & L. Hagley-Dickinson (Eds.), *Prisoner resettlement: Policy and practice* (pp. 174–196). Cullompton, England: Willan.

Ipsos MORI. (2009). *National survey of third sector organisations: Technical report, national survey of third sector organisations, 2008–2009* (UK Data Archive Study No. 6381). London: UK Cabinet Office.

Lewis, S., Maguire, M., Raynor, P., Vanstone, M., & Vennard, J. (2007). What works in resettlement? *Criminology & Criminal Justice*, *7*, 33–53.

Maguire, M. & Nolan, J. (2007). Accommodation and related services for ex-prisoners. In A. Hucklesby & L. Hagley-Dickinson (Eds.), *Prisoner resettlement: Policy and practice* (pp. 144–173). Cullompton, England: Willan.

Maguire, M. & Raynor, P. (2006). How the resettlement of prisoners promotes desistance from crime: Or does it? *Criminology & Criminal Justice*, *6*, 19–38.

May, T. (2001). *Social research: Issues, methods and process*. Buckingham, England: Open University Press.

Meek, R., Gojkovic, D., & Mills, A. (2010). *The role of the third sector in work with offenders: The perceptions of criminal justice and third sector stakeholders* (WP 34, TSRC). Retrieved from http://www.tsrc.ac.uk/LinkClick.aspx?fileticket=jpl0 uVVN90w%3d&tabid=500.

Mills, A., Meek, R., & Gojkovic, D. (2011). Exploring the relationship between the voluntary sector and the state in criminal justice. *Voluntary Sector Review*, *2*, 193–211.

Mills, A., Meek, R., & Gojkovic, D. (2012). Partners, guests or competitors: Relationships between criminal justice and third sector staff in prisons. *Probation Journal*, *54*, 391–405.

Ministry of Justice. (2008). *Third sector strategy: Improving policies and securing better public services through effective partnerships 2008–2011*. London: Ministry of Justice.

Ministry of Justice. (2012). *Offender management statistics: Quarterly bulletin January to March 2012, England and Wales*. London: Ministry of Justice.

Ministry of Justice. (2013a). *Proven re-offending statistics: Quarterly bulletin April 2010 to March 2011, England and Wales*. London: Ministry of Justice.

Ministry of Justice. (2013b). *Offender management statistics: Quarterly bulletin July to September 2012, England and Wales*. London: Ministry of Justice.

Ministry of Justice/NOMS. (2008a). *Working with the third sector to reduce re-offending: Securing effective partnerships 2008–2011*. London: Ministry of Justice.

Ministry of Justice/NOMS. (2008b). *NOMS third sector action plan: Securing effective partnerships to reduce re-offending and protect the public 2008–2011*. London: Ministry of Justice.

National Offender Management Service. (2011). *Annual report and accounts 2010–11*. London: Ministry of Justice.

Raynor, P. (2007). Theoretical perspectives on resettlement: What it is and how it might work. In A. Hucklesby & L. Hagley-Dickinson (Eds.), *Prisoner resettlement: Policy and practice* (pp. 26–42). Cullompton, England: Willan.

Ritchie, J. & Spencer, L. (1994). Qualitative data analysis for applied policy research. In A. Bryman & R. G. Burgess (Eds.), *Analysing qualitative data* (pp. 173–194). London: Routledge.

Social Exclusion Unit. (2002). *Reducing re-offending by ex-prisoners*. London: HMG Cabinet Office.

CHAPTER 8

Carceral Devolution and the Transformation of Urban America

Reuben Jonathan Miller and Gwendolyn Purifoye

Introduction

The expansion of the US prison population has been accompanied by a precipitous, equally historic, yet underexamined rise in the number of formerly incarcerated people living in the nation's most disadvantaged urban neighborhoods. By now, the statistics are familiar. On any given day, 2.2 million inmates are held in the nation's jails and prisons; yet 5 million formerly incarcerated people are managed through some form of community supervision, typically probation or parole services. The 600,000 adult inmates released from prison each year join thousands more processed through one of 1400 specialty courts, and nearly 12 million of their countrymen and women cycle between a police station holding facility or a local county jail and their disadvantaged home community (Minton & Golinelli, 2014; Peck & Theodore, 2008; Sampson & Loeffler, 2010; Wacquant, 2010). Even these figures are dwarfed by the 19.8 million people estimated to have a felony conviction and the 65 million Americans—a full third of the nation's adult population—who have a criminal record, constraining their participation in social, civic, and political life (Heck,

R.J. Miller, PhD (✉)
University of Michigan, Ann Arbor, MI, USA

G. Purifoye, PhD
Kent State University-Stark, North Canton, OH, USA

L.S. Abrams et al. (eds.), *The Voluntary Sector in Prisons*, Palgrave Studies in Prisons and Penology, DOI 10.1057/978-1-137-54215-1_8

2014; Uggen & Manza, 2006). Despite the prison receiving the lion's share of scholarly attention over the last two decades, the vast majority of those managed by the criminal justice system will never see the inside of a prison cell (Kohler-Hausmann, 2013). Given the disproportionate concentration of criminal justice efforts, actors and agencies within poor urban spaces (Miller, 2014), and vast disparities in criminal justice processing by race, class, and geography (Miller, 2013; Wacquant, 2010), we argue in this chapter that this new social arrangement has altered the urban landscape and transformed urban poverty in America.

The consequences of mass imprisonment are well documented. Criminologists have consistently shown that prisoners and former prisoners comprise a vulnerable group by almost any measure of population health (Drucker, 2006; Dumont, Brockmann, Dickman, Alexander, & Rich, 2012). Prisoners are overwhelmingly poor (Wacquant, 2009). Half are estimated to have a diagnosable mental-health issue (James & Glaze, 2006), and a recent study found that former prisoners are 147 times more likely to die of a drug overdose and 11 times more likely to die of any other cause within just 2 weeks of their release than members of the general population (Dumont et al., 2012). Moreover sociologist and demographer Evelyn Patterson (2013) found that for every year an inmate spends in prison, they lose up to 2 years of life expectancy. Further complicating matters, in the USA, former prisoners are largely released into notoriously disadvantaged urban spaces (Peck & Theodore, 2008; Sampson & Loeffler, 2010).

For example, Paul Street's (2001) examination of mass incarceration's impact on poor Black neighborhoods in Chicago revealed that neighborhoods where the highest concentration of prisoners were arrested were nearly identical to the neighborhoods where the prisoners were annually returned. The neighborhood effects literature has drawn similar conclusions (Sampson & Loeffler, 2010; Travis, Western, & Radburn, 2014). While these findings seem intuitive, former prisoners are a highly transient population who struggle to make ends meet, moving residences multiple times in a given year (Harding, Wyse, Dobson, & Morenoff, 2014). Put differently, prisoners are not necessarily returned to their home communities after their release, but to spaces *like* their home. These spaces, which service providers often describe as receiving communities, are among the few spaces willing to welcome former prisoners upon their release (Peck & Theodore, 2008). Thus, it is unsurprising that Street (2003) found that in some inner-city neighborhoods, no fewer than 70 % of the men have a felony conviction. In Illinois, where half of all prisoners return to the city of Chicago, a full one-third of all released inmates return to 6 out of 77 Chicago community areas (La Vigne, Mamalian, Travis, & Visher, 2003). Mirroring national trends, these neighborhoods have poverty, crime, and unemployment rates that triple the national average, with Black people representing no less than 90 % of their respective demographic, save one, which is 90 % Black *and* Latina/o (Miller, 2014). As human service agencies are tasked with meeting prisoners' complex and varied needs, prisoner reentry organizations are overwhelmingly concentrated within the inner city. While some may argue that this social arrangement is meeting a community need—that reentry programs are located in spaces where they are most needed—the place of reentry and the targets of reentry interventions raise important questions regarding voluntary sector involvement in the lives of the urban poor.

Given the sheer number of adults cycling between some form of confinement and the disadvantaged spaces where they reside, disparities in their health, socioeconomic, and criminal justice outcomes, and the costs associated with incarceration, prisoner reentry has become a normative social arrangement in the life-worlds of the poor. It has also become a veritable social institution, shaping former prisoners' behaviors, interactions, and understandings of themselves and others (Miller, 2014). With the reliance of the USA on its nonprofit and volunteer sector to manage social problems, we argue that the prisoner reentry organization is a salient, yet clearly underexamined urban organization.

This chapter examines the work of prisoner reentry programs, meaning the nonprofit and volunteer sector organizations operating within the inner city and tasked with addressing former prisoners' complex and varied needs, all the while supervising, monitoring, and managing them in the community. Travis, Solomon, and Waul (2001) describe prisoner reentry as an event that almost all prisoners undergo. Building upon and expanding this definition, Petersilia (2003) discusses the important role of organizations to address former prisoners' outcomes. These definitions of reentry are intentionally apolitical. Since roughly 90 % of all prisoners will eventually be released (Petersilia, 2003), community-based prisoner reentry programs play an important role in helping former prisoners navigate the barriers they face during reentry. Aligning reentry interventions with one political project or another would likely derail efforts to address returning prisoners' vast and complex needs. This body of scholarship highlights the important aftereffects of imprisonment, offering scholars and members of the concerned public a window into the world of returning prisoners. Moreover, better understanding the consequences of imprisonment and the efficacy of reentry organizations is important if we hope to alleviate the suffering of returning prisoners as they attempt to build prosocial bonds within their neighborhoods, desist from crime, and engage in the social, political, and civic life of their respective communities (Maruna, 2001; McNeill, 2006).

However, service provision of any kind is far from apolitical. Policymakers and reentry program planners view prisoners in particular ways—most often as a risk to public safety that must be managed upon their release (Miller, 2013). Their needs are envisioned accordingly, and the intervention strategies they design follow the ways in which these constructions occur (c.f. Schneider & Ingram, 1993). Therefore, to grasp the broader implications of reentry's emergence and proliferation, we must move beyond technical questions about whether or not reentry programs work and think carefully and critically about the role, force, and consequence of reentry policies and practices in the spaces that they target. Moving beyond a standard viewpoint, which often presents reentry as an apolitical process or an event in the lives of prisoners, we theoretically examine the broader implications of reentry's ascendance as the rehabilitative strategy of choice in the current age (Miller, 2014; Western, 2008). Prisoner reentry programs seek to address the cycle of incarceration, release, and rearrest through the provision of social services, targeting former prisoners' decision-making processes, identified needs, criminal-thinking patterns, and presumed antisocial behaviors (see Chap. 9, this volume; Chap. 10, this volume; Latessa & Lowenkamp, 2005; Petersilia, 2003; Visher & Travis, 2003). Reentry programs do not address the largely structural barriers that former prisoners face upon their release—there are simply not enough programs to meet the myriad and complicated needs of the millions of former prisoners living in community in the USA. Their strategy of human capital investment is instead designed to build skills and transform lives (See Chap. 9, this volume; Miller, 2014) rather than to remove barriers associated with having a criminal record, or to make significant enough changes in the labor or housing market to ensure former prisoners' full participation.

In the prevailing reentry program model, program planners and policymakers seek to enhance the skill sets of former prisoners, making them more employable in the modern economy (Miller, 2014). Following broader trends in US social welfare policy, the rehabilitative efforts of the state have been outsourced and privatized, moving from within prison walls into urban community-based organizations where prisoners are overwhelmingly arrested and released each year (Miller, 2014). A national study of former prisoners' access to prison-based and community services conducted by Faye Taxman and her colleagues shows that no more than 10 % of all former prisoners released on community supervision had access to treatment on any given day (Taxman, Perdoni, & Harrison, 2007). Since there are simply not enough reentry services to meet the needs of the vast and growing population of former prisoners, their family and community members become the resource of first and last resort. We argue that prisoner reentry is therefore a part of a larger process of responsibilization employed to broker a qualitative change in the lives of the urban poor, in effect offloading the responsibility of the state to ensure the social, civic, and political participation of its residents onto nonprofit organizations, community-based volunteers, prisoners' families, and ultimately, former prisoners themselves (Miller, 2014). This represents a break from older forms of prisoner rehabilitation, which used employment as the central lever of transformation and tasked prison officials and the community at large with the responsibility to ensure released prisoners' integration into society. We name this trend a process of "Carceral Devolution" where the responsibility and authority to rehabilitate (and to reintegrate) prisoners shifts from the state through prison-based rehabilitative programs and services to the very low-income communities from which prisoners are arrested and returned (see Chap. 9, this volume, and Miller, 2013, 2014 for more information about how these historical trends have unfolded). At the same time, the focus of reentry interventions is on the employability of the ex-offender, rather than the employment of the ex-convict. Thus, we theorize that the emergence and ascendance of prisoner reentry represents a broad shift in criminal justice policy and the operation of the state, taking place on geographic and conceptual levels. Geographically, rehabilitation has been outsourced and privatized, moving from within prisons and into third-sector community-based organizations (Miller, 2014). Private actors operating within poor urban neighborhoods now provide most services designed to aid former prisoners in their successful community reintegration. At the same time, the goals of this rehabilitative project have changed from the employment of the ex-convict to enhancing former prisoner employability, which should, in effect, make them more employable (Miller, 2013, 2014).

Despite reentry's ascendance as the rehabilitative strategy of choice, few studies have attended to the broader implications of its proliferation (for exceptions see Abrams & Lea, in press; Haney, 2010; Kaufman, 2014; McKim 2008; Miller, 2014). In this chapter, we argue that the rise of prisoner reentry represents one way the state has been reconfigured to manage poor populations and, borrowing from early prison reformers, show how reentry's ascendance represents one way that the power to punish has been more deeply embedded within the social body (Foucault, 1977).

Punishment, Sovereign Power, and the Rise of Rehabilitation

Prisoner rehabilitation was born out of calls from enlightenment-era prison reformers for restraint on the part of the sovereign, moving away from a retributionist framework that took crime out on the body of the accused to an efficient system of swift and sure, if moderately severe, punishment (Beccaria, 1995 [1764]; Foucault, 1977). In his famous booklet, *On Crimes and Punishment*, Cesare Beccaria, the Italian enlightenment philosopher and member of the Accademia dei pugni (the *Academy of Fisticuffs*) extended social contract theory, echoing Hobbes's assertion that the state of nature was a state of war, but infused utilitarianism within it (Harcourt, 2013). For Beccarria, the subjects of the nation were in need of a sovereign to use their power to punish to ensure the greatest degree of happiness for the largest number of people. Following Hobbes, subjects exchange their freedom to act in ways that they see fit, for example, to exact revenge on other subjects for causing them harm, for a contractual relationship with the sovereign who will use the power to punish to maintain the tranquility of the populous. On this note, legal scholar and political theorist Bernard Harcourt (2013) wrote, "It is punishment that keeps individuals from trying to seize back that small part of freedom that they relinquished.... But having bequeathed only the smallest portion of their freedom necessary to ensure their security, there is an inherent limitation to the extent, mode, and scope of punishment" (p. 6).

The right to punish, and by extension the role of the sovereign, was constituted through the "smallest possible portions," for in Beccaria's words, "everything more than that is no longer justice, but an abuse; it is a matter of fact not of right" (as cited in Harcourt, 2013, p. 7). That is, the sovereign is both staged (made present to its subjects) and legitimated through the use of punishment. However, the sovereign's power to punish must be limited to the smallest exertion of power necessary to ensure the "greatest happiness of the greatest number" (Harcourt, 2013, p. 5) which for Beccaria and the early prison reformers meant to deter the public from crime (general deterrence) and deter criminally minded individuals from crime (specific deterrence) to ensure the common good.

This treatise influenced utilitarian thought, prison-reform efforts, and political philosophy for the next 200 years, though it would fall in and out of favor (Harcourt, 2013). Jeremy Bentham (2012) would laud the precision that Beccaria called for in the punishment of offenders and the utilitarian premise he put forward in *On Crimes and Punishment* (1995 [1764]). Like Beccaria, Bentham (2012) wrote that the purpose of punishment was to deter the future crime of an offender and that excessive punishment was not simply unjust on humanitarian terms, but that it had limited to no deterrent effects. Put differently, these early utilitarian philosophers argued that punishment should be rigorous, it should be proportionate, it should be methodical and efficient, but above all, it should work. That is, punishment should operate on a kind of moral arithmetic where the state issued swift and sure punishments proportionate to the amount of harm the offender caused to the social body to deter crime and reform the offender.

Building on but departing from contractarian social thought, which called for the sovereign to act in ways that subdued the state of nature (which Hobbes described as a veritable state of war), Beccaria (1995 [1764]) sought to limit sovereign power to the realm of punishment. For punishment to be just, Beccaria argued, it must be based on a scientific calculus, rather than the passions of the sovereign. It must be equally applied, rather than applied differentially based on the preferences of the sovereign. It must produce a deterrent effect within the prisoner (specific deterrence) *and* the body politic (generalized deterrence), rather than act as retribution for an offense against the sovereign. This was one of the first and most influential arguments for deterrence as the primary function of punishment, opening the door for the rehabilitative ideals of nineteenth-century prison reformers and the use of the prison to accomplish those goals. Using *On Crimes and Punishment* (1995 [1764]) as a touchstone for the birth of disciplines, the prison, and eventually a vast carceral network, Foucault wrote that Beccaria advanced a "new strategy for the exercise of the power to punish… to make of the punishment and repression of illegalities a regular function, coextensive with society; not to punish less, but to punish better; to punish with an attenuated severity perhaps, but in order to punish with more universality and necessity; to insert the power to punish more deeply into the social body" (Foucault, 1977, pp. 81–82). Prisoner rehabilitation was central to this project.

From the Prison Yard to the Church Basement: Taking Rehabilitation to the Street

By the birth of the modern prison in the late eighteenth century, prison administrators and reformers viewed labor as the primary lever of moral reform. Employment was even a formal condition of parole in many US states prior to the punitive turn in criminal justice policy (Foucault, 1977; Simon, 1993). During the greater part of the nineteenth and twentieth centuries, probation officers spent the largest part of their days brokering employment relationships for prisoners, working with early prisoner-serving community-based organizations, known as prisoner-aid societies, to ensure former prisoners' successful reintegration into their communities and families upon release (National Prison Association, 1870). For example, speaking to the responsibility of the state in meeting the needs of prisoners upon their release, the declaration of principles states:

> More systematic and comprehensive methods should be adopted to save discharged prisoners, by *providing them with work* and *encouraging them to redeem their character* and *regain their lost position in society.* The state has not discharged its whole duty to the criminal when it has punished him, nor even when it has reformed him. Having raised him up, it has the further duty to aid in holding him up. And to this end it is desirable that state societies be formed, which shall co-operate with each other in this work. (National Prison Association, 1870, p. 3)

Here we see the roots of carceral devolution in not only the emphasis on rehabilitation as a guiding principle of imprisonment, but in the responsibilization of community-based actors and organizations in that process. Despite the prominent role these organizations played in the modern reentry landscape, it was the tough–on-crime movement that facilitated the full-throated expansion of community corrections and the decline of rehabilitative services offered inside prisons, effectively offloading the responsibility of the state to rehabilitate prisoners onto private, local, community-based actors and organizations. The story of how rehabilitation moved from within the prisons and into the community is a fairly complicated one. Trends in social welfare and criminal justice policy converged with a series of sociopolitical, cultural, and demographic shifts ushered in the rise of prisoner reentry as the rehabilitative strategy of choice (Miller, 2013).

Many popular accounts documenting the decline of prison-based rehabilitation begin with the publication of Robert Martinson's (1974) now famous essay "What works" in the 1974 edition of the *Public Interest.* Others have suggested that harsh penal policies were the result of racial backlash from Black Americans' progress during the civil rights era (Alexander, 2012). We concur that racial backlash in part explains the advent of harsh crime-control policies. However, some of the other forces that prompted this shift included the decline in demand for unskilled laborers, a real crime wave in the 1970s, and a largely unpredicted demographic shift in the US prison population.

From the 1970s to the 1990s, the prison census shifted from two-thirds White to nearly two-third non-White racial and ethnic minorities in just under two decades (Wacquant, 2001). In addition, US social welfare policy and scholarship on the urban poor was undergoing a series of dramatic changes during this period. The hard-fought expansion of welfare benefits to Black American families during the civil rights movement brought renewed attention to the social conditions of urban poverty, launching an industry of scholarship on the lives and living conditions of the urban poor (Kelly, 1997). This work examined the social forms and patterns of interactions of the Black poor, attempting to reveal the relationship between long-standing practices of residential segregation and labor market exclusion on the cultural expressions of marginalized groups (Harrington, 1997; Lewis, 1971; Moynihan, 1965; Stack, 1975). Despite their intentions, misreading of these works prompted reform-minded policymakers and public intellectuals to target the values and meaning-making strategies of the urban poor in an effort to shift their cultural practices toward what was referred to as the mainstream (i.e., White and middle class) (Kelly, 1997). This was at least in part due to the thick descriptions of the adaptive strategies that Black and Latino families used to survive and care for their children (Stack, 1975; Oscar, 1966; Moynihan, 1965).

Despite their best intentions, the very new deal-style government interventions that addressed the labor market, housing, and medical care for the poor that many of these authors called for eventually fell out of favor (Miller, 2013). Policymakers and program planners instead designed treatments targeting the presumed social pathologies of the Black poor. The goals of these interventions were to address Black dependence, rather than the poverty of Black Americans, Black deviance rather than policing practices in racially segregated neighborhoods, and Black Americans' work ethic, rather than their exclusion from the labor market, housing, and education. Put differently, the culture wars of the 1960s, which continued throughout the next two decades shifted the target of government intervention from the structures in which the Black poor languished to the individual pathologies of the Black poor (Miller et al., 2015).

At the same time, criminologists argued that efforts to control crime through rehabilitative programming inside prisoners were ineffective at best (Martinson, 1974; Wilson, 1975). Examined with assertions that access to welfare contributed to generational poverty (Murray, 1984), we see that the decline of rehabilitative services and the retrenchment of the welfare state that accompanied it was not simply a reaction to out-of-control spending on social welfare services or prisoner rehabilitation, but an attack on state intervention and the extension of benefits of any kind to the criminalized poor more broadly. Subsequently policymakers designed social welfare *and* crime-control policies in ways to contain crime and discourage dependence, rather than to address the root causes or systemic consequences of poverty or to reintegrate prisoners into the mainstream labor market (Miller, 2013, 2014).

A new actuarial strategy emerged to manage risky populations that could not be reformed, unseating the rehabilitative program that once sought to control and transform prisoners through labor and moral suasion (Feeley & Simon, 1992; Simon, 1993). By 1987, federal law codified this move by removing the rehabilitative potential of the prisoner from federal sentencing guidelines. Following this policy, rehabilitative services offered inside prisons were cut precipitously. Given prisoners' precarity, probation and parole offices, welfare state institutions, and most prescient for this analysis, a vast array of human service organizations located outside prison walls were then made responsible for managing prisoners, supervising them in the community, and meeting their service needs. This shift not only represented a vast structural change and a fundamental transformation in how the state managed released prisoners, but the wholesale embrace of a service model to address social problems associated with carceral expansion, extending the reach of the state further into communities through contractual relationships with third-sector organizations. With community groups now assuming this responsibility with the expansion of probation, parole, and nonprofit community-based services, the power to punish thus shifted from the state onto nonprofit actors and volunteer groups. Therefore, in the course of just a few years, the stakeholders responsible for the reintegration of prisoners changed from prison staff, prison officials, and actors working within formal arms of the state through welfare services, probation, and parole offices, to private, nonprofit actors operating within the human service agencies operating within the inner city.

From Employment to Employability

While the prison system has historically managed poor populations, the brokering of labor arrangements was central to the rehabilitative program. Today, although labor remains central to the *logics* that animate the practice of rehabilitation, shifts in the culture of punishment and changes in the political economy have prompted an important but underanalyzed development—the unseating of employment as the lynchpin of rehabilitative services and the advent of ***employability training*** as the rehabilitative strategy of choice. This shift is emblematic of a larger change in US social policy. Policymakers have come to embrace the development of human capital as an antidote to social problems such as poverty and unemployment (Miller, 2013). Consequently, the state is no longer responsible for the reintegration of released prisoners into the economy and, broadly speaking, into free society. Through human capital interventions, prisoners are instead made responsible for their own employment and other outcomes (Miller, 2014). They are trained to lift themselves out of poverty through the provision of services designed to make them employable, one former prisoner at a time (see Chap. 9, this volume, for an analysis of a reentry employment program in action). The combined series of events presented in this review set the stage for an unprecedented expansion of community corrections and the rise of reentry as the rehabilitative strategy of choice.

The Rise of Prisoner Reentry and the Revisioning of Rehabilitation

The decline of rehabilitative programming offered inside prisons was accompanied by a simultaneous increase in prisoner reentry services offered within prisoners' communities (Phelps, 2011). In her study of the practices of punishment and rehabilitation in prisons in the USA, sociologist Michelle Phelps (2011) operationalized rehabilitative programming as prison-based services that provide formal education or vocational training. Conversely, she operationalized reentry programs as prison-based services that address the practical skills associated with acquiring employment, such as resume preparation and interview training, the skill sets associated with meeting the demands of everyday life, like balancing a checkbook and paying bills, or the psychosocial skills associated with the acquisition and maintenance of prosocial relationships, such as anger management, parenting courses, or social skills training (Phelps, 2011). Rather than focus on the transformation of the ex-offender through employment and education, hallmarks of rehabilitation in the previous era, reentry programs address the practical skills associated with acquiring employment and the ways in which former prisoners understand their experiences and living conditions (Miller, 2014). Phelps (2011) found that while 64 % of all US prisoners' participated in rehabilitative services in 1991, just 31 % participated in these services by 2004. This decline in rehabilitative program participation coincided with an increase in participation in reentry-related services. Phelps (2011) found that in 1991 just 17 % of the US prison population participated in reentry-related services. That number increased to 34 % by 2004. Put differently, as rehabilitative programming offered inside prisoners declined, the number of prisoner reentry programs offered inside prisons increased.

The devolution and privatization of social welfare administration that occurred in this century is well documented. Nonprofit and voluntary sector organizations have not only precipitously expanded since the passage of welfare reform in 1996, but they have come to increasingly play roles that the government once played. Writing about similar trends already evident in the 1980s, Wolch (1990) described the operation of nonprofit and voluntary sector organizations as a shadow welfare state, receiving government funds to operate outside of the political system while remaining subject to the control of the state. Former President George H. W. Bush's famous speech invoking the thousand points of light, meaning the many faith-based and third-sector organizations contracted through the state to serve the needs of marginalized groups, was emblematic of this rationale (Bush, 1988). By 1996, third-sector organizations had nearly surpassed state-sanctioned organizations in the administration of welfare benefits and services, marking a shift away from state-mandated and state-administered social welfare programs to local community-based organizations and the ascendance of the public–private collaboration as policymakers' preferred model of community development. We suggest that these factors, more than any other, facilitated the diffusion of criminal justice institutions throughout the urban core and the series of formal and informal mechanisms associated with mass supervision throughout low-income urban communities (Miller, 2013). The massive growth in the number of reentry programs during this period provides some evidence of this shift (Miller, 2014).

Our examination of reentry programs showed that the number of registered community-based prisoner-serving organizations tripled between the 1996 passage of the welfare reform and the 2007 passage of the Second Chance Act (Miller, 2014). This increase, unsurprisingly, occurred in tandem with the rise of mass incarceration and the equally historical expansion of the population under correctional supervision. Today, reentry organizations provide training designed to get former prisoners ready for the worlds of work, fill perceived deficits in former prisoners, and build upon their interpersonal skills. All the while the worlds of work are not readying for them, and they are excluded from full participation in the social, economic, and political life of their communities through the mark of a criminal record (Pager, 2007). Thus, the power and responsibility to manage inmates and former prisoners, of which the responsibility to rehabilitate and reform them is central, has been offloaded onto local actors, community groups, and former prisoners themselves. Put differently, this shift represents the devolution of carceral power onto community-based actors and organizations. As such, following Foucault (1977), the rise of reentry is one way that the power to punish has been more deeply embedded within the social body.

Putting Prisoner Reentry in its Place: Final Thoughts on Carceral Devolution

Prisoner reentry programming is analogous to other social welfare programs of the welfare reform era in the USA that sought to intervene in the character, emotional stability, and decision-making processes of the urban poor. This is accomplished through the employment of psycho-social-skills groups, various cognitive interventions, and processes of socialization that occur within reentry sites (Miller, 2014; Western, 2008; see also Chaps. 9 and 10, this volume, for specific examples of this type of socialization). As the rehabilitative strategy of choice in the current age (Western, 2008), the ascendance and proliferation of prisoner reentry programming demonstrates the tentacular reach of the criminal justice system and represents at least one way that the state has been reconfigured to manage populations at the margins. Put differently, the state has devolved the authority and responsibility to rehabilitate prisoners onto local community-based actors and organizations. Since there are simply not enough reentry programs to meet prisoners' needs (Taxman et al., 2007) and given the individualizing strategies that many reentry organizations employ, prisoners, their families, and community members are made responsible for ex-offender reintegration. Thus the third sector now manages criminalized groups who were once the responsibility of the state, but they do so by shifting the responsibility of social reintegration onto the disadvantaged targets of the interventions themselves. Most reentry service providers cannot intervene in the labor market or address the barriers former prisoners face based on the mark of their criminal record. Thus, the effort of reentry programs to enhance former prisoners' skill sets in an effort to land work, housing, and manage their physical and mental health shifts the responsibility to fully incorporate released prisoners into the social, civic, and economic life of the city and lays it at the feet of former prisoners themselves. Miller (2014) finds that reentry programs frame the success or failure of former prisoners to fully reintegrate society as the direct result of their (in)ability to refrain from deviant behavior, change their outlook on life, or engage in prosocial relationships.

By getting out of the business of prisoner rehabilitation, the state has effectively offloaded its capacity to respond to the complex and varied needs of former prisoners, ceding the responsibility to ensure the successful reintegration of prisoners into society to former prisoners and the private actors from and operating within their home communities. Labeling this phenomenon "carceral devolution," we have argued that there has been a significant shift in criminal justice and social welfare policy occurring on geographic and conceptual levels. Geographically, rehabilitation has been outsourced, moving from within prison walls into the church basements and therapeutic spaces of the human service agencies that operate within low-income communities of color. Conceptually, the focus of efforts to rehabilitate prisoners has shifted from the social ecology of the ex-offender, with an emphasis placed on the acquisition and maintenance of employment, housing stability, and individualized substance abuse and mental-health treatment, to the inner life of the ex-offender—the meaning-making, decision-making, emotional management, and psychosocial skill sets of former prisoners (Haney, 2010; McCorkel, 2013; McKim, 2008, 2014; Miller, 2014). These initiatives are designed to modify their behavior and improve their decision-making strategies in the face of near intractable poverty, violence, and job insecurity, increasing their *human capital* and enhancing their employability for a service-oriented, highly competitive, and flexible labor market. Thus, the ascendance of prisoner reentry signals the transformation of the nature of rehabilitation, changing from an intervention into the social ecology of former prisoners, with at least a rhetorical focus on former prisoners' employment, to a dispositional intervention, seeking to address their meaning-making capacities and sense of psychological well-being (Miller, 2014). Put differently, prisoner reentry is a hyper local intervention, moving rehabilitation from inside prison walls into prisoners' home communities, and shifts the focus from the inner workings of the labor market to the inner workings of former prisoners' minds.

It is through the process of diffusion, where once centrally concentrated authority and sets of practices make their way into the social body, transforming it, that we can trace the emergence of novel social forms. Mass incarceration and carceral devolution are complementary institutions with productive capacities.

The activation of human service agencies in criminal justice administration has blurred the lines between punishment and welfare. Punitive logics have infiltrated most institutions of care, ranging from social welfare provision (Miller, 2014; Soss, Fording, & Schram, 2011; Stuart, 2013; Wacquant, 2009), education (Rios, 2011; Simon, 2007), and housing (Desmond & Valdez, 2013). The activation of third parties, such as landlords, employers, and public welfare agents, now reward and punish former prisoners through employment, housing, and social service policy (Miller, Miller, Zeleskoy Djoric, & 2015a). These mechanisms may include the eviction of prisoners and/or their families from rental properties because of their felony conviction, the exclusion of former prisoners from employment, housing, public welfare (Pinard, 2010), and the many good character clauses required for various employment licenses, limiting even former prisoners' entrepreneurial endeavors. Finally, carceral devolution includes the formal and informal crime-control efforts enacted by private agencies and actors, such as the proliferation of community corrections centers (state and federally funded halfway houses), the empowerment of neighborhood watches, and recent legislation that has effectively deputized private citizens to question, contain, and in some instances kill would-be criminals thought to hail from the nation's disadvantaged inner city (Anderson, 2013). As such, carceral devolution is not just a matter of social control, but of a recasting of the role, force, and consequence of the state. It has literally and figuratively reshaped the urban landscape.

References

Abrams, L. S., & Lea, C. H. (in press). Becoming employable: An ethnographic study of life skills courses in a men's jail. *The Prison Journal.*

Alexander, M. (2012). *The new Jim Crow: Mass incarceration in the age of colorblindness.* New York: The New Press.

Anderson, E. (2013). Emett and Trayvon. How racial prejudice in America has changed over the last 60 years. *Washington Review.* Retrieved from http://www.washingtonmonthly.com/magazine/january_february_2013/features/emmett_and_trayvon042036.php?page=all.

Beccaria, C. (1995) [1764]. *Beccaria: 'On Crimes and Punishments' and other writings* (Richard Bellamy, Ed. & Richard Davies, Trans.). Cambridge, England: Cambridge University.

Bentham, J. (2012) [1830]. *The rationale for punishment.* London: Robert Heward. Retrieved from http://www.laits.utexas.edu/poltheory/bentham/rp/.

Bush, G. H. W. (1988). *Acceptance speech at the Republican National Convention.* Miller Center Univeristy of Virginia. Retrieved August 15, 2015, from http://millercenter.org/president/bush/speeches/speech-5526.

Desmond, M. & Valdez, N. (2013). Unpolicing the urban poor: Consequences of third party policing on inner-city women. *American Sociological Review, 78,* 117–141.

Drucker, E. (2006). *A plague of prisons: The epidemiology of mass incarceration in America.* New York: The New Press.

Dumont, D. M., Brockmann, B., Dickman, S., Alexander, N., & Rich, J. D. (2012). Public health and the epidemic of incarceration. *Annual Review of Public Health, 33,* 325–339.

Feeley, M. & Simon, J. (1992). The new penology: Notes on an emerging strategy of corrections and its implications. *Criminology, 30*(4), 449–474.

Foucault, M. (1977). *Discipline and punish: The birth of the prison.* New York: Vintage.

Haney, L. A. (2010). *Offending women: Power, punishment, and the regulation of desire.* Berkeley, CA: University of California.

Harcourt, B. (2013). Beccaria's on crimes and punishments: A mirror on the history of the foundations of modern criminal law. In M. Dubber (Ed.), *Foundational texts in modern criminal law* (pp. 39–59). New York: Oxford University.

Harding, D. J., Wyse, J., Dobson, C., & Morenoff, J. (2014). Making ends meet after prison. Journal of Policy Analysis and Management, 33(2), 440–470.
Harrington, M. (1997). *The other America*. New York: Simon and Schuster.
Heck, M. (2014). *The testimony of Mathias H. Heck Jr. on behalf of the American Bar Foundation for the hearing on collateral consequences of criminal convictions and the problem of over-criminalization of federal law*. Washington, DC: Committee on the Judiciary Task Force on Over-Criminalization of the United States House of Representatives. Retrieved from http://www.americanbar.org/content/dam/aba/uncategorized/GAO/2014jun26_collateralconsequences_t_final.authcheckdam.pdf.
James, D. J., & Glaze, L. E. (2006). *Mental health problems of prison and jail inmates: Bureau of Justice Statistics Special Report*. U.S. Department of Justice Office of Justice Programs. Retrieved from http://www.bjs.gov/content/pub/pdf/mhppji.pdf.
Kaufman, N. (2014). Prisoner incorporation: The work of state and non governmental organizations. *Theoretical Criminology*. Retrieved from http://tcr.sagepub.com/content/early/2015/01/13/1362480614567172.abstract.
Kelly, R. D. (1997). *Yo mama's dysfunktional!: Fighting the culture wars in urban America*. Boston: Beacon.
Kohler-Hausmann, I. (2013). Misdemeanour justice: Control without conviction. *American Journal of Sociology*, *119*(2), 351–393.
La Vigne, N. G., Mamalian, C. A., Travis, J., & Visher, C. (2003). *A portrait of prisoner reentry in Illinois*. Washington, DC: Urban Institute Research Report. Retrievedfromhttp://www.urban.org/sites/default/files/alfresco/publication-pdfs/410662-A-Portrait-of-Prisoner-Reentry-in-Illinois.PDF.
Latessa, E. J. & Lowenkamp, C. (2005). What are criminogenic needs and why are they important. *For the Record*, *4*, 15–16.
Lewis, O. (1971). The culture of poverty. Scientific American, 215(4), 19–25.
Martinson, R. (1974). What works? Questions and answers about prison reform. *The Public Interest*, *35*(2), 22–54.
Maruna, S. (2001). *Making good: How ex-convicts reform and rebuild their lives*. Washington, DC: American Psychological Association.
McCorkel, J. A. (2013). *Breaking women: Gender, race, and the new politics of imprisonment*. New York: New York University Press.
McKim, A. (2008). "Getting Gut-Level" punishment, gender, and therapeutic governance. *Gender & Society*, *22*(3), 303–323.
McKim, A. (2014). Roxanne's dress: Governing gender and marginality through addiction treatment. *Signs*, *39*(2), 433–458.
McNeill, F. (2006). A desistance paradigm for offender management. *Criminology and Criminal Justice*, *6*(1), 39–62.
Miller, R. (2013). Race, hyper incarceration and U.S. poverty policy in historical perspective. *Sociology Compass*, *7*(7), 573–589.

Miller, R. (2014). Devolving the carceral state: Race, prisoner reentry and the micro-politics of urban poverty management. *Punishment and Society, 16*(3), 305–335.

Miller, R. J., Williams Miller, J., Djoric, J. Z., & Patton, D. (2015a). Baldwin's Mill: Race, prisoner reentry and the pedagogy of repression, 1965–2015. *Humanity and Society, 39*(4), 456–475.

Miller, R. J., Williams Miller, J., Djoric, J. Z., & Patton, D. (2015b). Baldwin's Mill race, punishment, and the pedagogy of repression, 1965–2015. *Humanity & Society, 39*(4), 456–475.

Minton, T. D., & Golinelli, D. (2014). *Jail inmates at midyear 2013—Statistical tables.* Washington, DC: U.S. Department of Justice, Office of Justice Programs: Bureau of Justice Statistics. Retrieved from http://www.bjs.gov/content/pub/pdf/jim13st.pdf.

Moynihan, D. P. (1965). *The Negro Family: The Case for National Action.*

Murray, C. (1984). *Losing ground: American social policy, 1950–1980.* New York: Basic Books.

National Prison Association. (1870). *Declaration of principles adopted and promulgated by the 1870 congress of the national prison association.* Retrieved from http://www.aca.org/ACA_PROD_IMIS/docs/1870Declaration_of_Principles.pdf.

Oscar, L. (1966). *La Vida. A Puerto Rican family in the culture of poverty, San Juan and New York* (p. 27). New York: Random House.

Pager, D. (2007). Two strikes and you're out: The intensification of racial and criminal stigma. In S. Bushway, M. Stoll, & D. Weiman (Eds.), *Barriers to reentry? The labor market for released prisoners in post-industrialized America* (pp. 151–173). New York: Russell Sage.

Patterson, E. (2013). The dose-response of time served in prison on mortality: New York State, 1989–2003. *American Journal of Public Health, 103*(3), 523–528.

Peck, J. & Theodore, N. (2008). Carceral Chicago: Making the ex-offender employability crisis. *International Journal of Urban and Regional Research, 32*(2), 251–281.

Petersilia, J. (2003). *When prisoners come home: Parole and prisoner reentry.* New York: Oxford University.

Phelps, M. (2011). Rehabilitation in the punitive era: The gap between rhetoric and reality in U.S. prison programs. *Law and Society Review, 45*(1), 33–68.

Pinard, M. (2010). Reflections and perspectives on reentry and collateral consequences. *Journal of Criminal Law & Criminology, 100*(3), 1213–1234.

Rios, V. (2011). *Punished: Policing the lives of Black and Latino boys.* New York: New York University.

Sampson R. J., & Loeffler, C. (2010). Punishment's place: The local concentration of mass incarceration. *Daedalus,* 139(3), 20–31.

Schneider, A. & Ingram, H. (1993). Social construction of target populations: Implications for politics and policy. *American Political Science Review*, *87*(2), 334–347.

Simon, J. (1993). *Poor discipline: Parole and the social control of the underclass, 1890–1990.* Chicago: University of Chicago.

Simon, J. (2007). *Governing through crime: How the war on crime transformed American democracy and created a culture of fear.* New York: Oxford University.

Soss, J., Fording, R. C., & Schram, S. F. (2011). *Disciplining the poor: Neoliberal paternalism and the persistent power of race.* Chicago: University of Chicago.

Stack, C. B. (1975). *All our kin.* New York: Basic Books.

Street, P. (2001). Race, prison, and poverty: The race to incarcerate in the age of correctional keynesianism. *Z Magazine*, 26.

Street, P. (2003). Race, prison, and poverty: The race to incarcerate in an age of correctional Keynesianism. *History as a weapon.* Retrieved from http://www.historyisaweapon.com/defcon1/streeracpripov.html.

Stuart, F. (2013). From rabble management to recovery management: Policing homelessness in marginal urban space. *Urban Studies*, *51*(9), 1909–1925.

Taxman, F. S., Perdoni, M. L., & Harrison, L. D. (2007). Drug treatment services for adult offenders: The state of the state. *Journal of Substance Abuse Treatment*, *32*(3), 239–254.

Travis, J., Solomon, A. L., & Waul, M. (2001). *From prison to home: The dimensions and consequences of prisoner reentry.* Washinton, DC: The Urban Institute. Retrieved from http://www.urban.org/UploadedPDF/from_prison_to_home.pdf.

Travis, J., Western, B., & Radburn, S. (2014). *The growth of incarceration: Exploring causes and consequences.* Washington, DC: National Academy's Press.

Uggen, C. & Manza, J. (2006). *Locked out: Felon disenfranchisement and American democracy.* New York: Oxford University.

Visher, C. A. & Travis, J. (2003). Transitions from prison to community: Understanding individual pathways. *Annual Review of Sociology*, *29*, 89–113.

Wacquant, L. (2001). Deadly symbiosis: When ghetto and prison meet and mesh. *Punishment and Society*, *3*(1), 95–134.

Wacquant, L. (2009). *Punishing the poor: The neoliberal government of social insecurity.* Durham, NC: Duke University.

Wacquant, L. (2010). Class, race, and hyperincarceration in revanchist America. *Socialism and Democracy*, *28*(3), 35–56.

Western, B. 2008. Reentry: Reversing mass imprisonment. *Boston Review.* Retrievedfromhttp://bostonreview.net/bruce-western-reentry-reversing-mass-imprisonment.

Wilson, J. Q. (1975). *Thinking about crime.* New York: Vintage Books.

Wolch, J. (1990). *The shadow state: Government and voluntary sector in transition.* New York: Foundation Center.

CHAPTER 9

From Ex-Offender to New Contributor: An Examination of How a Community-Based Reentry Program Addresses Racial Barriers to Employment

Charles H. Lea III and Laura S. Abrams

Introduction

The US penal population has increased more than fourfold since the 1970s and incarcerates more people per capita than any other nation (Wagner, Sakala, & Bagley, 2014). The massively expanded use of incarceration to control crime has resulted in an astounding number of adults who return to the community each year following their release from jail or prison. In 2010, over 700,000 adults were released from federal or state prison and over 9,000,000 were released from local jails. Recidivism rates for released adults are quite high; in the USA, an estimated 67 % of those who have exited a state or federal prison will be rearrested with three years (Bureau of Justice Statistics, 2010).

Communities of color in the USA are the most adversely affected by these sharp increases in the reentry population (Western, Pettit, & Guetzkow, 2003). In 2010, African Americans comprised 12.6 % and

C.H. Lea III (✉) • L.S. Abrams
University of California, Los Angeles, USA

L.S. Abrams et al. (eds.), *The Voluntary Sector in Prisons*, Palgrave Studies in Prisons and Penology, DOI 10.1057/978-1-137-54215-1_9

Hispanics comprised 16.3 % of the total population, yet accounted for 39% and 23 % of the jail and prison population, respectively (Guerino, Harrison, & Sabol, 2011). The high concentration of reentering adults in low-income communities of color has fueled a greater need for reentry and community reintegration services, particularly those related to education and employment skills. Whereas correctional staff historically provided reentry supports and programs for inmates prior to their release, prison overcrowding, unsafe conditions, and strapped state budgets have resulted in a shift of many of these services from the penal to the voluntary sector (Seiter & Kadela, 2003). Over the past decade, federal policies such as the Second Chance Act, the Severe and Violent Offender Reentry Initiative, and Department of Labor Workforce Initiatives have provided increased funding for the nonprofit sector to implement employment programs that target former inmates and those returning home from prisons and jails.

Empirical research has largely supported the inverse association between employment and recidivism (National Research Council, 2007). Yet still, the intersection of racial discrimination and a criminal record make legal employment opportunities difficult to obtain for people of color who have criminal records and histories of incarceration (Decker, Spohn, Ortiz, & Hedbeg, 2014; Holzer, Raphel, & Stoll, 2007; Pager, 2007). Thus, while reentry and job preparation training have largely become a voluntary sector enterprise, many ex-offenders remain marginalized from mainstream employment; studies have estimated 50–70 % unemployment rates for ex-offenders at 12 months postrelease (Pager & Western, 2009). These findings thus evoke a critical question: How does the voluntary sector address structural barriers to employment among formerly incarcerated individuals of color pursuing mainstream employment?

In this chapter, we critically examine how discussions of racism and racial discrimination are framed and negotiated in the context of a community-based reentry program. Within this program, both the participants and the instructors were nearly all African American and Hispanic. Using ethnographic methodology, we observed program sessions focused on job search skills to understand how the program frames its messages concerning opportunities and barriers to employment, and whether the program participants support or challenge these frames. Our research questions were

1. How do reentry instructors frame job search strategies to formerly incarcerated adult men and women of color in the context of a community-based reentry program?

2. Do the instructors address structural barriers to employment, such as racial discrimination? If so, how do they frame these messages?
3. How do the formerly incarcerated adult men and women respond to the instructors' strategies and messages concerning opportunities and barriers to employment?

Literature Review

Ex-Offenders, Race, and Employment

There are many reasons that ex-offenders are often unable to find or maintain steady employment, ranging from individual to more structural factors. As a group, more than two in five prisoners lack a high school diploma or equivalent (Harlow, 2003), which contributes to high rates of unemployment and low-wage or temporary work. In addition to low educational attainment, in many US states, convicted felons are outright barred from working in various industries (Rodriguez & Emsellem, 2011). Even without stated policies of exclusion, there are subtle ways that employers filter out applicants with criminal records. For example, one study of employer attitudes and practices in Los Angeles, California (n = 619), found that 40 % of respondents were unwilling to hire an ex-offender, and only 20 % were willing to accept ex-offenders' applications (Holzer et al., 2007). Moreover, the same study revealed that a large percentage of employers were more willing to hire individuals with other barriers in their work history, such as former or current welfare recipients and those with limited employment histories.

People of color, even with similar qualifications as white applicants, are also less likely to secure an interview or employment. For instance, Bertrand and Mullainathan (2004) argue that a racial/ethnic-sounding name on an equally qualified resume may bias a potential employer against an initial interview. As such, the intersection of race and a criminal record makes it particularly challenging for formerly incarcerated people of color to obtain a job interview, let alone be hired. The intersection of race and criminal record in forming barriers to employment is empirically supported. For example, Decker et al. (2014) study found that the odds of being contacted for a job interview for similarly qualified formerly incarcerated individuals were 125 % lower for African American men and 18 % lower for Hispanic men compared to white men. Similarly, Pager's (2007) study of employment and racial bias found that 14 % of nonoffending African

Americans received a "callback" following an interview, compared to 17 % of similarly qualified whites that had a criminal record.

The exclusion of formerly incarcerated individuals from legal employment often perpetuates further contact with the criminal justice system, as secure employment decreases the odds of recidivism (National Research Council, 2007). For example, one study of 6561 offenders returning to five metropolitan cities in the Midwest over 5 years found that unemployed ex-offenders were 1.5 times more likely to recidivate than an ex-offender who was employed (Lockwood, Nally, Ho, & Knutson, 2012). This study also found that those who were African American, younger, and less educated had higher risk factors for recidivism. However, a study in Florida found that while employment postponed the average time to recidivism, it did not reduce the overall odds of reoffending at 5 years postrelease (Tripodi, Kim, & Bender, 2010). Although the relationship between employment and recidivism may be moderated by additional factors such as substance abuse and homelessness, job preparation training and education toward employability are nevertheless a major focus of adult reentry programming in the voluntary sector.

Reentry and Employment Programs

Prisoners have historically returned to the same communities from where they were sentenced, in which they have to reestablish themselves as law-abiding individuals in order to prevent returning to the justice system. For much of the twentieth century, preparation for release was an important part of the prison experience. With indeterminate sentences, inmates could voluntarily participate in work or other release programs in order to improve their chances of release and to prove that they were indeed rehabilitated. Parole boards considered rehabilitation and planning for release an important component of a parole decision (Seiter & Kadela, 2003). Moreover, parole officers spent intensive time with released inmates to help them implement their plans upon their release.

However, in the era of mass incarceration and the War on Drugs (from about the mid-1980s onward), much of the emphasis on reentry and rehabilitation within prisons and jails shifted toward a primarily punitive model. First, since more money was spent in building new facilities in the "tough on crime" era of the 1980s and 1990s, funds for rehabilitative programs in federal and state prisons were dramatically reduced or even depleted (Seiter & Kadela, 2003). Moreover, a shift to determinant sentences reduced the incentive for prison inmates to participate in voluntary rehabilitation or reentry programs. Seiter and Kadela (2003) describe how this "new penology" shifted the focus of prisons and parole from "rehabilitation" to "risk management":

> For most of the 1990s, community supervision (probation and parole) underwent a transition from helping and counseling offenders to one of risk management and surveillance (Feeley & Simon, 1992). The focus on risk management is accompanied by new allocations of resources toward incarceration, rather than probation and parole, and management of internal system processes. (p. 70)

County jails, where offenders stay for shorter terms, offer even fewer rehabilitation services than state or federal prisons due to high turnover rates as well as limited resources, major overcrowding, and unsafe conditions requiring frequent lockdowns and cell confinement. All of these changes have carved a major gap in regard to prisoner education, rehabilitation, and job training: programs that have historically been effective in curbing recidivism (Adams et al., 1994; Aos, Miller, & Drake, 2006; National Research Council, 2007; Seiter & Kadela, 2003). While President Obama's administration has made some attempts to restore prisoner education and employment programs (e.g., a move to offer community college classes in prison), the major goal of the adult criminal justice system remains punishment and conformity (Carlson & Garrett, 2013).

Despite the punitive nature of the US adult criminal justice system, the complex social and economic effects of mass incarceration and efforts to drastically reduce the nation's penal population has ushered in many changes in criminal justice policy in the twenty-first century, including increased investments in community corrections and rehabilitation (Abarbanel, McCray, Newhall, & Synder, 2013). Substantial federal funding initiatives such as the Second Chance Reentry Act and the Severe and Violent Offenders Initiative have offered competitive grant opportunities for nonprofit organizations to establish and implement successful reentry programs. Moreover, large-scale foundations such as the Soros Foundation and the Robert Wood Johnson foundation have mounted parallel opportunities for the voluntary sector to increase its reach into employment and reentry training. This convergence of government funding strategies and philanthropic investments in community-based reentry has thus paved the way for the voluntary sector to contend with reentry barriers within low-income communities of color, from perhaps a different perspective than the penal system. Yet, even with this paradigm shift, it is unknown how the voluntary/nonprofit sector addresses issues of structural discrimination and racism while they tackle their main goal of preparing former inmates for employment.

Colorblindness and Justice

Throughout US history, people of color have commonly been conceived as deviants and threats to the social, economic, and political fabric of American society. The chief motive of dehumanizing people of color, often through the use of overt racial caste systems or systems of control, such as slavery and Jim Crow laws, was to maintain racial divisions and perpetual white dominance (Alexander, 2010; Horsman, 1981; Mills, 1997). Although major civil rights advancements such as the Thirteenth Amendment of the US Constitution legally barred overt racial caste systems, many view mass incarceration as replacing overt racism with more covert mechanisms of racial oppression (Alexander, 2010; Forman, 2012; Wacquant, 2000, 2002).

In her widely acclaimed book *The New Jim Crow* (2010), legal scholar Michelle Alexander argues President Ronald Reagan's War on Drugs initiative served as a key mechanism through which the mass incarceration of people of color, particularly African American men, was rationalized and implemented. Specifically, the War on Drugs enabled racially biased policing and drug operations in communities of color, which resulted in the disproportionate arrest, conviction, and sentencing of people of color. Moreover, by focusing on drug-related offenses, people of color are often unable to challenge criminal justice policies and procedures on the basis of race, which has aided in the development of this new, more covert racial caste system (Alexander, 2010).

The ideology of colorblindness has also subtly contributed to widespread public acceptance of mass incarceration. Colorblindness, a sociological term that evolved following the US Civil Rights Movement, suggests that racial characteristics of all groups should be ignored with regards to material and symbolic advantage and disadvantage, in order to ensure racial equality (Bonilla-Silva, 2010; Hanley-Lopez, 2010). Alexander (2010) argues that the gradual acceptance of a colorblind discourse, specifically as it pertains to the criminal justice system, has served to replace the stigma of race with the stigma of criminal, thus masking the racism that still permeates all aspects of the justice system.

Alexander (2010) further asserts that mass incarceration is "veiled by the cloak of colorblindness" (p. 223), such that conservatives can broadly assert that society should be concerned with individuals rather than groups, and liberals can maintain hope that the construct of race will eventually lose its significance. Following this logic, reentry programs, particularly those that are set within the institutional frame of the corrections system, will be likely geared toward the idea that "anyone can make it if they try" (Alexander, 2010, p. 245). In this sense, reentry programs, even those rooted in community-based organizations, may be likely to avoid topics such as race and racism as they may conform to the prevailing race-neutral discourse of the prison and reentry system.

Significance of the Study

To date, empirical research has established the existence of significant barriers to gainful employment for people of color with criminal records. Community-based reentry programs often focus on building skills toward employment, which is understandable given the connection between employment and recidivism reduction. Yet still, ex-offenders of color are likely to face bleak job prospects and discrimination. Thus the practice of preparation for employment in a community-based reentry program presents an interesting paradox: how do you train ex-offenders of color for employment when in all likelihood they may not be able to get a job? How do program instructors address issues of racism and discrimination in their training materials, conversations, and lessons? Do they follow some of the language of race-neutrality, or do they address contemporary racial realities more directly? These are some of the questions that we examine in this chapter.

Method

This study sought to understand how reentry instructors of color frame job search strategies and racial messages concerning opportunities and barriers to employment. To do so, two researchers, the first author of this chapter and a master's level social work graduate student, examined an 8-week community-based reentry program located in a low-income historically African American neighborhood in South Los Angeles. This program, which we will call "Empowered for Change" in order to maintain confidentiality, represented a partnership between a local law enforcement policing agency and a historic African American civil rights nonprofit organization. The two partnered in 2009 to develop and implement this community-based reentry program for adults returning from jail or prison. According to program records from the nonprofit partner, a total of 231 participants graduated from the program between 2009 and 2012. The racial/ethnic demographic of the program's participant base was also reported as representative of the neighboring community: 87 % African American, 10 % Hispanic, and 3 % other. The program setting was therefore well positioned to assist us in answering our research questions.

Empowered for Change targets and serves formerly incarcerated "system involved" individuals (i.e., under probation or parole supervision). Potential participants are referred to the program from criminal justice agencies such as law enforcement and probation/parole, as well as community-based organizations and former participants. The majority of participants are required to enroll and attend the program daily as a condition of their parole or probation plans. However, some ex-offenders participate voluntarily and are not held to these supervision requirements. The Empowered for Change program includes a cohort model, wherein over an 8-week period, participants are engaged in programming for 5 days per week, 3 hours per day, at a local church in South Los Angeles that provides a meeting space to the nonprofit partner. Throughout the 8 weeks, participants receive step-by-step training and support to personal growth and success, career development and job search and placement assistance, entrepreneurship training, and financial education (i.e., personal budgeting, basis banking, money and credit management) and are engaged in "therapeutic writing" exercise that uses the participant's personal life stories as a method to help them access and discover clarity, self-awareness, and empowerment. A blend of law enforcement and nonprofit instructors facilitate each program session, typically from a program workbook that was developed by the law enforcement instructors. Occasionally, invited community and faith-based volunteers facilitate and support program-related activities and discussions. The program concludes with a graduation ceremony and offers continued support to graduates such as bus tokens and access to interview clothes.

Sample

Collectively, the first author and a graduate student researcher conducted eleven 3-hour observations of the Empowered for Change reentry program. A total of 15 instructors, including five from law enforcement, four from the nonprofit, and six volunteers, were observed during the study period. Program participant attendance at each session ranged from a low of 13 to a high of 35. Additionally, the racial/ethnic composition of program participants at each session, including instructors, volunteers, and ex-offenders, were primarily African American (approximately 95 %). The other 5 % included Hispanic participants. With regards to the gender composition at each observed session, approximately 90 % of participants were men and the remaining 10 % were women. Table 9.1

Table 9.1 Summary of program sessions observed

Date of observation	*Law enforcement instructor*	*Nonprofit instructor*	*Volunteer instructor*	*Approximate number of participants*	*Observer(s)*
07/12/13	Mr. Reyes Mr. Thompson	Mr. Jones Mr. Turner	Mr. Williams Ms. Williams	35	Author 1 & Graduate student
07/16/13	Mr. Banks Mr. Thompson	Mr. Gonzalez Mr. Jimenez	Mr. Williams Ms. Williams	32	Graduate student
07/26/13	Mr. Banks Ms. Jackson Mr. Thompson		Mr. Scott Mr. Williams Ms. Williams	19	Author 1 & Graduate student
07/30/13	Mr. Banks Ms. Jackson Mr. Thompson		Ms. Walker Mr. Williams Ms. Williams	20	Author 1
08/02/13	Mr. Banks Mr. Thompson		Mr. Williams Ms. Williams	18	Graduate student
08/08/13	Mr. Banks Mr. Reyes Mr. Thompson		Mr. Williams Ms. Williams	19	Author 1
08/09/13	Mr. Reyes		Mr. Williams Ms. Williams	21	Graduate student
08/16/13	Mr. Thompson		Mr. Peters Ms. Roberts Mr. Williams Ms. Williams	19	Graduate student
08/30/13	Mr. Hall Mr. Thompson	Mr. Jones	Mr. Williams Ms. Williams	13	Graduate student
09/04/13	Mr. Banks Ms. Jackson Mr. Reyes Mr. Thompson		Mr. Williams Ms. Williams	11	Author 1
09/05/13	Mr. Banks Ms. Jackson Mr. Reyes Mr. Thompson	Mr. Gonzalez Mr. Jimenez Mr. Jones Mr. Turner	Mr. Williams Ms. Williams	26	Author 1

provides an overview of the program sessions observed, the instructors and volunteers, and the approximate number of participants (all names are pseudonyms to ensure confidentiality).

As we conducted our observations, we paid specific attention to program activities and discussions that surrounded opportunities for, and barriers to, employment, race, and racial discrimination. We also closely examined the interactions between and among the different participants (i.e., instructors, volunteers, and ex-offenders). Additionally, we conducted our observations on different days of the week in an attempt to observe each instructor and volunteer more than once, and to document a range of program-related activities and discussion. In accordance with our Institutional Review Board's stipulations, we obtained written consent from each instructor and verbal consent from each program participant, prior to conducting our observations. No study participants opted out of the observations.

Data Collection

Ethnography was the guiding methodology for this study. Specifically, we assumed the role of observer-participant in that we were part of the setting, yet had minimal interactions with participants (Lofland & Lofland, 1995). When requested we did participate in program activities and shared our opinions during large and small group discussions. However, our involvement was limited and thus our presence caused minimal reactivity bias.

We recorded our observations in the form of field notes. The field notes included our descriptions of the setting and participants, reports of events, behaviors and interactions, and transcriptions of participant conversations. We also included our impressions of our observations, including our experiences and reactions to the instructors' reentry discourses. Written field notes were expanded and typed within 2 days of each observation, and these notes were shared between the researchers to confirm accuracy, identify similarities, and to resolve any differences given our different racial and gender lenses (the first author as an African American man, and the other field researcher as a white woman). Program documents (e.g., handouts, reports, and the program workbook) were also collected and included in the overall analysis.

Analysis

The analytic process consisted of coding and memoing (Miles & Huberman, 1984). As coauthors (Lea and Abrams), we inductively coded each field note to identify and compare instances in the data where instructors' and volunteers' job search strategies and messages concerning opportunities and barriers to employment were discussed and negotiated. Following initial coding, we developed analytic memos to identify, classify, and categorize emerging and final thematic categories. Once we identified the major themes, we displayed excerpts from the field note data in a thematic matrix (Miles & Huberman, 1984) and discussed the initial and final categories to ensure we grounded our analysis and interpretation in the data. Findings from the analysis were also shared and discussed with a research group to ensure the trustworthiness of the findings (Lincoln & Guba, 1985).

Results

Although the Empowered for Change instructors of color often acknowledged the existence of structural barriers to employment, their reentry discourses constructed the formerly incarcerated men and women of color as self-transforming individuals who must pursue legitimate employment with a colorblind lens. The following excerpt from our field note data describes Mr. Thompson, an African American instructor from law enforcement, providing an overview of the 8-week reentry program. This example illustrates the individually focused, strengths-based approach embedded within this reentry program.

> Mr. Thompson stated that the purpose of the Empowered for Change program is to help the participants "get unstuck." He followed this statement with a question to the participants, asking, "how did you get the way you are?" An African American male participant said aloud, "bad decisions." Mr. Thompson responded, "you are your decisions." He then asked the participants, "what is the definition of insanity?" An African American female participant answered, "doing the same thing over and over, but expecting different results." Mr. Thompson thanked the participant for her response, and further explained the instructors' role over the next eight-weeks: "we are not committed to bringing you anything; we are committed to making things disappear. By making things disappear, as opposed to adding, you'll be able to get rid of old ways." He further questioned the participants by asking how many of them were fearful about something. Roughly

> 10 participants raised their hands, and Mr. Thompson followed his question by saying, "if you can disappear the things that make you fearful, then you can begin to find success. You have what you need to be successful."

Within this overarching finding, the analytic process yielded three major themes pertaining to job search strategies and barriers to employment for men and women of color participating in a community-based reentry program. The three themes include "be in the game," "get out of your own way," and "get out of the story of what it means to be black." We also discuss the men's and women's responses to the instructors' job search strategies and racial messages.

Job Search Strategies

"Be in the Game"

The first theme encompasses the practical job search strategies instructors provided to the Empowered for Change participants. Specifically, instructors encouraged the participants to focus on opportunities rather than barriers during their job search process. As one instructor stated, "failure is only present when you're performing." Instructors therefore suggested that the participants "get out of the stands of [their] life and into the game, because how [they] do anything is how [they'll] do everything." In other words, if you don't try, you can't fail.

One of the initial job search strategies to facilitate "being in the game" was to develop a career goal. Through lectures, videos, and program workbook assignments, the instructors assisted the participants with identifying and developing goals in several life domains (e.g., career, relationships, finance, travel, and family). In particular, instructors discussed the importance of developing goals that are specific, measurable, achievable, responsible (ecological), and time-bounded (S.M.A.R.T). As one instructor expressed, "when you know where you're going, it's easier to get there." Participants were therefore asked to develop and revisit their goals during the study period. Yet throughout this process, the instructors often belittled participants' concerns regarding employment barriers. In the following excerpt from our field notes, two instructors from the historic civil rights nonprofit organization used the personal barriers of one of the instructors to illustrate that their most significant barrier to employment lies within themselves:

> Two instructors from the non-profit organization, Mr. Jimenez, a mixed race man, and Mr. Gonzalez, a Latino man who used a wheelchair, facilitated an hour-long session focused on career goals, resume development, and interviewing. They also talked to the participants about developing a unique selling proposition. To help the participants with develop a unique selling proposition, they asked each of them to stand up and introduce themselves in 20 to 30 seconds without sharing any personal information about themselves. Each participant therefore introduced themselves by talking about their past work experiences. However, an African American male participant, prior to introducing himself, mentioned he's never worked before, and had either only been incarcerated or "on the streets." The instructors expressed to him and the other participants that "everyone has barriers to getting hired." Mr. Gonzalez shared that he has a criminal record with two convictions and a disability. He talked about identifying barriers as a first step, yet encouraged the participants to try to understand how focusing on barriers can contribute to fear. Mr. Jimenez echoed this statement, saying, "the way Mr. Gonzalez works and gets his job done you would never notice his disability or barrier." Mr. Gonzalez ended the discussion by reading a quote by Rosa Parks. After reading the quote, he said, "she [Rosa Parks] had fear; however, she still persevered to carry out her mission. Barriers are what we put in front of ourselves."

While the instructors' messages here concerning barriers to employment can be understood as empowering, the underlying message was that these barriers are personal, rather than structural. Using Rosa Parks' quote as a motivating example also acknowledges the racial composition and experiences of the participants as is fitting with the civil rights organization, yet within the context of the program, still maintains the focus on removing individual and mental barriers to "get in the game."

Quotes and affirmations included in the participant workbooks, such as "successful people overcome their excuses," supported the instructors' messages of personal responsibility for change. In nearly all program sessions we observed, the instructors recited these quotes and affirmations to remind the participants that they are solely responsible for the direction of their lives, regardless of the barriers they have or will continue to face. Thus in advising the participants to develop S.M.A.R.T career goals, instructors insisted they would be equipped to "play the game effectively," as they will eliminate their excuses and "remain loyal to [themselves] and not a game [they] did not create."

The job search strategy of "practice winning" provides another example of "getting in the game." In particular, participants were advised to reward themselves for activities that support goal attainment. To assist with the practice of rewards, the instructors introduced the "Mental Bank Program," a hands-on self-improvement activity that is based on the assumption that individuals can achieve their goals if these goals are reinforced. Through the mental bank process, participants developed a "Mental Bank Goal" (anticipated annual salary), identified "Value Events" (for example, applying for a job) that are productive toward their goals, and, each day, recorded completed value events on a "Mental Bank Ledger" worksheet included in their workbooks. Participants also developed an hourly rate to pay themselves for completing value events, as this was to ensure they completed the activity with a positive "Mental Bank Balance."

Although some participants raised concerns about the time-consuming nature of this activity, instructors encouraged them to commit to the process. For example, one instructor stated, "you have to get in the game and do the work in order for us to help you." In the following excerpt from our field notes, Mr. Thompson used a movie analogy to assist the participants with understanding the value in committing to a process of personal change:

> Following the mental bank video, some participants expressed concerns about the level of commitment required to complete the activity, as they mentioned they have a lot going on in their lives. Mr. Thompson responded to their concerns by expressing that while he is the instructor, he also struggles like them. He talked about having bills and even shared he has a disabled son. He concluded his response by saying, "while I have many things going on my life, I'm committed to excellence! You need to decide what game you're playing … going to jail is easy. Just do the work and don't worry about the how." He then referenced the movie "Karate Kid," and discussed how the young boy became frustrated by doing what he perceived as meaningless tasks his instructor told him to do. He also recited a line the karate instructor said to his young boy: "If I taught you karate the way you knew it, you'd manipulate the system."

To further assist the participants with their efforts to "practice winning," instructors told them to "under promise and over achieve," as presumably this strategy would set them up for success and not failure. For instance, Mr. Williams, a volunteer and life coach who attended every session we observed, informed the participants that they "must develop a format for how to successfully complete their goal." He viewed this as critical to their job search process, because "people who do 60 percent of what they say they will do will be successful." Mr. Williams further suggested to the participants that if they set a goal to call 10 companies each week to inquire about jobs, yet actually call 15, they've achieved 150 % of their goal. Instructors also reminded participants throughout the study period that the goals they set are personal, as a way to encourage them to practice winning.

Overall, in framing their job search strategies as "being in the game," the instructors attempted to help the participants to identify and build upon their own strengths and assets. Moreover, although the instructors utilized a strength-based approach in their reentry discourses, the message of personal transformation as the key to facilitate postrelease employment opportunities was most prominent. The process of personal change and growth was thus framed as an essential step to the participants' building resistance against employment barriers, as the scope of their employment opportunities, whether wide or narrow, could be increased overtime though mental positive reinforcement.

"Get Out of Your Own Way"

Along the lines of personal transformation and positive reinforcement, instructors also encouraged participants to address cognitive barriers to employment. Unlike the theme, "being in the game," which highlights the instructors' practical job search strategies, in this section, we discuss the instructors' strategies that aimed to assist the participants with addressing negative thought patterns concerning the job search process and postrelease employment opportunities. In particular, participants were instructed to "get out of [their] own way" by being attuned to their own thought patterns. More specifically, instructors suggested that the subconscious mind is inherently negative. Participants were encouraged to leave their prior knowledge at the door and to write down their goals and the information presented using a pen and pad, as the act of writing and viewing information on paper was promoted as critical to their personal cognitive transformation.

The role and influence of the subconscious mind was present in nearly every program session we observed. Instructors also exposed participants to therapeutic writing exercises during which each used their personal life story and the program activities "to access and discover clarity, self-awareness, and empowerment." For example, after showing a 75-minute video focused on the Mental Bank Program, Mr. Thompson emphasized the importance of facing the subconscious mind throughout their job preparation and search process. He explained:

> "The subconscious mind is constantly looking for ways to seek out the negative. We need to therefore replace that negative thinking because we are conditioned to move away versus towards something due to fear, lack and scarcity. The mind thinks in pictures so we need to imagine and hold onto a picture of what we want. That includes thinking and speaking success in order to positively fuel our mental thinking." Next, Mr. Thompson read a quote from the program workbook, which read, "the road to somewhere leads nowhere." The participants looked for it in their workbooks, and some recited the quote quietly to themselves. Mr. Thompson continued to talk about the subconscious mind stating, "it always puts our goals into tomorrow and pushes it out further and further." He followed this statement with two rhetorical questions, asking, "what am I going to do with what I want? And how do I keep a relationship or money or a job?" He answered, "73 percent of the information we take in everyday is negative.... Negative thoughts are immediate, and our thinking is attached to our physical being. Be present to your subconscious mind's responses. Your dominant belief is going to run the show."

In this example, Mr. Thompson described the function of the subconscious mind and its influence on the participants' perceptions and behaviors. He often repeated the mantra that "your perception is your projection," to suggest that their life chances and outcomes are determined by how they think. The instructors thus insisted that when participants wrote down information, including their career goals, using a pen and pad, the act of handwriting would counterattack from the critical mind and would "send that information into the right brain and positive goals w[ould] be implanted as a new program."

Instructors also encouraged the participants to "speak success" so as to ensure they would hold onto the positive thoughts they were developing in the course of the program. For example, a common lesson was to "change [their] conversations, because [their] words create [their] worlds." During one program session, Ms. Walker, an African American volunteer and life coach, facilitated an hour-long discussion focused on decision-making. She began by sharing several personal life experiences and challenges that were the result of poor decisions, such as "having a baby out of wedlock." As she shared her life narrative, Ms. Walker stated, "If you're wondering how you got to where you are, look at what you said

... you have created yourself to be exactly where you are today." To qualify this statement, she referenced Oprah Winfrey and Bill Gates to highlight that they are where they are financially not because of listening to the world external to them, but because of what they've said. Like many of the instructional themes, she thus emphasized the power of positive thinking and language in securing employment.

To assist the participants with understanding the role language plays in determining their life chances, Ms. Walker challenged them to examine how their words have created some predicament in their life. She engaged the participants in an activity during which they formed groups of two and shared how the language they've used in the past has prevented them from achieving success in some area of their life. Following the activity, Ms. Walker asked a few participants to share what they discussed with the large group. The excerpt below provides an example of the exchange we observed between Ms. Walker and two program participants, and her attempts to help them understand how their perceptions of opportunities and barriers are based on "lies." She also explains to them that they can create a new possibility of being if they transform how they think and speak:

> Following Ms. Walker's request for volunteers, one African American male participant said, "I've often said I can't get into college because I have a felony." After sharing, Ms. Walker asked him what his justification was. He responded, "because I have a felony. Because I've been to prison." She questioned him further, asking, "what are the facts or the truth you created?" He responded, "I can't get into college." Ms. Walker then said, "the fact that he has a felony and has been to prison is the story that he created about college, which is preventing him from going. This is the choice he made. No one told him to say that." She then asked him to rephrase what he said positively, following which he said, "I'm going to college." She proceeded by encouraging the participants to begin to speak things as though they already happened.
>
> After this interaction, another African American male participant shared, "I can't get a job because I have restitution fees." Ms. Walker responded to his statement by saying "can't is the story each of them created." She then asked the participant what is it about the restitution fees that are preventing him from getting a job. He mentioned that the restitution fees cost money, and that he's unable to pay because he does not have a job. Ms. Walker questioned him a bit more in an attempt to help him think about the story he was creating. The participant appeared to become frustrated by Ms. Walker's questions and comments, as he replied in a loud tone, "it's not that simple, the fees are just too much." Ms. Walker reminded this participant of an early statement she made, by saying, "we are given free will ... when you operate

from a high level of integrity, honoring your word and operating with discipline, you can live your best life."

The above excerpt illustrates the cognitive-behavioral frames that were explicit in program discourses. Like the law enforcement and nonprofit instructors, Ms. Walker's messages surrounding cognitively focused job search strategies suggested that barriers to employment are personal, or perceived, rather than structural. Here she apparently ignored some of the legitimate barriers to getting ahead, such as a felony record or restitution fees, both of which create complications for an ex-offender in their real-life circumstances. Participants were therefore encouraged to be conscious of, and present to, the beliefs they allow to influence their subconscious mind, as presumably this will empower them to develop and maintain habits that will help them to get out of their own way during their job search processes. Left unstated in Ms. Walker's reentry discourse was how to actually overcome real barriers to employment. The following section will examine how instructors recommended using personal transformation in the face of a particular type of barrier.

"Get Out of the Story of What It Means to be Black"

In the process of discussing practical and cognitively focused job search strategies, the group sometimes discussed racial barriers to employment. While the instructors acknowledged the existence of racial barriers, they discouraged participants from framing the scope of their job searches around them, as this would limit their chances of obtaining employment. The third theme, "get out of the story of what it means to be black," thus builds on the message of personal transformation included in the first two themes, as participants were frequently advised to reframe their thinking about what it means to be a formerly incarcerated job seeker of color.

In particular, instructors encouraged participants to face their fears, even those concerning racism or discrimination, as they pursue legitimate employment. In many sessions we observed, instructors referenced the mental bank activity to empower participants to face perceived racial barriers, as one instructor explicitly stated: "Fear is not real. Fear is a choice." Specifically, as discussed above, the mental bank activity includes cognitive and behavioral exercises that aim to support participants in their process of personal transformation. In the following example, Mr. Banks, an African American law enforcement instructor, references the mental bank program to highlight the utility of this activity and to relay a racial message concerning opportunities and barriers to employment:

> Following the mental bank video and debriefing session, Mr. Banks stated, "the mental bank process is like having a penny jar. It doesn't seem like much at first; however, over time, if you continually drop pennies in the penny jar you will accumulate a larger sum of money.... If this process is uncomfortable then that means that you are changing.... Doing uncomfortable and unfamiliar things lead to change.... Everything that's taught to us we know already. It's just some things have not been taught to us yet.... The only thing that separates us [African Americans] from people who live in Palos Verdes [an affluent community in Los Angeles County] is that they've been getting this information since they were young."

In comparing the mental bank process to having a penny jar, Mr. Brown illustrates the emphasis placed on cognitive-behavioral job search strategies rather than addressing any external or structural barriers to employment. Additionally, in suggesting that change occurs when individuals do "uncomfortable and unfamiliar things," Mr. Brown highlights the important role personal transformation played in the instructors' discourses. In asserting that a lack of knowledge or resources is the "only thing that separates" people in marginalized neighborhoods from those in affluent neighborhoods, Mr. Brown refuted the reality of a real or structural barrier to employment among formerly incarcerated individuals of color. Thus the underlying racial message was that formerly incarcerated individuals of color could overcome structural barriers to employment, if they commit to a process of personal change and growth.

While the message of personal transformation dominated the instructors' reentry discourses, they also framed their messages within a spiritually focused framework. In particular, instructors encouraged participants to "find a spiritual basis" so the positive cognitive-behavioral habits they are developing persist. Identifying a spiritual base would thus help to empower them to "rewrite the false stories" they've created regarding racial barriers to employment, such as "they won't hire me because I'm black." Participants were therefore advised to examine and change the structure of their belief systems, as this process would help them to live a life based on truth rather than lies. In the following excerpt from our field notes, Mr. Scott, an African American volunteer and spiritual leader, shared a personal life experience in order to help the participants understand how restructuring their belief systems can increase their life chances:

> Following the break, Mr. Thompson invited Mr. Scott to share a few "words of wisdom." Mr. Scott was an older African American man, who was maybe in his 50s, and had long dread locks that extended down his back. He walked to the front of the class very quietly, and began his talk by saying, "in 1992 my family divorced me because I was a drug addict!" He proceeded to share that he made the decision to commit suicide after his family divorced him. Yet, he decided to enroll in a drug treatment program prior to doing so.
>
> While Mr. Scott mentioned the drug program was helpful, he explained, "in order for me to change I had to find a spiritual basis. I needed to find my purpose in order to create a new life. I had to change what I was putting out, because I realized I couldn't lie to myself. I was trying to make something happen that wasn't happening." Mr. Scott further explained that by being still [meditating], he was able to see the areas in his life where he was lying to himself. He also expressed if it wasn't for his thinking, he wouldn't have been in the situations he was in.... "It was through self-forgiveness that I found peace within myself ... a person of spirituality has themselves and no one else." Mr. Scott continued with talking about spirituality and the "creator" by saying, "you're either what the creator made or something you made up. The creator makes things out of love. We make things out of lack and fear ... when you begin to question where you find yourself, look at your belief system. It is your belief system that threatens you."

In the above example, Mr. Scott's messages align with the dominant discourse of personal responsibility and change. He thus constructed the participants as spiritual beings who must allow a higher being to serve as the foundation of their lives. Through meditation, the participants can learn to forgive themselves and become aware of their life's purpose, as this process will assist them with restructuring their belief systems. Here the participants learn that by restructuring their belief systems, they can "get out of the story of what it means to be black" and begin to identify employment opportunities rather than barriers. Thus while race is mentioned and acknowledged, it is simultaneously downplayed as a potential barrier to successful reentry.

Responses to Job Search Strategies and Racial Messages

Throughout the observation period, participants typically appeared to buy into the instructors' strategies and messages concerning opportunities and barriers to employment. In particular, participants acknowledged that maintaining a colorblind lens and committing to a process of personal change and growth is necessary in their pursuit of postrelease employment. The program graduation offered numerous examples of participants' positive responses to the instructors' strategies and messages, as several were selected to share their program experiences at the ceremony. In the following example, an African American female participant read a statement she had prepared for the other graduates:

> "To my classmates, how many of you remember the question, if you can give up the story of what it means to be black for the possibility of it, would you? Well my story starts with three choices. My first choice, I chose my parents. This is a place where I picked up my spiritual upbringing, and where I first received some of my tools for my independence, strength, and knowledge. My second choice is that I chose to follow my niece's advice who told me [about the Empowered for Change reentry program], so I came.... My third choice, I chose change and thought modification. A total 180 for the renewal of the mind, because without renewal of the mind, transformation cannot take place. With that being said, basically my choice was to live versus to continue to exist. So with that, I chose and I still choose to have the right thoughts, to surround myself with the right people, in the right environment, at the right time, and for the right reasons, to obtain the right results. I am now renewed, refreshed, and restored."

In this example, the participant acknowledges that she had to make a personal decision to change in order for her to "obtain the right results." In expressing that she renewed her mind and changed her social networks to maintain positive external influences, she also supports the cognitively focused strategies. Her opening questions to the other participants also highlights the ways in which participants bought into the instructors' colorblind discourses.

In addition to acknowledging personal reform over system reform, participants also showed support for the instructors' strategies and messages by motivating others. For example, throughout the observation period, an African American female participant wrote an affirmation each day on the white board that was located on the wall at the front of the room. Some of her quotes and affirmations included:

- We are shaped by our thoughts; we become what we think. When the mind is pure, joy follows like a shadow that never leaves.
- Watch your thoughts, they become your words. Watch your words, they become your actions. Watch your actions, they become your

habits. Watch your habits, they become character and it becomes your destiny.
- Be who you really are, not who you are told to be. We are programed to be a certain way to fit into society. It is now time to reprogram ourselves so that today's society fits in with us.

Participants also responded positively to the instructors' strategies and messages by sharing them with nonprogram participants. For instance, during the last program session, the instructors asked each participant to share how the program has supported them in their change process. One African American female participant expressed that the program has helped her to change her conversations, in which she is now able to engage with and help other individuals from her neighborhood. She explained:

> "As a result of the class, I've started changing my conversations.... I was afraid of going back to the hood at first because my conversation didn't change. But since my conversation has changed I can now interact with people from the hood. I tell them about what I've learned to help them change their conversations. I don't stand in my story, I stand on it."

Overall, participants not only accepted the instructors' strategies and messages, they also used them to motivate and encourage others within and outside of the program setting.

Although participants typically demonstrated support for the program strategies and messages, in limited instances they raised questions about the ease with which they can apply these lessons beyond the 8-week program. For instance, during one program session, Mr. Thompson engaged the participants in an activity called "Things I am proud of are …" For this activity, the participants formed two small circles, and one person responded to the prompt aloud while the remaining group members listened. If the person speaking stopped or couldn't think of any other things he or she was proud of, the group members were to prompt them with the same statement, "Things I'm proud of are …" The following excerpt provides an example of an instance where a participant discussed the difficulty in applying the instructors' strategies and messages outside the comfort and safety of the reentry program:

> One African American man stated, "Things I am proud of are ... that I'm a family man to my mother and my brother; not being incarcerated or on probation; that I don't have to pay any more restitution; that I wake up and come to class; not being in jail; coming to class; showing change because I could be out in the streets; things I have, I appreciate them; to talk to my family not by phone cards." Once all of the participants shared, we went back to our seats and Mr. Thompson asked the participants what they thought about the exercises. The same African American male participant said, "this is the most relaxed time of my day." He expressed that he felt the freedom to be himself, but that "it's hard to face the streets when we leave because this program is a sanctuary."

In addition to raising concerns about the ease with applying the instructors' strategies and messages, participants also displayed some resistance to their teaching styles and methods that supported the job search strategies and messages. For instance, during one program session we observed, the instructors had asked program participants to read aloud the mental bank program contracts they developed for themselves. After one participant, an African American man, read his contract aloud, Mr. Williams, a volunteer, instructed him to rewrite his contract with a pen, as he noticed his contract was written in pencil. Mr. William's directive also supported the instructors' cognitive-focused job search strategy of writing information down using a pen and pad. Nevertheless, the participant expressed to Mr. Williams that he used a pencil because he "did not want to make any mistakes." Mr. Williams further questioned him, asking, "If it were a check would the bank accept it?" Appearing annoyed with inward-slanted eyebrows, the participant replied, "You're getting on my nerves." Mr. Williams then responded, "It's nothing personal, I'm just using you to teach the class. Not to embarrass you."

Overall, while participants typically supported the instructors' job search strategies and messages regarding opportunities and barriers to employment, the above example highlights some of the concerns and resistance participants displayed with regards to the instructors' reentry discourses or styles of teaching. Nevertheless, although participants would occasionally question or display some resistance to the instructors' strategies and/or messages, they remained engaged with all program-related activities, showing continual support for the dominant message of personal transformation as a strategy to increase their chances of obtaining postrelease employment.

Discussion

In this chapter, we sought to understand how issues of racism and barriers to employment are framed and negotiated in the context of a reentry program located in the hybrid space of the voluntary and carceral sectors. Specifically, we examined how instructors of color, including law enforcement, nonprofit workers, and community volunteers, framed their messages concerning opportunities and barriers to employment among a group of formerly incarcerated men and women of color. As a whole, we found that although the instructors, who fully facilitated the reentry sessions, and volunteers, who supported the instructors on a less regular basis, recognized the existence of racial barriers to employment, they discouraged participants from dwelling on or pondering issues of race and did not present strategies for directly breaking the barriers. Rather, they framed their employment and reentry discourses around practical, cognitive, and spiritually focused strategies. In doing so, they relayed messages that encouraged the participants to commit to a personal transformation that would enhance their success in postrelease employment. At times, the instructors evoked the language of civil rights or drew on cultural conventions in communities of color, such as prayer. While these strategies appeared to empower the participants in their pursuit of employment avenues, the instructors' and volunteers' strategies and messages also conformed to a colorblind discourse.

Given that low educational attainment has a strong connection to unemployment among ex-offenders (Uggen & Staff, 2001), it is not surprising that reentry program instructors and volunteers provided participants with practical job search strategies (e.g., career goal development, and then a mental bank). Yet in redirecting the participants away from acknowledging the importance of structural barriers, the instructors (who were themselves people of color) nevertheless diminished the reality that these factors often limit real-world opportunities. Thus, although the intersection of race and a criminal record pose major obstacles to even obtaining an initial job interview (Bertrand & Mullainathan, 2004; Decker et al., 2014; Pager, 2007), the cultural value of individualism was deeply embedded within and taught in the Empowered for Change reentry program.

The Empowered for Change program is an interesting hybrid resulting from the transfer of reentry services to the voluntary sector. It is housed within an historic civil rights organization yet also partnered with law enforcement. In this example, while the voluntary nonprofit organization took a leading role in providing community-based reentry services, it is still possible that the law enforcement instructors largely influenced the culture and structure of the reentry program. Thus even in this hybrid model, the language of law enforcement and colorblindness prevailed over possible alternatives.

For example, throughout the study period, instructors and volunteers continuously posed the question, "if you can give up the story of what it means to be black for the possibility of it would you?" This question not only provides an example of the way in which they support the cultural value of individualism, it also highlights how their reentry discourses in many ways support the notion of colorblindness. This was evident in their race-neutral discourses that promoted personal change and growth as a critical step to the participants securing employment. However, because race is socially constructed, social, economic, and political forces have a significant impact in shaping the meanings, ascribing qualities, and placing value on different racial/ethnic groups. These forces thus play an integral role in determining social and economic opportunities and outcomes, especially among people of color with a criminal record.

While participants occasionally displayed resistance or questioned the applicability of the instructors' strategies and messages outside of the program context, they generally supported the individual lens. It is likely the participants overwhelmingly supported the instructors' strategies and messages, as many identified the instructors' job search strategies and messages as beneficial to their job search and personal transformation process. Alternatively, because most participants were mandated to the Empowered for Change program, it is possible they supported the instructors' strategies and messages so as to not violate any aspect of their supervision requirements.

Moreover, while the Empowered for Change reentry program included instructors from disparate groups (i.e., law enforcement, nonprofit sector, community volunteers), there was little to no oversight or variability regarding the content or style with which the nonprofit and volunteer instructors presented their job search strategies and messages. This was observed in the cases of Mr. Jimenez and Mr. Gonzalez, two nonprofit instructors, and Ms. Walker, a community volunteer, who appeared to share a similar worldview as the law enforcement instructors, as they facilitated their sessions. Thus although this hybrid reentry program included the voluntary sector in the provision of reentry services, the law enforcement instructors were primary responsible for driving the program's messages concerning opportunities for and barriers to postrelease employment, as they not only developed the program workbook that guided nearly every session we observed, yet, often took the lead in setting the tone and structure for each program session we observed. For instance, from the initial orientation session to the graduation, Mr. Thompson, a law enforcement instructor, was present at nearly every session we observed and typically, opened and closed each session.

Additionally, while our analysis revealed that the instructors' and volunteers' strategies and messages conformed to a colorblind discourse of reentry, we also understand that their discourses can be viewed from a different perspective. For instance, Maruna (2001) argues that developing a sense of hope among ex-offenders is critical in their process to desist from crime, as individual empowerment can help them to move away from the feeling of being "doomed to deviance." McNeill, Raynor, and Trotter (2010) also assert that reentry program messages, such as those of hope, can help to increase ex-offenders' chances of obtaining postrelease employment as some may enter reentry programs with the knowledge, skills, and credentials needed to obtain legitimate employment. Race and structural barriers, such as racial discrimination, may therefore be less important to some ex-offenders of color as they pursue postrelease employment. Moreover, Burnett and Maruna (2004) found that those who leave prison with increased hope are less likely to recidivate. Yet, they also acknowledge that even the most hopeful may ultimately be discouraged if they consistently confront barriers, such as barriers to employment. Overall, although we take a critical stance regarding the instructors' job search strategies and messages, our findings also help to illuminate some of the positive and hopeful things that are occurring among and between law enforcement, ex-offenders, and communities of color, including the voluntary sector.

Limitations

With regards to limitations, we did not observe every session of the 8-week program and our study includes only one cohort. This selection may have limited the full range or transferability of our findings. Additionally, because we were confined to observation as our primary method, the exclusion of interview or focus group data collection methods prevented our ability to triangulate the findings to determine why the instructors framed their job search strategies and messages under an individually focused, race-neutral lens, or why the participants generally supported the instructors' reentry discourses. While studies using observation as the main mode of data collection may be prone to research bias, the inclusion of two researchers and analysts from different racial and gender backgrounds allowed us to document and interpret our findings from multiple perspectives, which helped to increase the rigor of the study.

Conclusion

The findings presented in this chapter contribute to the literature on the role of the voluntary sector in the criminal justice system. Specifically, our study highlights the ways in which the "colorblind" philosophy, one that assumes opportunities such as employment are equally attainable despite one's race, can influence the culture of a community-based reentry program and instructors' of color reentry discourses, including those from an historic civil rights organization. Further research should build on this study in a few key directions. It is important to examine how instructors and participants view this curriculum and its utility in the job search process. Is the program seen as being effective and what are the actual outcomes? On a more macro level, this study also illustrates an interesting way that the voluntary and criminal justice sectors intersect within the community, rather than within the jail or prison setting. The expanding reach of criminal justice system funding toward historically grassroots or civil rights organizations may have implications for building community trust among these agencies. It would be interesting to track, over time, how the positioning and/or expansion of these hybrid models affect the larger community.

References

Abarbanel, S., McCray, A., Newhall, K. M., & Snyder, J. (2013). *Realigning the revolving door: An analysis of California counties' AB 109 2011–2012 implementation plans.* Retrieved from http://law.stanford.edu/wp-content/uploads/sites/default/files/child-page/183091/doc/slspublic/Realigning%20the%20Revolving%20Door%20with%20updates%20for%2058%20counties%20(1).pdf.

Adams, K., Bennet, K. J., Flanagan, T. J., Marquart, J. W., Cuvelier, S. J., Fritsch, E., et al. (1994). Large-scale multidimensional test of the effect of prison education programs on offenders' behavior. *The Prison Journal, 74*(4), 433–449.

Alexander, M. (2010). *The new Jim Crow: Mass incarceration in the age of colorblindness.* New York: The New Press.
Aos, S., Miller, M., & Drake, E. (2006). *Evidence-based adult corrections programs: What works and what does not (#06-01-1201).* Washington State Institute for Public Policy. Retrieved from http://www.wsipp.wa.gov/ReportFile/924.
Bertrand, M. & Mullainathan, S. (2004). Are Emily and Greg more employable than Lakisha and Jamal? A field experiment on labor market discrimination. *American Economic Review, 94*(4), 991–1013.
Bonilla-Silva, E. (2010). *Racism without racists: Color-blind racism and racial inequality in contemporary American* (3rd ed.). New York: Rowman & Littlefield.
Bureau of Justice Statistics. (2010). *Recidivism of prisoners released in 30 states in 2005: Patterns from 2005 to 2010 (NCJ 244205).* Retreived from http://www.bjs.gov/content/pub/pdf/rprts05p0510.pdf.
Burnett, R. & Maruna, S. (2004). So 'prison works', does it? The criminal careers of 130 men released from prison under home security, Michael Howard. *Howard Journal, 43*(4), 390–404.
Carlson, P. M. & Garrett, J. S. (2013). *Prison and jail administration: Practice and theory* (3rd ed.). Burlington, MA: Jones & Bartlet Learning.
Decker, S. H., Spohn, C., Ortiz, N. R., & Hedberg, E. (2014). *Criminal stigma, race, gender and employment: An expanded assessment of the consequences of imprisonment for employment (2010-MU-MU-004).* National Institute of Justice. Retrieved from https://www.ncjrs.gov/pdffiles1/nij/grants/244756.pdf.
Feeley, M. M. & Simin, J. (1992). The new penology: Notes on the emerging strategy of corrections and its implications. *Criminology, 30*(4), 449–479.
Forman, J. (2012). Racial critiques of mass incarceration: Beyond the new Jim Crow. *N.Y.U. Journal of International Law and Politics, 87,* 21–69.
Guerino, P., Harrison, P. M., & Sabol, W. J. (2011). *Prisoners in 2010. US Department of Justice: Office of Justice Programs, Bureau of Justice Statistics.* Retrieved from http://www.bjs.gov/content/pub/pdf/p10.pdf.
Hanley-Lopez, I. F. (2010). Post-racial racism: Racial stratification and mass incarceration in the age of Obama. *California Law Review, 98*(3), 1023–1074.
Harlow, C. W. (2003). *Education and correctional populations. NCJ 195670.* Washington, DC: US Department of Justice, Bureau of Justice Statistics. Retrieved from bjs.ojp.usdoj.gov/content/pub/pdf/ecp.pdf.
Holzer, H. J., Raphael, S., & Stoll, M. (2007). The effect of an applicant's criminal history on employer hiring decisions and screening practices: Evidence from Los Angeles. In S. Bushway, M. Stoll, & D. Weiman (Eds.), *Barriers to reentry? The labor market for released prisoners in post-industrialized America* (pp. 117–150). New York: Russell Sage Foundation.

Horsman, R. (1981). *Race and manifest destiny: The origins of American racial anglo-saxonism.* Cambridge, MA: Harvard University.

Lincoln, Y. S. & Guba, E. G. (1985). *Naturalistic inquiry.* Newbury Park, CA: Sage.

Lockwood, S., Nally, J. M., Ho, T., & Knutson, K. (2012). The effect of correctional education on post-release employment and recidivism: A 5-year follow-up study in the state of Indiana. *Crime & Delinquency, 58*(3), 380–396.

Lofland, J. & Lofland, L. H. (1995). *Analyzing social settings: A guide to qualitative observation and analysis.* Belmont, CA: Wadsworth.

Maruna, S. (2001). *Making good: How ex-convicts reform and rebuild their lives.* Washington, DC: American Psychological Association.

McNeill, F., Raynor, P., & Trotter, C. (2010). *Offender supervision: New directions in theory, research and practice.* London: Routledge.

Miles, M. B. & Huberman, A. M. (1984). *Qualitative data analysis: A sourcebook of new methods.* Thousand Oaks, CA: Sage.

Mills, C. W. (1997). *The racial contract.* Ithaca, NY: Cornell University Press.

National Research Council (2007). *Parole, desistance from crime, and community integration (Committee on community supervision and desistance from crime, committee on law and justice, division of behavioral and social sciences and education).* Washington, DC: The National Academies.

Pager, D. (2007). Two strikes and you're out: The intensification of racial and criminal stigma. In S. Bushway, M. Stoll, & D. Weiman (Eds.), *Barriers to reentry? The labor market for released prisoners in post-industrialized America* (pp. 151–173). New York: Russell Sage.

Pager, D. & Western, B. (2009). *Investigating prisoner reentry: The impact of conviction status on the employment prospects of young men.* Washington, DC: US Department of Justice, National Institute of Justice, NCJ 228584.

Rodriguez, M. N., & Emsellem, M. (2011). *65 million "need not apply": The case for reforming criminal background checks for employment.* New York: The National Employment Law Project. Retrieved from http://www.nelp.org/page//SCLP/2011/65_Million_Need_Not_Apply.pdf?nocdn=1.

Seiter, R. P. & Kadela, K. (2003). Prisoner reentry: What works, what does not, and what is promising. *Crime & Delinquency, 49*(3), 360–388.

Tripodi, S., Kim, J. S., & Bender, K. (2010). Is employment associated with reduced recidivism? The complex relationship between employment and crime. *International Journal of Offender Therapy and Comparative Criminology, 54*(5), 706–720.

Uggen, C. & Staff, J. (2001). Work as a turning point for criminal offenders. *Corrections Management Quarterly, 5*, 1–16.

Wacquant, L. (2000). The new 'peculiar institution': On the prison as surrogate ghetto. *Theoretical Criminology, 4*(3), 377–389.

Wacquant, L. (2002). From slavery to mass incarceration: Rethinking the 'race question' in the U.S. *New Left Review*, *13*, 41–60.

Wagner, P., Sakala, L., & Bagley, J. (2014). *States of incarceration: The global context.* Washington, DC: Prison Policy Initiative. Retrieved from http://www.prisonpolicy.org/global/.

Western, B., Pettit, B., & Guetzkow, J. (2003). Black economic progress in the era of mass imprisonment. In M. Mauer & M. Chesney-Lind (Eds.), *Invisible punishment: The collateral consequences of mass imprisonment* (pp. 165–178). New York: The New Press.

CHAPTER 10

Penal Assemblages: Governing Youth in the Penal Voluntary Sector

Abigail Tsionne Salole

The objective of changing thinking patterns, along with terms such as "pro-social," "responsibility," and reducing "criminal thinking" are often linked to evidence-based practice in criminal justice programming. A common objective for these programs is to change the way offenders think by developing pro-social skills and reducing maladaptive behavior linked to criminal activity. For example, two testimonials from young people who have completed a voluntary sector program designed to reduce shoplifting for youth describe their development of a new perspective:

> "I learned to respect small and large businesses, they do me a favor by selling things I need so I do respect their property and them. This was a large eye-opener for me. I seemed to take things for granted."
>
> "I developed a whole new perspective on choices and learned that one mistake can change your life forever." (PVS organization Annual Report, 2011)[1]

The messaging behind these accounts is that young people involved with the voluntary sector learn "new ways of being." The phrases "whole new perspective" and "large eye-opener" connote a personal transformative experience and a departure from a former way of thinking and being.

[1] The names of organizations are confidential and unidentified.

A.T. Salole (✉)
Griffith University, Mt Gravatt, Queensland, Australia

L.S. Abrams et al. (eds.), *The Voluntary Sector in Prisons*, Palgrave Studies in Prisons and Penology, DOI 10.1057/978-1-137-54215-1_10

Temporally, these testimonials are a telling of the end of a narrative, what the young person's perspective is like after youth justice programming offered by the voluntary sector. If we are to imagine what came before these narratives, we might assume crime such as stealing and criminal attitudes.

While evidence-based practices are not a recent strategy, the discourse is increasingly prominent under neoliberalism and "contractual governance" (Crawford, 2003, p. 480) in which particular aspects of the criminal justice process are outsourced to the penal voluntary sector. Like Corcoran (2011) I use the term "Penal Voluntary Sector" (PVS) to refer to that segment of the voluntary sector that partners and delivers service in (and to) the traditional criminal justice system. The PVS has long since existed in Western industrialized states; however, under a neoliberal penal regime it is being reshaped and reconfigured as a site of punishment, correction, and rehabilitation. Contrary to beliefs surrounding the independence of the voluntary sector, PVS workers in this investigation do not experience their work as autonomous from the state. Instead, this chapter demonstrates how PVS work is conducted in relation and in reference to the traditional criminal justice system.

In this chapter I explicate discursive practices to provide insight on how PVS workers approach and conduct their work. Building on previous empirical investigations of the practice of punishment (cf. Barron, 2011; Franzén, 2015; Gray & Salole, 2006; Phoenix & Kelly, 2013; Singh, 2012; Thomas & Bull, 2013), I examine how local nonstate actors approach youth in conflict with the law and how their unique position within the youth criminal justice system shapes their work. Distinct from the chapters in other sections of this volume, the focus of this investigation is on paid employees within the voluntary sector. I begin with a brief historical overview of the role of the voluntary sector in Ontario, Canada, as it relates to the youth criminal justice system. Next, I outline the role of the PVS and contextual considerations in the modern youth justice system, while situating the prominence of cognitive behavioral approaches and risk frameworks within the context of "governing through freedom" strategies (Rose, 1999). Third, I explain my methodological framework, sample and data collection processes. Utilizing ethnographic observation and interview data, my findings section demonstrates how workers negotiate their institutional context within the contested terrain of the PVS.

The Role of the Penal Voluntary Sector in Shaping the Youth Justice System

European settlers understood Aboriginal children as the source of and the solution to Canada's "Indian problem." Initiatives to institutionalize the governance of Aboriginal children began with missionary education, which "paved the way for subsequent residential schools" (Smandych & McGillivray, 1999, p. 252). Indeed, McGillivray (1997) argued, "[the] colonization of Aboriginal childhood created a Foucauldian carceral archipelago whose institutions include the reserve, the residential school, the child protection system, young offender facilities and jail" (p. 136).[2] While the specific experiences of racialized youth in the establishment of the juvenile justice system in Canada requires further study, Chen's (2005) examination of child-saving in Toronto from the 1880s to the 1920s indicates that race was quite relevant to the child-saving movement. Though race was not often mentioned in official records Chen explains, "essentially, child-saving work at the time reflected anxiety about the size and quality of the predominant Anglo-Celtic population" (Chen, 2005, p. 15).

By the late nineteenth century, the voluntary sector was not only involved in providing services for juvenile delinquents, they were recognized and sought out as being providers of rehabilitative and pastoral care.[3] Chen (2005) documents the history of the "detention room" operated by the Toronto Children's Aid Society from 1894 until 1920. Chen's research reveals that several modes of power coexisted in the detention room: "the old punitive and despotic tradition of dealing with 'infant criminals,' discipline based on the identity of juvenile delinquent, and pastoral power over 'erring children'" (p. 110). Recognizing that pastoral care aspects of the detention room were missing, the Children's Aid Society involved volunteers from the Young Men's Christian Association

[2] It is beyond the scope of this chapter to provide a thorough history for Aboriginal children who were (and continue to be) governed differently from non-aboriginal children. For a specific examination of the governance of Aboriginal children and childhood see McGillivray's (1997) examination of the centrality of childhood in colonial and postcolonial Canadian policy and Miller's (1996) examination of residential schools.

[3] Foucault uses the concept of pastoral power to describe a benevolent form of power. For Foucault, the pastorate is a prelude to governmentality through procedures and "through the constitution of a specific subject, of a subject whose merits are analytically identified, who is subjected in continuous networks of obedience, and who is subjectified (subjectivé) through the compulsory extraction of truth" (Foucault, 2007, pp. 184–185).

(YMCA) and Big Brother and Big Sister Associations in order to provide these services. Chen (2005) notes how the presence of these volunteer workers reconfigured the power relations in the detention room. First, it meant the Children's Aid Society was

> under the gaze of outsiders, who not only owed their loyalty to parties other than the society but were a new breed of personnel in social service. Second, even though the Big Sisters and Big Brothers were also authorities so far as the children were concerned, they were nevertheless different from the Children's Aid staff, such as the "nightwatchman." The presence of Big Sisters and Big Brothers could work as a mechanism for children to exercise their agency, for example, by simply telling a Big Sister that she had been treated badly in the detention room. (p. 113)

The presence of voluntary organizations helped to reconfigure power relations by undermining the "relative autonomy" of more institutional power (Chen, 2005, p. 113). That the Children's Aid Society, a child protection organization, operated juvenile criminal detention illustrates the historical marriage between child welfare and delinquency. Child welfare work was imbued with crime prevention and treatment duties. Simultaneously, the prison reform movement greatly impacted child welfare (Chen, 2005; Maurutto, 2003). Based on this historical relationship, there was a slippage in the concepts of deserving (dependent) and undeserving (deviant). Chunn (1992) noted, "the stringent nineteenth-century ideological line of demarcation between the deviant and dependent of the province was obscured" (p. 21).

The lines between public and private institutions were similarly blurred. Many historical accounts of the governance of juvenile delinquency and child protection highlight the social control imperatives that belied social reforms. While the social control function of voluntary organizations is clear, it is also important to note that the trust and familiarity bestowed upon voluntary sector organizations did not always apply directly to the state (Maurutto, 2003). This unique familiarity aspect of the voluntary sector positioned them as attractive partners (albeit sometimes silent and invisible) with the state. The slow social reform process toward a separate youth justice system and child protection statutes witnessed the emergence of strategies such as reformatories, training schools, detention rooms, and later a deinstitutionalizing trend in favor of probation and community corrections. The voluntary sector was an important force of reform and change throughout this process.

Concern over juvenile delinquency helped to galvanize the voluntary sector to protect children from neglectful parents (Chen, 2005; Chunn, 1992; Maurutto, 2003). In addition to pastoral power, voluntary organizations and nonstate actors regularly participated in a range of other rationalities and technologies. From supervising juvenile delinquents on probation to managing and classifying juvenile delinquents in industrial schools to advocating for policy change, the participation of voluntary organizations in the criminal justice system is complex and contradictory. The role of the voluntary sector in the governance of juvenile delinquents in Canada pre-dates the establishment of a federally mandated separate youth justice system, which was enacted with the Juvenile Delinquents Act in 1908. Recognition of this historical pattern of contested terrain is needed to understand the more recent context for the PVS in Canada. It also raises important questions about the role of the voluntary sector in the justice system. Has the PVS maintained the ability to disrupt institutional power as it did in the detention room? More broadly, how does the PVS relate to the traditional criminal justice system? How does the role of the PVS relate to the shifting social and political context? What is the role of the frontline worker in the PVS?

Compared with previous youth justice polices, the current Canadian Youth Criminal Justice Act (YCJA) names "community" as an actor and stakeholder in youth justice policy; however, the concept remains malleable (Hogeveen, 2005). While collaborations and partnerships with the state are often couched in the discourse of community, nonprofit organizations in the PVS have often filled the role of community as partners to the state. The YCJA applies to youth between the ages of 12 and 18 and is federally legislated and operationalized by the provinces and territories of Canada. The legislation adopts a bifurcated approach to youth in conflict with the law—specifying one approach for offenders who are deemed serious and another for those who are minor or first-time offenders. These two approaches to young offenders have important consequences including "an assumed division of responsibility between the state and *the community* in managing them" (Campbell, 2005, p. 19, *emphasis added*). In addition, the enhanced role of community-based sanctions under the YCJA like attendance centers, community circles, and community-based justice programs have contributed to a reconfiguration of partnerships between the state and the PVS.

Partners in Crime: Youth Crime Statistics and the Role of the PVS under the YCJA

Across Canada, police-reported crime statistics show that numbers and rates of youth accused of a Criminal Code offense have decreased steadily since the implementation of the YCJA in 2003. In 2014 approximately 94,100 youth were accused of a Criminal Code offense nationally (Boyce, 2015). Almost half (45 %) of these youth were charged by police and processed through the traditional criminal justice system. The remaining 55 % were processed through other means including being warned or referred to a PVS organization. The total number of accused represents a 42 % reduction since the enactment of the YCJA. Following these numbers, the proportion of youth sentenced to custody has also decreased substantially. In the 2011–2012 fiscal year, 15 % of youth found guilty of crimes served a jail sentence (Dauvergne, 2013). Most of these custody sentences were 3 months or less (74 %), and less than 2 % of youth court custody sentences exceeded 1 year. Despite the overall reduction in youth incarceration, there are continued indications of the overrepresentation of racialized youth at every stage of the youth criminal justice system. In Ontario, this overrepresentation manifests in the disproportionate representation of Aboriginal and black youths (McMurtry & Curling, 2008; Rankin & Winsa, 2013).

In the province of Ontario there are approximately 250 organizations that receive funds from various governmental branches in order to provide programs under the provision of the YCJA. The Ministry of Children and Youth Services (MCYS) has primary responsibility for administering youth justice services in Ontario and funds 207 organizations that serve more than 37,000 youth in conflict with the law annually in the province (Ministry of Children and Youth Services, 2014). The MCYS funds PVS organizations that run programs like open custody facilities, attendance centers, intense supervision programs, extrajudicial sanctions, and extrajudicial measures.[4] Referrals to these PVS organizations come from various points within the traditional criminal justice system (police, courts, and probation). Most organizations in Canada's PVS are funded

[4] Extrajudicial sanctions and extrajudicial measures are alternatives to traditional criminal justice programming made available under sections 6, 8, and 10 of the YCJA. Extrajudicial measures refer to pre-charge proceedings outside of the formal court system. Extrajudicial sanctions divert charged young people in conflict with the law away from the traditional criminal justice system.

as transfer payment organizations, which means what the phrasing implies: Governmental ministries transfer funds to organizations in the provision of their state mandate. This funding stream accounts for over half of the total amount of the youth justice services' budget in Ontario. According to the Auditor General's (2014) audit, in the 2013–2014 fiscal year the Ministry spent $352 million on the Youth Justice Services programming. This amount includes $180 million in transfer payment funding. PVS organizations are diverse and range considerably in size, mandate, and funding and are disparate across the province. From 2008–2013,[5] the MCYS youth justice services funded approximately the same 205 organizations over 5 years. The highest transfer payment amount to one organization in the 2012–2013 fiscal year was $9,508,349. The lowest transfer payment amount in that same fiscal year was $3434. An examination of the MCYS funded organizations revealed that while there remains some organizations that provide a combination of child welfare services, developmental services and justice services, there is an increasing specialization of youth services for youth in conflict with the law as reflected in programming that is exclusive to young people as a result of being accused of crime.

PVS workers have a range of job titles, descriptions, and educational backgrounds. For example, Youth Court Workers conduct much of their work in youth court and aim to represent their PVS organization to court personnel and youth in conflict with the law. Others are group facilitators who provide offense-related programming as part of an extrajudicial measure program. Residential or primary workers supervise youth while they serve a custody sentence or are in pretrial detention. Frontline PVS workers often have their bachelor's degree or diploma in paid helping professions such as social work or child and youth work.

Young people in conflict with the law in Ontario, like many advanced liberal democracies, are often assessed through risk assessments tools. The risk/need assessment most commonly utilized in Ontario is the Level of Supervision Inventory—Ontario Revised (LSI-OR) version (Andrews, Bonta, & Wormith, 1995). This assessment focuses on lowering particular risks in the areas of: criminal history, education/employment, family, leisure/recreation, antisocial peers, substance abuse, and attitudes/orientation. Standardized assessments are rooted in actuarial research and based on the premise that these assessments will also lead to evidence-based interventions with youth in conflict with the law (cf. Whyte, 2009). One of the

[5] This information was gathered as result of a Freedom of Information request.

critiques of the prominence of governing through risk is the consequence of limiting individualized treatment and programming options. Hannah-Moffat, Maurutto, and Turnbull (2009) explain:

> The "risk principle" directs practitioners to assign offenders to a limited set of programs that target criminogenic needs and demonstrate an impact on rates of recidivism. For institutions faced with declining resources, risk logics provide a convenient rationale for restricting and streamlining programming options. Thus, risk assessment is more than the management of offenders; it essentially limits the number and range of treatment options available to practitioners. (p. 396)

Risk assessments are intrinsically linked to treatment options. One of the more popular treatment frameworks used to reduce risk is cognitive behavioral therapy (CBT), which is a vast area of therapeutic intervention employed by those in the helping professions (including social workers, psychologists, and other counseling professionals). The approach is widely researched and empirically validated, making it a favored evidence-based practice for a variety of mental health issues such as addictions and depression (Butler, Chapman, Forman, & Beck, 2006). Using this approach in youth justice settings assumes that young people in conflict with the law have distorted thinking and impaired social and interpersonal skills that contribute to offending behavior. Similar to risk assessments, this treatment option has also been met with a range of critiques. One critique is that CBT ignores larger social realities that construct offending behavior and therefore contribute to a compromised understanding of rehabilitation (Balfour, 2000; Barron, 2011). Another observation is that, under a cognitive behavioral approach, youth in conflict with the law are encouraged to simultaneously practice submission and responsibility (Cox, 2011; Franzén & Holmqvist, 2014) and there is absence of interventions that would actually result in a change in their social position (Gray, 2013).

Risk discourse and CBT are aligned with technologies of "governing through freedom" (Rose, 1999) since they are preoccupied with the future and how choices can impact the future. If a young person does not exhibit behavior that is assessed as conducive to their becoming an autonomous, mature, and responsible adult citizen, then experts will govern them "according to the new regime of autonomy and choice, utilizing a tool-bag of techniques ... to install the capacities for self-determination and self-mastery" (Rose, 1999, p. 89). These strategies, which are often linked to neoliberal governance, also produce particular subjectivities (cf. Franzén, 2015). This current research focuses on how PVS workers negotiate issues tied to subjectivity and explicates how responsibilization is practiced in a modern penal assemblage.

Methodology: Mapping Social Relations

Drawing on Smith's institutional ethnography and Foucault's theories of governmentality, this research explores the everyday realities and multiple rationalities that are available in the PVS. Despite ontological and epistemological differences between Smith and Foucault, there remains utility in combining methodological aspects of the two scholars (Satka & Skehill, 2012). To understand various institutional contexts, I conducted 24 interviews with respondents from a range of employment contexts from 2012–2014. Sixteen respondents were frontline PVS workers, four were PVS managers/executive directors, and four were professionals in the traditional criminal justice system, such as probation officers or police officers. The lines between these professional categories are not always clearly demarcated. That is, some PVS research participants had also worked in the traditional criminal justice system and some police and probation respondents report having worked in nonprofit organizations and the PVS. In addition, two PVS frontline workers had temporary employment experiences in the traditional criminal justice system and then moved to working in the PVS. Two PVS workers identified that they have also had interactions with the traditional criminal justice system as offenders, and this experience of conflict with the law formed an important part of how they established rapport with young people.

For frontline workers, I examined how they spent their time at work and conducted interviews at their place of employments, an alternate worksite (such as court) or another agreed upon location. I asked questions about their professional accountability and the relationships they forged in order to conduct their work. Interviews were about 1 hour in length. At times, I asked questions about what would be considered a breach of social and institutional norms. For example, I would ask questions like, "Would you share that type of information with a probation officer? "How do you determine case management process and group curriculum topics?" Answers helped me to ascertain how decisions were made and specifically how external actors and polices inform the local context. Following the method of institutional ethnography (Smith, 1987) I took particular interest in forms, policies, memos, and the institutional sequencing of PVS work. While social characteristics like race, class, and gender were an important part of this examination, I did not collect social demographic information and relied on research participants to make connections with how their identity informs their work. I developed a data dialogue sequence in order to inform my research problematic and read the transcripts and other data sources with multiple purposes (Doucet & Mautner, 2008). In the next section I delineate how PVS workers navigate and are an important part of the penal assemblage of the youth justice system. I demonstrate how these PVS workers resist, accommodate, subvert, extend, and negotiate state goals and rationalities with a particular emphasis on how risk governance and cognitive behavioral approaches are practiced and negotiated within the PVS.

Findings: Hybrid Assemblages and the PVS

The concept of an assemblage collates multiple discourses, acts, and identities and helps to organize seemingly conflicting ideas that are not binary or temporal in nature. Newman and Clarke (2009) explain that the term assemblage:

> ... provides some conceptual leverage for understanding both the work of assembling (the building of assemblages in and through which governing is enacted) and the vulnerability of assemblages to coming apart (under the strain of maintaining their internal connectedness or apparent coherence). (p. 68)

The concept of a penal assemblage is useful to understand the *practice* of youth justice, which is often a departure from the policy of youth justice. PVS work like most criminal justice practice is complex, contradictory, and based on hybrid models of punishment (Franzén, 2015; Gray & Salole, 2006). These findings are divided into two main parts. First, I explain how PVS workers strategically accommodate and approach risk discourse and assessments. Second, I explore how PVS workers negotiate a mandate to offer CBT programming in the PVS.

Strategic Accommodation/Acceptance: Risk Discourse

PVS workers espoused varying degrees of support for risk discourse; however, all PVS workers were made to somehow accommodate the discourse in order to conduct their work. Some research participants expressed a degree of confidence in the risk assessment tools and their ability to drive case management decisions. PVS worker Ray[6] explained that he thinks that risk assessments have authority, and while he does not consider himself an expert in "that kind of stuff," he "knows that a lot of research went into it. And it's probably the best thing we got in the science of young people getting in trouble." Ray went on to explain that he "hasn't really looked into it because it's not as if it would make any difference. They [probation] seem to think it's important. So guess what? It's important."

By contrast, PVS worker Aziza explained, "They [LSI scores] don't really mean anything to me. I read them but then I go on to get to know the youth. That's where the answers are. Not on some piece of paper." For Aziza, risk assessment tools undermine her caring and authentic approach to young people in conflict with the law. Aziza also questioned the authority and legitimacy of the LSI as a tool:

> At risk. What does that even mean? From what I can tell it means how marginalized a young person is and I don't think the answer to that marginalization should be to treat youth like they are a number. They are so much more than that.

Other research participants noted that the LSI is not aligned with their approach to working with youth. As one frontline worker Arundeep explained,

> Well, I have a problem with how those things are done. Most of the time they want you to sit down with a kid and ask them a bunch of questions. And it's really hard to make it sound natural. And when you're trying to build a rapport with a young person, the last thing you want to do is just drill them with questions. And then, well, and then what? You can't even say it was worth it. Because you go through all these questions and then the conclusion is this number that really doesn't mean anything to them. I guess that's my problem with it. My problem with it is that's so obviously a professional exercise that my clients don't care about. It's not for them. It's for probation. It's for the professionals.

[6] Pseudonyms were used for research participants.

Importantly, PVS workers expressed indifference or skepticism toward risk assessments when they felt alienated from the process. They reported frustration when probation officers did not share the entire risk assessment and only shared the goals that are understood as the outcome of the assessment. Regina indicated that there had been instances where she had long-standing relationships with a young person and she was not interviewed as part of the probation officer's assessment and presentencing report. She lamented,

> So if they are not going to ask me, their worker who has seen them [the youth client] almost every week for the last two years about what's been going on with them [the youth]. What's going on at home? What's going on at school? What's going on with court dates and whatever? If they are not going to ask me, then quite frankly I just don't think that probation takes them very seriously. They obviously are just going to write what they want to write. But it's such a piss off. Because here I am in the probation office, seeing [this particular probation officer] and he doesn't even want to ask me. Because you know those reports [presentencing reports] are important. Judges read them. And, well it's not because I'm hard to find. I'm right in front of his face all the time.

For Regina, being excluded as a key-informant for a presentencing report undermines the legitimacy of the process. While PVS workers are often positioned as working alongside the traditional criminal justice system, they unanimously agreed that they needed to be recognized by the courts, police and probation.

As a result of lack of information from probation, some PVS workers conducted their own risk/need assessment. Sadie expressed some ambivalence about that process:

> so in essence when [PVS organization], when we complete a risk/needs assessment they have no weight, whatsoever anywhere in this universe. Nowhere, nowhere but within our organization. And the reason why we even conduct them is that we can be on the same page as probation. So it's to, at the end of the day, come out with a risk/need assessment that is pretty similar to what probation came up with.

In a slightly different vein, Ray found the assessment tools useful and a form of leverage with probation officers that he works with. He describes, "I always refer to the LSI score. It means that I'm speaking the same lingo as the P.O. It gives us some common ground and shows that we are looking at what they are sending over." According to Ray and Sadie, the risk/need assessment, then, is embedded within a particular knowledge base that carries legitimacy with probation officers.

One probation officer who formerly worked in the PVS indicated that she often completed risk/need assessments as part of her routine work in the PVS. But only as a probation officer did she understand the purpose of the tools. She explained: "As a probation officer I go to training, like days of training, on how to do these assessments. Working at [a PVS organizations] they give you some old unofficial photocopied version that's just a form and not one day of training. You just kinda figure it out."

Connected to Arundeep's ambivalence and frustration with the official rationales for risk assessments, Arundeep explained that she used risk/need scores to meet other goals. In the quote below, she refers to the risk score (and therefore reconstitutes the risk score), not because of blind adherence to risk rationality, but to meet her client-centered goals. She explained:

> So I don't pay much attention to those scores for what I do. But when I need to write a letter for probation or when I'm doing my summaries, I do refer to them. Especially, if it helps to rationalize something that the youth actually needs… An example would be family counselling, home visits that sort of thing. I mean probation is very formulaic when it comes to goals. It's always education. It's always anger management. And it becomes the same thing again and again, but, I see these guys as different. I try to tailor what I do for them…. I say to the probation officer that this is really aligned with the risk/need assessment even if I think some other language would be better to use for the sort of work that I do.

Regardless of the PVS workers' perceptions of validity of the risk/need assessment, the narratives of the workers indicated that they engaged in a form of *strategic accommodation*. In doing so, they recognized that it was an important part of their work, particularly as it applied to their work with probation. Some workers like Arundeep were able to use assessment scores to ensure that helping goals were met. As opposed to probation officers who might partially engage in and/or embrace risk discourse for the defensible decisions it creates, PVS workers do not have to defend their case management with the young person as much as they need to establish legitimacy and broker a relationship with probation officers who are the official case managers. While risk discourse is important to probation officers and the MCYS, PVS workers also felt that risk discourse was easy to understand and comply with for the purposes of their work. Indeed, in this case strategic accommodation can be easily accomplished by aligning PVS work with the case management goals that the probation officers set.

Prior research has indicated that probation officers have a complex relationship with risk assessments (Hannah-Moffat et al., 2009) in which they maintain discretionary power in the utilization of risk-needs-assessments. However, the PVS workers in this study explained that they negotiated their relationship with probation officers based on the premise that the officers strictly adhered to risk assessments. That is, for PVS workers, the myth of the monolithic and comprehensive risk discourse, as it applies to probation officers, remains. There are a few possible explanations for these different findings. One possibility is that it is simply easier for probation officers to communicate certainties to PVS workers. Indeed, while the presences of fissures and exceptions to rules are a reality, it is more difficult and time-consuming to communicate the particularities of when and why exceptions should occur. Put another way, that discretion exists in every facet of the criminal justice system is not contested; rather, discretion becomes problematic when there is a negative unintended consequence to that use of discretion. Another possibility is that since probation officers are the case managers for the purpose of having to defend decisions, it is also likely that they do not want there to be a second layer of "black box" (opaque) decision-making residing in the PVS. Rather, if the probation officers have to defend decisions made, they would prefer all decisions to be theirs.

Changing Minds (Within Reason)

PVS workers expressed that there was a certain functionality to the cognitive behavioral approach that was aligned with the work that they do with people in conflict with the law. Citing literacy levels of the clients, effectiveness, and the punitive functions of their work, PVS workers explained that CBT has both legitimacy and utility in their work with young people in conflict with the law. For Meredith, the expert role and the hierarchy associated with the cognitive behavioral approach, and its distinction from a "feel good" approach invoked the punishment role of the PVS. Meredith indicated how CBT fits with her approach to young people in conflict with the law because you can just be like "um nope, you're wrong." She explained,

> For a lot of these kids, we are seeing them pretty short term. It's kinda punishment to see us and we also need to give them some new skills so if they want to use this as an opportunity to turn things around, at least they got some skills to do that. So our programs need to send that message, they need to be about taking responsibility and giving them options and to make better choices.

Other research participants explained how the cognitive behavioral approach is aligned with evidence-based practice. Aziza stated:

> Well, counseling young offenders is tricky. A lot of the times I know I am doing some good with them just because they have someone to talk to. I know it, they know it. But how do you prove that? You can't really. So I think that we end up doing a lot of stuff here that we can't prove. So we give them a pre-test and post-test so we can prove we are making a difference and it just so happens that CBT fits well with that model. So it wins.

The verifiable efficacy of CBT was also pointed to as one of the reasons why PVS workers adhere to the principles behind the cognitive behavioral approach. Mandy explained:

> Well probation is pretty clear that they want us to use a thought-feelings-action approach. This seems to be what works and that's what they think that we do. So we just have to keep on doing it... And I would have to say that I think it does work. I think it's easy for them [the PVS clients] to understand. If you look at our pre/post scores, I can tell that it does make a difference. It gives the tools they need to take responsibility. I know it doesn't work for everyone but at least we can have some answers for them. A lot of these kids come from pretty tough homes and so it if they want to make a change and maybe treat their kids differently, well here are the tools. They really need to change the way they think.

CBT resonated with many workers for various reasons, including the simple premise of the modality fitting well to ease of tracking measurable outcomes. For some research participants like Meredith, CBT's focus on individual responsibility is connected to the rationality of the criminal justice system. For her, it is important to extend that rationality that is core to the criminal justice system and neoliberal governance alike.

Another observation from PVS workers' assessments of cognitive behavioral approaches are that some of them, like Aziza and Mandy, are acutely aware that it is often factors which stem from outside their PVS work setting that inform their work. From a management perspective, Kandy explained that it was important that group sessions be standardized so that referral organizations know what to expect from the PVS. She explained,

> But, so now we've moved to very standardized groups. This is the curriculum we offer. Make sure you do these exercises, make sure you do these worksheets. Following this, it's part of your job. Because we are not going to get referrals if people don't know what they are referring folks to.

Participants largely agreed that there is a certain degree of functionality in standardized group curriculum. At the same time, some PVS workers felt as long as the learning objectives were met in a session, there was still room for the facilitator to make modifications as they saw fit.

> I've been doing this for so long that I end up using the "best of" series. We've purchased a lot of different kits over the years. And each of them has something that it's good at. So I choose what we do based on what I've seen to be the most successful and by that I often mean they understand it. Quite honestly, that's what we are dealing with here. You'd be surprised at the number of these guys that can't read. I have one guy now who is in grade 11 and he is at a grade 5 reading level. What are you supposed to do with that?

Other participants concurred that modifications could be made to the curriculum or the general cognitive behavioral approach, "within reason" (as Regina stated). Importantly, the permission or personal agency of PVS workers to veer away from set curriculum had to do with their personal context within the PVS organization they worked for and whether they considered the modification to be reasonable. Examples of modification "within reason" were: adding material from other group prepackaged group modules, discovering new material that fit (even loosely) within the cognitive behavioral framework, and adding popular culture references (one PVS worker used crimes committed by celebrities as an example to apply to the cognitive behavioral framework). The PVS workers indicated that "within reason" translated to keeping the cognitive behavioral framework clear and intact.

There were also elements of group programming that fell out of the bounds of "within reason." For example, participants did not consider it appropriate for PVS workers to discuss race or racism in group sessions or individual counseling sessions. Aziza shared an experience when she had all young black in men in her anger management group:

> So this was the first time this happened to me. This was the first time I ever had when every single participant was a black boy. And I just couldn't do it the same. I tried, because it was early on and I thought there might be trouble, and I've got mouths to feed at home, so I'm not trying to draw attention to myself… but, I was like unable to. It was like my body would not let these young black boys leave this class without some sort of race analysis. So the first couple sessions were the same and then one day, I was just like this is the day. And it was all about why are young black men angry? What is happening to them? And also, why are people so scared of black men? I thought it went great. Yeah, it was great until [the youth] went up to his probation officer citing Malcolm X. Well, let's just say I got spoken to. Let's just say I don't do that in groups no more.… But I still do it. But I do it when I know that they [youth] know that most people around here are going to be scared when we start talking about Malcolm [Malcolm X]. I ain't trying to start no revolution. I just want them to connect the dots. And it's sad. It's sad that they can be in a room with all young black men who got into trouble and they still need me to connect the dots for them. What's happening there?

Aziza's experience indicates that she took a risk to do something outside of the curriculum or the bounds of group sessions. She knew it was professionally risky to depart from a CBT approach to a more structural analysis; however, she felt a moral imperative to change the material. Her rationale for stepping outside of this scope was that she thought it would be helpful for the young black men in her anger management group to link their experience of criminalization to a historical and ongoing criminalization of black men. This connection contradicts the individualized framework and calls into question assumptions of individual responsibility.

This tension regarding racism in the criminal justice system and a shared social identity based on race for young people in conflict with the law seemingly undermines approaches seeking to fix or reform individual thinking patterns (e.g. see Chap. 9 in this volume, Lea & Abrams). Aziza further clarified that what was problematic about the breach in her conduct was not that she went off the cognitive behavioral script. Rather, the precise problem was that the youth's probation officer called her PVS manager to express discontent when her youth client cited a subversive narrative (Ewick & Silbey, 1995) of racism in the criminal justice system. Drawing from this experience, subversive narratives become problematic when youth become more difficult to control and/or challenge the notion of individual responsibility.

It is important to note that this encounter did not result in Aziza abandoning what she considered an important part of her work. Instead, she reconfigured her work to ensure that that these subversive narratives were undetected by probation by providing further background to youth in individual sessions of how subversive narratives can be used. Specifically, she taught youth that probation officers would not be amenable to hearing about these subversive narratives; however, they can still be empowering ("Use it so you can see that people who look like you can have power") and educative ("You got to find this stuff out. There is a lot that is not taught in schools").

Cognitive Behavioral Approaches in the PVS: The ABCs of Compliance

In this section I examine a worksheet used by PVS workers as a case study of how cognitive behavioral approaches play out at the local level of the PVS organization. In response to my query about forms and texts that would help me to understand frontline PVS work, several research participants produced examples of therapeutic interventions they use as tools in either group or individual sessions.[7] In the middle column of Table 10.1 I have replicated a worksheet described as rooted in CBT by Shannon, a PVS worker. This worksheet was representative of others worksheets I viewed within the purview of this research. Shannon spoke favorably about cognitive behavioral approaches for youth in conflict with the law and saw it as a tool to "help them figure out different ways to think about what they did." Shannon also saw CBT as a way of showing her clients that they should take responsibility for their actions. In my interview with Shannon I used this worksheet as an opportunity to understand more about how PVS workers determine whether a young person in conflict with the law is compliant and/or rehabilitated. In the left-hand column are some observations and generalizations that would apply to a compliant response from a youth in an interaction centered on this worksheet. Inversely, in the right-hand column is a summary of observations from noncompliant responses by a youth. Quotes in Table 10.1 are from an interview with Shannon.

[7] Notably, despite the standardized approaches in programming that many of the PVS workers identified as prevalent, research participants chose to engage activate texts (Smith, 1987) as part of a data collection process with worksheets that they created. Research respondents cited various reasons for this choice including being concerned about sharing trademarked documents that were part of packages and feeling that their own worksheets were more exemplary of their work with clients.

Table 10.1 Text–worker activation conversation: ABC worksheet

Example compliant responses	*Text of original document*	*Example noncompliant responses*
– Youth is authentically willing to engage with questions by asking clarification questions and answering the question appropriately/pertinently – Youth is aware of feelings and uses correct and appropriate words to describe feelings (e.g. "A kid might say I was really grumpy that day because I did not get enough sleep") – Youth response is considered exemplary if they are comfortable and accept this line of questioning. This comfort might be because they have considered the answer to this question previously and have a pro-social story for what they are telling themselves about how their thought impacted their actions	1. Antecedents: What happened before your crime? What were you feeling? What was your day like?	– Youth does not think what happened before their crime is relevant to their commission of the crime – Youth thinks that committing the crime was the only option available to them – It is difficult to get youth to talk and engage in the conversation. They might answer with one or two words. They might speak in generalities. ("Upset is not a correct answer. It doesn't tell me anything") – Youth discusses life events which fall outside short temporal inquiry. ("A lot of these kids, they have had tough lives. It hasn't been easy for them for sure. And so when they are doing this form, I don't let them go too far back like what their childhood was like. I want to know what's happening lately. We can't do anything about the past") – Youth "makes" the PVS worker do all the work by asking probing questions with possible answers like: Were you feeling this? Were you getting along with your parents?
– Youth accepts responsibility for their crime. They do not implicate someone else – Youth demonstrates an understanding that what they did was wrong – An exemplary youth is able to connect this transgression of the criminal charge to a pattern of behavior	2. Behavior: What did you do? Had you done this before?	– Youth minimize, deny, or rationalize their crime ("If they assaulted their victim, they might say they tapped them. If they threatened their victim, they might say they were just kidding") – Youth explains difficulty with the process by which he/she "got caught" ("Someone told on them, someone was watching them more carefully or someone doesn't like them")

(*continued*)

Table 10.1 (continued)

Example compliant responses	*Text of original document*	*Example noncompliant responses*
– Youth can easily make the connection between their actions and consequences – An exemplary youth would take full responsibility for their actions and consequences and think that it is fair	3. Consequences: what happened as a result of your behavior	– Youth struggles to make connections between behavior and consequences. He/she may think the two are not related
– Youth believes that there are things that he/she can do to prevent future crime – An exemplary youth is particularly optimistic about their ability to prevent future crimes	What actions can you take to make sure this does not happen again?	– Youth doubt or has a negative attitude about whether he/she can prevent future crime – Youth does not believe that a pro-social life is within their ability or future

Worksheet title: Pro-social thinking! it's as easy as ABC, 1-2-3

Prerequisites to Shannon completing this worksheet are that there has been a general review of cognitive behavioral approaches—without actually naming the words cognitive behavioral approach with the youth. Shannon's employment in the PVS has involved her being a Residential Counselor in an open custody facility, an Alternative to Custody caseworker, Youth Bail Supervision caseworker, and more recently a frontline worker in an Attendance Centre. Shannon indicates that she has used versions of this form with young people in all of these frontline positions. Shannon used this worksheet as part of a larger pro-social curriculum where the crux of the curriculum was "your thoughts impact feelings which consequently influences actions." She explained that she sometimes asked her youth clients to complete a worksheet (with the text replicated in the middle column of Table 10.1) as homework; however, more often, she guides youth through the completion of the worksheet because it is often one of the first ones they complete.

From my interview with Shannon, it became clear that there was a difference between acceptable and rehabilitated. Indeed, a youth who she mostly understands as being noncompliant and not rehabilitated can attend and successfully complete her group or individual sessions on criminal thinking. Shannon understood the expression of noncompliance as an opportunity to correct a young person's thinking errors by identifying them as such and it was important for her to not react punitively to these thoughts and instead approach them as a learning opportunity. Once Shannon corrects noncompliant thinking, it then becomes the young person's responsibility to adopt a new line of thinking that the PVS workers consider compliant or pro-social. Shannon also explained that what I've described here as "compliant" youth are rare. Shannon explained, "Most of these guys have a ton of thinking errors. But, even if they learn just a little something.... That's okay." She further explained that she was only expecting "baby steps of change ... for me the main thing is that they are open and willing to shift. To probation I report on their attitude, participation levels and if they are open. Whether or not they get it, well I don't really know. All I can do is try and hope they will too."

Referring to Table 10.1, Shannon explained that the title of the worksheet was a mnemonic device that she hoped her young clients would invoke in risky situations. The offense-specific focus of this worksheet is indicative of a narrow focus of rehabilitation. As Garland (1996) noted, "Where once the individual's personality or social relations formed the object of transformative efforts, that object is now offence behaviour and the habits most closely associated with it" (p. 176). Since this worksheet focuses on the offense (not the offender), there is a short temporal inquiry: PVS worker Shannon is interested in what happened on that particular day and/or recent history. She explained, "And so when they are doing this form, I don't let them go too far back like what their childhood was like. I want to know what's happening lately. We can't do anything about the past." For Shannon, focusing on the present is a way to control the scope of her sessions with youth in a way that she understands as fitting with a CBT model. In addition, she also believed that a short temporal scope will be helpful to the young person in conflict with the law. Deeper social relations (e.g. colonialism, childhood abuse, child welfare history, victimization, etc.) would not be relevant to the frame created in this worksheet.

Despite there being a separate youth justice system based on "diminished moral blameworthiness or culpability" (YCJA, Section 3[b]), there is little recognition that young people are less responsible than adults. This responsibilization of the young person in conflict with the law also seemingly contradicts the juvenile title of the worksheet. In addition, that the same therapeutic intervention (Table 10.1 worksheet) is used for youth in confinement and those in community-based settings raises questions about the differentiation between intervention modalities according to punishment. That is, while the different level of punishment and control between a custody sentence and probation sentence can be presumed, the messaging about responsibilization and the subject positioning in probation or the PVS is less clear.

Moreover, there is an embedded assumption that offenders can learn to anticipate and make more pro-social choices if they are equipped to do so and this omits that crime can be the result of rational thinking (cf. Fenwick & Hayward, 2000). More than taking responsibility for past conduct, this worksheet posits that young people should take responsibility for their future selves and engage in personal crime prevention. Similar to research examining youth confinement, the task for the PVS worker is to coach youth into being "simultaneously responsibilized and self-governing" (Franzén, 2015, p. 274, see also Cox, 2011). While this suggests a wide scope of inquiry and involvement for the PVS worker, there is simultaneously a detachment and a "self-serve" approach to youth clients in the PVS. Indeed, according to the practice of punishment in this investigation the cognitive behavioral approach vis-à-vis the PVS worker can only offer answers to *modifying* criminal behavior but does not make claims to *addressing* underlying needs and marginalization. This finding is aligned with Phoenix and Kelly's (2013) observation that young people in conflict with the law receive the message that:

> ... being responsibilized meant that they understand they (as opposed to anyone else) were responsible for themselves (as in there was no one else who could effect change in their lives), despite the fact that many of the conditions that shaped their offending were outside of their control to change. (p. 433)

In line with "governing through freedom" youth are experiencing a governing regime that represents a shift from Foucault's panoptican. Rather than a constant disciplinary power (such as that of a prison guard), the PVS workers and the cognitive behavioral approaches employed are aligned with a more relinquished intrusion in the lives of young people in conflict with the law. This is not to say that the youth experience in the PVS is necessarily less coercive or intrusive. Rather, the workers' discourse and understanding of their role is that the choice ultimately lies with the young person in conflict with the law to choose pro-social thinking and the PVS worker is seriously constrained on whether the young person makes this choice.

Discussion

While PVS workers pride themselves on their pastoral and caring power, their strategic accommodation of risk discourse and cognitive behavioral approaches can also be understood as helping to (re)produce neoliberal strategies that blame and responsibilize the individual young person in conflict with the law. The voluntary sector and helping professions have a long history of focusing on individual reform. Finn (2001) argued that social work as a profession is built on interventions based on individual reformation and adaptation to social conditions. Furthermore, these individualizing and often pathologizing interventions that aim to reproduce white middle-class values have been central to social work and social services in Canada and the USA since the profession was founded in the early twentieth century (Graham, 2005). This recognition of long-standing individuation in social services is in stark contrast with concerns that somehow the institutionalization of the PVS (in which the PVS will become simply an extension of the state) will cause a rupture in service—as though the state and the PVS inherently have different ways of governing. While social work has some history of antioppressive, critical, and social justice praxis (cf. Mullaly, 2006; Sakamoto & Pitner, 2005), there are also social workers and other helping professionals [including in the PVS] who are willing and active participants in the individualization of social problems. Participating in discourses and practices of individuation, normalization, and even disciplinary practices does not preclude PVS workers from expressing concern about structural issues such as racism and poverty. Aziza, for example, reported switching from cognitive behavioral approaches when another approach seemed particularly salient as with the example of her integrating a critical race analysis into her group session. All research participants in this investigation valorized their work in the PVS as helping young people in conflict with the law and held well-meaning intentions for their youth clients. Issues related to the limits of individualized approaches in the PVS are important to discuss, although difficult to resolve without further research and investigation.

One certainty is that individualized approaches to working with young people in conflict with the law are pervasive and dominant in the PVS, an approach that mirrors the mostly individualized criminal justice system. While outside the scope of this chapter, it is important to note that youth are also situated actors. Young people in conflict with the law also adapt, subvert, and negotiate the criminal justice system and the PVS alike. For example, Abrams and Anderson-Nathe (2012) in their ethnographic examination of incarcerated youth demonstrate how contradictory frameworks (and/or technologies) require "residents anticipate and differentiate when they would be expected to assume responsibility for their own actions and when they would be expected to account for their behaviors based on their family problems" (p. 59).

This chapter demonstrates how some workers within the PVS are positioned as double agents within the youth criminal justice system. Indeed, it is possible that those who work in the PVS enable neoliberal governance through a form of a double alliance. That is, they can "ally themselves with political authorities" and simultaneously form alliances with those in conflict with the law while offering "to teach them techniques by which they might manage better" (Rose & Miller, 1992, p. 189; see also Bull, 2008) that are also aligned with the neoliberal governance. Thus, through the role of an intermediary expert, responsibilization strategies can align the personal choices of offenders "with the ends of government" (Rose & Miller, 1992, p. 189). Frontline PVS workers remain "situated agents"[8] influenced by social context and capable of acting as result of their own intentionality; however, these alliances are often not made visible. Indeed, there is considerable effort and energy expended by PVS workers to ally themselves with institutional discourses of the criminal justice system while subversive narratives are submerged so as to be undetected.

Conclusion

In the late nineteenth century, one of the roles of the voluntary sector in the criminal justice system in Ontario was to disrupt the coerciveness and punitive nature of the criminal justice system. Indeed, the mere presence of the voluntary sector ruptured the disciplinary power of the detention room (Chen, 2005). In contrast, the more modern role of the PVS in the youth criminal justice system raises new questions of autonomy within the current neoliberal context. While PVS workers' helping/pastoral rationalities are often contorted by the hierarchal relationships PVS organizations have with the state, fissures and subversion do exist. Corcoran (2011) explains that:

> It would be premature to announce the wholesale assimilation of the voluntary sector, although neoliberal social capitalist discourse has disarmed elements of the pluralist, solidaristic consensus of the voluntary sector mainstream. Modernization entails an ideologically charged and contested, rather than seamless, discourse. There are limits to disavowing the voluntary sector's distinction from states or markets without jeopardizing its public legitimacy.... Resistance by voluntary workforces to micro-management indicates a durable disposition towards social democratic and solidaristic concepts of justice and citizenship. (p. 47)

In other words, it seems possible for neoliberal rationalities to coexist with other forms of rationalities within a penal assemblage. Neoliberalism has not completely engulfed the PVS; resistance and negotiations continue. While

[8] Bevir (2013) explains, "To say that people are situated agents is to say only that their intentionality is the source of their conduct; they are capable of using and modifying language, discourse, or tradition for reasons of their own. It is not to say that their intentionality is uninfluenced by their social context" (p. 37).

the PVS is not completely encompassed by being a service provider to the state, the inherent hierarchy in relation to the state seriously compromises the ability of PVS organizations to be visible advocates and social reformers. In addition, the shift in focus from offender to offense within the penal assemblage for young people in conflict with the law results in a more individualized approach for young people in conflict with the law. This individualized approached is especially problematic considering the marginalized social location of young people in conflict with the law.

References

Abrams, L. & Anderson-Nathe, B. (2012). *Compassionate confinement: A year in the life of unit C.* New Brunswick, NJ: Rutgers University.

Andrews, D. A., Bonta, J., & Wormith, J. S. (1995). *The level of service inventory: Ontario revision.* Toronto, ON, Canada: Ontario Ministry of Correctional Services.

Auditor General of Ontario (2014). *Youth justice services program follow-up.* Retrieved from http://www.auditor.on.ca/en/reports_en/en14/412en14.pdf

Balfour, G. (2000). Feminist therapy with women in prison: Working under hegemony of correctionalism. In K. Hannah-Moffat & M. Shaw (Eds.), *An ideal prison? Critical essays on women's imprisonment in Canada* (pp. 94–102). Halifax: Fernwood.

Barron, C. (2011). *Governing girls: Rehabilitation in the age of risk.* Halifax: Fernwood.

Bevir, M. (2013). *A theory of governance.* Berkley, CA: University of California Press.

Boyce, J. (2015). Police-reported crime statistics in Canada. *Juristat, 35*(1). Ottawa. Statistics Canada. Catalogue no. 85-002-x.

Bull, M. (2008). *Governing heroin: From treaties to treatment.* Hampshire: Ashgate Publishing.

Butler, A. C., Chapman, J. E., Forman, E. M., & Beck, A. T. (2006). The empirical status of cognitive behavioural therapy: A review of meta-analyses. *Clinical Psychology Review, 26*, 17–31.

Campbell, K. (2005). Introduction: Theoretical overview. In K. Campbell (Ed.), *Understanding youth justice in Canada* (pp. 1–19). Toronto, ON, Canada: Pearson Education.

Chen, X. (2005). *Tending the gardens of citizenship: Child saving in Toronto,1880s-1920s.* Toronto, ON, Canada: University of Toronto.

Chunn, D. (1992). *From punishment to doing good: Family courts and socialized justice in Ontario, 1880–1940.* Toronto, ON, Canada: University of Toronto.

Corcoran, M. (2011). Dilemmas of institutionalization in the penal voluntary sector. *Critical Social Policy, 31*(30), 30–52.

Cox, A. (2011). Doing the programme or doing me? The pains of youth imprisonment. *Punishment & Society, 13*(5), 592–610.

Crawford, A. (2003). Contractual governance of deviant behaviour. *Journal of Law and Society, 30*(4), 479–505.

Dauvergne, M. (2013). Youth court statistics in Canada 2011/2012. *Juristat.* Ottawa. Statistics Canada. Catalogue no. 85-002-x.

Doucet, A. & Mautner, N. (2008). What can be known and how? Narrated subjects and the listening guide. *Qualitative Research, 8*, 399.

Ewick, P. & Silby, S. (1995). Subversive stories and hegemonic tales: Toward a sociology of narrative. *Law and Society Review, 29*, 197–226.

Fenwick, M. & Hayward, K. (2000). Youth crime, excitement and consumer culture: The reconstruction aetiology in contemporary theoretical criminology. In R. Smandych (Ed.), *Governable places: Readings on governmentality and crime control* (pp. 163–190). Aldershot, England: Ashgate Publishing.

Finn, J. L. (2001). Text and turbulence: Representing adolescence as pathology in the human services. *Childhood, 8*, 167–192.

Foucault, M. (2007). *Security, territory, population: Lectures at the collège de France, 1977–1978, Trans. Graham Burchell.* New York & Basingstoke: Palgrave Macmillan.

Franzén, A. G. (2015). Responsibilization and discipline: Subject positioning at a youth detention home. *Journal of Contemporary Ethnography, 44*(3), 251–279.

Franzén, A. G. & Holmqvist, R. (2014). From punishment to rewards? Treatment dilemmas at a youth detention home. *Punishment & Society, 16*(5), 542–559.

Garland, D. (1996). The limits of the sovereign state: Strategies of crime control in contemporary society. *British Journal of Criminology, 36*, 445–471.

Graham, J. (2005). *History of Canadian social welfare.* New York: Oxford.

Gray, G. C. & Salole, A. T. (2006). The local culture of punishment: An ethnography of criminal justice worker discourse. *British Journal of Criminology, 46*(4), 661–679.

Gray, P. (2013). Assemblages of penal governance, social justice and youth justice partnerships. *Theoretical Criminology, 7*(4), 517–534.

Hannah-Moffat, K., Maurutto, P., & Turnbull, S. (2009). Negotiated risk: Actuarial illusions and discretion in probation. *Canadian Journal of Law and Society, 24*(3), 391–409.

Hogeveen, B. (2005). Toward 'safer' and 'better' communities: Canada's youth criminal justice act, aboriginal youth and the process of exclusion. *Critical Criminology: An International Journal, 13*(30), 307–326.

Maurutto, P. (2003). *Governing charities: Church and state in Toronto's catholic archdiocese, 1850–1950.* Montreal, QC, Canada: McGill-Queens University Press.

McGillivray, A. (1997). Therapies of freedom: The colonization of aboriginal childhood. In A. McGillivray (Ed.), *Governing Childhood*. Dartmouth, England: Dartmouth Publishing Company.

McMurtry, R. & Curling, A. (2008). *The review of the roots of youth violence.* Toronto, ON, Canada: Queens Printer for Ontario.

Miller, J. R. (1996). *Shingwauk's vision: A history of native residential schools.* Toronto, ON, Canada: University of Toronto Press [Kindle DX version] Retrieved from amazon.ca.

Ministry of Children and Youth Services. (2014). Three year review: Response to AGO recommendation. Youth Justice Services Division.

Mullaly, B. (2006). *The new structural social work: Ideology, theory, practice.* New York: Oxford University Press.

Newman, J. & Clarke, J. (2009). Narrating subversion, assembling citizenship. In M. Barnes & D. Prior (Eds.), *Subversive Citizens: Power, agency and resistance in public services* (pp. 67–82). Bristol, England: Policy Press.

Phoenix, J. & Kelly, L. (2013). You have to do it for yourself: Responsibilization in youth justice and young people's situated knowledge of youth justice practice. *British Journal of Criminology, 53*, 419–437.

PVS Organization Annual Report. (2011). Youth justice testimonials, PVS annual report 2010/2011.

Rankin, J., & Winsa, P. (2013, March 1). Unequal justice: Aboriginal and black inmates disproportionately fill Ontario jails. *Toronto Star.* Retrieved from http://www.thestar.com/news/insight/2013/03/01/unequal_justice_aboriginal_and_black_inmates_disproportionately_fill_ontario_jails.html.

Rose, N. (1999). *Powers of freedom.* Cambridge: Cambridge University Press.

Rose, N. & Miller, P. (1992). Political power beyond the state: Problematics of government. *British Journal of Sociology, 43*(2), 173–205.

Sakamoto, I. & Pitner, R. (2005). Use of critical consciousness in anti-oppressive social work practice. *The British Journal of Social Work, 35*, 435–452.

Satka, M. E. & Skehill, C. (2012). Michel Foucault and Dorothy Smith in case file research: Strange bed-fellows or complementary thinkers? *Qualitative Social Work, 11*(2), 191–205.

Singh, R. (2012). When punishment and philanthropy mix: Voluntary organizations and the governance of the domestic violence offender. *Theoretical Criminology, 6*(3), 269–287.

Smandych, R. & McGillvray, A. (1999). Images of aboriginal childhood: Contested governance in the Canadian west to 1850. In R. Halpern & M. Daunton (Eds.), *Empire and others: British encounters with Indigenous peoples, 1600–1850* (pp. 238–259). London: University College, London Press.

Smith, D. E. (1987). *The everyday world as problematic: A feminist sociology.* Toronto, ON, Canada: University of Toronto Press.

Thomas, N. & Bull, M. (2013). Negotiating the challenges of coerced treatment: An exploratory study of community-based service providers in Queensland, Australia. *Contemporary Drug Problems, 40*, 569–594.

Whyte, B. (2009). *Youth justice in practice: Making a difference.* Bristol, England: The Policy Press.

PART IV

Supporting the Supporters: The Voices of Volunteers

CHAPTER 11

"Volunteers Welcome, That Is, Some Volunteers": Experiences Teaching College Courses at a Women's Prison

Kristenne M. Robison

Prison volunteers provide unpaid labor and social capital to prisons. The collective contributions of volunteers are a seemingly valuable asset at a time in the USA when declining budgets create the need to do more with less in prisons. Volunteers with specialized skills, such as educational training, should be very appealing to prison administration as prison education budgets have been dramatically cut over the last 5 years (Clarke, 2014). The Rand Corporation found that states reduced their prison education budgets by an average of 6 % between the fiscal years of 2009–2012. The states with the largest prison populations slashed their education budgets by 10 %, and those with mid-sized prison populations slashed their education budgets by 20 % (Davis, Bozick, Steele, Saunders, & Miles, 2014). Cutting prison educational budgets might have the unintended consequences of increasing recidivism rates, as Davis et al.'s meta-analysis (2014) found that inmates who participated in correctional education programming had a 43 % less chance of recidivating compared to those

K.M. Robison (✉)
Westminster College, USA

L.S. Abrams et al. (eds.), *The Voluntary Sector in Prisons*, Palgrave Studies in Prisons and Penology, DOI 10.1057/978-1-137-54215-1_11

who did not participate in prison educational programming. Intentional recruitment and utilization of prison education volunteers not only benefit the inmates and prison budgets, but also the prison administration. Moreover, educational volunteers who can teach higher education courses are valuable to prisons seeking accreditation from the Correctional Education Association (Correctional Education Association, 2004).

So what do we know about prison educational volunteers? The answer is very little. The largest percentages of prison volunteers are typically those who participate in religious programming. Tewksbury and Dabney's (2004) survey of 72 volunteers at one medium-security prison in the southern USA found that 91.4 % of prison volunteers surveyed were involved in Chapel programming, with the remaining 8 % volunteering in educational and recreational programming. The authors subsequently called for scholars to explore the world of prison volunteers, yet 11 years later we find little has been accomplished. It is important to better understand the motivations and experiences of prison volunteers to reduce attrition and improve the quality and consistency of volunteer programming within prisons.

This study uses an autoethnographic, magnified moment methodology (Hochschild, 1994) to highlight various cultural and structural factors that shaped the experience of one prison educational volunteer offering college courses at a women's prison. I am a trained sociologist who was entering the prison to teach a sociology course and conduct focus groups with incarcerated women on their educational experiences, but I also was a volunteer who was met with resistance and suspicion. A goal of this chapter is to elevate my personal experiences as a prison educational volunteer into a meaningful analysis, but I also want it to convey the emotional side of the experience, which often included hope, confusion, frustration, and anger. This study is not meant to make sweeping generalizations about educational prison volunteers nor the factors that shape all volunteer experiences, but instead through focusing on these magnified moments take the reader on a journey to consider larger theoretical questions of **which** volunteers attain access into prison, or on the flipside, which volunteers do not get into prison? What are the implications of who gets in and who doesn't get in? Who gets in, but walks away? This book highlights some of the innovations in the voluntary sector in prisons, but this chapter pushes us to think about **what** innovative volunteer programs might never have the chance to flourish, **why** they might not make it into prison, and **why** some volunteers might not come back. The experiences and lessons learned add to the paucity of literature on volunteers in prison, particularly on the experiences of volunteers themselves in the intersection of the educational and correctional sectors. This chapter will provide insight to better understand the experiences of educational volunteers and to help bridge the gaps between volunteerism and the vast need for prison education.

Literature Review

Prison Education

Scholars, policymakers, and practitioners generally agree that access to and participation in prison educational programming contributes to the success of inmates who are eventually reentering society (Davis et al., 2014; Vacca, 2004; Wilson, Gallagher, & MacKenzie, 2000). Inmate "success" is typically measured through recidivism and employment rates post-release. Across many rigorously designed empirical studies, Davis et al. (2014) report a 43 % lower recidivism rate and 13 % higher rate of post-release employment for inmates who participated in prison educational programming. Prison education can take on many forms including adult basic education (ABE), high school/GED, post-secondary education, and vocational education. Davis et al.'s (2014) meta-analysis found that all four types of prison education programs are associated with reductions in recidivism. Their explanation for this is that these four types of education span a spectrum of abilities with ABE addressing the needs of academically lower achieving prisoners and post-secondary education programs serving the academic achievers in prison. Davis et al. (2014) also calculated the odds ratio of success according to method of instructional delivery. They found that five of the seven methods of instructional delivery, particularly whole class instruction, class taught by college teacher, class taught by correctional employee, class taught by outside employee, and program with post-release services all are associated with a reduction in recidivism. They singled out classes taught by college teacher, classes taught by outside employee, and programs with post-release services as being particularly important in that they connect inmates with the outside community, directly and indirectly.

Prison education also saves money when considering long-term costs of crime and incarceration. Esperian (2010) argues that with prison education comes a reduction in recidivism, which means a decline in the number of prison inmates. From 2008–2009, Nevada saw a reduction of 1.6 % in prison inmates, which translated to a savings of $38 million in addition to avoiding $1.2 billion in prison construction costs. Esperian correlates the reduction of Nevada inmates and spending with accessible prison educational programming available to the inmates.

Post-secondary Prison Education

In 1994, President Bill Clinton signed the Violent Crime Control and Law Enforcement Act (1994), which eliminated prisoners' access to Pell Grants.[1] Pell Grants help college and university students afford post-secondary education. The elimination of this funding shaped prisoner access to post-secondary education. There were about 350 established college or university prison education programs leading up to the 1994 decision and now only 12 remain (Murphy, 2014). Not all post-secondary education was in the form of structured programs, as much of the educational programming was in the form of a course being offered here and there. However, all post-secondary education in prison, whether formal or informal, took an immediate and indisputable hit with this ruling. In the last year of Pell Grant eligibility for the incarcerated, about four-fifths of state correctional systems offered post-secondary prison education, but just 3 years later only about half offered the same options (Tewksbury, Erickson, & Taylor, 2000). Prison administrators were left scrambling to find ways to maintain post-secondary prison education programming because the cost was now out of reach for many inmates.

Despite the change in Pell Grant eligibility, a number of initiatives continue to make post-secondary education possible in prisons. One of the most famous is the Bard Prison Initiative (BPI). The BPI, started in 1999, offers degree-granting programs to inmates in six prisons in New York State. As of 2013, 300 inmates had received degrees with a total enrollment of 700.[2] One aspect unique to the BPI is that they offer enough courses for students in the prisons to earn an associate or bachelor's degree in liberal arts, while most post-secondary programs focus on a technical

[1] "The Federal Pell Grant Program provides need-based grants to low-income undergraduate and certain post-baccalaureate students to promote access to post-secondary education. Students may use their grants at any one of approximately 5400 participating post-secondary institutions. Grant amounts are dependent on: the student's expected family contribution (EFC) (see below); the cost of attendance (as determined by the institution); the student's enrollment status (full-time or part-time); and whether the student attends for a full academic year or less" (http://www2.ed.gov/programs/fpg/index.html).

[2] www.bpi.bard.edu

or applied degree. Since the development of the BPI, the Consortium for the Liberal Arts in Prisons initiated similar liberal arts programs in colleges across the country.

Another well-known post-secondary prison education program is the grassroots Inside-Out International Exchange Program.[3] Founded in 1997, the Inside-Out program trains college and university instructors to run post-secondary courses inside prison walls to a combination of incarcerated "inside" students and college "outside" students. The program is notable in that it facilitates interactions between those on the inside with those on the outside of prison, which Davis et al. (2014) found to be beneficial post-release.

The Prison Education Project (PEP) is another model prison volunteer program. According to the website, "the overarching philosophy of PEP is to use resources, for example, university student and faculty volunteers, in the backyard of each of California's prisons to make change. There is a college within a 25-mile radius of the majority of the state's 35 prisons."[4] The Prison University Project[5] at San Quentin State Prison in California is significant in that it emerged after the elimination of Pell Grants for prisoners,[6] it offers college prep and associate of arts degrees, and it actively recruits volunteer instructors, teaching assistants, and tutors. Despite the Pell Grant ruling, some successful higher education prison education programs have clearly emerged and persisted.

Individuals who teach within these types of post-secondary education programs are typically defined as volunteers as they are not paid employees of the prison. As these programs rely quite heavily on volunteers, it is important to better understand their experiences. Ideally the programs want trained volunteers to return for the sustainability of the program as well as to maintain and increase the quality of the programming offered. However, little is known about the institutional factors that retain, promote, and encourage sustained volunteerism.

[3] www.insideoutcenter.org

[4] http://www.prisoneducationproject.org/

[5] http://www.prisonuniversityproject.org

[6] At the date of this publication, President Obama has introduced legislation that would provide a limited number of prisoners the opportunity to use Pell Grants at a select group of colleges and universities (Anderson, 2015).

Prison Education Volunteers

Just a few scholars have examined the experiences of prison educational programming volunteers. Tewksbury and Dabney's (2004) survey of volunteers at just one medium-security prison in the USA found that approximately 8.6 % of all volunteers (n = 72) volunteered in the educational and recreational activities of the prison. The authors do not speculate on the rationale for the low percentage of educational programming volunteers. The majority of volunteers reported their motivation for volunteering was their religious faith; however, it is unknown how many of the educational programming volunteers cited religious beliefs as their primary motivation for their service. The authors also found that in general, the volunteers at this prison were white men with high levels of education (Tewksbury & Dabney, 2004). Volunteers with 4-year college degrees or more of education were generally less satisfied with their volunteer experiences, particularly as related to their communication with staff. Tewksbury & Dabney (2004) interpreted this finding as a result of post-secondary education that encourages "critical thinking and higher expectations regarding other individuals and organizations" (p. 178). While this is a credible study it is one study of 72 prison volunteers from the southern USA. Scholars should be encouraged to further investigate the experiences of prison volunteers and in particular, educational programming volunteers, who seemingly have much to offer incarcerated individuals in a time of reduced prison education budgets.

Structure and Culture

The experiences of educational programming volunteers are shaped by the structures and cultures in which they interact, both at the prison and in outside contexts and settings. Hay's (1994) conceptualization of social structure consists of two interconnected elements: systems of social relations and systems of meaning. "Systems of social relations consist of patterns of roles, relationships, and forms of domination according to which one might place any given person at a point on a complex grid" (p. 66), for example, incarceration status, age, gender, race, and more. Systems of meaning are also known as culture, "including not only the beliefs and values of social groups, but also their language, forms of knowledge, and common sense, as well as the material products, interactional practices, rituals, and ways of life established by these" (p. 65). While it is common that the concepts of structure and culture are thought of as distinct from one another it can be difficult to disentangle them. This definition embeds culture, or systems of meaning, within larger social structures.

In this chapter, I use Hay's concept of social structure to analyze a series of magnified moments. Systems of social relations largely place me, as the volunteer, in a hierarchical relationship with Department of Corrections' administration and correctional officers where I am near the bottom of the power structure, perhaps only being located above prisoners. Other players involved include the Correctional Education Association and the State Corrections Officers Association, at least in this particular state prison system. Systems of meaning, or culture, are embedded in the systems of relations, including beliefs about the role of volunteers and their place in the prison, as well as beliefs about what types of prisoner educational programming should be offered.

Method

This authoethnographic study (Ellis, 2004) uses a magnified moment methodology to elucidate structural and cultural factors that shaped the process of offering and teaching college classes in a women's prison. According to Hochschild (1994) magnified moments are "episodes of heightened importance, either epiphanies, moments of intense glee or unusual insight, or moments in which things go intensely but meaningfully wrong. In either case, the moment stands out; it is metaphorically rich, unusually elaborate and often echoes" (p. 4). In this chapter, I will analyze a series of magnified moments. These moments occurred over a timeframe of approximately 3.5 years from September 2011 to April 2015. These moments stemmed from my interactions with prison administration, which occurred through in-person communication, phone calls, e-mails, and observations at the prison. I also had significant interactions with incarcerated women in focus groups I held on their educational experiences. The focus groups were useful in learning more about the culture of the institution, as well as perceptions of the programming that was offered. Observations and interactions were recorded as qualitative research notes that were then coded and analyzed to form the findings for this chapter.

Since the fall of 2011, my college, Westminster College,[7] has offered two sociology courses, as well as courses in political science, history and

[7] Westminster College (Pennsylvania) is a small, liberal arts college with an enrollment of 1500 students. The author of this study initiated Westminster's involvement at the women's

psychology at the women's prison. I taught the two sociology courses and my colleagues taught the political science, history, and psychology courses. My role was initially as instructor, but that role expanded to liaison for the other faculty who teach at the prison. I have provided an orientation to the faculty on what to expect at the prison, as well as worked with the prison School Principal to make all arrangements for the courses.

Study Site

The data from this autoethnographic study largely emerged from my volunteer experiences at a women's prison[8] located in the Northeast USA. It is one of two women's prisons in the state and houses approximately 1000 incarcerated women. The facility is located in a rural, politically and socially conservative area of the state. Residents of the town and region rely on the prison for employment, so many of the employees are politically and socially conservative holding conservative beliefs about the incarcerated, including what benefits prisoners deserve while being incarcerated.

Despite budget cuts and reduced educational programming, the school at the prison was persevering largely due to the dedication of the School Principal. The School Principal created a dynamic learning environment for the women that included vocational, GED, and English as a Second Language programming, as well as the classes offered by Westminster College. Nevertheless, the Principal and the incarcerated women conveyed through informal conversations and focus groups that while doing time was easier at this institution compared to the other women's facility in the state, it came with a cost: less access to educational programming. The difference in educational offerings was partially due to attrition in that positions that previously existed were not filled when employees vacated those positions. The School Principal was always looking for ways to provide educational opportunities for the women, but he was keenly aware of the conservative environment he was working within.

Volunteers play an important part in the State Department of Corrections (DOC). The volunteer and internship coordinator at the women's facil-

prison. The author also had to convince Westminster administration of the importance of offering higher education courses at a reduced cost to incarcerated women so the resistance to programming was not necessarily one-sided.

[8] I purposely choose to not name the prison or the state it is located within to protect the confidentiality of the individuals in my study.

ity is also the Prison Chaplain, which is common in other facilities in the state. State DOC data from 2012 convey that 77 % of volunteers in the state were involved in religious programming, while 1.5 % of volunteers were involved in educational programming. The State DOC categorizes volunteers into two categories: volunteers and public visitors. Both are deemed volunteers but the volunteer category suggests repeated contact with inmates while the public visitor category suggests a "one and done" (i.e., one-time only) interaction with inmates. In the year 2012, 1155 religious volunteers and 2280 religious public visitors entered the walls of the state's prisons. In that same year there were 23 education volunteers and 37 education public visitors (State Department of Corrections, 2012). Data was not available for each institution, but I am assuming that data is fairly representative of the volunteer composition at the women's prison.

As an institution, Westminster College never pushed for a relationship with the prison. The college administration was resistant to the relationship, feeling that they should not pay for prison educational programming as that was the responsibility of the State DOC. However, because the programming fit within aspects of its mission,[9] I pushed successfully to create a relationship with the prison, highlighting the benefits it would have for our students who could act as teaching assistants for the classes and gain internships through the program. Nevertheless, every time I propose a new course I still have to get permission from Westminster College administration, which has proved to be challenging. I mention this to highlight that I continue to face similar structural and cultural barriers at Westminster as I do at the prison.

Findings

My gut reaction to my experiences as a volunteer is that I was met with suspicion as a sociologist who wanted to teach college courses that would educate and empower the incarcerated women. But that would be a reductive and unfair assessment of the larger picture, which is far more complex. The magnified moment methodology allowed me to piece together some of my moments that "went intensely but meaningfully

[9] Specifically "to acquire knowledge of self, society, human cultures, the natural world, and human relationships to God" and "to demonstrate moral and ethical commitments to neighbor, society, and the natural world" (https://www.westminster.edu/about/mission.cfm).

wrong" (Hochschild, 1994, p. 4) while highlighting how culture and structure shaped those moments. This section includes three magnified moments that assisted me in identifying the multiple layers of cultural and structural factors that were shaping my access to the prison as an educational volunteer. The first moment occurred during a face-to-face interaction with the School Principal when he noted that religious programming volunteers are welcomed with open arms. The second moment occurred after a tense phone call I had with the then Superintendent of the women's prison. The third happened when I was eating dinner with the Secretary of the State DOC. He stated his desire to get as many outsiders on the inside as possible, within reason. It should be noted that two of the three of these were moments when things went intensely wrong and one was a moment of joy, but the moments of teaching and interacting with the incarcerated women were joyful and propelled me to continue the fight for education for the women. Throughout this chapter I will highlight and tie together the systems of social relations and systems of meanings that shape one's volunteering experience, but as importantly I hope to convey the very emotional and personal experience I had as an educational programming volunteer that potentially has implications for which volunteers might stay and which might go.

"Volunteers Welcome, That Is, Some Volunteers"

The first magnified moment occurred when the School Principal uttered the above quote to me in a conversation we were having about gaining prison administration approval for a college course at the facility. The timing of this comment came just after we had successfully offered our first sociology course with no security problems or other issues that might slow down the approval process. The School Principal followed up this comment, clearly frustrated, with his observation that groups of religious volunteers enter the prison with few questions asked, yet the one educational volunteer was being scrutinized and discouraged. Gaining access to prison is possibly the most precarious and tedious process for some volunteers, as it was for me. Prison access can be determined by a number of factors, including the perceived benefit of programming to prisoners, perceived motivation of the volunteer wanting to get on the inside of prison walls, supervision of the volunteer, and safety. All of these were certainly considered when I was trying to access the prison, but there were additional factors taken into account on the basis of my being an educational programming volunteer. Prison administration considered if I would be taking a paid, unionized position away from a staff member, if my presence created more work for current employees, and if I helped the prison and administration meet their accreditation goals. Reflecting on the process as I have been doing in this chapter elucidates these many concerns, but in the moments, hours, days, weeks, and months that I was advocating for access I felt frustrated and disheartened. I saw myself as a volunteer offering a free and useful program. What was preventing the program and me from being welcomed?

The Correctional Educational Association (CEA) offers accreditation to prison schools, which places each individual prison, the DOC, and the CEA in a system of social relations involving power. The State DOC requires each prison school to acquire CEA accreditation. The CEA has a set of required and mandatory practices that must be met for each school to be accredited. Access to higher education is viewed as a required practice by the CEA, despite the removal of Pell Grant access for inmates. The required higher education practice can be met by offering one 30-day fiber optics course or other trade-related course per year, eliminating the need for any other post-secondary programming. Offering a three- or four-credit college course is seen as going above and beyond the call of duty for accreditation purposes.

As such, while there is a need for higher education courses, this requirement can be met by a trade program that has a compact time frame that prison administrators may view as being more beneficial to the women. For example, if the prison has a fiber optics program where they are making products in the prison they can get paid on the inside for their fiber optics work and then ideally use that skill for paid work when they reenter society. So educational programs that offer more "bang for the buck" for the women may be prioritized The higher educational program I was offering had no cost to the DOC, but was likely not prioritized above the trade school options.

I experienced resistance to offering courses in the prison despite being the only college or university in the region willing to offer post-secondary courses in the women's prison. In my case I offered the prison a series of social science and humanities courses that were not configured to work toward a degree, but instead would provide lower level electives that the women could use toward a degree upon their release. Since they are not vocational degree-granting courses, the administrators may have viewed them as less important or not worth the time or security risks. In my time at the prison I observed the high work volume of the School Principal such as completing yearly audits of the school, investigating grievances by educational programming staff or prisoners within the educational programming, overseeing all programming, and substituting for absent employees. My observations forced me to ask myself what I would do if I was understaffed and overworked. Would I push for the programming when it created more work for myself? This particular School Principal did, but I suspect not all do. And would all volunteers stay around for the arduous process? I suspect not.

The commissioning of educational programming volunteers might also conflict with the policies of the State Corrections Officers Association (COA). Educational volunteers are more likely to run into conflicts with the COA than religious volunteers due to the potential for teachers or educational program staff to fall into the category of a unionized position. Correctional officers occupy many educator positions in the state, which means they are unionized positions with regular pay and benefits. When officers leave these positions, some do not get filled due to budget constraints. I learned that a computer teacher left for the Army, so the position went unfilled. At the women's prison not only did computers go unused, but also other vacancies left a business program without any teaching staff. Fortunately my classes did not interfere with correctional officers' positions, but verifying that did slow down access into the prison.

After I observed the unused computers with dust on them, I suggested that some Westminster students could volunteer to teach short classes on basic computer skills. The administration met this request with caution and eventually denied it. Other positions continue to go unfilled due to budget constraints and COA conflicts, which is unfortunate as inmates lose opportunities for additional programming and for making more contacts on the outside. These policies also keep volunteers out. The systems of social relations between the CEA, the COA, the prison, the prison school, the DOC, the volunteer, and the higher education institution demonstrate a complex web of power relations with differing bodies wielding the power at different times, but the volunteer or the higher education institution would rarely hold power unless the prison school was desperate for a higher education course to meet CEA accreditation standards.

As I return to those comments by the School Principal I sympathize with his frustration as he observed an endless stream of religious volunteers enter prison while he struggled to get me, his one educational volunteer, access. This was partly structured by the prison's relationship to the COA and the CEA. The quote used as the title of this section, "Volunteers welcome, that is, some volunteers," compared educational volunteer experiences to religious programming volunteer experiences. However, little is known about the religious volunteers' experiences so more research is needed to determine if they, too, are experiencing resistance in accessing the prison. For example, the Prison Chaplain is a paid position. It is possible that there might be some resistance if the COA feels that the Chaplain position is threatened by the presence of volunteers. Volunteers fit into a power grid based on institutional need and potential threat to jobs, but they also fit into the larger grid of structured relationships with other organizations. Further magnified moments demonstrated additional structural and cultural factors that influenced volunteers' access to this particular prison.

There's No Crying in Prison Education

The second magnified moment occurred in my office at Westminster College during a phone call with the then Superintendent of the prison, the second Superintendent in my three and a half years of interactions with the facility. At that time I was experiencing increased resistance to offering more college classes at the women's prison. It would have been easier to throw in the towel, but I forged ahead partly because I am persistent by nature and partly because I was fighting for more opportunities for the incarcerated women. The School Principal said the best way to get a "yes" from the Superintendent was to arrange a meeting in her office. I called to make an appointment with her and her administrative assistant scheduled me on her calendar. Within minutes my phone rang. It was the Superintendent. She asked why I wanted to meet her. I was caught off guard, as even though I knew what I wanted to talk about I wanted time to strategize my approach. I explained I wanted to discuss offering more educational programming at the prison. She said in a short, terse voice, "I'm not interested." So I attempted to ask her rationale for denying the programming. She responded, "I said no. I don't have to explain myself." In that moment I did not know how to respond as I could not recall the last time I was treated in a way that preempted having a constructive conversation with someone. She then hung up on me. I sat in disbelief and then I did something I did not predict: I cried. To this day I don't know why I cried. I imagine it was because of how I was treated and how I let her treat me. It was because of the investment in programming for the women that I thought would never materialize. Honestly, the experience left me feeling disheartened with little hope for additional programming for the women, but as a volunteer I was dismayed, sad, and angry. Why would any volunteer continue to provide service after that exchange?

Prison administration is similar to the military in that there is a chain of command that one must follow, particularly when decisions about policies or programs are involved. The terminology of prisons reinforces this with terms such as Superintendent, Deputy, Captain, and subordinates. The chain of command sets in place a system of social relations of power within the prison. I found that the School Principal played a significant role in knowing and communicating the chain of command, but also in informing me of what I could or could not ask or do. However, there were times when I felt that the School Principal either assumed I knew things I did not or just let me find out for myself. It was clear to me that the School Principal not only cared for the women, but he advocated for them and he went out of his way to secure as much programming as possible. Through my observations of the School Principal I learned how much difference one person can make on the inside of prisons, but it is a cautionary tale as people transition out of positions. In an environment of budget constraints, employees are being asking to do more work with the same pay. In order to get a college class approved, the School Principal must write up a plan of action to be submitted to the Deputy in charge of educational programming. The Deputy must first approve it then it is submitted to the Superintendent, who has the ultimate decision whether they want to allow the programming or reject it. Even though I never encountered a Deputy or Superintendent in person during my time teaching at the women's prison, they ultimately decided the fate of the programming. As outsiders, the volunteer is clearly placed in a position with no power in the chain of command, even if what they have to offer is valuable. But valuable to whom? When at first I got a "no" I eventually learned if I waited it out, a new administration would be around the corner, potentially bringing with it opportunity, but also more red tape. By contrast, the loss of supportive administrators can be devastating for volunteer programming already underway.

Administration turnover has been a common theme in my experience, as the Superintendent from the above story was the second of three in my almost 4 years at the women's prison. The first was on medical leave not long after I arrived, so the initial course was approved by the then Acting

Superintendent. The third Superintendent began in the fall of 2014. The School Principal recently left, too, which has been a huge loss of cultural and social capital for me. He taught me a lot about the prison culture including beliefs, language, knowledge, and interactional processes that have proven invaluable in the access process, but more importantly he was the one who achieved access for my programming. From his new position within DOC administration he still regularly contacts me to check on the state of the programming. This not only highlights how much he continues to care for the women, but that he also continues to advocate for my access to the prison.

In my conversations with the former School Principal I have also learned more about why there is so much administrative turnover within the state's prisons. The DOC has a policy on retirement that encourages and possibly leads to a short tenure as a Superintendent of a prison. In the State DOC, employees who work within prisons are awarded with an earlier retirement than employees who work outside of prisons. This policy might possibly shape short administrative tenure as individuals who desire to retire early might take a short stint as a prison Superintendent or administrator to accelerate their retirement clock. Additionally, working in a prison is not easy. The benefits of being a volunteer who shows up once a week is that you show up for a limited amount of time, and then leave. But working "eight in the gate" or doing one's 8 hours a day is a different story (Johnston, 2014). During my first conversation with the former School Principal after beginning his new position in state-level administration, I asked him how he liked his job. He responded, "I get to bring in my own lunch and my cell phone." I was astounded that these were the first two things that he reported as they conveyed a lot about working within prisons from the viewpoint of one former worker.

What I have since learned about the second Superintendent, with whom I shared the tense phone call, has provided me with perspective on the role of the Superintendent more generally. Quoting a worker at the women's prison, "Superintendents are either inmate-focused or security-focused, it is rare when you find one who is both." The second Superintendent was known to be risk-averse and security-focused, perhaps to a flaw. Scholarly literature would define this as custodial/prison order model (Cullen, Latessa, Burton, Jr., & Lombardo, 1993). Cullen et al. (1993) found that even those who prioritized a custodial/prison order model supported rehabilitation, but that this focus is usually superseded by order and security. It is possible that the Superintendent saw too much risk with extra educational programming, even though she valued it. This may originate from the DOC level, as there is likely pressure to be security-focused. Considering the explanation that the second Superintendent was overly security-focused returns me to the first magnified moment. If, indeed, religious programming volunteers were welcomed with little resistance and minimal safety concerns, why was a program offering free college classes, with only a few volunteers, experiencing such resistance and being denied at times? The phone conversation and the ensuing emotional response have provided me a springboard to discuss the role of prison administration in my volunteer experience. This interaction was the most personal of all of the magnified moments, as I felt personally attacked and disrespected. Prison volunteers likely have plenty of other activities to consume their time so what motivation would volunteers have to continue advocating for access for their programming after such an interaction?

In the summer of 2015 my colleague was teaching a Psychology of Women course at the prison. A mutual student of ours from the prison asked her to convey a message to me. "Could you could set up an Inside-Out class for us next year? The timing is good with the Superintendent, but she may be retiring soon. So please try to squeeze it in while it is likely to be approved." I was excited to receive this message from the student which additionally serves to highlight awareness among the incarcerated women of the impact that turnover has on programming. But, after 3 years plus of resistance I am fatigued from the access process. The jury is out on whether I will pursue this request.

So far I have discussed mostly structural explanations for the resistance experienced during the process of gaining access, which highlights the DOC's relationships to other organizations, administrative turnover, workload concerns, and administrative style. Cultural explanations play a role in the process as well, as highlighted by the next magnified moment.

"Anytime I Can Get People from the Outside on the Inside, It's a Good Thing"

In 2013 I had the opportunity to have a meal with the Secretary of the State DOC, which is the highest position in the state appointed by the Governor. Over dinner, I informed him about the two courses that I had offered in the women's prison to date partly out of pride and partly out of politics. Through this conversation I was probing his position on such programming. He seemed genuinely interested in the classes and the role that Westminster College students took as teaching assistants in the courses. He stated the above quote after hearing about our role at the women's prison. He explained that he believed the prison and the inmates benefitted from outsiders being on the inside. I proceeded with caution and explained that I encountered some resistance to future courses. He responded with: "Let me know what you need as I have a way of making people do things I want them to." I felt a glimmer of hope, as this is what I was looking for. I was looking for someone who could make it happen, but I was hesitant to take him up on his offer. Instead I reflected on how difficult life would be for me, the School Principal, and the students if I forced my way in. The Secretary's comments provided me a moment to really reflect on some of the cultural aspects of the resistance I was encountering, while also demonstrating how out of step with the Secretary's vision the agenda in a particular prison may be.

The other women's prison in the state had multiple educational volunteers and a thriving Inside-Out program. One of their educational volunteers was even named statewide volunteer of the year by the DOC. At the prison where I volunteered, I was struggling to get an additional college class established. While all of the structural factors I have been discussing certainly shaped my experience, there was obviously more to the story beyond structural concerns. Cultural influences also likely shaped my experiences, as individual belief systems appeared to be playing a role in the process.

The women's prison where I have taught is located in a rural, conservative area of the region. There are four prisons within a sixty-mile perimeter, so working in prisons is a popular and likely necessary source of employment in this area (Courtright, Packard, Hannan, & Brennan, 2010). It is worth noting that the other women's prison, while located in a rural area, is in close proximity to the State DOC and a large metropolitan area, where individuals are more likely to hold progressive views on issues such as prison education. Providing free or low-cost education to inmates is not generally a well-supported initiative. For example, in 2014 New York State Governor Andrew Cuomo announced a statewide initiative (State of New York, 2014) to offer college education to inmates at ten facilities across the state. While his proposal was based on evidence and made fiscal sense, there was considerable resistance to the plan, largely from Republicans, forcing him to drop the proposal (Kaplan, 2014). The occasional comment from a correctional officer questioning the value of the programming or the low-cost of the four-credit course made me wonder how much of the resistance I was experiencing was due to cultural beliefs systems. But I also had to ask myself, how much of the resistance was because of me? Getting access to the inside of prisons is a privilege that can require specific forms of cultural knowledge and a particular location in the hierarchy of social relations. I often am awarded privilege on a day-to-day basis, as I am a white woman with a PhD, but that social status was not rewarded in this particular setting.

Reflecting back on the Secretary's comments about maximizing the number of people on the outside who get inside made me wonder if religious programming volunteers really do find their way into prisons more easily, or if they also experience resistance. Are they able to persevere when there is resistance? How often do educational volunteers find their way into prisons? The data provided from the State DOC suggests that few educational volunteers actually get in. So who does get in? Some get in. Some do not. Some are persistent. Some are not. Some individuals might question why someone would want to volunteer their time in prison, but I wonder why more people do not volunteer in prisons. Quoting Tyrone, an inside student from Inside-Out, "that wall isn't there just to keep me in, but to keep you out."

Discussion

In this chapter, I did not intend to position my experience as a volunteer to represent those of all other educational volunteers. Instead, I wanted to shed light on the structural and cultural factors shaping access to a prison and to encourage the reader to think more broadly about who does and who does not get into prisons, as well as the implications of who does and does not get in. I also wanted the reader to see the emotional toll that I experienced in this process.

Hay's (1994) definition of structure embeds the concept of culture into structure through the ways that systems of meaning are built into systems of social relations. Tewksbury and Dabney (2004) point out that volunteers with higher levels of education tend to be more critical of the institution and ask more questions, which might be another reason that educational volunteers do not fit into the systems of social relations as seamlessly as other volunteers. In particular it must be noted that I am a sociologist who is trained to analyze and critique institutions, so that might add another layer to this reflection. I did not choose this as one of my magnified moments, but in one conversation with the School Principal, when he was experiencing fall-out from the Superintendent, he asked me why I asked so many questions. After that exchange I trained myself to ask fewer questions, I laid low when I thought it would benefit the programming initiative, and I began to associate the programming with other faculty at Westminster so that if I was part of the problem some of the resistance might subside. I realized that the School Principal was absolutely required for access for my programming so I needed to heed his warning.

A liaison, like the School Principal, who knows the chain of command, who knows the institutional language and knowledge, as well as the appropriate interactional practices, is priceless. But this is not the end of the line because if it was, I would have had endless access. At the end of the chain of command must be an administrator, such as the Superintendent, who is accepting of programming and is willing to take risks on programming that provides value to the inmates.

Noticeably absent from this chapter is the argument that the programming is for the inmates. In my interactions in class and in focus groups I found the women to be excited about the college classes, especially since a local community college left the prison years before, and because they appreciated the benefits that the classes offered. The classes provided them a space where they could speak and share ideas freely. They stated this space made them feel like they were not in prison. They were initially cautious of our presence, but quickly accepted us. If participation in educational programming and programming that promotes connections with the outside of prison is known to reduce recidivism (Davis et al., 2014), it seems that making room for educational volunteers is indeed an important practice for preparing inmates for a life outside of prison. Most recently I was in negotiations with the prison to offer a Psychology of Women course. Since the prison was, again, in the midst of administrative turnover, I was waiting to hear who would be chosen as the new School Principal. At the time, I informed my colleague who would be teaching the course that there were no guarantees that I would get the course approved. In an e-mail communication with my colleague she wrote, "Why would anyone think that education for prisoners is a bad thing!? If you can explain that to me sometime, I would be interested to know what the issue is." I have attempted to answer that very question in this chapter or at least shed light on some of the barriers for educational programming and volunteers. Besides trying to answer that question we also need to start to conceptualize the potential role that educational programming volunteers might play in prisons, especially if teacher positions are being cut or not replaced.

Politically the time does seem right to expand educational volunteer programs. Recently Republicans and Democrats in the US Congress reached across the aisle to support a platform for criminal justice reform at the Bipartisan Summit on Criminal Justice Reform as the current trajectory of spending on mass incarceration is unsustainable. Perhaps economics holds the power to change beliefs and practices around incarceration and prisons. In the meantime there is an educated volunteer force in the waiting. Many colleges and universities have community service written into their mission statements. A college education has in some ways become more accessible, yet at the same time exclusive. If colleges and universities took a small amount of their resources to offer classes on the inside of prison walls they could be contributing positively to educating all of our citizens, while also reducing recidivism rates. But of course State DOC's and prisons would need to be open to these volunteers. The Prison Education Project in the state of California offers a model that other states could adapt. University students and faculty volunteers could provide valuable programming to prisons.

The Inside-Out program has a group of volunteers who have been trained to navigate the prison system and to teach on the inside of prison walls. I recently taught my first Inside-Out class, although not at the women's prison. At the graduation ceremony the prison Warden complimented the group, saying that he had not heard anything about the class. What he was indirectly conveying was that he had not heard of any safety issues or problems within the class, which to him was a good thing. So not only do we need college and universities to be willing to offer their resources to teach classes in prisons, we also need prisons to open their doors to educational programming volunteers, and we need a volunteer force that is trained to teach within jails and prisons. In addition, we need to promote policies that allow inmates to earn credits for the courses and be able to attain degrees while in prison. As an example, the state of Ohio allows incarcerated students to get credits for "advanced job training" although they said "no liberal arts. No more general studies. Not more giving degrees, per se" (Pant, 2013). This is most likely a reflection of the beliefs and values that education, particularly a college education, does not resonate with the penal system we have developed, but also that they want courses to be job-focused. However, as Davis et al. (2014) highlight, participation in post-secondary education correlates with the largest reduction in recidivism for inmates. Offering college credits to inmates for vocational programming is a good policy, but it would benefit inmates even more if they could earn college credit for liberal arts courses.

As access to outside contacts reduces recidivism it seems indisputable that correctional facility administrators should work harder to integrate educational volunteers. In the DOC volunteer and intern handbook for this particular state, there is a clause that indicates that each individual area head is responsible for recruiting volunteers and that "the facility should utilize volunteers, public visitors and interns in as many diverse program areas as possible." I certainly recognize how overworked many prison employees are which leaves little time to recruit volunteers on top of the work they are already tasked to complete. In addition, not all programs or people are ideally suited to volunteering in prisons. Nevertheless, the risks associated with the programs and volunteers need to be weighed against the benefits, particularly when experienced volunteers are willingly offering their services. Moreover, we must aim for consistency between DOC policies and what actually happens within individual prisons, regardless of leadership changes within those facilities.

Conclusion

University-Prison partnerships seem to offer the potential to achieve the goals of less recidivism and increased job placement for the incarcerated. The US prison system is at a tipping point so now is the time to act. We should embrace volunteers, increase the number of people on the outside who get access to the inside, and increase prison education, as it is good for all of society. A number of structural and cultural issues need to be addressed to ease this process for prison volunteers so we no longer have to ask who does and who does not get in.

References

Anderson, N. (2015, July 31). Feds announce new experiment: Pell grants for prisoners. *The Washington Post.* Retrieved from http://www.washingtonpost.com/news/grade-point/wp/2015/07/31/feds-announce-new-experiment-pell-grants-for-prisoners/.

Clarke, M. (2014, May 19). Prison education programs threatened. *Prison Legal News.* Retrieved from https://www.prisonlegalnews.org/news/2014/may/19/prison-education-programs-threatened/.

Correctional Education Association (2004). *Correctional Education Association Standards Commission: Performance standards for correctional education programs.* Elkridge, MD.

Courtright, K. E., Packard, S. H., Hannan, M. J., & Brennan, E. T. (2010). Prisons and rural Pennsylvania communities: Exploring the health of the relationship and the possibility of improvement. *The Prison Journal, 90*(1), 69–93.

Cullen, F. T., Latessa, E. J., Burton Jr., V. S., & Lombardo, L. X. (1993). The correctional orientation of prison wardens: Is the rehabilitative ideal supported? *Criminology, 31*(1), 69–92.

Davis, L. M., Bozick, R., Steele, J. L., Saunders, J., & Miles, J. N. V. (2014). *Evaluating the effectiveness of correctional education: A meta-analysis of programs that provide education to incarcerated adults.* Washington, DC: Rand Corporation.

Ellis, C. (2004). *The ethnographic I: A methodological novel about autoethnography.* Walnut Creek, CA: Alta Mira.

Esperian, J. H. (2010). The effect of prison education programs on recidivism. *The Journal of Correctional Education, 61*(4), 316–334.

Hay, S. (1994). Structure and agency and the sticky problem of culture. *Sociological Theory, 12*(1), 57–72.

Hochschild, A. R. (1994). The commercial spirit of intimate life and the abduction of feminism: Signs from women's advice books. *Theory, Culture, & Society, 11*, 1–24.

Johnston, T. (2014). Eight in the gate: Organizational impact of prisons on correctional officers. Senior Capstone Project. Westminster College.

Kaplan, T. (2014, April 2). Cuomo drops plan to use state money to pay for college classes for inmates. *The New York Times.* Retrieved from http://www.nytimes.com/2014/04/03/nyregion/cuomo-drops-plan-to-use-state-money-to-pay-for-college-classes-for-inmates.html?_r=1

Murphy, C. (2014, April 7). New York Governor drops prison education plan. *Colorlines News for Action.* Retrieved from https://www.colorlines.com/articles/new-york-governor-drops-prison-education-plan.

Pant, M. (2013, November 10). Ohio expands prison education program to fill gap left by others. *Dayton Daily News.* Retrieved from http://www.correctionsone.com/facility-design-and-operation/articles/6581504-Ohio-expands-prison-education-program-to-fill-gap-left-by-others/.

State Department of Corrections. (2012). Source remains confidential.

State of New York. (2014, February 16). Governor Cuomo launches initiative to provide college classes in New York prison. *Governor's Press Conference.* Retrieved from https://www.governor.ny.gov/news/governor-cuomo-launches-initiative-provide-college-classes-new-york-prison.

Tewksbury, R. & Dabney, D. (2004). Prison volunteers: Profiles, motivations, and satisfaction. *Journal of Offender Rehabilitation, 40*(1/2), 173–183.

Tewksbury, R., Erickson, D. J., & Taylor, J. M. (2000). Opportunities lost: The consequences of eliminating Pell Grant eligibility for correctional education students. *Journal of Offender Rehabilitation*, *31*(1/2), 43–56.

Vacca, J. S. (2004). Educated prisoners are less likely to return to prison. *The Journal of Correctional Education*, *55*(4), 297–305.

Violent Crime Control and Law Enforcement Act of 1994. (1994). 103 U.S.C. & 20411. Retrieved from http://www.gpo.gov/fdsys/pkg/BILLS-103hr3355enr/pdf/BILLS-103hr3355enr.pdf.

Wilson, D. B., Gallagher, C. A., & MacKenzie, D. L. (2000). A meta-analysis of corrections-based education, vocation, and work programs for adult offenders. *Journal of Research in Crime and Delinquency*, *37*(4), 347–368.

CHAPTER 12

Crossing the Color Line into America's Prisons: Volunteers of Color Reflect on Race and Identity in a College Service Learning Project

Jennifer R. Tilton

One day 15 college students were walking into a Southern California juvenile hall when two guards approached the group and singled out Anthony, the darkest-skinned African American volunteer. He had left his identification card at home as had another White woman, Joan. But they ignored her as they asked him a series of probing questions about what he was doing in the facility. When they left, they politely asked him to dress differently next time so he would be easier to distinguish from the incarcerated minors.

When I asked Anthony about the incident several months later, at first he struggled to remember it, "I'm sorry, I forgot about that." But eventually he told the story, described it as "funny," and said he just "laughed it off." He explained: "That's something that I've also experienced many other times in life.... I don't take offense to it. It's something I'm used to, being...a dark-skinned male in our world." He said that it wasn't worth getting mad "because it's like, it's not going to change ... but I also

The research for this chapter was in part funded by the University of Redlands. The volunteer program discussed in this paper is supported by the Will J. Reid Foundation

J.R. Tilton (✉)
University of Redlands, Redlands, CA, USA

L.S. Abrams et al. (eds.), *The Voluntary Sector in Prisons*, Palgrave Studies in Prisons and Penology, DOI 10.1057/978-1-137-54215-1_12

understand where they are coming from. At the end of the day, that's their job. They have to make sure their premises are secure."

These volunteers had come face to face with a particular twenty-first-century version of what W.E.B. DuBois (2005) described as "the problem of the color line." The probation staff unconsciously expressed their assumption that our college volunteers were White and that Black young men looked like juvenile delinquents. This unconscious stereotype is broadly shared in America today and continues to both reflect and shape structures of opportunity for young people (Eberhart, Purdie, Goff, & Davies, 2004; NAACP Legal Defense Fund, 2005; Pager, 2007). America's prisons and juvenile justice facilities are filled with black and brown bodies. In contrast, although US colleges are becoming more racially diverse, White students are still overrepresented on most 4-year selective campuses (Carnevale & Strohl, 2013). College volunteers like Anthony and Joan were stepping across what Michelle Alexander (2010) might call the new Jim Crow color line created by mass incarceration. For Anthony, volunteering in juvenile hall was just one more time he was forced to confront the question DuBois (2005, p. 8) famously posed: "What is it like to be a problem?"

This chapter explores how volunteers of color make sense of race and construct their own racial identities as they cross the color line embodied in the walls of America's juvenile and adult correctional facilities. I build on Mitchell and Donahue's (2009) call for scholars to pay more attention to the experiences of volunteers of color in community service projects because too often the literature on volunteerism presumes that volunteers are White and middle-class. Exploring the diverse experiences of Black and Latino volunteers enables us to see the distinctive form and contours of the color line in twenty-first century America and the ways the criminal justice system is reshaping our ideas about race.

As college volunteers walk into prisons or juvenile justice facilities, they see one of the most visible pieces of evidence that we do not live in a postracial society, but instead that race matters in shaping life chances. Youth of color are massively overrepresented in the juvenile justice system, just as adults of color are in the criminal justice system. The facility where we conduct community service is 47 % Latino, 35 % Black, and just 17 % White. Latino youth are only slightly overrepresented in this facility as the county youth population is predominantly Mexican American. However, in this county, like nationally, African Americans are massively overrepresented, as they are four times more likely to be detained than

White youth (Haywood Burns Institute, 2015). Boys also outnumber girls in the juvenile justice system almost 10:1. Private 4-year colleges present a stark contrast. In the residential undergraduate college where I am on faculty, Black and Latino youth are significantly underrepresented: only 3 % of students are Black, 22 % are Latino, and 53 % are White.

Volunteers see these stark racial contrasts, but they struggle to understand how exactly race matters in an ostensibly colorblind era, when racial boundaries are both more porous and flexible than in the Jim Crow era of US history. As Latino youth have become a majority in many Southern California counties, a Black–White color line clearly fails to account for the workings and meanings of race. Indeed in the southwest of the USA it never could. Black and Latino staff fill America's juvenile halls and prisons, as do increasing numbers of Latino and Black college student volunteers, visible representatives of the growing, if still fragile, Black and Latino middle class throughout the Los Angeles suburbs. And yet, Black students like Anthony are all too aware that their class status and educational attainment does not fully insulate them from the dangerous image of the "criminal blackman" (Russell-Brown, 2008; Tilton, 2011).

The shifting nature and ongoing significance of these racial boundaries raise significant questions for all volunteers in America's prisons. But volunteers do not interpret or experience crossing the color line embodied in our prisons in the same way. Race, class, and gender shape experiences of volunteering in distinctive ways, as does the degree to which volunteers have themselves engaged in studying or reflecting on questions of race and racism. As Mitchell and Donahue (2009) argue, there are significant differences in how White volunteers and volunteers of color understand their volunteer service. White volunteers usually see their work as a chance to learn from and to help young people radically different from themselves; students of color often see their volunteer work as a chance to give back to their home communities or to reconnect to a shared racial identity.

The emerging literature on race in service learning often focuses on the important question of whether volunteer experiences are effective in challenging racial stereotypes and promoting a deeper awareness of racism and privilege (Caro, Porfillio, & Valeri, 2009; Dunlap, Scoggin, Green, & Davi, 2007; Mitchell, Donahue, & Young-Law, 2012). However, this growing body of literature misses a vital opportunity to delve more deeply into how volunteers make sense of race and construct their own sense of racial identity through the experience of volunteering. These questions are particularly important for volunteers in the criminal justice system because this system is one of the central race-making institutions in the post-Civil Rights era, shaping the boundaries and meanings of racial categories. Just as slavery, Jim Crow laws, and the ghetto were "race-making institutions," sociologist Loic Wacquant (2001) has argued that mass incarceration is one of the core race-making institutions of the post-Civil Rights era (see also Alexander, 2010). The particular racial contours of mass incarceration in the USA have made encounters with the criminal justice system almost the paradigmatic racial experience. Police profiling has become the clearest, most pervasive, and publically recognized example of Black and, in Southern California, Latino racial marginalization.

The importance of policing and incarceration to race-making has important impacts on the ways volunteers of color think about race and understand their own racial identities. Anthony faced a particularly stark encounter with racial stereotypes in juvenile hall. But all volunteers of color had to craft an identity for themselves within a minefield of what Patricia Hill Collins (1990) calls "controlling images." Volunteering in juvenile hall brought students face to face with young people who embodied some of the most pernicious racialized images of youth: the teenage mother, the high school dropout, and especially the thug or gangster, an image that makes the bodies of young men of color targets for policing, surveillance, or even vigilante violence in contemporary public spaces as the high-profile murders of Trayvon Martin and Tamir Rice make all too clear. This set of images has racial, class, but also spatial components, defining youth of color as problems located in the ghetto, the barrio, or more generically "the inner city."

As this chapter will show, Black and Latino college volunteers had sometimes felt the power of these racialized stereotypes in their own lives. Many had been affected by police profiling themselves or watched family members cycle in and out of the justice system. But not all college students of color experienced the race-making operations of the criminal justice system in the same way. Race, class, gender, neighborhood, and particular family strategies of social mobility shaped their level of contact with the paradigmatic racial experiences of police profiling and the criminal justice system. Indeed some more privileged volunteers of color saw their work in the juvenile justice system as a way they could learn about, and connect to, the reality of racism and to their own Black or Latino identities.

On a broader level, paying attention to the experiences of volunteers of color within the penal sector can help us understand the contradictory meanings of race in contemporary America. Black and Latino college graduates embody our national hopes that race no longer constrains opportunity in America. But comparing their experiences to those of incarcerated youth makes visible the way race, class, and place interlock to constrain opportunity in the post-Civil Rights era (Wacquant, 2010). The racial contours of our prisons have also exacerbated racial stereotypes, creating new barriers and dilemmas even for upwardly mobile students of color. Listening to volunteers of color struggle against these stereotypes can provide important insights for people who run volunteer programs in prison, who may want to recruit more volunteers of color, but may not have developed ways to support and retain those volunteers.

Method

Community Service Learning in College

This research draws on interviews, reflections, and field notes about the experiences of college volunteers in the Read Empower Attain Create Hope (REACH) project, a volunteer community-service-learning project that brings undergraduate students into a juvenile detention center (juvenile hall) in Southern California. REACH has two main parts. In the volunteer program, 25 to 30 students conduct weekly discussion and writing workshops in juvenile hall and periodically publish incarcerated student writings with a national magazine called *The Beat Within*. Students work in small groups to design and lead these workshops on topics of their choice and do not generally receive course credit. As the faculty founder and program supervisor, I provide some training in facilitation techniques and lesson planning, but do not directly supervise student volunteers in juvenile hall. The second component of REACH is built into the academic curriculum through a course I teach based on the "Inside Out" model that brings 15 college students together with 15 incarcerated students to look at whether there is a cradle to prison and cradle to college pipeline and what we might do about it.[1] Students move fluidly between these two parts of REACH, sometimes starting as a REACH volunteer and later taking an Inside Out class, or becoming a volunteer after taking the Inside

[1]The "Inside Out" Prison Exchange Model was started by Lori Pompa (2002) at Temple University.

Out class. Many stay on as volunteers for 3 to 4 years, but others only take one Inside Out class and then do not continue on as volunteers.

The REACH program is located within the Race and Ethnic Studies (REST) Program at my university in order to encourage students to link their work in juvenile hall to academic coursework that explores the significance of race in their own lives and in American society. In the students' end of semester reflections and exit interviews, I ask them explicitly to think and talk about how race mattered in the context of their work in juvenile hall and how their work in juvenile hall shaped their understandings of their own identities and the significance of race and class in America. We aim to challenge the colorblindness that characterizes most volunteer programs in and out of college and to craft a model of social justice community service learning (Green, 2001; Mitchell, 2010).

Volunteer Population

For most of the 7-year history of REACH, White students and women have comprised the clear majority of volunteers (i.e., 60 to 70 %). In this respect, REACH has been similar to most college volunteer programs (Butin, 2006; Chapman & Morley, 1999). However, we have actively recruited students of color as volunteers, and particularly men of color given the institutional demographics of juvenile hall. Over the last 2 years these efforts have been fairly successful in racially diversifying REACH so that now 50 to 60 % of REACH volunteers are students of color, with 11 to 16 % Black and 33 to 40 % Latino. Black and Latino men are 11 to 17 % of our volunteer core, a fairly good representation given the numbers of men of color on our college campus, but a small percentage compared to the numbers in juvenile hall. And we have often struggled to retain Black and Latino male volunteers, a struggle which inspired many of the questions this chapter aims to answer.

Data Collection

I have been conducting research on the effects of this volunteer project both on incarcerated youth and on college volunteers since 2011 when I secured human subjects approval. This research focuses on how the relationships and dialogues forged through volunteering affect how young people, both inside and outside of the juvenile justice system, make sense of race, class, and citizenship in contemporary America. This particular chapter draws on student-written reflections and interviews with college student volunteers.

I conducted 1 to 2 hour open-ended interviews with 34 REACH volunteers, including 14 White students and 20 students of color who are the primary focus of this chapter. There were four Black students, two students who alternated between identifying as Black and biracial, ten Latino students, two Asian students, and two students who alternated between identifying as multiracial and as White.[2] The interviewees represented a good sample of our volunteers. Sixty-five percent were women, and Latinas significantly outnumbered Latinos and African Americans of both genders as they do in our volunteer pool. Over 45 % of all participants and 55 % of participants of color were REST majors or had race as a core part of their course of study in another interdisciplinary major. Most of these students saw their work in juvenile hall as an integral part of their academic study. However 40 % of all volunteers, and 25 % of the volunteers of color who participated in the study, had taken few classes that focused directly on racism or encouraged the exploration of the significance of race in their own lives.

The questions I asked were intentionally very open-ended to capture volunteers' own perspectives on what they learned from their volunteer experience and how they came to understand their own racial, class, and gender identities as they moved between campus and juvenile hall. My own identity as a White middle-class woman and my position as a professor and project supervisor certainly played a role in these open-ended interviews. My role as founder and supervisor of REACH may have inhibited students from speaking more critically about their experiences in, and the design of, the program. In order to mitigate this possibility. I expressed my interest in their critical perspectives and my hope that they could help us improve the program. My close relationships with many students in the program also offered benefits in the research process. I knew 75 % of the participants very well, having taught them in multiple classes and mentored them as volunteers for several years. These personal relationships enabled the kind of open discussion of race that might not have been possible otherwise.

I transcribed all interviews, and then coded the interviews, my field notes, and the weekly response papers from two of my Inside Out classes.

[2] I use students' descriptions of their own racial and ethnic identities to place them in racial categories.

I identified the key themes for this analysis from this process of coding, writing analytic memos and discussing my emerging analysis with long-term volunteers in REACH. Although my analysis is fundamentally qualitative and ethnographic, I also calculated some basic descriptive percentages to enable me to more carefully compare key themes within the narratives of volunteers across race, class, and gender lines. For example, I calculated the frequency of women and men talking about their own experiences confronting racial stereotypes or police profiling and the percent of White volunteers compared to volunteers of color who spoke of family and close friends in the criminal justice system.

Geographic Context

The distinctive spaces of the greater Los Angeles region shaped this volunteer project and the analyses of race volunteers brought with them to juvenile hall. The vast majority of REACH volunteers grew up in California, with 12 of the 20 students of color in this study growing up in the greater Los Angeles metropolitan area. A few grew up in neighborhoods like "South Central" or "East Los Angeles" that popular culture has turned into symbols of gang-filled Californian ghettos or Mexican barrios. But many more grew up in the sprawling suburbs that extend across five counties and represent the new face of suburban inequality in America, a patchwork quilt of new luxury tract homes, modest houses, apartment buildings, historic town centers, and trailer parks. These suburbs have always been both racially diverse and divided (O'Mara, 2005). Some communities are the leafy green, predominately White, privileged towns that dominate the image of American suburbia, while others are long-standing Mexican American working-class suburbs, new multiracial middle-class boom towns hit hard by the subprime housing crisis, and older cities or suburban communities that have become spaces of concentrated poverty filled with Black and Latino families living alongside scattered poor White families. By 2010, Whites had become a minority in much of this region, and suburban poverty had grown significantly as it has all over America (Frey, 2011, p. 7; McGirr, 2012).

Volunteers of color came from every kind of community across this complex racial and class geography, and many had moved across the region as their families sought safer neighborhoods, better educational opportunities, and social mobility for their children. As volunteers talked about this shifting landscape, they often used the culturally powerful, if often incongruous, labels of ghetto and suburb to distinguish between cities they defined as good and those they saw as bad or "sketchy." These distinctions relied heavily on race, despite the ostensibly colorblind language, but volunteers' analyses also highlighted subtle understandings of race, class, and place in the twenty-first century.

Findings

Feeling at Home and the Intimacy of Mass Incarceration

The problem of mass incarceration was not a distant academic question for many REACH volunteers, particularly for volunteers of color. As the number of people in jails and prisons has skyrocketed over the last few decades, incarceration has touched more and more American families (Mauer & Chesney Lind, 2002). Seventy percent of the students of color I interviewed talked about family members or close friends who had been incarcerated. White volunteers were less affected, but also not immune to the effects of mass incarceration, with almost 25 % of White volunteers having family members or close friends who had been locked up.[3] These volunteers often chose to work in juvenile hall because they wanted to understand the experience of their loved ones. They came with urgent questions in the back of their minds. Why had their cousins or uncle ended up in the system? What had their boyfriend gone through? They wanted to get beyond the confines of the visiting room to get a more intimate view of life inside the juvenile justice system.

The racial contours of mass incarceration often led volunteers of color to experience the strange sensation of feeling more at home in juvenile hall than on our predominantly White college campus (Mitchell & Donahue, 2009). This sense of homecoming was especially true of Mexican American students who found themselves able to share the pleasures of speaking Spanish and sharing stories of family traditions with students in juvenile hall. One Latina volunteer was struck by how "I fit in more with the inside students than with the outside students that go to the same college as I do." Another young woman commented, "We're similar so it was like easy to get a conversation going and like talk about our past and families and

[3] Students volunteered this information without being explicitly asked so the numbers may be higher. Interestingly, two White volunteers had served time on juvenile probation themselves, while no students of color had, an indication of the ways White privilege could pave the way to college in spite of a history of criminal trouble.

parties and all that stuff.... We had like a lot in common with some of the teens there." As these quotes suggest, volunteers of color relished the connections and community they forged with students in juvenile hall. But this experience of feeling at home in a correctional facility did not come without some significant emotional costs. After all, what does it mean for a student of color to feel a sense of belonging as they walk into a prison or juvenile jail?

Feeling at home in juvenile hall made students more aware of the ways they felt "out of place" as students of color at the University of Redlands. Several students described feeling "culture shock" when they arrived on campus from their predominantly Latino neighborhoods or high schools. They described feeling judged or hypervisible and out of place in classes that were predominately White. Luis, who grew up in South Central, explained that being on a predominantly White campus,

> makes me feel a little weird, awkward, insecure sometimes.... Going to juvie hall and talking to them about stuff that I'm used to, it felt like going home in a way. I felt more comfortable there sometimes than here because of the obvious demographics.

Sometimes this feeling of connection left students of color with a kind of survivor's guilt when they left incarcerated students behind in juvenile hall every week. Anjelica explained:

> I am Latina, and I can freely leave the facility. Yet these boys who are seen as racial minorities as well, are placed there.... Most of these kids grew up where I did. They went to [a] similar school as I did, and I feel a lot of guilt being here [at the University] and living the life I do.

This guilt and sense of responsibility encouraged her to volunteer and to work toward a future career as a teacher in low-income schools.

Trauma of Going Back Home

Occasionally the experience of going into juvenile hall was much more traumatic for volunteers. As Mitchell and Donahue (2009) explain, for students who feel like college is "an escape" from a difficult home or neighborhood, "going back 'in the name of service' may be a challenging experience that neither the student, course facilitator or community partner is prepared to handle " (p. 177). This was the case for DJ, a biracial young man who grew up poor in the same tough neighborhood as many inside students. He stopped volunteering after a year and spoke eloquently about how painful it was for him to connect back to the hometown which he had "tried so hard to escape." "I remember walking through the doors and being super nervous. Back in my mind...I was transported back to when I was like a teenager, how nervous and how on guard I had to be all the time." He valued connecting with the inside students, but all their stories made him relive traumatic childhood experiences of his own. He stated:

> One student talked about just leaving a party and how one of his friends got jumped and eventually got hospitalized and ended up losing his life. And I'm like, it brought me back to when I saw [my friend] get shot and passed away, and it was just a horrible situation. Or I hear another student say they were kicked out of the house, and they were homeless for a couple of days, and it brought me back to being homeless and how horrible...the day to day survival of that is.

Finally DJ quit participating in the workshops, overwhelmed by the feeling of going home and reconnecting to his neighborhood:

> I hated my neighborhood.... When I left, I left.... I have gone back ... a handful of times ... and I always feel this extreme despair and anger ... towards everything, years of being picked on, years of having to take the long way home, nights of not being able to eat, nights of fighting for hours on end with everyone, being randomly stopped by the police for just walking home from school, having someone try to jump me right after school with a brick.... No, I hate almost every part of my city.

DJ wanted to be a role model for young people in juvenile hall, but he also felt powerless to offer meaningful guidance or advice to incarcerated youth. He felt like he only made it out of his neighborhood through sheer luck. He had a special second grade teacher, who "got him interested in school" by showing "an active interest" in him. "She would go over to my house and check up on me." And then he was lucky enough to win one of the lottery slots in a higher-achieving middle school that got him interested in the arts and into track. He explained, "It's almost like I got plucked out of a group and I was allowed to do something greater." But the rest of the students in his community were left behind "like they were just part of the mass." DJ said he felt he couldn't honestly tell the incarcerated young men that they had options because "a lot of those options are like luck of the draw" or "rolling the dice." He recognized, "That's not advice." "If you are in a situation, you don't want to hear that."

Understanding Success: Racial Exceptions and Social Mobility

First-generation college students like DJ were conscious of their own identities as exceptions in their families, neighborhoods, and schools. Antonio, a Chicano Ethnic Studies major, described this experience:

> When I went to Redlands, it'd be like, okay this is where all the White students are and then Juvenile Hall this is where all the people of color went. This is the way that we're funneling people. It's a very clear visual that I never had before. It was simply textbook at that point.

As volunteers of color moved between our college campus and juvenile hall, they struggled to understand the overwhelming incarceration of Black and Latino youth alongside their own educational success. Why had they ended up in college when so many members of their family and other people of color ended up in jail? Exactly how did race matter when so many kids of color were on a track to jail, and yet their own success suggested that mobility was possible?

This line of questioning was especially common among students of color who had grown up in working class or poor communities and who were the first of their family to go to college. As DJ explained,

> I never really understood why I wasn't in there, how I didn't get arrested. It was weird, not that I felt guilty … I just didn't understand how I was able to get out and so many of these kids were talking about the exact same experiences I did, but they were arrested.

Students like DJ began their volunteer experience assuming that they came from very similar backgrounds to the students inside. They grew up in poor, underresourced communities and went to "ghetto" schools, where they faced the racism of low expectations from teachers. But as these students compared their experiences to those of the inside students, they often developed nuanced understandings of the structures of opportunity in poor- and working-class neighborhoods. They came to understand the complex ways gender, sexuality, family dynamics, and class divisions shape the paths young people take to adulthood, enabling some to escape over structural barriers to mobility, but leaving many others trapped.

This detailed kind of analysis distinguished the reflections of students of color who were first-generation college students. White students and upper-middle-class students of color more often just remarked that they felt "lucky" or privileged when they compared their childhoods to those of kids in juvenile hall. But they less often probed the specific dimensions of their "luck" or privilege. As Carlos, a Mexican American working-class student commented, "Slowly my questions as to why I made it and others have not are being answered."

Volunteers of color who grew up in working class or poor neighborhoods slowly realized that their families had significant class privileges that distinguished them from young people incarcerated in juvenile hall. Most, though not all, grew up in two-parent households. Their parents may have had working-class jobs, cleaning houses or working in construction, but they generally had stable work. Their parents often insulated them from worries about money and could pay for structured sports or after-school programs. One young woman talked about how significant it was for her that her mom didn't work and so could provide the daily supervision that helped pull her out of some early experiments with trouble in the dangerous streets in her neighborhood.

Students identified ways that their own academic successes were enabled by specific parental strategies to create upward mobility. Their parents had insisted that "college was not optional" for their children because they themselves had struggled without higher education. Their families moved to safer neighborhoods or hustled to get their kids into better schools outside of the neighborhood. Often they simply forbade any play or hanging out on the street especially as their children entered the pre-teenage years. For example, Carlos' mother always knew "college was a way out." Despite her limited English and long days cleaning houses, she was very active in her kids' schools, drove them to college prep programs they found, and even managed to send some of her kids to private school.

Students also identified the ways that gender or sexuality had insulated them from particular kinds of trouble on the streets. Latina women whose brothers or male cousins were incarcerated discussed how gendered expectations in their family insulated them from physical discipline or from participating in cultures of street violence. Carlos said, "Being gay saved me." He lived in a neighborhood surrounded by gangs, drugs, and prostitutes. "I was always confused as to why I didn't venture into it, and believe me

I had the opportunity…At least for me, I think it was because I'm gay." Instead of exploring the street culture all around him, he got involved in the gay community, in the "PRIDE club" at his school, and believed that this gay community saved him.

Students of color who had grown up working class invariably had the common experience of having been identified in school as someone with academic potential. They had been chosen by a teacher, often at a young age, and subsequently had been plucked out of the regular educational track in school and placed into a more academically rigorous program. Robert remembered one teacher who just told him, "You're smart" and encouraged him to ask questions and think of his biracial identity as an asset. His whole sense of self changed as he started to get good grades. Without that experience, he thought, "I don't know what I'd be doing. I could be back home with a lot of the kids that I know that aren't doing nothing." These teachers or counselors often helped connect students to college preparatory programs that gave them the knowledge and cultural capital to negotiate the college application process.

Good Kids and Bad Kids: The Role of Exceptions in the Post-Civil Rights Era

Some volunteers of color saw their own mobility as proof of the dominant discourse that equal opportunities were available across racial lines if only you were motivated to make the right choices. Julio, who grew up in a safe lower-middle-class neighborhood thought that "opportunities are there. It's just a matter of taking them and learning to take advantage of them." But other volunteers came to critique the way they had been plucked out and offered educational opportunities, while so many other youth of color were left behind. Anjelica described becoming increasingly uncomfortable with how she had been privileged by an educational culture that identified a few kids as worthy of investment and abandoned the others as "a waste of time and space." Volunteering in juvenile hall reminded her of how she "was always treated differently than others" in high school.

> My AP class got new books every year, while my friends kept reading tattered books, written in, and falling apart in their hands. It makes me feel like people don't care about these kids; we classify them all as potential dropouts, and let them fulfill the prophecy.

She felt a lot of guilt as she began to become aware of many ways "society has rejected these kids, lost hope in them, while I was handed opportunities."

Back in high school, students had often embraced their own exceptional status as "good kids" who deserved the academic opportunities that "bad kids" would just throw away. These labels, learned through school tracking, encouraged academically successful students of color to distance themselves from "bad kids" or troublemakers. Norma, a Mexican American young woman who grew up in a very poor urban community, explained that she had been resentful of the "bad kids" in her school and always thought kids dropped out and ended up in juvenile hall "because they didn't care.... They're bad kids. They don't want to do anything."

Luis was also encouraged to distance himself from the image of "the thugs" and "bad kids" as he forged an identity as a working-class student pursuing his education. Luis grew up in South Central, but from a fairly young age, his parents and schools taught him to draw a clear boundary between himself and the "thugs" he saw in the neighborhood. He stated:

> I couldn't have spiky hair because it looked gangsterish. I couldn't have it bald because it looked like a gangster. I couldn't wear baggy clothes because it was gangster. I couldn't have skull shirts. I couldn't really have the gold chain.

Getting to know students in juvenile hall made Luis and Norma recognize the ways they had themselves embraced many of the negative stereotypes of poor youth of color. Luis remembered wishing the "cholos"[4] in his school would just drop out and get out of their way, "Why are you wasting your time being here if you don't want it?" But getting to know kids in juvenile hall "made me understand a lot more and it makes me feel a little bit bad why I was judging them so harshly back in high school."

Volunteers of color sometimes developed a deep critique of the ways teachers, school tracking, and other community institutions created the simple distinction between "good kids" and "bad kids" that they took for granted in high school. Anjelica explained that working in juvenile hall,

> taught me to not judge the way I did when I was in high school. I thought all those kids were dumb and should drop out because all they did was

[4] This is a common term for the cultural style of street-affiliated Mexican American kids.

> hold the smart ones, like me, back. I realize now that not all of the youth in America are treated fairly or even expected to "make it." Most of the students in my school were not expected to graduate college.

Luis realized that his school had constructed a real separation between kids on the college track and the regular track. He remembered when one teacher casually dehumanized the majority of students in his school, saying how lucky he was to teach the gifted students so he could be a teacher instead of a "zookeeper."

These volunteers' stories make visible one of the central ways racial inequalities are maintained in an ostensibly colorblind era. When we treat good kids and bad kids as if they are naturally occurring kinds, we ignore the ways concentrated poverty, school discipline and tracking practices, and the juvenile justice system work together to create "bad kids" (Ferguson, 2001; NAACP Legal Defense Fund, 2005). On the flip side, we ignore the ways magnet schools, honors classes, and college prep programs enable small numbers of working-class kids of color to be plucked out of poor schools or neighborhoods to become living examples, but also powerful ideological symbols, of the possibility of social mobility.

America needs the social mobility of a few exceptional Black and Latino young people, like those who end up in selective 4-year colleges, to believe that the American dream is possible for all. This faith in a (mostly) colorblind America was common among White volunteers in REACH, but often rejected by volunteers of color. Indeed our White volunteers sometimes pointed to the presence of Latinos or Blacks on campus (and as REACH volunteers) as evidence that equal opportunity was a reality and that race couldn't itself be a real barrier to opportunity. Samantha, a White volunteer, talked about her feelings of guilt as she thought about the opportunities that she had experienced that the kids in juvenile hall hadn't. Yet still, she didn't think that "whiteness" explained it. "We have tons of Latino students here...[at the University]. I truly believe that it's possible for anyone to go to college, but it's the want, their support system, and if it's possible." White volunteers often returned to this refrain that what really determines success or failure was desire, whether they "want it" badly enough. In contrast, volunteering in juvenile hall encouraged students of color to reject this discourse of racial exceptionalism, recognizing how it divided communities of color and used the success of some to condemn those left behind.

Developing Racial Identity in a Field of Stereotypes

College students are at a crucial age of racial identity development, as they leave home and transition to adulthood. For many, volunteering in the juvenile justice system became an important space for them to reflect on and to develop their own sense of racial identity. The stories of volunteers of color make clear that the ghetto and barrio remain symbolically central spaces in defining race, even as Black and Latino populations have spread widely throughout the suburbs of America. But they also highlight the strange effects of the criminal justice system as a race-making institution as police profiling and incarceration have become paradigmatic experiences of race in contemporary America, but not all young people of color experience the criminal justice system in the same way.

For Black and Latino volunteers, working in juvenile hall sometimes brought back powerful memories of their own encounters with racial stereotypes that equated race, class, and education. They told stories about teachers who expected them to drop out or were surprised to see them in honors classes, counselors who told them they should only apply to community college because they couldn't afford a 4-year college, and fellow students who were surprised at their academic prowess at the university. Students of color had overcome these stereotypes and made it to college. But in the lives of young people in juvenile hall, they could see how these kinds of interactions produced dropouts and pushed people into the criminal justice system. They could see the broad ways racism constrained opportunity, and had endangered their own success, in ways they hadn't fully noticed before.

Paloma, a Latina student who grew up in a Northern California barrio, connected with the inside students over stories about teachers' low expectations of themselves as minority students. One inside student told her that "he was expected to be stupid, to flunk out of school and probably end up in jail. I told him I was expected to get pregnant and just turn into a Latin breeding baby machine." Sharing these stories made her reflect on the power of these stereotypes to shape actions. "When we are told that that is how our life is supposed to be, we give up and we follow what we are told to do, and in this way we become stereotypes." She realized how precariously close she herself had come to becoming that stereotype.

Antonio too remembered a time in his own education that he went from being an A student to getting Ds and Fs because of a racist teacher who treated the Latino students "very poorly" and regularly made fun of one of the ESL learners in the class. Antonio began to reject school, explaining,

> I didn't really know [how] to put words to it, but I was like fuck this guy. I had been having B's and A's in my class and in that class, I had D's and F's because I saw the way the teacher was treating other students who were Mexicano or Latino.

Shortly after this experience, Antonio's parents moved him into a more middle-class community, and he began again to excel in school. But working in juvenile hall made the consequences of low expectations and racism in schools painfully visible. Antonio often found himself thinking: "where would I have ended up?" if his parents hadn't moved.

Robert was frustrated in college as he was still forced to confront White classmates' stereotypes that all (or "real") Black men came from poor backgrounds, had street credibility, and were academically unprepared. He described the "crushing" weight of the stares and looks he received from classmates who seemed to assume he "was still not as smart, still not as qualified." He felt he had to "work three times harder" than his peers to prove that he belonged at the university.

> Not only do I deserve to be here, but I'm going to show you up. I'm going to work for it. I'm going to earn it, and I'm going to be better than you. I'm coming with a force. I'm not representing myself. I'm representing a lot of underrepresented Black males as a whole.

As he crafted an oppositional identity as a Black intellectual, he also faced challenges from White (and some Black students) that he now wasn't Black enough and assumptions (in his case false) that he came from economic privilege.

While stereotypes of poor barrios and ghettos often stigmatized college students of color, these stereotypes could also lead to a strange form of cultural capital on our predominately White suburban campus. White students sometimes saw men of color who had grown up "in the hood" as exciting and cool, in part because of how hip-hop has commodified urban (particularly Black) masculine street cultures as the epitome of "ghetto cool" (Halnon, 2011; Hooks 1992; Kelley, 1998). Luis talked explicitly about how many White students responded when they found out he grew up in South Central, a neighborhood made famous by gangster rap. They'd want to hear his stories, sometimes asking, "Is it really like how NWA says it was?"[5] The image of his neighborhood gave him an aura of tough mas-

[5] Famous gangta rap group of the 1980s and 1990s from South-central Los Angeles.

culinity, making many people misread his shyness as a street-savvy toughness. As Luis explained, "I've been told I dog people." A White friend told Luis he understood the cold reception he felt at their first meeting. "You're from South Central. You're just sizing me up." This interpretation did not at all fit Luis' own experience or self-conception since he had grown up a self-described "good kid" radically insulated from the streets. But he could sometimes enjoy the ways his neighborhood earned him respect, a form of status, and an aura of cool among men at the university. "I get this automatic, instant credibility that I'm from the hood. And I got street smarts. So every once in a while I'm like, 'Yeah, I'm from South Central,' and I get that look, you know." He played with the tough image, chuckling as he added, "Respect me or you'll get your ass beat."

The Complex Contours of the New Jim Crow Color Line

While volunteers of color identified and shared experiences of racial stereotyping as they worked in juvenile hall, some also became aware, even self-conscious, about the radical differences between their experiences and those of incarcerated youth. This was particularly true as they reflected on experiences with the police and the criminal justice system. Police profiling may have become the most publically recognized example of Black and Latino racial marginalization, and the criminal justice system has certainly codified the definition of Black and Latino youth as problems (Rios, 2011). But hyperincarceration and stereotypes of criminality do not affect all Black and Latino young people the same way. While Black and some Latino male volunteers often talked about their experiences with police profiling and criminalization, other volunteers of color had never been stopped by the police and identified few direct personal experiences with racial stereotyping or discrimination in their schools or neighborhoods. The same factors that propelled volunteers of color on a track to college protected some of them from experiencing the full force of criminalization in their schools and neighborhoods.

As Loic Wacquant (2010) argues, class and place intersect with race to shape patterns of policing and incarceration. In the USA, the weight of the criminal justice system falls most heavily on poor Black men, and to a lesser degree Latino men, growing up in neighborhoods of concentrated poverty. Heavy policing and prosecution focuses on Black ghettos and Latino barrios, disproportionately drawing in young people with little education. This means that many Black and Latino women and even some young men, particularly those who grew up in middle-class neighborhoods or attended magnet schools, did not experience the same level of contact with criminal justice authorities. Indeed for Black men with a college education, the lifetime chances of incarceration have declined over the last 30 years while they have sky-rocketed for high school dropouts, most markedly for Black men but also significantly for all men without a high school diploma (Western & Petit, 2010). This reality has led some Black and Latino volunteers to see their work in juvenile hall as a way to connect to these foundational experiences of racism and thus to forge a clearer sense of belonging to Black and Latino communities that have been decimated by mass incarceration.

Even though Black women and girls also face disproportionate policing and school discipline, as Crenshaw, Ocen, and Nanda (2015) have found, women of color among our volunteers generally described themselves as insulated from experiences of criminalization. For them, like for many White students, getting to know students in juvenile hall made racism feel more real to them. It now affected people they knew and came to care about, encouraging them to speak out about racism more. Melinda grew up in a primarily Mexican community and went to "the ghetto high school." However, as she was insulated in college prep classes, she herself had faced little racism and no contact with the criminal justice system. She was really shocked to hear many inside students express a fundamental lack of faith that the police or even ambulances would serve their community. When she heard an inside student say simply, "They don't care about us," she explained that that statement "hit me the most because it was their stories that they shared. It is someone I know that is being discriminated against…I feel like I'm being exposed to a reality that society doesn't want me to see."

Some middle-class and upwardly mobile working-class male volunteers had also, at least partially, been insulated from experiences with police profiling. For example, although Luis was a dark-skinned Latino young man with immigrant parents from South Central Los Angeles, he identified no experiences of racial profiling in his teenage years because he simply wasn't ever "on the street in South Central." He went straight to and from his high school in a wealthier White neighborhood and his parents carefully controlled his dress and use of space to protect him from the real dangers, and from the stigma, of criminality in his neighborhood. When he first heard stories of police harassment from inside students, his reality was challenged. He explained:

> That to me was a big shock… because I was always taught police are going to help you. All my encounters with the police have always been friendly. When I started hearing like, "Police, cops harass me, and I'd be just walking down the street, and then they're saying stuff." That, I hadn't really heard about it. I might've read about it or heard about it in songs, but not personal knowledge. That definitely helped me like change to a different perspective; like they're probably living in a different world, different mentality.

Volunteering in juvenile hall and hearing these personal stories of police profiling reshaped how Luis understood his own racial identity and how he located himself within a racial community. He rejected his earlier identity as a "good kid" defined in opposition to "the thugs" in his school and neighborhood and began to identify more with the kids in juvenile hall. "It got really comfortable to me. Just the way they look, I feel like I look like them, and I know where they're coming from too because they grew up in [the same city as many incarcerated youth]." He had started to hang out with his cousin in a nearby skate park and learned that his family there had "problems" with cops as well.

> They don't like cops. Cops tried shutting down their skate park. They've always had like, beef or whatnot…I'm hanging out with my cousin. I'm getting this mentality, and I'll go back to juvie and it's like the same mentality, so it's like I'm going home. I'm going back to the people I know how to hang out with.

As Luis built relationships with students in juvenile hall and with his own extended family, he began to forge a broader sense of belonging to a community of color that was engaged in a shared struggle against criminalization.

Ghetto Authenticity and Black Middle-Class Dilemmas

Many Black volunteers grew up middle class in predominantly White communities, in neighborhoods that did not fit dominant definitions that equated blackness with economic struggle and inner-city communities. They would not describe going into juvenile hall as "returning home," but their volunteer experiences did help them to develop a clearer sense of their own identity as Black. Their narratives highlight the complex ways volunteers of color construct racial and class identities as they move between predominantly White middle-class spaces and prisons and jails that are filled with poor people of color.

Some Black middle-class volunteers seemed to define incarcerated students as embodying a kind of ghetto authenticity, which helped them identify more strongly with Black culture. Mari, in a written reflection, described how she had often laughed along with the racist jokes of her White suburban friends and had not actively identified herself as Black in high school.

> I joked about my race, right along with them; stepping into their grasp. I was being fake. It reminds me of a lyric from a Kanye West song: 'As long as I'm in a polo and smilin' they think they've got me, but they'll try to crack me if they ever see a Black me. Being proud of who I am … is something I am seriously working on. I am doing this because my juvenile justice classmates are the realest people I have ever met; and I am striving to be more like them.

This idea that young people in juvenile hall were "real" and could help Black middle-class students understand their own blackness draws on the widespread equation of blackness with urban poverty, struggle, and street cultures. As Kelley (1998) argues, young men involved in ghetto street cultures have long been framed as authentic representatives of "real Black culture."

Black middle-class college student volunteers thus had to construct an identity in dialogue with these stereotypes that located "real" Black identity in the experience of poor inner-city youth. Anthony described working in juvenile hall as "something that "brought me back to my identity" because it connected him to foundational Black experiences of ghettoization and criminalization. He grew in a predominantly White community and had not embedded himself within Black social networks at his predominately White high school. "I wasn't so in tune as I'd like to be with my race." Working closely with students in juvenile hall made him think more about himself "as an African American male in this community and how I was perceived." He described talking with incarcerated youth as "a learning process." Although he had "a lot of family from the inner city," he explained that "doesn't mean you directly understand what's going on in their shoes and everything." Anthony's language moved between defining Black culture as his own and as something he learned about at a distance, in part through the stories of incarcerated youth. "I still have a lot of learning to do with my, with the African American culture." Volunteering in juvenile hall became a way for middle-class Black students like Anthony to feel more connected to Black communities and to their own Black identity.

Black college students regularly talked about their struggles with this narrow definition of Black authenticity, which often led people to label them as "not really Black" or "white washed." Anthony described watching Black friends on campus "feel that they had to prove their blackness" through "the way they dress, the way they talk, or by fighting or the music they listen to or just doing outlandish things." He explained, "Sometimes, the kids with the good education and opportunities want to act as though they're from struggle."

Going into juvenile hall helped middle-class Black students resolve these perceived tensions between their class and racial identities. As Mari explained, "When I'm here [at the university], it's easy for me to think I'm around all of these White people," and "they just don't understand what I'm talking about." She often felt "alienated" and was tempted to distance herself from the White middle-class spaces she grew up in, to think, "I have nothing in common with these people, and I have everything in common with people that look like me." But when she went into juvenile hall, she had to acknowledge that was "not true" because her privileged childhood was so different than that of incarcerated youth. "I share commonalities with both. I share experiences with both. And that's something I need to recognize."

Cass, another African American woman, also thought students in juvenile hall helped her identify more with being Black and to expand her definition of blackness. She grew up feeling like she didn't fit in with other Black kids and wasn't "Black enough" because she grew up in an upper-middle-class, mostly White, neighborhood. But working in juvenile hall "probably made me more okay with what I am...with the blackness that I portray to the world. So I'm not stereotypical Black, but I think I realized there are many different ways to be Black and that the kids allowed me to express that part of my identity." As Cass became more conscious of and comfortable with her blackness, however, she became "hyperaware" of the ways she was affected by racism. She started to recognize racism in those times "when I wasn't sure what was going on. I thought I'd never experienced it, but then I realized I did." With this awareness, Cass became more concerned with how she was perceived and how she presented herself. She said: "I guess I worry now about how I'm being, how I'm presenting myself to different situations."

For privileged students of color, like Cass, going into juvenile hall led to this kind of heightened double consciousness, which DuBois (2005) defines as "this sense of always looking at one's self through the eyes of others, of measuring one's soul by the tape of a world that looks on in amused contempt and pity" (p. 9). For students who grew up with the ideal of colorblindness, working in juvenile hall often prompted their most substantive (and sometimes first) reflection on the significance of race in their own lives and in America. They became more aware of racial tensions that surrounded them and felt increasingly responsible for speaking up against racism in predominantly White settings. They found themselves choosing to identify with young people behind bars on the wrong side of the new Jim Crow color line, which heightened their own awareness of racism. Thus, they began consciously to negotiate their own sense of racial identity in dialogue with young men and women in juvenile hall and, more broadly, with the racial stereotypes that shaped and constrained their lives.

Discussion and Implications

This research has some significant implications for those of us who run programs that support volunteers in correctional facilities. Volunteering in prisons and juvenile corrections is an intense experience for all volunteers. They are often confronted with stories of deep personal suffering that emerge out of conditions of poverty, family dysfunction, and the failures of schools, courts, and social welfare systems to support young people and their families. Volunteers in prison are also crossing one of the clearest racial divides in America. They struggle to understand what they see and to cope with the diverse emotional reactions this work can produce. As is clear from the research presented in this chapter, however, these struggles take distinctive forms for volunteers across race, class, and gender lines.

Juvenile hall presented a set of unique challenges for men and women of color, and this may account for some of our difficulty recruiting and retaining men of color as volunteers. Most women of color described going to juvenile hall as "the high point" of their week. They valued the relationships they forged, but they were rarely forced to imagine themselves literally in the shoes of the incarcerated students who were overwhelmingly men. Indeed women of color were able to play the culturally overdetermined role of community caretaker, as they nurtured students in juvenile hall (Ferguson, 2001). Many played this role already in their families and communities, sharing stories of how they tried to help their cousins, brothers, or friends get back on their feet or stay on the right track when they came home from juvenile hall or prison.

In contrast, men of color were face-to-face in a much more personal way with the racialized stereotype of "the thug." For some, their own experiences of being stereotyped as criminals made the experience of going into juvenile hall much more personally charged and exhausting. Many men said they couldn't leave juvenile hall behind when they left the facility. DJ was struck by how White students left juvenile hall with "an extreme sense of hope" while he left exhausted because he felt "all that pressure and depression from the students." Antonio agreed,

> A lot of the White students could go home and that would be it. It'd be, "Oh damn that sucks." But for me, it would be like I would go home, but I would still be pulled over [by the police] in Redlands. I would still hear things about my racial identity in Redlands. People would yell things at me like racial slurs or whatever or homophobic slurs. So there's always these reminders of who I am.

Juvenile hall even haunted his dreams as he imagined being beaten by police and ending up in our local juvenile hall.

Several men of color who were part of the Inside Out class chose not to continue as volunteers despite many efforts to convince them otherwise. One of these students, Robert, ultimately decided not to continue volunteering because he found himself so frustrated when he saw students in the hall embrace the thug stereotype. In an interview, he enacted an imagined dialogue begging the young men he had met to leave the gang life. "'Come on, man.' I just don't want them to … fit that stereotype, or just live that life in general. It's hard for me, when I know. 'You can't do this. Just don't. Please God. Don't.'" This was really personal to him, a painful reminder of the ways he was linked to, and continually judged by, a racial stereotype that framed him as a dangerous and uneducated thug. DJ talked about his own efforts to get other Black men to join him in REACH. They said they were committed to service and to showing kids of color that they could overcome racial barriers and make it to college. But he often saw students hesitate, "Wait you want me to go to prison?" He described how they seemed to see volunteering in prison as a threat to their own successful college path, "They say wait a minute so you want me to take a step backwards?"

Volunteer programs need to think carefully about how to best support the diversity of our volunteers and how to encourage volunteers to develop the knowledge they need to understand the complex social dynamics they see reflected inside our prison systems. Without structured reflection, many more privileged volunteers rely on dominant cultural narratives for why people are poor or incarcerated. They focus insistently on the bad choices of individual kids or the terrible parents who have failed them. Their analyses reproduce common sense cultural, and implicitly racial, explanations for crime and violence in America. The intimacy of volunteering and mentoring can actually make this problem worse because getting to know individual kids in the system focuses volunteers' attention on individual choices and often chaotic family lives (Tilton, 2013).

Volunteers of color, especially those from working-class communities, developed complex analyses of the structures of opportunity that enable and constrain success for many poor kids of color. But they also struggled with a sense of powerlessness in the face of the massive structural constraints they saw reflected in the lives of incarcerated youth. Volunteers of color, and especially Black and Latino men, carried distinctive personal and emotional burdens as their volunteer experiences often brought back painful memories of their own experiences with racism or make them newly aware of the ongoing significance of race in America.

In thinking about supporting volunteers to do the much-needed work in the prison voluntary sector, this chapter lends itself to some concrete ideas. Teachers and program leaders need to create the space and support for volunteers to explore the range of emotional impacts and analytic questions volunteering in corrections raises. We should cultivate explicit conversations about how race and class shape volunteers' expectations and experiences coming into prisons and juvenile halls. Volunteers also need a basic understanding of the structural forces and criminal justice practices that have produced significant racial disparities in America's prison system. Sometimes these conversations should take place in separate identity-based groups so that students have the space to reflect on their distinctive experiences of race. This could help build communities of support for volunteers of color, whose experiences confronting race inside and outside of juvenile hall can be exhausting and demoralizing. But this is also important for White volunteers, who are often unused to and uncomfortable with exploring their own racial identities and deeply held stereotypes. They may be able to more directly explore their own racial experiences and stereotypes among other White volunteers. This can also avoid putting volunteers of color in the uncomfortable position of having to confront the racial stereotypes of their White colleagues as this can intensify feelings of alienation many students of color experience on predominately White college campuses (Mitchell, Donahue, & Young-Law, 2012).

The analysis presented in this chapter offers important insights into the complex ways race, class, and gender shapes daily experiences, life chances, and the ways we all craft identities. The problem of the color line remains a central twenty-first-century problem, taking a distinct form that is embodied most visibly in the walls that surround the prisons and jails that dot our landscape. This New Jim Crow color line is not a clear or simple Black–White racial divide, but one muddied by the shifting and messy ways race intersects with gender and class. Volunteers in prison have the opportunity to reflect on, understand, and potentially work to dismantle that color line but only if they have spaces of support to think about their experiences inside and out of America's prison system.

References

Alexander, M. (2010). *The new Jim Crow: Mass incarceration in the age of colorblindness.* New York: The New Press.

Butin, D. (2006). The limits of service-learning in higher education. *The Review of Higher Education, 29*(4), 473–498.

Carnevale, A., & Strohl, J. (2013). *Separate and unequal: How higher education reinforces the intergenerational reproduction of White racial privilege.* Retrieved from https://cew.georgetown.edu/wp-content/uploads/2014/11/SeparateUnequal.ES_.pdf.

Caro, R., Porfilio, B., & Valeri, A. (2009). Critical service learning confronts homelessness. *Academic Exchange Quarterly, 13*(3), 101–112.

Chapman, J. & Morley, R. (1999). Collegiate service-learning. *Journal of Prevention & Intervention in the Community, 18*(1), 19–33.

Collins, P. H. (1990). *Black feminist thought: Knowledge, consciousness, and the politics of empowerment.* New York: Routledge.

Crenshaw, K. W., Ocean, P., & Nanda, J. (2015). *Black girls matter: Pushed out, overpoliced and underprotected.* Retrieved from http://www.aapf.org/recent/2014/12/coming-soon-blackgirlsmatter-pushed-out-overpoliced-and-underprotected.

Du Bois, W. E. B. (2005). *The souls of Black folk.* New York: Barnes & Noble Classic.

Dunlap, M., Scoggin, J., Green, P., & Davi, A. (2007). White students' experiences of privilege and socioeconomic disparities: Toward a theoretical model. *Michigan Journal of Community Service Learning, 13*(2), 19–30.

Eberhardt, J. L., Purdie, V., Goff, P. A., & Davies, P. G. (2004). Seeing Black: Race, crime, and visual processing. *Journal of Personality and Social Psychology, 87*, 876–893.

Ferguson, A. (2001). *Bad boys: Race and the construction of Black masculinity in a public school.* Ann Arbor, MI: University of Michigan.

Frey, W. (2011). *Melting pot cities and suburbs: Racial and ethnic change in metro America in the 2000s.* Retrieved from http://www.brookings.edu/~/media/research/files/papers/2011/5/04%20census%20ethnicity%20frey/0504_census_ethnicity_frey.pdf.

Green, A. (2001). "But you aren't White:" Racial perceptions and service-learning. *Michigan Journal of Community Service Learning*, *8*(1), 18–26.

Halnon, K. (2011). So-called Black ghetto cool: From the color line to colorblind. *Consumers, Commodities and Consumption*, *12*(2). Retrieved from http://csrn.camden.rutgers.edu/newsletters/12-2/halnon.htm.

Haywood Burns Institute.. (2015). *Unbalanced juvenile justice* [California County level data 2011]. Retrieved from http://data.burnsinstitute.org/.

Hooks, B. (1992). *Black looks: Race and representation.* New York: South End.

Kelley, R. (1998). *Yo mama's dysfunktional! Fighting the culture wars in urban America.* New York: Beacon.

Mauer, M. & Chesney-Lind, M. (2002). *Invisible punishment: The collateral consequences of mass imprisonment.* New York: The New Press.

McGirr, L. (2012, March 12). The new suburban poverty. *New York Times.* Retrieved from http://campaignstops.blogs.nytimes.com/2012/03/19/the-new-suburban-poverty/?_r=0.

Mitchell, T. (2010). Challenges and possibilities: Linking social justice and service-learning. *Michigan Journal of Community Service Learning*, *17*(1), 94–97.

Mitchell, T. & Donahue, D. (2009). "I do more service in this class than I ever do at my site": Paying attention to the reflections of students of color in service-learning. In J. Strait & M. Lima (Eds.), *The future of service-learning: New solutions for sustaining and improving practice* (pp. 174–192). Sterling, VA: Stylus.

Mitchell, T., Donahue, D., & Young-Law, C. (2012). Service-learning as a pedagogy of whiteness. *Equity and excellence in education*, *45*(4), 612–629.

NAACP Legal Defense Fund. (2005). *Dismantling the school to prison pipeline.* Retrieved from http://www.naacpldf.org/files/publications/Dismantling_the_School_to_Prison_Pipeline.pdf.

O'Mara, M. (2005). Suburbia reconsidered: Race, politics, and property in the twentieth Century. *Journal of Social History*, *39*(1), 229–243.

Pager, D. (2007). *Marked: Race, crime and finding work in an era of mass incarceration.* Chicago: University of Chicago.

Pompa, L. (2002). Service-learning as crucible of change: Reflections on immersion, context, power and transformation. *Michigan Journal of Community Service Learning*, *9*(1), 67–76.

Rios, V. (2011). *Punished: Policing the lives of Black and Latino boys.* New York: New York University.

Russell-Brown, K. (2008). *The color of crime: Racial hoaxes, White fear, Black protectionism, police harassment, and other macroaggressions*. New York: New York University.

Tilton, J. (2011). *Dangerous or endangered? Race and the politics of youth in urban America*. New York: New York University.

Tilton, J. (2013). Rethinking youth voice and institutional power: Reflections from inside a service learning partnership in a California juvenile hall. *Children and Youth Services Review*, *25*(8), 1159–1296.

Wacquant, L. (2001). Deadly symbiosis: When ghetto and prison meet and mesh. *Punishment & Society*, *3*(1), 95–133.

Wacquant, L. (2010). Race, class and hyperincarceration. *Daedelus*, *139*(3), 74–90.

Western, B. & Pettit, B. (2010). Incarceration & social inequality. *Daedelus*, *139*(3), 8–19.

CHAPTER 13

Developing Support and Self-Care Strategies for Volunteers in a Prison Writing Program

Tobi Jacobi and Lara Rose Roberts

Introduction

> "My own personal history with abuse made me a better volunteer because I was able to better understand some of the trauma the girls had been through." (Tina)
>
> "You know, literacy is really important, but it's not a fix for the problems that cause a lot of the incarceration." (Karen)
>
> "I had no preparation or expectation about how awful being locked up is." (Viva)

In the above quotes, the volunteers relay the reality that work inside prisons inspires connection and makes visible the gravity of—and challenges of working within—the US carceral system. Indeed, compassion fatigue is all too real for volunteer writing teachers who encounter difficult disclosures of violence, rape, and loss week after week. While self-care is a regular component of social work and counseling training and a practice that social service organizations (e.g., hospice, child advocacy, elder care) encourage, it is less common to talk about in conjunction with literacy outreach programs behind bars.

T. Jacobi (✉) • L.R. Roberts
Colorado State University, Fort Collins, CO, USA

L.S. Abrams et al. (eds.), *The Voluntary Sector in Prisons,* Palgrave Studies in Prisons and Penology, DOI 10.1057/978-1-137-54215-1_13

SpeakOut! writing workshops were developed in 2005 following an informal needs assessment that revealed a paucity of opportunities for extracurricular literacy programming for underserved and at-risk populations, particularly those enmeshed in the criminal justice system. Each workshop meets weekly for 1 to 2 hours and runs for 12 to 14 weeks under the guidance of three or four volunteer facilitators. As we illustrate in this chapter, self-care has emerged as a primary volunteer training concern in our writing outreach program. Open interviews with volunteers revealed themes of anxiety, frustration, and longing for support, and these concerns underscore the need for ongoing training in writing response theory, community engagement, and self-care.

As writing teachers and practitioners, we turn to writing itself as a method of support for volunteers responding to the tensions emerging from encounters with institutions like jail. Drawing upon the reflections of community writing group facilitators like Tina, Viva, and Karen, this chapter argues that volunteer training programs have a responsibility to recognize secondary trauma and make self-care training available to volunteers. Reflective writing exercises and narrative therapy strategies (Adams, 1998; Bolton, 2011; Pennebaker, 2004; Thompson, 2010) offer a ready set of tools for volunteers to name, share, and process the challenging disclosures and situations they may encounter behind bars as well as methods for understanding how volunteer experience might fit into the larger system of incarceration and justice work.

Literature Review

Volunteers behind bars often bear witness to inmates' stories of personal trauma, much like counselors, therapists, and social workers receive clients' stories. Terms such as vicarious traumatization, secondary traumatic stress, and compassion fatigue all describe the negative psychological and physiological responses of helpers who are exposed to others' trauma through their work in volunteer, therapeutic, or caregiving roles. While some researchers have used terms like compassion fatigue, vicarious traumatization, and secondary traumatic stress synonymously, Stamm (2010) delineates compassion fatigue that is felt due to burnout (associated with feelings of exhaustion, anger, and depression), and compassion fatigue based on secondary traumatic stress (characterized by negative feelings of fear based on shared stories of others' personal trauma). Regardless, each of these concepts implies that trauma-based work has the risk of causing a fundamental shift in one's worldview due to empathetic involvement with someone who has experienced trauma. This shift can impact the helper's sense of self, others, or the world, and this risk is present whether trauma is witnessed—as in the case of emergency room nurses—or shared as a story—such as in writing groups or therapy (Pearlman & Mac Ian, 1995; Sansbury, Graves, & Scott, 2015). In general, these traumatic exposure responses can be referred to as the ways in which "the world looks and feels like a different place to you as a result of doing your work" (Lipsky & Burk, 2007, as cited in Sansbury et al., 2015, p. 114).

Vicarious traumatization describes how a helper's worldview may be shifted in five areas: safety, dependency/trust, power, esteem, and intimacy. Helpers are most susceptible to traumatization if a story or experience taps into one or more of the five needs that they might currently be lacking (Sansbury et al., 2015). For instance, a person who struggles with feeling safe in their own life is more likely to internalize stories that reinforce the idea of safety as impossible. Early research on vicarious traumatization was conducted through a survey of therapists who self-identified as doing trauma work (Pearlman & Mac Ian, 1995). More than half of survey respondents (60 %) indicated that they themselves had personal trauma history. Their results also found that these therapists with personal trauma history had a significant negative disruption in their worldviews (or schemas) in the categories of safety, self-esteem, and trust. These results would indicate that individuals with a personal trauma history must be especially careful to maintain mental boundaries between their own lives and the stories they might hear within their work within helping professions, including healthcare providers, social service workers, and prison volunteers.

Without maintaining proper boundaries, volunteers are not only at risk for vicarious traumatization, but also for burnout. Sansbury et al. (2015) define burnout as "an occupational syndrome in systems of care characterized by high demands and little support" (p. 115), and self-care is considered a necessary component to preventing burnout among volunteers. In an initial study on mental health professionals who work with adolescent sex offenders, Kraus (2005) found that self-care alone did not directly increase resilience to compassion fatigue or burnout, though it did significantly increase helpers' level of compassion satisfaction. These high levels of compassion satisfaction—the joy one receives from helping others—were correlated with low levels of burnout, but self-care is most effective in helpers who also work to sustain interpersonal relationships.

Studies assessing recognition of both compassion satisfaction and fatigue suggest that volunteers perceive and experience both positive and difficult outcomes of their work (Kraus, 2005; Stamm, 2002). Figley's (1995) self-assessment tools for compassion fatigue, later adapted to include compassion satisfaction (Stamm, 2002), suggested that satisfaction awareness and self-care tools encourage responses that sustain volunteers and potentially counter the effects of fatigue and burnout. Conrad and Kellar-Guenther (2006) similarly found that compassion satisfaction played a role in mitigating compassion fatigue, trauma, and burnout in child-protection staff in Colorado, a workspace where workers encounter narrative disclosures and circumstances similar to those experienced by volunteers working with incarcerated writers in correctional facilities.

Over the past two decades, various forms of narrative therapy have emerged as techniques for responding to primary and secondary trauma (Adams, 1998; Bolton, 2011, DeSalvo, 1999; Pennebaker, 1990, 1997, 2004; Thompson, 2010). Pennebaker's (1997) landmark work on the value of writing identified the potential for wide-ranging therapeutic effects of guided writing activity. Simultaneous and subsequent work by researchers and practitioners in counseling, social work, psychology, and therapy have further developed Pennebaker's work into a robust set of curricular techniques and exercises for reflection and narrative-based self-care with applications for both those experiencing trauma and caregivers. Such techniques can offer prison and jail volunteers tools for both grappling with the competing needs of individual writers and the tightly controlled environments they reside in and for navigating their own complex responses to the stories of violence, sadness, injustice, and inequality that come with this kind of volunteer work. This research on vicarious trauma, compassion satisfaction/fatigue, and narrative therapies has converged as we consider how best to strengthen our training and support for volunteers working with confined youth in rehabilitation centers and adult writers in a county jail.

Program Background and Volunteer Perspectives

Since 2005, a community literacy center in northern Colorado has recruited and trained volunteers to facilitate SpeakOut! workshops, which are weekly creative and expository writing groups for teens in a rehabilitation center and adult prisoners in a local jail. The program has grown substantially since then; in spring 2015, six concurrent workshops were facilitated in two youth rehabilitation centers, at a women's community corrections unit, and with both men and women's groups at a county jail. Youth groups are mixed gender and the adult groups are single gender only. Workshop sizes range from 5 to 15 writers and participation varies weekly since all partner facilities are units through which youth and adults actively move on their way to recovery, release, or, in some cases, prison.

In 2010, research was begun with the aim of investigating the writing histories, motives for participation, and outcomes for participating prisoners and volunteer teachers through analysis of program materials, biannual evaluations, and targeted interviews. This chapter draws primarily on a grounded theory analysis of semistructured interviews conducted with workshop volunteer facilitators between the years of 2010 and 2014. They confirm much of what we might suspect about the role of writing/literacy in our lives: it can be painful and rewarding, difficult and necessary, which reinforces the tension between compassion satisfaction and compassion fatigue that we suspect is felt by many volunteers who work in the prison sector. Beyond personal affective experience, though, many of the narratives that emerged from the data reflect the tensions volunteers experience when engaging with writers whose tangled life histories and experiences move far beyond labels like "inmate" and "criminal." This chapter draws upon those semistructured open interviews with facilitators as a way to understand facilitators' experiences with and perceptions of their work as weekly volunteers in writing workshops with confined youth and women and men in jail.

We came to this research as the founder and director of the Colorado State University Community Literacy Center (CLC) and SpeakOut! workshop program and as a first-year graduate student holding a CLC internship involving facilitation of a workshop with incarcerated women. Through the years, Tobi, as SpeakOut! director, has been privileged to receive and respond to hundreds of stories and poems written by women and men who participate in the workshop. With this accumulation of narratives has also come the responsibility and burden of caring for them ethically. As is the case with so many professions that require staff members to keep personal information confidential, work with incarcerated writers mandates attention to disclosure and program safety. For Tobi, this also extends to the emotional well-being of all the writers—including volunteer facilitators.

Lara's emphasis on self-care began organically, when the biweekly staff meetings for the SpeakOut! interns were not sufficient to understand the emotions resulting from the work inside the jail. She started journaling but also found that the experience in the workshop was much easier to manage when she began to carpool with one of the volunteers. The ability to sort through the stories she and the volunteer had just heard was a powerful decompression tool, as was articulating shifting worldviews and guilt from respective privilege. This experience revealed the importance of training volunteers on self-care methods, as the volunteers (unlike the interns) do not meet outside of workshop. Without a time or place to meet and discuss the workshops, volunteers should be encouraged and trained to take their emotional health into their own hands.

In trying to understand how best to serve the SpeakOut! volunteers and interns, we drew upon our 11 years of collective experience with the program as well as interviews with 14 current and former volunteers to engage these key concerns:

- Volunteer self-awareness of factors contributing to compassion satisfaction and fatigue;
- Emerging need for structured group and individual writing-based self-care strategies; and
- Ethical responsibility for prison volunteer program administrators and coordinators to support volunteer training in compassion satisfaction and fatigue.

These concerns remained forefront in our minds as we aligned interview data from SpeakOut! writing workshop volunteers and current literature on volunteer sustainability alongside our own experiences in order to understand how volunteers might be more fully supported through writing-based self-care and training.

Interview Methods

Volunteer Interviews

Fourteen semistructured interviews were conducted with current and past SpeakOut! volunteer writing workshop facilitators. Interviews were recorded and took between 45 and 90 minutes. We asked the volunteers a series of open questions focused on their understanding of their volunteer work and their perceptions of its impact on themselves and others. Participants completed informed consent and their identities are protected through pseudonyms. Participants were both male and female volunteer facilitators and identify as either students or faculty at a local university or as community members; they joined the SpeakOut! community after expressing interest in literacy-based volunteer work and completing the training. All interviewees had completed at least one semester of volunteer work, and participants were recruited based upon work completed between 2010 and 2014 through e-mailed interview invitations. Fourteen volunteers, whose identities cut across gender, race, and professional affiliation (some based at the university, others in the community), were interviewed for this project.

Program Reflection and Interview Analysis

As active workshop leaders, Tobi and Lara write both from the perspective of invested teaching volunteers at the jail and as researchers interested in volunteer perspectives. Participation in all aspects of the writing workshop design and facilitation as well as the training process influence how the program—and particularly the volunteer training activities—has developed. We recognize this inextricable tie to the program and its development as necessary participatory action that influences how self-care strategies emerged. For this chapter, we analyzed data from all 14 interviews using an open coding scheme in order to establish volunteers' perceptions of their experiences as community workshop facilitators and the impact of that work. Emerging themes generally fell into and crossed between categories of compassion satisfaction and compassion fatigue, and these themes informed an emerging set of volunteer support practices as the research and program coordination continued.

Volunteer Perspectives on Working Behind Bars

Volunteers in our SpeakOut! writing programs come to us with a wide range of experiences. Some are driven by a passion for writing, creativity, and self-expression; others are motivated by a desire to engage in literacy work or to contribute to opportunities for incarcerated people. Some join our efforts through undergraduate or graduate internships and practicums while others work in our community in a wide range of nonprofit, teaching, and editing positions. All participate in an orientation and training session and have opportunities to participate in face-to-face additional training and access online resources and support.

Our experiences as both an experienced program director/facilitator and first-year graduate student/facilitator suggest that most volunteers experience both compassion satisfaction and compassion fatigue, often in close proximity since difficult disclosures and interactions often inspire myriad responses. As Louise DeSalvo (1999) suggests, work with people experiencing trauma (like many who are in jail and prison) is risky work—necessary, engaging, and difficult—but risky nonetheless.

Volunteer Perspectives on Satisfaction with Experience

Though not the primary focus of this chapter, we do want to first acknowledge that various facets of compassion satisfaction fuel volunteers' excitement and energy for work behind bars. This positive satisfaction often stems from an understanding that this type of work is necessary and can be further stimulated by intentional self-care practices, like those we offer as an appendix to this chapter. We offer brief evidence of satisfaction expressed through formation of communities, creative growth, and recognition of human connection.

Writing Builds Community

As Anderson & MacCurdy (2000) have argued, writing can reveal commonalities that bring together people who have experienced different, but nonetheless painful or emotional traumas. Several volunteers echoed the importance of group and communal spaces. Margaret, for example, described her experience in the workshop:

> When you sit in a circle and everybody is there to create something new, it is just like a little miracle because of all the stuff that gets poured out in the space of an hour and a half while we are there, it didn't exist before we sat together.

Viva's words also supported this theme: "The best moments were doing the songwriting workshop, having this moment where everyone created something together. I felt like we were all in the room together as creative people, creating a thing together." Both Margaret and Viva describe the physical space of the workshop ("in a circle," "in the space," "in the room"), undoubtedly because, in the confines of a jail, the notion of space is impossible to ignore. However, both volunteers felt that this space was filled with a positive energy, because they were *creating* something together. The power of creative individual and group energy emerged as a strength of the volunteers' experiences that can be channeled into functional self-care tools for volunteers.

Writing Inspires Creative Growth

The act of writing itself also creates space for creativity, understanding and empathy, and community between groups of people who might not otherwise interact, a reality that is often the case for people who volunteer behind bars. Both Samantha and Margaret offered their reflections on writing with the group:

> It also helped me feel more connected to the ladies (on a whole) by being a writer WITH them. I felt like I could be vulnerable in the workshop. Seeing other women share in such a strong way encouraged me to write my own work that speaks to my strengths as a woman.... It's also inspired me to pursue publication more. It's great to see the women's reaction when they get the publication. I want to feel that a bit more myself! (Samantha)
>
> I get community from it [and] I get friends from it. I am linked to something outside of my own little sphere. I work at home so it is good to have the time to go out. I get as much from it as we give when we go. (Margaret)

Others translated their growing sense of community into the language of teaching and growth. Marli and Samantha both found satisfaction in the learning they observed in writers—and in the ways the act of writing functioned within the group.

> I think the most rewarding times were when you could see a piece of literature they responded to and were excited about, and also seeing them grow as a writer or even as a class participant. There was one guy who got dragged there on his first day, and to compare that to the work at the end of the workshop you could see he was digging deeper into his feeling and was enjoying the writing. He was really prolific about the work. He submitted each work and he would go back to the pod and continue writing there. That was really rewarding to see some kind of change for him. (Marli)
>
> I learned a lot about myself as a teacher, a writer, and a person. I learned that writing could be more open and therapeutic. And that as a teacher, we often have a certain "way" of teaching set in our minds. The program showed me there are many methods and approaches.... It's helped me learn how to better critique others' work and how to receive critique myself—how to mold my work. (Samantha)

Writing itself extends beyond a teaching or expressive act for many facilitators, occupying roles of creativity, connection, and change. For some volunteers, this work led to new creative projects (e.g., a memoir or novel); for others, inspiration was found for rethinking university courses or methods for responding to traditional student writing.

Writing Reveals Human Experience

Volunteers also reflected on the ways that leading the workshop helped them to deepen their understanding of writers' sense of self and the ways they hoped to be understood as a humanist approach to confinement emerged. They spoke about how their workshop facilitation fit into a larger social justice approach to education and the circulation of writing from behind bars. In many cases, facilitators shifted their language about justice and incarceration to include a broader definition of humanity and creative spirit. Also, they understood the importance of publishing the SpeakOut! journal and actively worked to circulate copies widely as a method of instituting change.

> It really helps me understand not only the person behind the inmate, but also that they deserve an opportunity and they deserve a second chance. And if we give them an opportunity, maybe they will find success out there rather than returning to the old ways that got them in trouble.... There is definitely some activism going on, especially with the publication. When people read this, they think, "holy cow, I didn't realize that these people went through this, I didn't understand. I think it helps to build awareness, absolutely. (Samantha)
>
> I do talk to people about the workshop and people just look at me and they're like, "Wow." They're really fascinated and they want to experience it in some way too because it's so different from their image, and so I think there's a lot of educational responsibility that comes with working in this way. (Karen)

Samantha's musings suggest she recognizes not only individual depth of character within the incarcerated writers but also the need for public compassion. Karen expressed her desire to actively participate in shifting the dominant identity narratives of prisoners, drawing in part from the responsibility that she felt as a facilitator. She went on to reflect on her own conflicted view of how participants understand the role of jail in their lives:

> Something that's really been weighing on me since I heard it at the last reading, [was] that one of the women said that jail was the place she felt most accepted. And that was heartbreaking and wonderful at the same time. Another thing I don't know how to process just yet. But it was so sad she would say that. But it was also so good that she felt that she could have support within the jail.

Karen expressed some internal conflict when she said it is "weighing on her" and she doesn't "know how to process it yet," and we can see that the conflict continued in her shifts between "heartbreaking" and "wonderful" and "sad" and "good." While an opportunity for candid conversation on the relative safety that some inmates might feel while inside may have been useful for Karen and the writer, writing-based self-care strategies such as imagined dialogue (see Sample Writing Exercises in the appendix) might also offer needed space for critical reflection on these tensions that might otherwise contribute to compassion fatigue.

Volunteer Perspectives on Challenges Faced

While facilitators revealed important points concerning satisfaction and motivation related to their volunteer writing work, we also recognize the link between sustainability and compassion fatigue. We turn now to the tensions, stresses, and traumas that regularly emerge for literacy volunteers working through (and sometimes around) institutional rules and regulations in jail. We highlight five common challenges faced by volunteers: human confinement, difficult disclosures, participant recidivism, feelings of isolation, and activist tensions.

Participating in Human Confinement

Longtime volunteer Margaret described her emotional reaction every week in having to walk through the prison:

> I feel it definitely in the walk through the hallways. I hold my breath through that whole thing; I don't like it. I can understand the need for that kind of regimentation and the women certainly, for the most part, seem to take to it, like "we know we're supposed to walk on the right side and stop on the corners and if a guy's coming." They know it all and, for the most part, deal with it. I'm just not comfortable with it because it seems to underscore the fact that we're in an institution, which we can't get away from. Plus, we're walking along [with] a human being that you can't really talk to.

It can be difficult for volunteers to move between the roles demanded by the jail (hall monitor), by the program (writing program facilitator) and one's own autonomy (independent person with free will). Margaret's reflection not only highlights the split between the "institution" and "a human being," but also spotlights the intense physical reaction of holding her breath every week. Without exploring these tensions and reactions, such as through the guided writing exercises that we will suggest, Margaret risks becoming overwhelmed by the realities of volunteering within a carceral institution.

Managing Difficult Disclosures and Relationships

The disclosure of challenging experiences, including graphic violence, abuse, and loss, and description of unfamiliar life choices are ever-present behind bars, particularly in writing workshops. This reality must remain in the forefront since volunteers in the prison sector may have experienced their own trauma and thus may be at a higher risk for secondary traumatic stress if they do not receive proper support. In our interviews, one volunteer specifically acknowledged her own trauma: "One of the greatest challenges that I faced was when my own life collided with the writings of the girls, which I knew was a risk coming in." Not only did Tina have a history of trauma in her life, but also she had been concurrently dealing with a friend's death. She stated:

> I did not anticipate the girls' writing to overlap with those triggers. However, one of the poems a girl wrote was focused around a gravestone and this triggered me because the funeral was the next day and I began to cry. The girls were aware I was crying and I was embarrassed.

Although Tina's words, such as "collide," "triggered," and "embarrassed," seemed to insinuate that her feelings of safety and self-esteem have been compromised, she continues on to say that she used this experience as a "teachable moment." "After [exposing myself]," she says, "We became a closer group." This seems to suggest that intimacy shared in a group, though challenging, can be a foundation through which trauma workers can build trust and thus resiliency to vicarious trauma.

Marli, the men's group volunteer quoted in the prior section, stated: "The most difficult thing towards the end is that they write about a lot of raw stuff. I got a little tired of reading it. There was a lot of positive stuff, but that was the most difficult part. There was some really positive, happy writing, but some depressing stuff too." These words illustrate Marli's growing feelings of burnout: she was tired of reading the "raw stuff"; it was "difficult." However, her interview also revealed how she wants to acknowledge the positive experience of the workshop. Earlier in the interview, she discussed how it was "rewarding to see some kind of change for [a writer]" and how one writer had told her "it gave him a lot of confidence, and he said when they get out of [the facility] the one thing they're going to need is confidence." Notably, when Marli responded to questions about self-care, she did not actually mention self-care strategies, but rather that her emotional health was bolstered by the nature of the workshop. She said, "the workshop being once a week and for an hour was good," and both Margaret and Karen also mentioned the time limit as a positive boundary for their work. Creating temporal boundaries in terms of time inside and how deeply one might engage with multiple writers emerged as a strategy that bolsters empathy, as identified by volunteers when asked to reflect upon their experiences.

Others, like Karen, struggled with disclosure in a different way: "There was a moment when, and I'll never forget this, when somebody asked me, one of the men asked me where I run, and I said, 'Oh I run along the Powder Trail in Windom.' And then I thought, 'Oh my gosh! Should I have said that?'" Cumulative interactions with jail guards and staff, metal detectors, sliding steel doors, and institutional training often collide with myriad media portrayals of criminality to create anxiety about how much personal information to reveal when writing with people inside. Disclosure becomes an issue of emotional safety from the perspective of receiving challenging information and needing to create boundaries that are comfortable without compromising potential professional and creative relationships.

Observing Recidivism

Although we know both intuitively and through research on prison education that educational opportunities do reduce the likelihood of recidivism (Skorton & Altschuler, 2013; Vera Institute of Justice, 2015), prisoners do return, often for failing to maintain the terms of their parole. And while volunteers sometimes celebrate a familiar face during a writing session, a return can also feel discouraging. When asked about what feels most difficult, Samantha relayed this feeling: "seeing some of them return when they wrote (repeatedly) about never wanting to come back. You desperately want them all to get out and find happiness and success."

As the program director, this sentiment resonates with Tobi as well. Ten years of facilitating SpeakOut! writing workshops sometimes weighs heavily on the psyche when the same faces appear in the workshop every couple of semesters. Perhaps even more difficult to bear is the generational cycle that surfaces when writers move from the youth rehabilitation centers to the adult jail workshops or when participants request back issues of journals so they can review work by their mothers, uncles, and cousins. Although it is gratifying to see the program (and the print journals) as highly valued and stable forms of support and programming for participants, it is also discouraging to see people struggling to find their way, especially when that struggle is multigenerational.

Longing for More Communal Reflective Space

Although some volunteers celebrated the community formed by SpeakOut! groups, others did not find time/energy/space to develop adequate communal spaces for reflection. Viva wrote:

> One of the struggles of being a volunteer, not necessarily an intern, is that you are not connected to a community of people to talk to about stuff; you sort of just come in to do the workshop. I think a big challenge is not feeling like there were spaces to talk through and process that stuff, not knowing how to ask.

In contrasting volunteers and interns, she highlighted an important opportunity for support that we recognized in the SpeakOut! program. We realized that the interns were receiving much more support, because they earn university credits from their role as a workshop facilitator. As part of the internship requirements they meet biweekly as a group to discuss workshop successes and difficulties; they are presented with readings on topics like literacy, activism, and incarcerated populations; and they are required to write biweekly reflections on individual blogs sites. The interns are supported in person, online, and they support themselves through writing prompts. In contrast, the SpeakOut! volunteers, as Viva stated, simply show up to the jail each week and leave after the workshop. This leaves them undersupported, which we have recognized and tried to temper through meet-ups at coffee shops and monthly newsletters. As important as it is to create a sense of workshop community *inside* the jail, it is equally as important to bring a community together *outside* the jail as well in order to prevent volunteer burnout.

Understanding the Role of Activism and Privilege

Although some volunteers characterized their participation as activist, others grappled with how a writing workshop contributes to contemporary prison activism more broadly. Viva, for example, pressed the distinction between activist and ally to more fully examine the tensions that inevitably emerge from working inside a repressive system. She wrote:

> Are you an activist or an ally? Are you perpetuating an unjust system? Being able to tease out those underlying assumptions about what the work means.... To explore something like prison abolition. And maybe just having a space for having conversations about understanding the work of a writing workshop fitting into these larger conversations about prison and incarceration.

Participants also brought up the productive tensions that their work within what Goffman (1961) calls a "total institution" can inspire. For example, the weekly act of leaving jail after a workshop session often inspires reflection embedded with relief, guilt, hopefulness, and even anxiety. Just as the incarcerated writers in our groups sometimes claim that jail feels safe, a known quantity compared to the chaos of an unpredictable outside world, so too must our volunteers confront an expanded world as soon as they pass through the heavy metal doors that mark the return of keys, phones, identification cards, and jackets in winter. As Sandra wrote:

> I remember the first night, somebody stole a pen and it was a big deal, and I left thinking I can have as many pens as I want, I have all this freedom and I can do whatever and they can't.

The work of being intentional about privilege is a fatigue that we might struggle through—and celebrate—as we face the inequities that incarceration produces and makes visible. These very real stresses and productive tensions that emerge out of both compassion satisfaction and fatigue revealed additional opportunities for developing training and support for volunteers. As writing and literacy specialists, we turn to writing as both a functional tool for personal and economic survival and as a viable self-care resource for working through the complicated nature of compassion.

Implications for Volunteer Coordinators and Programs

Effective writing-based self-care (as offered below and detailed in the appendix) depends upon strong support from volunteer organizations. Given the high risk of compassion fatigue facing volunteers working with incarcerated writers, it is vital that volunteer programs establish clear and ongoing training that includes a diversity of support opportunities. Stamm (2012) suggests multiple strategies for encouraging awareness of both satisfaction and fatigue for people working in contexts where trauma is present and even a normalized discourse. These strategies include education about the risk of grappling with the negative and positive aspects of their work, guidance regarding tools for addressing these challenges, an understanding that distress is a normal and often regular part of witnessing and experiencing trauma, support for emotional responses to such trauma, training in cultural competence, and establishment of clear expectations and boundaries for volunteer expectations. These structural supports are particularly important for volunteers working inside correctional settings since human imprisonment is disturbingly common in the current US justice system. It is also one of the more mythologized institutions in a culture that has largely embraced a "lock' em up and throw away the key" approach to human criminality. Volunteers entering jails and prisons often confront their own curiosity, cultural exposure, nervousness about the physical confinement, fear of unknown criminal personas, and personal histories.

As our above analysis indicates, many SpeakOut! volunteers confront such apprehensions as they participate in writing workshops and respond to writing and experiment with self-care strategies. As program coordinators and administrators, we have developed a continuum of support tools that include both overt training opportunities and self-care techniques to encourage a healthy balance of satisfaction and fatigue as volunteers move through the weekly workshops. We have recognized the value of ongoing training and reflection, practices that shift and develop across the trajectory of a volunteer's experience with the program including initial orientations, informal self- and peer-care conversations, and online communications and resources. We offer them here as an example of one program's training system for volunteers.

Formal Training Opportunities

Initial Program Training and Orientation

We offer several orientation and training sessions annually to fill positions within our community-writing workshops. We emphasize community and flexibility in both practical application and theoretical orientation. This often requires that volunteers translate their own classroom-based experiences with writing into a community literacy approach that values process and product differently than a traditional evaluative system. The training weaves the language of self-care and community throughout the orientation activities and support materials to emphasize the vital role that volunteer commitment plays in the success of carceral literacy programming.

Volunteer Training Manual

Print and online manuals offer opportunities for volunteers to affirm the program philosophies and practices that trainings introduce. They also offer space for illustrations of practice through sample lesson plans, response methods, and institutional procedure. Even recognition of the need for self-care as an intentional component of training can be powerful within a familiar document like a volunteer manual. Outlining a set of practices and a continuum of potential responses to community workshop outcomes can provide volunteers with both a valuable acknowledgement of their experiences as well as strategies for responding to traumatic events, tensions, or fatigue. Best practice suggests that an integrated model of self-care is more effective than an invitation to reflect or offer feedback at the conclusion of a volunteer experience (see Adams, 2013). A manual can encourage a set of practices that can precede and follow sessions to provide volunteers with an engaging tool kit for understanding the traumas that can emerge from work inside prisons and jails.

MidYear Volunteer Development Workshop (Trauma, Art Therapy, Restorative Justice)

In addition to a training orientation, we offer a midyear volunteer development session that highlights the traumatic potential of work with confined youth and adults. In recent years, we have turned to colleagues in music and art therapy, narrative therapy, and restorative justice to offer volunteers additional strategies for both planning their workshop sessions and understanding the direct and indirect outcomes of their time with incarcerated writers. Space for individual reflection and self-assessment is incorporated into these training workshops to allow volunteers to move beyond individual SpeakOut! sessions and toward a wider understanding of their experiences and the impacts that this experience may have beyond the workshop. For example, employing the "unsent letter" exercise (Adams, 2011) encourages volunteers to imagine ways to talk back to a tension or trauma that emerged in a session in order to name that tension explicitly rather than allowing it to trouble accumulating memories of past sessions. Such professional development sessions also provide a needed space for volunteers from across different workshop sites to gather and share both commonalities and differences in experiences. Too, administrative/program evaluations from volunteer development sessions can offer program staff with valuable feedback on program successes and challenges, a checkpoint that can inform evolving practice and potentially identify crises before they escalate.

Informal Training and Outreach Efforts

Brief Pre- and Post-workshop Meetings with Co-facilitators
The facilitation team for each site meets in advance of each session for 30 to 60 minutes to review and revise the weekly lesson plan and to generally touch base with one another. This work sometimes occurs a few days before the session, but often just before the actual workshop when all the volunteers gather. While this time is often filled with the technical details of the facilitation, it is also a terrific and consistent opportunity for naming and discussing facilitation and response to challenges. For example, if a submitted writing (i.e., a poem turned in the week before) has been particularly difficult to respond to, facilitators often consult with each other about the best strategy for offering appropriate comments. This is also a useful space for anticipating the kinds of topics that a specific lesson might invite. Similarly, the walk through the halls and brief gatherings in the lobby often invite immediate reflection and session feedback. These pre- and post-workshop moments are important spaces for each facilitator to voice concerns, enthusiasms, revision suggestions, and/or pose questions to jail staff.

Individual Appointments/Informal Reflection and Assessment
Volunteers come from university and off-campus community contexts, a diversity that we welcome, but that also makes scheduling meetings

challenging. One simple support mechanism we offer is individual reflection sessions with volunteers as requested. Support staff reaches out to all volunteers several times throughout each workshop series to invite dialogue and feedback. These one-on-one sessions often result in improved practice for the program as a whole.

Monthly Volunteer Newsletter

We began circulating a SpeakOut! newsletter to volunteers and facilitator alumni in 2012 after some volunteers expressed concern about program communication and resource access. Each issue offers a spotlight on a current writer and volunteer, a self-care idea column, shared workshop ideas, and a featured article. The aim is to create a cohesive experience for volunteers as well as fostering a sense of shared purpose and community. The newsletter both celebrates the accomplishments of the program participants who face a myriad of challenges as they live through rehabilitation, jail, or prison as well as recognizes the tensions that emerge when working with institutions driven by often rigid scheduling and security measures.

Coffee Shop Stops

These bimonthly informal meetings are drop-in sessions for volunteers. They are co-hosted by a volunteer and staff member and offer volunteers an informal space for reflection and conversation with others from across the six community workshops. Each session is loosely organized around a theme and includes at least one new workshop lesson idea for volunteers to take away.

Online Access to Program and Self-Care Materials

Although the Internet provides a treasure trove of writing prompts and activities, volunteers often ask for guidance in designing effective lesson plans. We continue to build an online repository for tested lesson plans, activities, and handouts. This is also an effective space for encouraging self-care activities such as those highlighted earlier in this chapter. Reflective writing prompts, simple self-tests, and surveys and visual mapping exercises can be linked to program web resources to encourage volunteers to check in with themselves throughout their volunteer service.

Within our SpeakOut! program, we have been slowly building this collection of resources and developing varied training sessions to meet the needs of volunteers who move through our writing workshops. We offer these examples of our own volunteer training and support as integral to the support of compassion satisfaction and reduction of fatigue as a way to underscore the importance of offering meaningful training and support for all prison volunteers, whether volunteers reside within or beyond institutional walls.

Developing a Writing-Based Self-Care Plan for Volunteers

Self-care strategies based in writing emerged as a valuable resource because they are self-directed and can be customized based on individual needs, and they are private, which alleviates emotional vulnerability (Pennebaker & Memon, 1996). As noted above, volunteers who lead the SpeakOut! writing workshops demonstrate these advantages, as they often turn to writing themselves as they seek to understand the impact of their work. Samantha and Viva both situate writing not simply as a tool for expression, but also as a tool for understanding and self-care:

> I write myself. Often, delving into a fictional world helps you forget the problems of "now." Also, getting online and looking for poetry and fiction that is similar to something the participants shared (with a similar topic or theme) is helpful. Knowing that you can show them something the next week that speaks to what they experienced makes you feel like you can do something—however small. (Samantha)
>
> Sometimes it is the only space I get to do creative writing and share with other people. On that level, it was a creative outlet for me too. Hearing where other people were willing to go and how much they were willing to share and how vulnerable they were willing to make themselves in their writing, it was really inspiring. Because I am in the program, trying to understand myself as a writer is really tied to trying to understand myself as a teacher. (Viva)

Both theoretical frameworks and interviews centered on volunteer experience have underscored the importance of establishing community and communication in order to sustain the psychological and physiological health of volunteers. Without funding or resources though, proper levels of support are often difficult to achieve, thus it is important to examine methods of self-care that can augment organizational support.

Purposeful and intentional journaling can increase awareness of a situation, provide self-care, and be used to explore internal or external conflict. The key of the journaling technique is to writing purposefully and intentionally, with an awareness of the outcome one hopes to achieve

(Adams, 2011). Writing to achieve a goal is form of self-supervision. According Shohet (2008), the concept of supervision—which includes individual supervision, group supervision, peer supervision, or personal supervision—is aligned with coaching and mentoring, and all "desire to improve practice through some kind of reflection" (as cited in Thompson, 2010, p. 2). In therapeutic contexts, supervision is a necessary practice to ensure proper boundaries between client and therapist, and the concept can be applied to any context where facilitators have close interactions with clients.

However, many prison volunteer programs do not have the infrastructure to provide individual supervision. Instead, this sector must often find ways to create self-supervision. Thompson (2010), of the Therapeutic Writing Institute, posits that journal writing can function as self-supervision by "developing intimacy with and knowledge of the self," which will "help practitioners to stay connected and grounded in their own experience and practice" (pp. 3–4). A benefit to this practice is that it can help a volunteer create a mental separation between different clients, stories, and experiences so that each can be managed on its own, rather than considered in one overwhelming group. Then, each experience can be regarded with greater focus.

Thompson also discusses the importance of managing countertransference, defined as "when thoughts and feelings from previous relationships or situations in the practitioner's life become revived in the present therapeutic relationship" (p. 6). For example, a client might share a story that reveals their disappointment in their child, which may activate feelings of parental disapproval that the practitioner may have dealt with in his or her own life. Countertransference is a large risk in volunteers who work with stories of personal trauma, and at SpeakOut!, we see journal writing as a tool to manage this countertransference by writing about moments of interaction in which discomfort was felt. We suggest that volunteers ask questions such as "what is the discomfort that I feel in my interactions with this person?" and "where does that feeling come from?"

Basic self-care writing strategies encourage self-awareness as a priority, as that awareness allows personal emotions to be extricated from others' trauma. Emotions become manageable through this separation and can be further investigated through a structured writing process (Adams, 1998; Bolton, 2011; Pennebaker, 2004; Thompson, 2010). To find ways to grapple with these questions productively, we offer three examples of written self-assessment tools and writing-based activities.

Assessing Compassion Satisfaction and Fatigue with the Professional Quality of Life Scale

Adams (2011) and Pennebaker (2004) advise that journal writing must remain structured, in order to stave off feeling out-of-control or experiencing despair as a result of confronting a situation. Self-assessments offer a way to focus journal exercises. The Professional Quality of Life Scale (ProQOL) (Appendix 13.1) (Stamm, 2012) asks individuals to consider their current work or volunteer situation, and the results are evaluated to determine the participant's levels of Compassion Satisfaction and Compassion Fatigue (either Burnout or Secondary Trauma).[1] With these results, volunteers can understand specific areas of focus in order to combat secondary trauma and burnout.

Creating a Self-Care Plan

Where the ProQOL assesses areas of risk and need, writing can be used to help a volunteer understand their current self-care practices as well as assist in brainstorming new methods. The Self-Care Plan Worksheet (Appendix 13.2) (Reiser and Butler, n.d.) provides a structured, manageable outlet for this understanding to which the volunteer can continually refer. The worksheet asks the participant to consider their current methods for self-care within six domains that affect an individual's sense of well-being: mind, body, emotions, spirit, work, and relationships. By comparing current practices (if any) to the results of the ProQOL Scale, it becomes possible to identify which domain of self-care has the greatest effect on personal well-being and thus create a focus for which aspects of self-care should be altered or improved. For example, if the ProQOL Scale indicated a high score for both Compassion Satisfaction and Burnout, the volunteer likely feels satisfied in their work but should focus on self-care methods in which they make themselves a priority (using the categories of Body, Mind, or Spirit) before helping others (which would fall under the categories of Work or Relationships).

Writing-Based Self-Care Techniques: The Journal Ladder and Writing to Heal

Both the ProQOL Scale and the Self-Care Plan Worksheet provide a structured understanding that can then create a framework through which to

[1]The measures to evaluate results can be found at proqol.org/uploads/ProQOL_5_English_Self_Score_3-2012.pdf

confront the situation through journal writing. It is recommended that this self-supervision process begins with structured exercises before moving to writing within abstract realms, and Adams (2011) created The Journal Ladder (Appendix 13.3) to develop journaling techniques that range from very structured (Sentence Stems) to not structured at all (Free Writing). These journaling techniques are followed by a reflection of the writing process that begins, "As I read this, I notice …" (p. 7). This self-reflective writing technique mirrors those that Pennebaker (2004) recommends in *Writing to Heal* (Appendix 13.4). He recommends four consecutive days of 20-minute writing, followed by a set of four reflection questions to gauge the emotional effect the writing process caused. Techniques and tools such as these are highlighted in more detail in the appendix (including sample self-care writing exercises) and can illuminate volunteer awareness of both the emotional joys and stressors that inevitably come with work behind bars. Writing can encourage a healthy understanding of experience that can tip the scales in favor of compassion satisfaction while also recognizing the reality of fatigue.

Conclusion

The training and support of volunteers should be a paramount concern for any organization that undertakes noble and necessary work within the criminal justice system. In our organization in which we facilitate weekly writing groups for incarcerated populations, the practice of writing as self-care materialized as a simple evolution of the work in which we were already participating. However, by incorporating writing as self-supervision, any organization can assure that their volunteers are more likely to find their work sustainable, rather than cause for compassion fatigue, burnout, or secondary trauma. Volunteers risk these detrimental psychological stressors through their willingness to interact with inmates—interactions that often result in the sharing of stories of traumatic pasts filled with violence, substance abuse, and poverty. Rather than avoiding or fearing these powerful experiences that create bonds across difference larger than "inside" versus "outside," volunteers should be encouraged to reflect on these encounters through writing in order to appreciate the shared intimacy while protecting their own emotional health. Organizations that work behind bars have not only an ethical duty to provide this fundamental support for their volunteers, but also they should encourage writing practices that will stimulate a further sense of satisfaction derived from the volunteer work. This will ensure the continued success of the voluntary sector in prisons.

APPENDIX 13.1: ASSESSING COMPASSION SATISFACTION AND FATIGUE

Professional Quality of Life Scale (ProQOL)

Compassion Satisfaction and Compassion Fatigue
(ProQOL) Version 5 (2009)

When you *[help]* people you have direct contact with their lives. As you may have found, your compassion for those you *[help]* can affect you in positive and negative ways. Below are some-questions about your experiences, both positive and negative, as a *[helper]*. Consider each of the following questions about you and your current work situation. Select the number that honestly reflects how frequently you experienced these things in the *last 30 days*.

1=Never	2=Rarely	3=Sometimes	4=Often	5=Very Often

_____ 1. I am happy.
_____ 2. I am preoccupied with more than one person I *[help]*.
_____ 3. I get satisfaction from being able to *[help]* people.
_____ 4. I feel connected to others.
_____ 5. I jump or am startled by unexpected sounds.
_____ 6. I feel invigorated after working with those I *[help]*.
_____ 7. I find it difficult to separate my personal life from my life as a *[helper]*.
_____ 8. I am not as productive at work because I am losing sleep over traumatic experiences of a person I *[help]*.
_____ 9. I think that I might have been affected by the traumatic stress of those I *[help]*.
_____ 10. I feel trapped by my job as a *[helper]*.
_____ 11. Because of my *[helping]*, I have felt "on edge" about various things.
_____ 12. I like my work as a *[helper]*.
_____ 13. I feel depressed because of the traumatic experiences of the people I *[help]*.
_____ 14. I feel as though I am experiencing the trauma of someone I have *[helped]*.
_____ 15. I have beliefs that sustain me.
_____ 16. I am pleased with how I am able to keep up with *[helping]* techniques and protocols.
_____ 17. I am the person I always wanted to be.
_____ 18. My work makes me feel satisfied.
_____ 19. I feel worn out because of my work as a *[helper]*.
_____ 20. I have happy thoughts and feelings about those I *[help]* and how I could help them.
_____ 21. I feel overwhelmed because my case [work] load seems endless.
_____ 22. I believe I can make a difference through my work.
_____ 23. I avoid certain activities or situations because they remind me of frightening experiences of the people I *[help]*.
_____ 24. I am proud of what I can do to *[help]*.
_____ 25. As a result of my *[helping]*, I have intrusive, frightening thoughts.
_____ 26. I feel "bogged down" by the system.
_____ 27. I have thoughts that I am a "success" as a *[helper]*.
_____ 28. I can't recall important parts of my work with trauma victims.
_____ 29. I am a very caring person.
_____ 30. I am happy that I chose to do this work.

Appendix 13.2: Creating a Self-Care Plan

Maintenance Self-Care Plan Worksheet
Instructions: Consider what you do now for self-care and list those activities within each dimension of self-care on this worksheet. Identify new strategies that you will begin to incorporate as part of an ongoing maintenance self-care plan—pay particular attention to domains that you have not been addressing in the past. On the last page, identity barriers that might interfere with ongoing self-care, how they can be addressed, and any negative coping strategies that should be targeted for change.

Body Current Practice: New Practice:	Mind Current Practice: New Practice:
Spirit Current Practice: New Practice:	Emotions Current Practice: New Practice:
Work Current Practice: New Practice:	Relationships Current Practice: New Practice:
Other:_______________ Current Practice: New Practice:	Other: _______________ Current Practice: New Practice:
Barriers to maintaining my self-care strategies:	How I will address these barriers and remind myself to practice self-care:
Negative coping strategies that I would like to use less/not at all:	What I will do to cope instead:

Appendix 13.3: Writing-Based Self-Care Technique No. 1

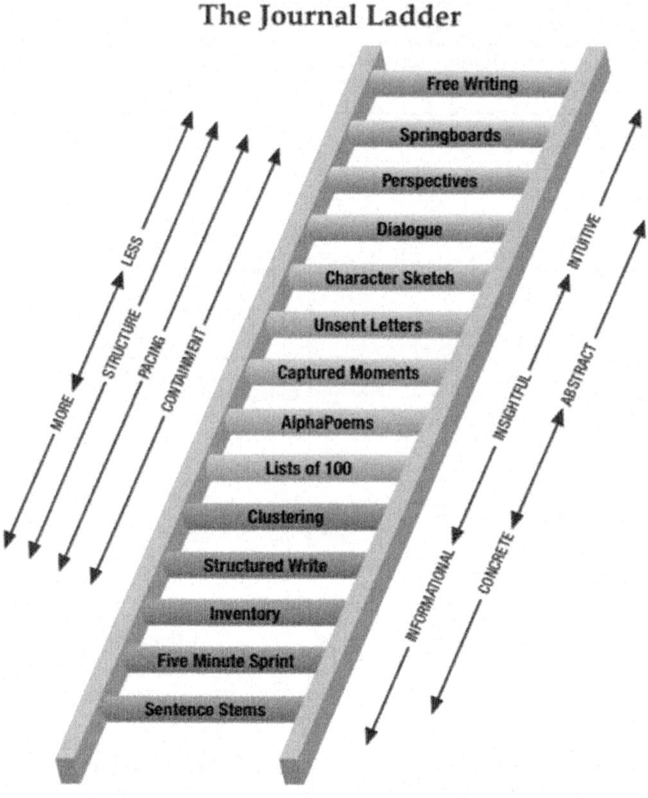

Kathleen Adams LPC, Center for Journal Therapy, Inc.

Structure	Foundation, form, sequenced tasks, orderliness
Pacing	Rhythm, movement, timing
Containment	Boundaries, limits, shape
Concrete	Easy to understand and attempt, external, reality-based
Abstract	Symbolic, metaphoric, internal, imaginal
Informational	Practical, immediately useful
Insightful	Connections, patterns, awareness
Intuitive	Sudden knowing, internal wisdom, quiet voice within

Appendix 13.4: Writing-Based Self-Care Technique No. 2

Adapted from James W. Pennebaker's *Writing To Heal.*

The Basic Technique:

1. Write for 20 minutes per day for four consecutive days.
2. Pick the same topic all 4 days, or write about a different event each day.
3. Write without stopping and without worrying about spelling or grammar.
4. Write only for yourself. Plan to destroy or hide the exercises once complete.
5. If you feel that a particular topic will push you over the edge, do not write about it. Deal with situations you can handle in the present.
6. You may feel depressed after writing. This is normal, though reflecting on the process may help.

The Reflection:

Place a number between 0 and 10 by each question, where 0 means "Not At All," 5 means "Somewhat," and 10 means "A Great Deal."

7. To what degree did you express your deepest thoughts and feelings? ____
8. To what degree do you currently feel sad or upset? ____
9. To what degree do you currently feel happy? ____
10. To what degree was today's writing valuable and meaningful for you? ____
11. In the space below, briefly describe how your writing went today:

Appendix 13.5: Sample Self-Care Writing Exercises

The previous appendices offer tools for designing a writing-based self-care tool kit for volunteers working in prison. Combining these handouts with exercises like those sampled below can result in self-care practice that provides volunteers with a feasible, structured method for critically reflecting on working with incarcerated people. Below are specific writing exercises that apply ideas presented in Appendices 1–4.

Unsent letters. The technique of Unsent Letters (Adams, 2011) dictates that the volunteer writes a letter to someone with whom they experience conflicting emotions. This technique can help a volunteer understand what they want to communicate to the population they serve, their supervisor, or their peer group. By writing directly to someone with no danger of them reading the words, a space of honesty is created where both negative and positive feelings can be acknowledged and examined. Writing a letter can help identity a frustration, work through a way to communicate an idea, or process lingering feelings of unfinished business.

For those who work with an incarcerated population, with individuals who may leave abruptly without forewarning, writing a letter may provide closure for the volunteer. This tactic may have been useful for Tina, who mentioned that "The most difficult part was not knowing where and what happens to the girls once they leave. We created relationships with the girls and when they leave (at times unannounced), it feels as if there is something lost and it's upsetting despite the positive potential of moving beyond a halfway house." Had Tina written a letter to one of the girls she bonded with, she may have identified other feelings or may have seen that the difficulty she felt was because she did not have an opportunity to say goodbye or thank them for the writing they had done.

Dialogue: Creating an imagined Dialogue requires a suspension of belief in order to examine responses to someone not present. Thompson (2010) claims that writing an imagined dialogue "can help us think our way forward, to access different points of view and to hear our own thoughts more clearly" (p. 11). She recommends writing an imagined dialogue with a feeling (such as guilt), with a client, with an internal supervisor (perhaps starting with the question "What could I do better?"), and with our volunteer self (who may be drastically different from one's personal self).

Switching perspectives: Switching perspectives is based on the notion that writing about a personal experience in the third person creates a greater distance to the situation, from where one can examine it safely and objectively, removing some of the negative power of strong personal feelings. Pennebaker (2004) recommends writing about the same experience four times for five minutes each. The first 5 minutes, write about the situation broadly: Who was there? What happened? What are the effects of the situation as they are currently present? The second time, examine the situation using only your perspective: I felt this.... I think ... It has affected me in the following ways. My behavior affected others by ... Third, take the perspective of only the other people involved: What did they think or feel? What do they want other people to know about their experience in that situation? Lastly, write about the entire situation again. What didn't you consider the first time you wrote about it that taking other perspectives allowed you to see? What are values that you and the others can take from the situation?

Identifying the image: Grey, Young, and Holmes (2002) work within the psychological framework of cognitive behavioral therapy to help their patients understand how recurring mental images perpetuate posttraumatic stress. Based on the nature of jail work, volunteers may be exposed to stories that spark mental images of traumatic situations. In order to objectively evaluate and move past the effects of these images, begin by writing, "The image that represents the worst moment of the situation is...." Then, reread the description of the image, and rate your emotional response from 1 to 100. From there, appraise the image by writing responses to these questions: "What does this image mean to me?" "What did I believe in that moment?" Finally, reread everything that you wrote about the situation and answer "What do I understand now about this image or my response to it?" The volunteer perspectives revealed through quotes in this chapter reaffirm the direct application and utility of self-care practices that are situated in a generative writing process.

References

Adams, K. (1998). *The way of the journal.* Brooklandville, MD: Sidran Press.

Adams, K. (2011). *The journal ladder: A developmental continuum of journal therapy.* Denver, CO: Center for Journal Therapy.

Adams, K. (Ed.) (2013). *Expressive writing: Foundations of practice.* Lanham, MD: Rowman and Littlefield Press.

Anderson, C. & MacCurdy, M. (2000). *Writing and healing: Toward an informed practice.* Urbana, IL: National Council of Teachers of English.

Bolton, G. (2011). *Write yourself: Creative writing and personal development.* London, UK: Jessica Kingsley.

Conrad, D. & Kellar-Guenther, Y. (2006). Compassion fatigue, burnout, and compassion satisfaction among Colorado child protection workers. *Child Abuse & Neglect, 30*(10), 1071–1080.

DeSalvo, L. (1999). *Writing as a way of healing: How telling our stories transforms our lives.* Boston: Beacon Press.

Figley, C. R. (1995). Compassion fatigue as secondary traumatic stress disorder: An overview. In C. R. Figley (Ed.), *Compassion fatigue: Coping with secondary traumatic stress disorder in those who treat the traumatized* (pp. 1–20). New York: Brunner-Routledge.

Goffman, E. (1961). *Asylums: Essays on the social situation of mental patients and other inmates.* New York: Anchor Books.

Grey, N., Young, K., & Holmes, E. (2002). Cognitive restructuring within reliving: A treatment for peritraumatic emotional "hotspots" in posttraumatic stress disorder. *Behavioural and Cognitive Psychotherapy, 30*, 37–56.

Kraus, V. I. (2005). Relationship between self-care and compassion satisfaction, compassion fatigue, and burnout among mental health professionals working with adolescent sex offenders. *Counseling and Clinical Psychology Journal, 2*(1), 81–88.

Lipsky, L. & Burk, C. (2007). *Trauma Stewardship: An everyday guide to caring for self while caring for others.* Seattle: Las Olas Press.

Pearlman, L. A. & Mac Ian, P. S. (1995). Vicarious traumatization: An empirical study of the effects of trauma work on trauma therapists. *Professional Psychology: Research and Practice, 26*(6), 558–565.

Pennebaker, J. W. (1990). *Opening up: The healing power of expressing emotions.* New York: Guilford.

Pennebaker, J. W. (1997). Writing about emotional experiences as a therapeutic process. *Psychological Science (Wiley-Blackwell), 8*(3), 162–166.

Pennebaker, J. W. (2004). *Writing to heal: A guided journal for recovering from trauma and emotional upheaval.* Oakland, CA: New Harbinger Publisher.

Pennebaker, J. W. & Memon, A. (1996). Recovered memories in context: Thoughts and elaborations on Bowers and Farvolden. *Psychological Bulletin, 119*(3), 381–385.

Reiser, S., & L. Butler. (n.d.). *My maintenance self-care plan worksheet.* Adapted from S. Lopez. Retrieved from http://socialwork.buffalo.edu/content/dam/socialwork/home/self-care-kit/my-maintenance-self-care-worksheet.pdf.

Sansbury, B. S., Graves, K., & Scott, W. (2015). Managing traumatic stress responses among clinicians: Individual and organizational tools for self-care. *Trauma, 17*(2), 114–122.

Shohet, R. (Ed.). (2008). *Passionate supervision.* London: Jessica Kingsley Publishers.

Skorton, D., & Altschuler, G. (2013). College behind bars: How educating prisoners pays off. *Forbes.* 25 March. Retrieved from http://www.forbes.com/sites/collegeprose/2013/03/25/college-behind-bars-how-educating-prisoners-pays-off/.

Stamm, B. H. (2002). Measuring compassion satisfaction as well as fatigue: Developmental history of the compassion satisfaction and fatigue test. In C. R. Figley (Ed.), *Treating compassion fatigue* (pp. 107–119). London: Taylor & Francis.

Stamm, B. H. (2010). *The concise ProQOL manual* (2nd ed.). Pocatello, ID: ProQOL.org.

Stamm, B. H. (2012). Helping the helpers: Compassion satisfaction and compassion fatigue in self-care, management, and policy. In A. D. Kirkwood & B. H.

Stamm (Eds.), *Resources for community suicide prevention [CD]*. Meridian and Pocatello, ID: Idaho State University.

Thompson, K. (2010). Using your journal as a supervision tool. *Seminar Series*. Denver, CO: Therapeutic Writing Institute. Retrieved from https://csuclc.files.wordpress.com/2015/02/using-your-journal-as-a-supervision-tool.pdf.

Vera Institute of Justice.. (2015). *Pathways from prison to postsecondary education project*. Retrieved from http://www.vera.org/project/pathways-prison-post secondary-education-project.

Afterword

Laura S. Abrams, Emma Hughes, Michelle Inderbitzin, and Rosie Meek

We want to end this book with a message of hope for the men and women in prison, for the volunteers striving to bring services to those who are incarcerated, and for the larger prison system itself. We know we can both encourage and create personal and institutional change; we see shining examples of innovative programs and selfless contributions every day. In this book, we have highlighted both obstacles in volunteering and small victories in empowering those who wish to take up—and continue—the fight to make prisons less harmful and more humane. Our own research and experiences have long taught us the importance of the voluntary sector in providing hope and opportunities to the men and women living in prisons and youth correctional facilities. Our work in putting together this book has only amplified our admiration for the volunteers and paid outsiders who help make prisons bearable.

Each volunteer who gives up his or her time—and too often a bit of his or her dignity—to enter prisons brings humanity into the prisons with them. They offer those living inside the walls respect and empathy along with new skills, fellowship, and alternative ways of thinking. By partnering with the men and women inside, we can begin to transform prisons into "schools for life, thereby improving the lives of inmates, prison staff and the community at large" (Helliwell, 2011, p. 255). We believe this is a worthy goal, and one we as editors, researchers, and community members will continue to work toward.

L.S. Abrams et al. (eds.), *The Voluntary Sector in Prisons*, Palgrave Studies in Prisons and Penology, DOI 10.1057/978-1-137-54215-1

We wish to reiterate our belief that prisons are overused and that states should provide many of the services that have fallen to volunteers in this era of mass incarceration. Yet, even as we hope for more innovative programs and alternatives to incarceration to be developed and implemented, we applaud the efforts of the thousands of volunteers from inside prisons and outside communities in their determination to make something positive of the time inside. Your efforts are being noticed. You are making a difference.

Reference

Helliwell, J. F. (2011). Institutions as enablers of wellbeing: The Singapore Prison case study. *International Journal of Wellbeing*, *1*(2), 255–265.

Index

A
AA. *See* Alcoholics Anonymous (AA)
Abrams, L., 268
Adams, K., 352, 353
adult basic education (ABE), 279
African Americans, 215–16, 220, 241, 301, 303
age, prisoners, 56
Alcoholics Anonymous (AA), 40, 68–9, 116
Alexander, M., 220, 302
Anderson, C., 338
Anderson-Nathe, B., 268
Anglo-Celtic population, 247
anti-bullying mentors, 119
arrival and orientation (A&O), 94
Ash, E., 78
Asian Pacific family, 69
Athletic Club, 69–70
Authoethnographic study, 283

B
Bard Prison Initiative (BPI), 280
beneficial programs, 47–8
Bentham, J., 201
Berry, P.H., 91
Bertrand, M., 217
Bible studies, 43
Big Brother and Big Sister Associations, 248
black middle-class dilemmas, 321–4
black students, 303
black-white color line, 303
Blagden, N.J., 122
book projects, 95–7
Boothby, M., 121
bottom-up approach, prison commitment, 161–3
BPI. *See* Bard Prison Initiative (BPI)
Braun, V., 126
British prisoners, 22
  primary motivation for, 27
British resettlement policy, 175
Brown v. Plata, 25
Burnett, R., 31, 138, 240
Bushway, S., 138

L.S. Abrams et al. (eds.), *The Voluntary Sector in Prisons*, Palgrave Studies in Prisons and Penology, DOI 10.1057/978-1-137-54215-1

C
Cain, Joshua, 12
California Department of Corrections and Rehabilitation (CDCR), 24–5, 39, 45
California prisons, 35
CaliforniaVolunteers, 11
caller care, 118
CARAT S (counseling, assessment, referral, advice, and through care services), 185
carceral devolution, 199, 207–10
career criminal, 43
CBT. *See* Cognitive behavioral therapy (CBT)
CDCR. *See* California Department of Corrections and Rehabilitation (CDCR)
CEA. *See* Correctional Educational Association (CEA)
Cernkovich, S.A., 29
challenges, communication, 111
charitable sector, 173
charity-based provisions, 32
charity-funded education, 31
Chen, X., 247, 248
Children's Aid Society, 247
Christian leadership, 33
citizenship, 59–61, 63–6
  benefits of, 75–6
  opportunities, 78–9
Citizens United for the Rehabilitation of Errants (CURE), 104–5
civic engagement, 57
CJS. *See* Criminal justice system (CJS)
Clarke, J., 254
Clarke, V., 126
Clinks, 191
Clinton, Bill, 280
Cloyes, K.G., 91
club leaders champion, 68
cognitive behavioral therapy (CBT), 252
Collins, Patricia Hill, 304
Comfort, M., 60
communication
  with community agencies, 102, 111
  e-mail, 295
  International Red Cross, 149
  leadership development, 64, 70, 94
  online, 346
  peer-based approaches, 146
community, 88, 249
  agencies, 102–6
  impact meetings, 106–8
  members and men inside, interactions, 106–10
  outside investment, 72–5
  writing, 338–9
community-based reentry programs, 221
community engagement, 332
community-led prison ministries, 30
community members and men inside, interactions
  annual car and bike show, 109–10
  community groups, 108–9
  debate teams, 108–9
  entertainers into one-time meetings, 108–9
  hosting victim impact and community impact meetings, 106–8
  sports teams, 108–9
community partners
  Citizens United for the Rehabilitation of Errants (CURE), 104–5
  Family First program, 105–6
  HOME Youth Resource Center, 103
  Oregon Youth Authority (OYA), 103–4
community sector, 173
community volunteers, 22, 23, 34, 35, 38

community writing group, 332
Corcoran, M., 269, 289
correctional educational association (CEA), 278, 287, 288
creative writing, 95–7
Crenshaw, K.W., 320
criminal blackman, 303
criminal code offense, 250
criminal justice policies, 4
criminal justice system (CJS), 5, 56, 174, 218
criminal thinking, 198, 245
criminologists, 204
Cullen, F.T., 291
culpability, 266
cultures of learning, 34–6
CURE. *See* Citizens United for the Rehabilitation of Errants (CURE)

D

Dabney, D., 23, 278, 282, 294
data collection, 306–8
Davis, L.M., 277, 279, 296
Dead Man Walking (Prejean), 108
Decker, S.H., 217
democracy, 56, 60, 67–8
democratic citizenship, 56
Department of Corrections (DOC), 284–5, 292, 293
Department of Labor Workforce Initiatives, 216
DeSalvo, Louise, 338
Dickinson, G.E., 91
distance learning, 32, 33
DOC. *See* Department of Corrections (DOC)
Donahue, D., 302, 303, 310
drugs policies, 4
DuBois, W.E.B., 302

E

earning trust, 137
Economic and Social Research Council (ESRC), 7
educational opportunities, 57
education provision, 26
employability training, 205
employment, 217–18
employment to employability, 205
empowered for change, 241
empowering ripple effect, 59
England, prisons in
  health promotion activities, 144
  interviews, adult prisons, 22
  population in, 144
  prisoner education programs, 26
  RAPt Mentors, 120
Esperian, J.H., 279
evidence-based practices, 246
ex-offenders, 217–18
ex-offender to new contributor
  analysis, 225
  data collection, 224
  job search strategies, 226–37
  limitations, 240–1
  racial messages, 234–7
  sample, 222–4
  significance of study, 221
expository writing groups, 334

F

family first program, 105–6
Figley, C.R., 334
Finn, J.L., 267
formal training opportunities
  initial program training and orientation, 347
  MidYear Volunteer Development Workshop, 347–8
  volunteer training manual, 347
Foucault, M., 207

G

geographic context, 308–9
ghetto authenticity, 321–4
Giordano, P.C., 29
Gojkovic, D., 14, 176
Gottschalk, M., 55
governing through freedom strategies, 246
Grant, Pell, 281
Grey, N., 359
guided writing activity, 334

H

Hacker, J.S., 57
Hannah-Moffat, K., 252
Harcourt, B.E., 56, 200
Hayner, N.S., 78
Hay, S., 282, 294
health and first aid prison volunteer scheme, 149
health outcomes, 146
health trainer roles, 149
Helliwell, J.F., 137
Her Majesty's Prison (HMP), 120
Hispanic, 215–16
HIV testing campaign, 150
HMP. *See* Her Majesty's Prison (HMP)
Hochschild, A.R., 282, 283
Hoffman, H.C., 91
Holmes, E., 359
homelessness, released prisoners, 58
homeless youth, 103
HOME Youth Resource Center, 103
hospice, 91–3
human capital, 209
human confinement, 341–2
humanizing quality, 34–6

I

imprisonment, 57
incarceration rates, 4
informal mentoring, 97–9
informal social safety net, releasing prisoners, 58
informal training and outreach efforts
  bimonthly informal meetings, 349
  co-facilitators, pre-and post-workshop meetings with, 348
  individual appointments/informal reflection and assessment, 348–9
  monthly volunteer newsletter, 349
  online access, 349–50
  self-care materials, 349–50
Inside-Out International Exchange Program, 281
Inside-Out Prison Exchange Program, 94–5
insiders programme, 117, 119
interview analysis, 336–7
interview methods
  program reflection, 337
  volunteer interviews, 336–7
investment, prisoners connections with, 72–5
Ipsos MORI, 176
Irish Red Cross volunteer inmates programme, 149–50
Irwin, J., 25, 60

J

Jacobi, Tobi, 16, 17
Jim Crow color line, 319–21
Jim Crow laws, 220, 304
job search strategies, 234–7
Josh, C., 77
The Journal Ladder, 352–3
justice, 220–1
Justice, B., 56, 60

K

Kadela, K., 219
Kellar-Guenther, Y., 334

Kelly, L., 267
Kraus, V.I., 333

L

Lakota Club, 70–2
Latino Culture Club, 70
Laub, J.H., 133
leaders
 of clubs, 63
 and cognitive-behavioral programs, 63–4
 peer-taught classes, 64
 of prison gangs, 64
 and teachers of educational classes, 63–4
leadership, 63–6
 benefits of, 75–6
 opportunities, 78–9
 of prisoners, 61
 risks of, 76–8
LeBel, T.P., 138
Lee, H., 60, 80
Level of Supervision Inventory-Ontario Revised (LSI-OR) version, 251
Lewis, G., 191
Lifers' Club, 62
Lifers' Unlimited Club, 69, 86–7, 102
Listener scheme, 117–19
literacy outreach programs, 331
literacy volunteers, challenges faced
 communal reflective space, 344–5
 difficult disclosures and relationships, 342–3
 human confinement, 341–2
 observing recidivism, 343–4
Loury, G.C., 81

M

MacCurdy, M., 338
marketable skills, 57
Martinson, Robert, 203
Maruna, S., 31, 39, 42, 131, 138, 240
mass imprisonment, consequences of, 196
mass incarceration, 4, 309–10
mature coping, 34
Maurutto, P., 252
McNeill, F., 240
MCYS. *See* Ministry of Children and Youth Services (MCYS)
Mead, S., 116
Meares, T.L., 56, 60
medium-security prison, 278
Meek, R., 14, 176
mental-health issue, 196
MidYear Volunteer Development Workshop, 347–8
Miller, R., 208
Mills, A., 14, 176
Ministry of Children and Youth Services (MCYS), 250–1
Mitchell, T., 302, 303, 310
modern prison, 202
moral blameworthiness, 266
Mullainathan, S., 217

N

Nanda, J., 320
Narcotics Anonymous (NA), 40, 68, 120
National Offender Management Service (NOMS), 124, 174
National Survey of Third Sector Organizations (NSTSO), 176
The New Jim Crow (Alexander, Michelle), 220
Newman, J., 254
NOMS. *See* National Offender Management Service (NOMS)
nongovernmental sector, 173
non-profit and criminal justice sectors, 7, 14–16
non-profit and voluntary sector provisions, 29

non-profit organizations, 21, 38
  British resettlement policy, 175
  procedure, 177–8
  qualitative interviews, 179–80
  reducing re-offending national action plan, 174
  social exclusion unit's (SEU), 174
  survey participants, 178–9
NSTSO. *See* National Survey of Third Sector Organizations (NSTSO)

O

Offender Management Act, 9
On Crimes and Punishment (Beccaria, Cesare), 200, 201
Oregon State Penitentiary (OSP), 56, 61, 62, 68–92
Oregon Youth Authority (OYA), 103–4
outside community, prisoners connections with, 72–5
Owens, M.L., 81

P

Pager, D., 217
Patterson, Evelyn, 196
peer-based approaches
  aim, 146
  analysis, 152–3
  auxiliary healthcare service, 157–8
  civic duty, 154
  design, 151
  gaining status and credibility, 154–5
  information and support, 156–7
  Irish Red Cross volunteer inmates programme, 149–50
  personal development, 153–4
  personal health gains, 154
  prison health trainer scheme, 146–9
  Samaritans' Listener scheme, 150
  sample, 152
  social environment, 160–1
  thematic analysis, 152
  utilising peers, 155–8
peer-based health scheme, 163
peer motivations, 158–9
peer-support roles
  analytic technique, 126–7
  change and transition, 127–33
  channelling, 135–6
  and criminal desistance, 121–3
  data collection, 125–6
  Insiders programme, 119
  Listener scheme, 117–19
  prisons in UK, 116–23
  RAPt Mentors, 120
  setting and participants, 123–5
  Toe-by-Toe, 119–20
peer teachers
  inside-out prison exchange program, 94–5
  prisoner-led classes, 93–4
penal voluntary sector (PVS), 246
  changing minds, 258–62
  cognitive behavioral approaches, 262–7
  hybrid models of punishment, 254
  mapp ing social relations, 253–4
  strategic accommodation/ acceptance, 255–8
  YCJA, 250–3
  youth justice system, 247–9
Pennebaker, J.W., 334, 352–3, 358, 378
PEP. *See* Prison Education Project (PEP)
Perrin, C., 122
Petersilia, J., 197
Phelps, Michelle, 206
Phoenix, J., 267
Picking Cotton (Thompson-Cannino), 108

political places, 66–7
Porter, L.C., 60
post-Civil Rights era, 305, 314–16
post-secondary prison education, 280–1
poverty
  of Black Americans, 204
  released prisoners, 58
  and unemployment, 205
pre-and post-workshop meetings with co-facilitators, 348
Prejean, Helen, 108
prison democracy, 60
prison education, 277, 279–80, 289–92
  post-secondary prison education, 280–1
  study site, 284–5
prison educational budgets, 277
Prison Education Project (PEP), 281
prison education volunteers, 282–3
prisoner awareness, 190
prisoner-led classes, 93–4
prisoner-led clubs, 67–90
prisoner reentry, 197, 198, 200, 203, 205–7
prisoner rehabilitation, 199
prisoner-run clubs, 56
prisoners
  decision-making processes, 198
  fundraising for, 95
Prisoners' Education Trust (PET), 22, 28, 36, 37
  potential significance of, 29
prison healthcare, 145
prison health, peer-based approaches
  Irish Red Cross volunteer inmates programme, 149–50
  prison health trainer scheme, 146–9
  Samaritans' Listener scheme, 150
prison health trainer scheme, 147–9
prison hospice program, 91
prison jobs, lead men in, 64–6
prison, partnership with voluntary sector, 79–82
prison politics, 60
prison's magazine, 44
prison volunteers, 277
prison wardens, 45
privilege level determines, 61
Professional Quality of Life Scale (ProQOL), 352, 354
program reflection, 337
pro-social, 245
punishment, 200–2
  affected families and communities, 55
  discourses of, 7
  hybrid models of, 254
  primary function of, 201
  purpose of, 201
  rehabilitation in prisons, 206
PVS. *See* penal voluntary sector (PVS)

R

Race, 217–18
Race and Ethnic Studies (REST) Program, 306
race-making operations, 304
racial discrimination, 216
racial exceptions, 312–14
racial identity, 317–19
racial messages, 234–7
Raynor, P., 240
Read Empower Attain Create Hope (REACH) project, 305, 306
Reagan, Ronald, 220
recidivism, 10, 26, 69, 175, 215, 216
Red Cross Volunteers, 164
Reducing Re-Offending National Action Plan, 174
reentry and employment programs, 218–20

reflective writing exercises, 332
rehabilitation, 219
  revisioning of, 205–7
  rise of, 200–2
  to street, 205
Rehabilitation of Addicted Persons Trust (RAPt), 120
rehabilitation revolution, 26
released prisoners, 58
religious inspiration and spiritual guidance, 41
resettlement policy, 175
responsibility, 245
REST Program. *See* Race and Ethnic Studies (REST) Program
risk management, 219
Roberts, Lara, 16, 17
Robert Wood Johnson foundation, 219
Robison, Kristenne, 16
Rosenkranz, S.J., 91
Rudolph, J.L., 29
Rumgay, J., 39

S

Samaritans Listener scheme, 118, 150
Sampson, R.J., 133
Sansbury, B.S., 333
Scharf, P., 60, 78
Second Chance Act, 207, 216
Second Chance Reentry Act, 219
Seiter, R.P., 219
self-care strategies, 332–6, 338. *See also* writing-based self-care
Self-completed prisoner surveys, 178
Seventh Step club, 69
Severe and Violent Offender Reentry Initiative, 216
Shannon Trust programme. *See* Listener scheme
Sibley, D., 59
slavery, 220
snowball sampling technique, 23
social environment, 160–1
social exclusion unit's (SEU), 174
social media, 58, 88
social mobility, 312–14
social welfare administration, 206
social welfare and crime-control policies, 204
society
  encourage citizenship of prisoners, 78
  positive contributions to, 88
Society of Captives (Sykes, Gresham), 58
sociological perspective, 88–90
Sohet, 351
Solomon, A.L., 197
sovereign power, 200–2
special housing units (SHUs), 95
Stamm, B.H., 346
state-contracted substance abuse treatment program, 29
stigmatism, released prisoners, 58
strategic accommodation, 257
Street, Paul, 196
Substance Dependence Treatment Program (SDTP), 120
Supiano, K.P., 91
survey participants, 178–9
survival mode, 42
Sykes, Gresham, 58

T

Taxman, Faye, 199
Tewksbury, R., 23, 278, 282, 294
third sector, 173
third-sector community-based organizations, 199
third sector organizations (TSOs), 9, 175–7
  and offenders, 180–3
  prisoner self-reported awareness, 181
  qualitative interviews, 181

reentry services, 177
resettlement pathway, 184–9
Thompson-Cannino, Jennifer, 108
Thompson, K., 351, 358
Tilton, Jennifer, 16
Toastmasters International, 70
Toe-by-Toe, 117, 119–20
traumatic for volunteers, 310–12
traumatization, 333
Travis, J., 197
Trotter, C., 240
true humanity, 92
Turnbull, S., 252

U
Uhuru sasa, 69
Understanding Self Equals Life's Foundation (U-SELF), 94
unemployment rates, 216
urban community-based organizations, 199
US Civil Rights Movement, 220
US prison population, 195

V
Vaughan, B., 122
veterans association, 70
Violent Crime Control and Law Enforcement Act, 26
voluntary provision, 44–7
voluntary sector, 173
voluntary sector working, partnership with prisons, 110–13
volunteer coordinators and programs, 346–53
formal training opportunities, 347–8
volunteer interviews, 336–7
volunteerism, role of, 5
volunteer-led programs, 44
volunteer-led provision, 31
volunteer population, 306
volunteers of color, 326
volunteers welcome, 286–9
volunteer training manual, 347
volunteer writing teachers, 331
vote, prisoner opportunities to, 67

W
Wacquant, Loic, 304, 319
Wales, prison system, 24. *See also* England, prisons in
Walraven, Trevor, 12
Waul, M., 197
Weaver, V.M., 57, 58
Wildeman, C., 57
Will J. Reid Foundation, 301
Wisdom within the Pen (James), 96
Wolch, J., 206
Wold, D., 91
women's prison, 278, 279, 283, 284
work behind bar, volunteer perspectives on
challenges faced, 341–5
satisfaction with experience, 338–41
writing
community, 338–9
creative growth, 339–40
human experience, 340–1
writing-based self-care, 346, 357–9, 370–1
dialogue, 358
image identifying, 359
interview analysis, 336–7
professional quality of life scale, 352
program background, 334–6
program reflection, 336–7
self-care plan, 352
switching perspectives, 358–9
unsent letters, 358
volunteer interviews, 336–7
volunteer perspectives, 334–6
writing/literacy, role of, 335
writing outreach program, 332

writing response theory, 332
writing to heal, 352–3, 357
writing workshops, 332, 335
writing workshop volunteers, 336

Y

YCJA. *See* Youth Criminal Justice Act (YCJA)
young adults, prison, 144–6
  chronic health conditions, 145
  mental health issues, 145
  substance abuse disorders, 145
Young, K., 359
Young Men's Christian Association (YMCA), 247–8
Young Offender Institution (YOI), 145, 150, 152
  behaviour change, 159
Youth Criminal Justice Act (YCJA), 249–53
youth empowerment programs and speaking panels, 100–1

Printed by Printforce, the Netherlands